THE
GREAT
HINDU
CIVILISATION

Pavan K. Varma is a writer-diplomat and was till recently an MP in the Rajya Sabha. He was earlier Advisor to the Chief Minister of Bihar, with the rank of Cabinet minister. He has been India's Ambassador in several countries, also Director of the Nehru Centre in London, Official Spokesperson of the Ministry of External Affairs, and Press Secretary to the President of India. Author of over a dozen successful books, Pavan K. Varma was conferred an Honorary Doctoral Degree for his contribution to the fields of diplomacy, literature, culture and aesthetics by the University of Indianapolis in 2005. He was also conferred the Druk Thuksey, Bhutan's highest civilian award, in 2012.

PAVAN K. VARMA

THE GREAT HINDU CIVILISATION

ACHIEVEMENT, NEGLECT, BIAS AND THE WAY FORWARD

WESTLAND
NON·FICTION

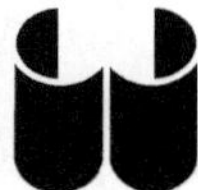

First published by Westland Non-Fiction, an imprint of Westland Publications Private Limited, in 2021

Published by Westland Non-Fiction, an imprint of Westland Books, a division of Nasadiya Technologies Private Limited, in 2022

No. 269/2B, First Floor, 'Irai Arul', Vimalraj Street, Nethaji Nagar, Allappakkam Main Road, Maduravoyal, Chennai 600095

Westland, the Westland logo, Westland Non-Fiction and the Westland Non-Fiction logo are the trademarks of Nasadiya Technologies Private Limited, or its affiliates.

ISBN: 9789395073288

10 9 8 7 6 5 4 3 2 1

Typeset by SÜRYA, New Delhi

Printed at Nutech Print Services - India

To the remarkable unknown sage who wrote this
shloka in the *Isha Upanishad*:

Om poornamadah poornamidam
Poornat poorna mudachyate
Poornasya poorna maadaya
Poorna meva vashishyate

All this is full, all that is full
From fullness, fullness comes.
When fullness is taken from fullness
Fullness still remains.

Om sarve bhavantu sukhinah, sarve santu niramaayah
Sarve bhadrani pashyantu, Maa-kashchid-dukha-bhaga bhavate
Om shaantih, shaantih, shaantih.

May all sentient beings be at peace, may all be free from illness
May all see what is auspicious, may no one suffer
Om, peace, peace, peace be on all.

The most effective way to destroy a people is to deny and obliterate their own understanding of their history.

– George Orwell

A nation that forgets its past has no future.

– Winston Churchill

Janani janmabhoomischa swargadapi gariyasi: Mother, and motherland, are superior to heaven.

– Lord Ram in the Ramayana

Contents

Preface

From my point of view, the fact that a great Hindu civilisation existed, and continues to exist, is not in doubt. It is marked by great antiquity, substantial—even unprecedented—refinements, audacity of thought, and achievements both in the spiritual and secular realms. This does not mean it is unblemished, and objectivity demands that the blemishes too must be taken into account. Nor does it mean that it evolved in an insular silo or untouched by outside influences. On the contrary. And yet, this intermingling has not diluted or erased its essential identity as a verifiable civilisation. Unlike many other great civilisations of the past, the Hindu civilisation has not become a historical relic, an antiquary of the past, but has survived as an unbroken continuum to the present.

It is important to know more about this civilisation, most of all for Hindus themselves. The civilisation faces a rather unfortunate paradox. On the one hand, it is notable for its resilience and continuity, and its spillover into every aspect of a Hindu's life; and, on the other, Hindus themselves show little real curiosity or interest in knowing more about it. This indifference is a matter of concern, not least because, if Hindus do not know about their own civilisational legacy, their authenticity as Hindus—based on knowledge—is stunted and reduced to ritualistic tokenism.

It is true that Hinduism is a way of life rather than a prescriptive religion like the Abrahamic faiths. In Hinduism, there is no one

Pope, no one text, no inflexibly mandatory ritual, no compulsory congregations, and no one presiding temple. But this is no reason for Hindus to be unaware of the remarkable philosophies and deeper meanings that animate their religion. It is important to always remember that a civilisation evolved in parallel with the evolution of Hinduism. To have only a vague idea about what it was, and what an extraordinary degree of cerebration inspired it, is to do disservice to a great and abiding legacy.

The need for Hindus to be more knowledgeable about their heritage also exists because there is an influential section of western Indologists who question the very existence of this civilisation. One of the more specious arguments is that because Hinduism and Hindu civilisation have so much internal diversity and freedom of expression, there is no definitive core to it. Hindus who do not take the trouble to know a little more about their past are likely to become unintentional accessories to this untenable—and sometimes mischievous—point of view masquerading as academic scholarship.

In this book, I have sought to rebut arguments that question the existence of Hindu civilisation, and deal also with the notion that the narration of history should expediently exclude Hindu religion and its civilisational consequences. I have also discussed in some detail the philosophical, cultural, social, political, scientific and other aspects of this civilisation, as also the impact on it of the Islamic invasion and the British conquest. Finally, I have discussed the way forward, and what the imperatives of a real Hindu Renaissance should be.

Today, the need for Hindus to become confidently aware of what their religion and heritage stand for has become critically important because there is an attempt by some to posit themselves as the sole interpreters of this great legacy. Distortion can only be countered by knowledge. As Adi Shankaracharya said: Satyam Jnanam; Anantam Brahman: Knowledge is Truth and Brahman is Eternal.

This book was written in the enforced solitude of the Covid lockdown. Fortunately, in the digital age, there was always access to information and the opportunity to discuss matters with people more knowledgeable than me. In September 2020, my wife, Renuka, got the virus, and for two weeks I hardly wrote, concerned only with her well-being and full recovery, which fortunately happened. But for this interregnum, for months I remained absorbed in the intensely rewarding task of discovering and reinterpreting the precious legacy that Hindus and non-Hindus alike are heir to. Notwithstanding the morbidities of the pandemic, it was a most rewarding period.

I would like to record my gratitude to my editor, Karthika V.K., at Westland. Always perceptive and encouraging, she was a source of strength. There are many friends and scholars of Hinduism and Indian history whom I would like to thank for their unfailing readiness to discuss issues with me and provide advice. Finally, my family was a great pillar of support. And, above all, as always, I have no words to express my gratitude to Renuka for her love, care, support and literary solidarity.

1

HINDU CIVILISATION

MYTH OR REALITY?

The origins of civilisations are often shrouded in mystery and speculation. Current legatees of that civilisation seek to unravel this mystery, use scientific tools to establish what may have been the truth, set aside historical prejudice, discount colonial interpretations, weigh the facts, analyse with passion but objectivity, and find the right balance between a simplistic glorification of the past and a legitimate sense of pride in what once was.

It shall be my attempt to show, through evidence and reason, that there was, once upon a time, a great Hindu civilisation. This civilisation commenced at the dawn of time and lasted as a verifiable homogeneity for thousands of years without extensive or invasive foreign intrusion until the coming of Islam in around the tenth century CE. This civilisation was a living continuity beyond the formative years that defined it and, in spite of the historical vicissitudes it went through later, survives even today—not exclusively or with the same intensity as in the past, but as a living entity in the life of Hindus. In this sense, the Hindu civilisation is unique—compared to the other great foundational civilisations of the world, it did not fade away after its apogee and become a museum relic, a mere antiquary or only a fossilised memory.

Above all, it is my premise that this Hindu civilisation has few parallels in terms of the cerebral energy invested in it. All its documented refinements—about which I shall talk in detail subsequently—were underpinned by the grandeur of thought. It was sustained by the unrelenting application of mind, in every field— metaphysics, philosophy, art, creativity, polity, society, science and economics. Nothing in it was random or happenstance. There was a holistic interconnectedness that informed it, and this unified vision permeated all aspects of its highly complex intellectual construct.

This civilisation broke new conceptual ground with its sustained spirit of enquiry, the conscious absence of dogmatism, the sanction to uninhibitedly question, dissent and interrogate, the freedom for the fullest expression of diversity within the framework of a unitary vision, the harmonious interface between the secular and the spiritual, the absence of a false binary of the sacred and the profane, and the remarkable—even surprising—ability to reinvent itself. A triad defined this civilisation—first, the elaboration of a concept; then, the expression of that concept in profoundly diverse ways; and, lastly, over millennia, the permeation of both the concept and its expression in every level of society. This civilisation must therefore be seen as the triumph of irrepressible ideation. In fact, because its origins lay in the self-conscious realm of cognition, it was incapable of destruction. That is why it became—and is—sanatan or eternal and imperishable.

This is not to assert that this civilisation was without blemish. Like any complex structure, some faults crept into it—some of them grave—including oppression, social discrimination, economic inequity and institutionalised gender inequality. In evaluating the remarkable achievements of this civilisation, these drawbacks must also be taken into account. However, nothing can be judged only by its faults. No civilisation anywhere in the world has been entirely an epitome of perfection. In all of them there has been, in varying degrees, exploitation, oppression and discrimination. The call here is for historical objectivity, uninfluenced by ideological biases, so that the historian's microscope is not focused only on the negatives.

The thesis of this book is that, in spite of the negatives that it acquired over a period, the Hindu civilisation is without parallel in the world for the sheer robustness of its cerebration, and the creative output that is its consequence. The key question then is, why have Hindus themselves not made enough efforts to discover the grandeur of their past? This is an important question because no other great civilisation of the world, even if no longer alive, has suffered from such inglorious indifference, amnesia and neglect. This book will seek to answer this question too.

Gurcharan Das, a product of Harvard University, who took early retirement as CEO of Procter & Gamble to become a full-time writer, has an interesting anecdote to tell about the reaction at a typical upper-crust dinner in Delhi when he decided to research Hindu epics and philosophy. His aggressive interlocutor was a 'self-proclaimed leftist and secularist, who had once been a favourite of former prime minister Indira Gandhi, [and] had the gruff, domineering accent of an English aristocrat, not surprising in a former civil servant of the old school. I admitted reluctantly that I had been thinking of reading the Mahabharata, the *Manusmriti*, the *Kathopanishad* perhaps and ... "Good Lord, man," he exclaimed. "You haven't turned saffron have you?"'[1]

The inference that any interest in our Hindu past is tantamount to being communal is the ludicrous reaction of the rootless anglicised elite in our country, and of people of a certain ideological persuasion. For them, millennia of our history, and of the undeniable and unparalleled achievements of ancient India, must lie buried, unexplored, inert and forgotten, because to show an interest in them—and even more dangerously, appreciation for them—turns you automatically into a 'Hindu' fundamentalist. The tragedy is that such reflex 'secularists' know close to nothing about our ancient past. They can quote Shakespeare but have never read Kalidasa or Thiruvalluvar; their knowledge of our epics, the Mahabharata and the Ramayana, has been gleaned from comic books and they have only the scantiest idea of the basic storyline. They have no idea when Adi Shankaracharya lived, what he wrote, no clue of the six systems of Hindu philosophy or the three foundational texts of Hinduism, not even a notion about the remarkable principle of aesthetics of that period, no knowledge about the intellect that went into such concepts as dharma, no concept about what the four purusharthas are, and are largely ignorant about the unprecedented scientific achievements of that time.

Why does the elite of a country turn against its own culture and civilisation? This is an interesting question to ponder, and the answers to it lie in recent political history, the mental servility of the postcolonised, and the carefully nurtured and prolonged institutional neglect. I shall deal with these subsequently. For the moment, it is sufficient to say that there must be very few nations which have such a rich past, but whose opinion-making elite, cocooned in their Western notions of 'modernity', are so ignorant or unconcerned about it. The irony is that while those in the West, and other developed nations, who are the role models of this desired modernity, continue to enthusiastically explore their own past, Indians, who genuinely need to do so because they have been severed from it against their will, make indifference to it a virtue.

The ingrained hostility to India's Hindu civilisation also stems from the ill-informed claim that this is essential to preserve the nation's secular fabric. Amartya Sen, the Nobel laureate, is an ardent votary of this school of thought. In his book *The Argumentative Indian,* he argues that those who speak of a Hindu civilisation 'are the promoters of a narrowly Hindu view of civilisation'.[2] While conceding that 'these old books and narratives have had an enormous influence on Indian literature and thought'—a rather supercilious way of describing thousands of years of civilisational achievement— he nevertheless views 'the harking back to ancient India with the greatest suspicion'. The key to his thinking lies precisely in this inadvertent confession. For him, the very attempt to revisit ancient India is ab initio a tainted exercise, a matter of the greatest suspicion. This is an a priori conclusion, influenced by factors extraneous to the independent value and need of such a project. For a person of his intellectual calibre, to dogmatically label anyone wanting to 'hark back' to ancient India as a Hindu fundamentalist is, to put it politely, deeply disturbing. It implies a blind rejection on the assumption that any such attempt has to be imbued with the ulterior motive of promoting 'a narrowly Hindu view'. Sen's choice is the view of the 'integrationists', who 'are not wrong to question the factional nature of the choice of "Hindu classics" over other products of India's long and diverse history. They are also right to point to the counterproductive role that such a partisan selection can play in the secular, multi-religious life of today's India.'[3]

The historian Romila Thapar seems to share Sen's Hindu phobia. She defines 'communal historical writing' as something 'narrowed down to projecting the history of a particular community, identified by a monolithic religion being preeminent, and excludes the study of others'.[4] Why should the 'study of a particular community', if it has played a definitive role in a verifiable period of history, be communal? Why should the study of religion, if it has played a dominant role in influencing the world view of a historical period, be communal? Thapar is, of course, entitled to a personal point of view that the study of religions should not be a part of historical enquiry. For her, to identify a historical period on the basis of religion, even if this is not done to the exclusion of other factors, is to appeal to 'emotion' and 'faith' and 'can threaten the intellectual foundations of historical discourse'.[5] Are religions, and their evolution and content, especially when—as in ancient India—they are interlinked with society, culture and the polity, not a factor in the making of history? Her assumption is that the study of Hinduism as a part of the study of ancient India would ipso facto 'exclude the study of others'. However, this will never be the case in any truly intellectual enquiry. I suspect that, like Sen, her main problem is about a focus on Hinduism, and she would be quite willing to discuss Islam and Christianity as influential elements in the narrative of Indian history.

The obvious question is, does an appreciation of India's genuine achievements in the foundational period of our history, which are dominantly an aspect of Hindu civilisation, simply translate to hatred of other religions, or politically motivated 'over-glorification'? Are those who make this argument even remotely aware of the eclecticism and spirit of religious tolerance that characterised this period of our history? A miniscule number of overzealous Hindu propagandists do invoke Hindu civilisation to argue for a Hindu India. But the tenets of Hinduism itself—if one cares to find out—are the best counter to such demands for religious exclusion. Moreover, more than seven decades into a plural republic, where respect for all faiths is guaranteed, this would appear to be the cause of a lunatic, ultra-right fringe, rather than of the mainstream Hindu opinion. In reality, the so-called 'integrationists', in their smear campaign against anyone daring to speak of a Hindu period of history, are exclusionists who want to obliterate from public memory and historical appreciation the legitimate analysis of a long and identifiable part of our history. Objective history is for them a dispensable tool to be sacrificed on the expediently conjured fantasy of a 'secular' India. So obsessed are they with the admittedly unwarranted shenanigans of a miniscule Hindu fringe, that they will reflexively condemn even a genuine exploration of ancient India, because, according to them, Hinduism cannot be excluded from it.

The truth is that the opposition to the study and rediscovery of Hindu civilisation is based on an entrenched bias—conscious or otherwise—of a definable 'establishment' that had till recently political backing as well as the endorsement of prominent historians. We need to examine on merit what the arguments of this establishment are.

The first argument falls into what Jawaharlal Nehru dismissed as 'the deadwood of the past'. It was—and is—used by those impatient for the benediction of 'modernity', defined essentially in terms of a rupture from the past. Their conviction is that only when India finds freedom from the shackles of its ancient heritage can it adopt the 'scientific temper' and 'rationality' to develop a truly 'modern' outlook and vision. This kind of thinking was prevalent in influential segments of the intelligentsia in the period leading up to Independence in 1947, and after that as well. Long years of colonial servitude, the severance from one's cultural roots and the internalisation of the myth that modernity and scientific progress are possible only for those who emancipate themselves from the baggage of history influenced this approach. Ancient India was seen as largely obscurantist, riddled with archaic superstition, exploitative prejudice, meaningless rituals and irrational speculations. The future of India lay in emulating the British—and the West in general—for their scientific prowess and technological achievements. Nehru put it bluntly: 'India's ancient culture has outlived itself. Silently, desperately, it is struggling against a new and all-powerful adversary, the civilisation of the capitalist West. It will be defeated because the West brings with it science—and the West brings that antidote which is the principle of socialism.'[6] Nehru could still assert that 'the principles which India will espouse must be in contact with its roots in the soil'.[7] But most others who echoed him were hopelessly deracinated, adrift from their cultural roots, adept more in English than in their own mother tongue and largely unaware of India's civilisational achievements. It was also a matter of self-interest. Their cultural milieu was—as Macaulay had predicted—far more in consonance with the departing British. Their personal gain lay in perpetuating the same anglicised ethos that guaranteed their social dominance. They, therefore, had little incentive to encourage new knowledge, such as objectively revisiting the past, because that could threaten their hegemony.

It is nobody's case that Hindu civilisation did not have any superstition and prejudice and a great deal of meaningless rituals, largely perpetuated by an elite Brahmanical class. But, it is farcical— and grossly inaccurate—to argue that India's ancient past was only ritual and superstition. Ancient and complex civilisations are not unidimensional—either this or nothing else. 'Except for a handful, Indian intellectuals' ... approach to the past is characterized more by intellectual and emotional inertia than by critical selectivity.'[8] In this ill-informed binary, 'the relationship between tradition and modernity is allowed to remain in a state of perpetual dichotomous tension; no encouragement is given to conceiving this relationship as dialectical, creative, rejuvenating'.[9] The projection of ancient India encompasses an entire ecosystem of vested interests. Its disdainful dismissal is based as much on ignorance as on transparent personal interest.

The second argument is that there is no such word as 'Hindu'. How can there be a Hindu civilisation if those who constitute it do not have a word to describe themselves as Hindus? Such an argument is prima facie facile. If a people, with a verifiable philosophical vision, religious practice, social norms, kinship rules, creative expression, political thought, ethnic overlap and geographical location, are aware of their unified identity and can differentiate themselves from others on this basis, does a name tag alter the fact of their existence? Most of the ancient civilisations of the world, which have been identified as such today and given labels to describe them, were not, at the time of their origin, self-consciously aware — or concerned — about by what name they will be known to posterity.

Historical evidence clearly shows the recognition by outsiders of a civilisation called 'Hindu'. Dr Upinder Singh, in her magnum opus, *A History of Ancient India and Medieval India: From the Stone Age to the 12th Century*, testifies to this. It is important to remember that Dr Singh is no ultra-right demagogue. She is a professional historian of impeccable credentials, and the daughter of Dr Manmohan Singh, the former prime minister of India who belongs to the Congress party. She writes that the words 'India', 'Hindu' and 'Hindustan' originate from the river Indus (or Sindhu, which originates in the Tibetan plateau, and flows 3,200 km south-west across fertile plains before it merges with the Arabian Sea). Ancient Chinese sources refer to the land of 'Shen-tu', Greek texts mention 'India', and Persian inscriptions describe 'Hidu' as one of the subject countries of the Achaemenid king, Darius. These terms initially referred only to the lower Indus valley but their connotations expanded rapidly. For Megasthenes, who visited the court of Chandragupta Maurya in the fourth century BCE, 'Hindu' meant the entire subcontinent. When exploring the ancient history of South Asia, it is necessary to ignore the modern political boundaries and to treat the Indian subcontinent and its many regions and subregions as a single canvas.[10]

American Indologist Wendy Doniger — we shall have more than one occasion to critically dissect her approach to Hinduism and Hindu civilisation — first denies the Hindu appellation, and then confirms its existence. In a somewhat condescending manner she asks: 'If we can agree that there is something out there worth naming, what shall we call it? The main objections to calling it Hinduism or to calling the people in question Hindus are that those were not always the names that Hindus used for themselves or their religion and that they are geographical names.'[11] But even she cannot overlook the historical evidence. Even if Hindu is not a 'native word'—as she describes it—it 'comes from a word for the "river" (Sindhu) that Herodotus (in the fifth century BCE), the Persians (in the fourth century BCE), and the Arabs (after the eighth century) used to refer to everyone who lived beyond the great river of the Northwest of the subcontinent'.[12] Her conclusion is that it is 'not uncommon for one culture to take from another a word to designate a concept for which the original culture had a concept but not a word'.[13] The Hindus recognised themselves as such, irrespective of where the word originated.

But even if the word 'Hindu' existed, was there anything that can be called a Hindu civilisation? Sunil Khilnani, who wrote a very readable book, *The Idea of India*, quotes the British writer John Stratchey as an example of the dominant colonial view. 'There is not, and never was an India, nor ever any country of India, possessing according to European ideas, any sort of unity, physical, political, social or religious; no nation, no "people of India" of which we hear so much.' Khilnani rightly labels this kind of dismissal as 'the humiliation inflicted by colonial views'.[14] But, strangely, he comes close to endorsing this approach. 'After all, before the nineteenth century, no residents of the sub-continent would have identified themselves as Indians. There existed intricate, ramified vocabularies of common understanding, which classified people by communities of lineage, locality and sect; but "Indian" would not have figured among its terms.'[15] Romila Thapar reinforces this 'sectoral' view, denying a civilisational identity. 'Identity in pre-colonial India,' she writes, 'was dependent on various factors such as caste, occupation, language, sect, region and location.'[16]

Historian Sanjay Subrahmanyam, in his book *Is Indian Civilization a Myth?* examines two conceptions of India. The first, which for some inexplicable reasons he calls the 'constructivist approach', believes that 'India as we know it was invented in not too distant a past, probably by the British, or perhaps by Indians and Britons acting together in the period of colonial rule'.[17] The second view is that 'some very stable and autarchic notion of India has been around for a very long time, indeed from the time when a classical Indian civilization put down its roots in the Indo-Gangetic plain'.[18] His contemptuous conclusion is that 'we need to see India not as a civilization but as a crossroads, as a space open for external influences'.[19] What was before medieval India was only 'intellectual constructions and wishful thinking', and thus, 'ancient India is not a reality for us in the same way as medieval India, and it can never achieve the same state'.[20] Ancient Indian civilisation then is 'just a hybrid, a crossroads, a mixture of elements derived from chance encounters and unforeseen consequences', and anyone who contests this is taking 'the path to xenophobia and cultural paranoia'.[21]

Ultimately, we are back to the same bogey of 'xenophobia', which is shorthand for Hindu fundamentalism. To admit that there could have been an identifiable civilisation where Hinduism was dominant, is to unleash forces of 'cultural paranoia'. Why is this automatic conflation made ignoring historical objectivity? The approach of the naysayers is not to examine the possibility of an ancient Indian civilisation, but to immediately conclude that to even essay such a possibility is a conspiracy of Hindu fanatics. Sanjay Subrahmanyam was, at the time of writing of this book, Distinguished Professor of History at the University of California at Los Angeles. We are told that he had earlier taught in Paris and Oxford. For a person of his credentials in history, it is surprising that, ignoring the mass of textual, historical and archaeological evidence available, he cursorily concludes that the entire notion of an ancient Indian civilisation is just a 'hybrid', and 'a mixture of elements derived from chance encounters'.

Indeed, history can certainly have 'chance encounters'. It can also be a 'mixture of elements'. The question is whether, from these 'chance encounters' and 'mixture of elements' was melded a civilisation with identifiable attributes and—in spite of the diversity—an underlying unity. To disdainfully dismiss our ancient past as just 'intellectual constructions and wishful thinking' is, as I shall subsequently show, sheer intellectual laziness influenced by the fashionable notion that such ill-informed rejection best establishes your liberal credentials. It is a viewpoint that has the admiring support of many in the academic establishment of the West. To pander to that bias, even more flagrantly than some Western (and Indian) academics do is, for people like Dr Subrahmanyam, a way of strengthening their personal acceptance within that tribe. Subrahmanyam's thesis that to talk of a past civilisation is 'the same as the notion of a closed India' must take the cake in unhistorical generalisations. It is a classic example of extrapolating current prejudice on historical evidence, for even the worst critics of ancient India will admit that it was, at the intellectual level, an extraordinarily eclectic civilisation, and very far from being 'closed'. Again, why should historical memory be limited to medieval India, as Subrahmanyam would like it to be? His academic bias may sustain only such arbitrary selectivity, but there is tangible evidence to incontrovertibly profile what actually existed earlier. Shutting your eyes to it neither establishes your credentials as a liberal nor as a historian.

Jawaharlal Nehru had a well-intentioned but romantic view of Indian history, which he presented with considerable literary verve in his book, *The Discovery of India*. He saw India as 'an ancient palimpsest on which layer upon layer of thought and reverie had been subscribed, and yet no succeeding layer had completely hidden or erased what had been written previously'. Khilnani interprets this to argue that in Nehru's imagination, 'India appeared as a space of cultural mixing, its history a celebration of the soiling effects of cultural miscegenation and accretion'.[22]

The problem arises precisely here. The dictionary defines

palimpsest as 'a manuscript or a piece of writing matter on which later writing has been superimposed on effaced earlier writing'. Can millennia of history, with Hinduism as the principal religion, and with defined civilisational attributes (which I discuss in detail in the next chapter) be a palimpsest where what once was is effaced by what happened later? Nehru concedes that it was not completely hidden or erased. But, in his world view there is, implicitly, a reluctance to give due recognition to the pivotal role played by the longest foundational period of our history, and to gloss over it as just one phase overwritten by another. True, the history of India has been one of many strands coming together. But the argument of a palimpsest also presupposes that there was never a period of civilisational history that, far from being overwritten, played a foundational role in determining the subsequent course of history. Essentially, Nehru—for well-intentioned reasons—did not wish to dwell too long on the ancient past lest it become a reason to underplay the politically desirable goal of projecting a 'syncretic' India. The mention of an ancient Hindu India was assumed to be discordant to such a goal. For him, it was much better to view Indian historical structure as a successive 'layering', rather than to acknowledge, with any degree of emphasis, the foundations on which the subsequent layering was built.

The invocation of local factors, lineage, locality, region, sect, occupation, caste and community was also done precisely for this purpose. If the micro is the only source of identity, it rules out any sense of belonging to a macro entity. Not that there is any irresolvable contradiction between the two. One can have local fealties, and also a sense of being part of a larger loyalty. But, the dichotomy was created deliberately, so as to debunk any claim to civilisational consciousness. An ancient civilisational footprint would lead to the verifiably factual claim that it was dominantly Hindu, and that would jeopardise the present-day need to downplay this in the interest of 'preserving secularism'. Hence, historical objectivity must be sacrificed on the altar of a perceived sense of political correctness.

Objective historians are today willing to accept this reality. Dr Upinder Singh writes: 'One of several explanations of the name Bharatvarsha connects it with the Bharata people, descendants of the legendary king Bharata, son of Dushyanta and Shakuntala. Cosmography blends with geography in the Puranas. Bharatvarsha is said to consist of nine divisions (khandas), separated from one another by seas. But the mention of its mountains, rivers and places — some of which can be identified — suggests that the composers of such texts were familiar with various areas of the sub-continent, *and perceived them as part of a larger cultural whole* [emphasis mine]'.[23] Surprisingly, for all his protestations, Khilnani also accepts this. He says: 'Equally significant was India's archive of images of political community, which related culture to polity. In the Brahminic traditions, for instance, the Puranic literature expresses a sense of the sub-continent's natural geographic frontiers, reflected in a sacred geography mapped out by *tirthas*, pilgrimage points scattered across the land, and encompassed by the idea of mythic realms like Aryavarta or Bharatvarsha.' Moreover, he contradicts himself when he seeks to confine this cultural polity only to 'Brahminic traditions'. Ancient India, he concedes, 'did share intelligible, common cultural forms, derived from *both* [emphasis mine] Brahminic traditions and non-Brahminic sources. The storehouse of shared narrative structures embodied in epics, myths and folk stories, and the family resemblances in styles of art, architecture and religious motifs — if not ritual practices — *testify to a civilizational bond* [emphasis mine].'[24]

Even so, his conclusion is that 'the moments of actual unification in India's past were achieved under the yoke of imperial rule'.[25] But this too is factually incorrect. Political unity — even if not in the modern sense of a nation state — was achieved as far back as the fourth century BCE, in the reign of Chandragupta Maurya. His contemporary, the legendary Chanakya, defined that unity as the 'Charkravarti Kshetra'. 'The area extending from the Himalayas in the north to the sea and a thousand yojanas wide from east to west is the operation of the King-Emperor.'[26] Scholars of ancient India endorse this territorial unification. 'Chandragupta Maurya, Ashoka and Samudragupta are fully historical rulers who approached the ideal of uniting the whole sub-continent. … There aren't many countries which had a sense of national unity 23 centuries ago on the basis of the same boundaries which (disregarding the Partition) are valid today.'[27]

Of course, the British wanted the 'natives' to believe that it was they who created the concept of India. This is precisely what John Strachey, quoted earlier, disdainfully said. But for the British, India was a non-existent entity—an inchoate collation of random diversities—with no self-consciousness of cultural (or political) unity dating back millennia. Many modern Indian 'liberals' indirectly endorsed this imperialist point of view, because to not do so would encourage Hindu 'cultural paranoia'.

But the mistake such commentators make is to conflate a political state, in the modern sense, with a past civilisational construct that transcended merely political frontiers. Author Amish Tripathi explains this simply: 'India as a cultural and civilizational entity has existed for millennia. There are enough examples and documentation to prove this. … And, in any case, before the treaties of Westphalia in the seventeenth century, "nations" did not exist as political units, but as cultural entities. In sixteenth-century England, if you were loyal to England rather than King Henry VIII, you could have been beheaded as a traitor. But the cultural concept of England existed at the time. Just like the cultural concept of India did.'[28]

Mahatma Gandhi says the same thing in his first book, *Hind Swaraj*. The book was written in a gush of outrage in ten days, between 13 and 22 November 1909, on board the ship *Kildonan Castle* on his return voyage from England to South Africa. During his brief visit to England, Gandhi had had enough of the smug opinion among Britishers that they were responsible for the creation of India. Nor was he amused at their attempt to devalue India's civilisational past. In *Hind Swaraj*, he expostulates: 'What do you think could have been the intention of those far-seeing ancestors of ours who established Shvetbindu Rameshwar in the South, Juggernaut in the

South-East, and Haridwar in the North as places of pilgrimage? You will admit they were no fools ... they saw that India was one undivided land so made by nature. They, therefore, argued that it must be one nation—and fired the people with an idea of nationality in a manner unknown to other parts of the world. Any two Indians are one as no two Englishmen are.'[29]

Aurobindo makes the same point. 'The "nation idea" India never had. By that I mean the political idea of the nation. It is a modern growth. But we *had* in India the cultural and spiritual idea of the nation.'[30] Even Amartya Sen, who is wary of any attempt to 'hark back' to ancient India, reluctantly concurs on this point. 'Obviously, we could not expect to see, historically, a pre-existing "Indian nation" in the modern sense, lying in wait to form a nation-state, but it is difficult to miss the social and cultural linkages and identities that could serve as the basis of one. The cultural transmissions across the land have been swift and comprehensive for millennia, and the economic and social connections too close to be missed in understanding Indian history.'[31]

Another critique is that ancient India's civilisational self-consciousness was a 'fiction' created by Indian nationalists in response to British rule. No doubt, nationalist fervour could have, in some instances, triggered an over-glorification of the past. But an objective examination of the truth cannot become an inert victim to two extremes of opinion—either India was only a creation of the British, or it was solely a creation of overzealous nationalists. The rise of nationalism in the eighteenth and nineteenth centuries led to a legitimate desire to rediscover Indian history. A nation seeking to salvage its pride after centuries of subjugation sought historical validation. Bankimchandra Chattopadhyaya believed we must have a history, and soon many educated Indians were enthusiastically taking up the task of historical rediscovery.

Inadvertently, the British fuelled this pride in India's civilisational past. Some of the early British colonisers were genuine admirers of the ancient culture of the 'natives' (I shall discuss this in more detail in

Chapter 5). Sir William Jones (1746–1794), who arrived in Calcutta in 1783 to take up his assignment as a judge of the Supreme Court, was the most important figure of this scholarly investigation. Within four months of his arrival, on 15 January 1784, he founded the Asiatic Society. For the next several decades, the members of the Society did pioneering work in studying different aspects of India's lost past and translating its important works. Although later in British rule there was a rabid denunciation of Indian culture, especially Hindu culture, many among the early colonisers found enough evidence to testify to the remarkable achievements of ancient India.

Nationalism, thus, did not invent India's civilisational foundations. As more and more facets were reawakened from historical somnolence, it reinforced the consciousness of an ancient past, and a desire, as Mahatma Gandhi put it, 'to cling to the old Indian civilization even as a child clings to its mother's breast'.[32] When Gandhi spoke about our 'far-seeing ancestors' establishing tirthas or pilgrimage spots across the length and breadth of the subcontinent, he could have also mentioned the amazing example of Adi Shankaracharya (788–820 CE), arguably Hinduism's greatest philosopher of this era. Shankaracharya was born in Kaladi, in Kerala, at the southern tip of India. He died in Kedarnath, in the lap of the Himalayas, in the far north. His short life unfolded long before the Islamic conquest, or the coming of the British. Yet, apart from his prodigious output on Hindu philosophy and the Advaita school, he set up mathas or monasteries at Sringeri in the south, Dwarka in the west, Puri in the east and Joshimatha in the north. If there was no consciousness of an identifiable Hindu civilisation, why would he, cutting across different kingdoms, confidently walk the length and breadth of the subcontinent, from Kaladi to Omkareshwar along the Narmada in central India, to Kashi on the Ganga, and right up to Badrinath and Kedarnath in the Himalayas? The four mathas he established were the four extremities of this notion of a pan-Indian Bharatvarsha, the geographical coordinates of the civilisational map of India.

Arun Shourie argues that although 'the Mahabharata and the Ramayana describe warring states *they are the epics of one people* [emphasis mine]',[33] and, indeed, in the Ramayana, Rama goes across the subcontinent, from Ayodhya in the north to Sri Lanka at the very southern tip. Shourie bolsters his reasoning by a fascinating study of many Hindu rituals which clearly indicate this pan-Indian consciousness. 'Only Namboodiris from Kerala are to be priests at Badrinath, those in the Pashupatinath temple at Kathmandu are always from South Kanara in Karnataka, those at Rameshwaram in the deep south are from Maharashtra. ... Every Diwali the sari for the idol of Amba at Kolhapur comes from the Lord at Tirupati. The Sankalpa Mantra with which every puja commends the prayers in the deities, situates the yajyaman (the person organizing the puja) with reference to the salients and sacred rivers of the entire land.'[34] Commenting on this, Dr Koenraad Elst says: 'From hoary antiquity, the Sankalpa locates the Hindu worshipper in time and space, notably in Bharatvarsha, in a decreasing scale of geographical regions down to the city or region where the ritual is performed.'[35]

The truth is that, although it may be expedient for some people to deny an ancient Hindu civilisation, such a civilisational awareness was millennia old, and has had a lasting and verifiable impact on the evolution and, indeed, the very character of India. To admit this is not to invite 'xenophobia' or 'cultural paranoia'. Nor is it the febrile imagination of Hindu enthusiasts. It is, simply, borne out by the facts of history, and cannot be controverted by superimposing the political attitudes of today on the cultural integrations of the past. Sudhir Kakar, one of India's most respected psychologists—and certainly no Hindutva-vadi—writes: 'Indian-ness is about similarities produced by an overarching Indic, pre-eminently Hindu civilization, that has contributed the lion's share to what we would call the "cultural gene-pool" of India's peoples.'[36] The fact, or memory or acceptance, of such a civilisation can be devalued, marginalised, forgotten or ignored, but it cannot be erased. Beyond the recent chronology of historical events, 'the lives of human beings involves many other phenomena which cannot figure in the film of events: the space they inhabit, the social structures that confine them and determine their existence, the ethical rules they consciously or unconsciously obey, their religious and philosophical beliefs, and the civilization to which they belong. These phenomena are much longer lived than we are. ... To study the great civilizations as an exploratory background to the present means stepping aside from the headlong rush of history ... it invites us to reflect on history with a slower pulse-rate, history in the longer term. Civilizations are extraordinary creatures, whose longevity passes all understanding. Fabulously ancient, they live on in each of us; and they will still live on after we have passed away.'[37]

But if the word 'Hindu' to describe a given set of people in a defined territorial space existed, and if a civilisation was verifiably hyphenated with it, why should it be called Hindu, and not Buddhist, or Jain, or any other name so long as it is not labelled 'Hindu'? This is the argument of those of the 'cultural paranoia' school, who suspect a Hindu agenda behind any move to prefix the word 'Hindu'. They are afraid of historical and cultural appropriation by Hindu extremists, which they believe must be resisted in the name of preventing 'xenophobia'. The claim of a dominantly Hindu civilisation must be refuted, not on grounds of historical analysis or factual veracity, but on the basis of a political viewpoint that is deeply suspicious of any attempt to 'hark back' to the past, because such an attempt is synonymous with Hindu revivalism and, therefore, inimical to their selective definition of 'secularism'.

Historical analysis must then compartmentalise the continuum of a civilisation, and see it as consisting of separate or irreconcilable elements, mutually opposed to each other, so that no one aspect— in this case, religion—can claim a defining role. This can only be done by deliberately overlooking the similarities, commonalities and overlapping elements, and projecting a competitive and antagonistic milieu qua religions. Religions, for the sake of a post facto motivation to justify 'secularism', must necessarily be shown to be hostile to one another, admitting of no inclusive interface, even if it is clear that in spite of obvious differences, they are part of the same metaphysical search, as is clearly the case of the ancient Indic faiths. Thus, Hinduism, Buddhism and Jainism must be pitted against one another, for if it is admitted that they are all a part of the overarching Hindu ethos, it will lead to Hindu 'glorification' today. To propound the clash of religions then becomes, ironically enough, the argument of those who as 'secularists' should normally, one would have thought, believed in the ultimate unity of all religious faiths.

Romila Thapar argues that the religion of political dynasties should not be the only criteria to label ancient India with Hindu, and medieval India with Muslim. 'The equation of Ancient with Hindu, and Medieval with Muslim, was based on the fact that many dynasties of the first period were Hindu while those of the second period were Muslim. ... But such a periodization of Indian history is misleading in its emphasis, apart from being questionable in its assumptions. The religious affiliation of rulers was not the pre-eminent motivating factor of change in Indian history, as these categories would imply: it was one among a number of factors.'[38]

Thapar is right. The assertion that ancient India was Hindu because most of its rulers were Hindu is not the only criteria to label this period as Hindu. Ancient India's civilisational ethos was not a consequence of political factors alone. It was Hindu because of *cultural* reasons. A central pillar of this culture was to accommodate, within the larger Hindu world view, a great deal of heterogeneity. This heterogeneity included 'protest' religions like Buddhism and Jainism, and many more schools of thought which, prima facie, seemed to contradict what some would call the basic tenets of Hinduism. For instance, the Charvaka school of materialist thought, which bluntly rejected the sanctity of the Vedas, or the Tantric way, which followed esoteric practices and an ideology different from mainstream Hinduism, were also Hindu because Hinduism, and the culture it nurtured, did not consider such differences to be antithetical to its self-assured ideological generosity. 'Hindu India has had no history of book burning, of executing heretics, or confining heretics to lunatic asylums.'[39]

But although Thapar makes a valid point with regard to political dynasties, the real fear lurking in her mind, it appears, is the old one of 'cultural paranoia'. If ancient India is labelled as 'Hindu', would it not feed hyper Hindu nationalism? She admits this when she says: 'Nationalism seeks legitimacy from the past and history, therefore, becomes a sensitive subject.'[40] The misuse of history is not an irrational fear. But it is equally irrational to allow this fear to distort the reality of the past. If ancient India was overwhelmingly Hindu in the civilisational sense, and if today this leads some overzealous Hindus towards xenophobia, then the right thing to do is to condemn such bigots, and not dilute the indisputably inferable facts of history to suit an extraneous purpose.

Amartya Sen takes this fear to unsustainable lengths. His obsession with countering the possibility of ancient India being Hindu leads him to say that 'the dominant religion in India was Buddhism for nearly a thousand years'.[41] This is a historical distortion. Buddhism, and indeed Jainism, were remarkably enlightened offshoots of Hinduism, one of the many examples of significant heterodoxy permitted by Hinduism itself. Hinduism provided the cultural substratum even in the reign of Ashok, who officially adopted Buddhism. And, as I shall discuss in greater detail in the next chapter, philosophically Buddhism and Hinduism had so much in common that Adi Shankaracharya, rightly credited with reviving Hinduism in the eighth century CE, was described by his Hindu critics as being a 'klepto' Buddhist.

Sen himself accepts that there is 'a well-established view of a broad and generous Hinduism'.[42] But he does not want this acceptance to lead to the acceptance of Hindu India, for that would strengthen Hindu bigotry. His aim, therefore, is to somehow break up the religious continuum of ancient India, and he ties himself in knots in trying to do so. For instance, he writes: 'Indeed, even in terms of Vedic and

Upanishadic contributions, Buddhism and Jainism are as much the inheritors of that tradition as are later forms of Hinduism.'[43] Perhaps so, but in saying this, is he not acknowledging that Buddhism and Jainism were inheritors of the Vedic and Upanishadic contributions? To establish ancient India as Buddhist—or, at least, not dominantly Hindu—he resorts to seriously disputable statements. Nalanda, he says, 'happened to be a Buddhist university'.[44] Such a description was contradicted by none other than Xuanzang, the Chinese traveller, who actually studied at Nalanda. At Nalanda, Xuanzang says, 'There were ten thousand students who studied not only the Buddhist literature in all its branches, but other works such as the Vedas (including *Atharva Veda*), Logic, Grammar, Medicine, Sankhya philosophy etc., and discourses were given from hundred pulpits every day. Piety of generations of kings not only adorned the place with magnificent buildings, both residential and lecture halls, but supplied all the material necessities of this vast concourse of the teachers and the taught.'[45] Many of these kings were Hindus.

Sen's concerted attempt to puncture the claim of Hindu civilisation sometimes assumes laughable proportions. Panini, the great grammarian, who lived in the fourth century BCE was, he says, an Afghani, because his village was on the banks of the Kabul River![46] Does Sen not know that at that time, large parts of modern Afghanistan were part of an Indian empire and closely integrated with Hindu civilisation? By using current political frontiers to categorise one of the greatest Sanskrit scholars as a foreigner seems to be a desperate attempt to devalue our indigenous culture merely because it would enable the 'Hindutva movement' as he calls it, to 'glorify' it. He considers it 'convenient' for Hindu zealots that even cultural theorists like Samuel Huntington describe ancient India as a 'Hindu civilization', but is adamant in maintaining that India was not a 'Hindu country even before the arrival of Islam'.[47] India, for him, was Buddhist for a millennium. In addition, he argues, there were Jews, Parsees, Christians and Arabs, progressively from the first century CE. This is argument for the sake of argument. Firstly, such non-Hindu communities, including Muslims (mostly Arab traders), were present in very limited numbers before the Islamic invasion in the twelfth century CE. Secondly, their presence neither dented nor invalidated the established Hindu ethos, which welcomed their presence in the first place. Somewhere Sen himself realises this, for in calmer moments, he says quite the opposite. 'Those who argue that the Indian identity has to be in some way derived from a Hindu identity point out not only that the Hindus constitute a large majority of the people in India, but also that, historically, Hinduism has been the mainstay of the Indian civilization. These descriptions can, to a considerable extent, be taken to be true.'[48]

Sen is a classic example of a distinguished scholar caught in the trap of using history as convenience—because he feels there is a need to counter current hardline Hindu politics today. With due respect to Dr Sen, I think this is intellectual dishonesty. In rebutting him (and his supporters), the aim is not to assert the superiority of Hinduism over Buddhism or Jainism. These are great religions too. However, there is no doubt that they were organically linked to Hinduism, especially at the level of philosophy, metaphysics, logic and empirical enquiry. Some hostility between the followers was inevitable, but there was never an irreconcilable antagonism between them, as was the case between religions elsewhere. As I have argued, Hinduism permitted a great deal of heterodoxy within its own capacious folds. Buddhism and Jainism remained a part of this diversity, even if they also established a separate identity of their own. Most importantly, the followers of all three religions did not see themselves as viscerally opposed to each other. The followers of one faith respected the others, and kings who were Hindus provided patronage to the other two. Thapar testifies to this. 'In India,' she writes, 'diverse and multiple religions were practised, with royal patronage extending to more than one.'[49] Lay people followed one faith, supported the second and bowed before the saints of the third. This non-confrontational milieu—with negligible exceptions—was essentially a part of the religio-cultural ethos of the foundational Hindu civilisation.

Historical evidence provides abundant proof of this. Early Buddhist relief carvings borrowed freely from the cultural symbols and ornamentation of Hindu worship, such as yakshas, yakshis, nagas and naginis. A frequently recurring symbol in Buddhist shrines was the taurine or nandi-pada, and this has been interpreted as a fire symbol, the Vedic vajra (thunderbolt) or Shiva's trident.[50] Even the rites of worship were similar to that of Hinduism, since the element of bhakti was very much assimilated by the new faith.[51] 'The few metal sculptures of the Gandhara school include a metal reliquary found in a large destroyed stupa at Shah-ji-ki-dheri (near Peshawar), the site of the capital Kanishkapura. The lid of the box bears three figures—a Buddha sitting on a lotus flanked by Indira and Brahma.'[52] A certain interchangeability between the three faiths was witnessed in practice, not only in the behaviour of common people but also royalty. For instance, while the Gupta kings were associated with the promotion of Hinduism, they also extended their patronage to Buddhism. 'Paramartha, a Buddhist scholar of the period, states that king Vikramaditya sent his queen and prince Baladitya to study under the famous monk and scholar Vasubandhu.'[53] Later, the Gupta kings Kumaragupta and Budhagupta built monasteries at Nalanda. Then, in post-Gupta times, Nalanda enjoyed patronage from Harshavardhana and the Palas, both Hindu rulers. Similarly, the Cholas, although Shaiva, 'protected and enriched both Shaiva and Vaishnava temples, as well as Jain and Buddhist establishments'.[54]

Evidently, the non-permeable barrier that Sen asserts against Hinduism, and Buddhism and Jainism, so as to deny one at the expense of the other, is largely incorrect. The two faiths emanated from Hinduism; in their practice and thought they overlapped in myriad ways and certainly did not erase the continuing influence of the parent faith. 'Hindus, Jains, and Buddhists all told their own versions of some of the same stories. Hindus and Buddhists (and others) in the early period shared ideas so freely that it is impossible to say whether some of central tenets of each tradition came from one or the other; often two Hindu versions of the same story, composed in different centuries, have less in common than do a Hindu and Buddhist version of the same story. ... Many of the same images too were used by Buddhists and Jains as well as Hindus.'[55]

The fact is that Hinduism was the chronologically older progenitor of both Buddhism and Jainism. The three religions mostly coexisted peacefully, as part of the larger diversity of thought that Hinduism nurtured, not only within its own fold, but also in its interface with the religions that emanated from it. It is near impossible to compartmentalise any period in ancient India, as Sen is wont to do, exclusively as the domain of either of the later faiths, or to view them separately from Hinduism. The manner in which this actually played out is brought out evocatively by the filmmaker and art historian Benoy K. Behl, who has visually documented the religious sites in ancient India. His commentary, based on extensive ground research, is revealing of the remarkably multifaceted milieu of those times, and of the fact that far from Buddhism establishing its hegemony over Hinduism, the latter continued, even at the high tide of Buddhism, to be its support and patron. It is instructive to quote Behl's full findings:

> By the 8th or the 9th century BCE, the Upanishads were composed, out of the early philosophic traditions of the land. The thoughts contained in the Upanishads were to form the basis of all major Indic faiths thereafter.
>
> This is a view of the world which sees a harmony in the whole of creation. It sees the same which is in each of us, in the animals, the flowers and the trees. All that there is, is seen to be a part of the One.
>
> In this period, there were large numbers of ascetics who gave up the material attractions of the world to seek the truth beyond. The names of two historical 'renunciators' of this tradition became most prominent: Gautama Buddha and Mahavira.
>
> Both taught the philosophy of the Upanishadic age and there are striking similarities in their teachings. In later times, the followers of these teachers formed large religious groups, which continue till today as two of the great religions of the world, with millions of followers: Buddhism and Jainism.

Emperor Ashoka's inscriptions show that he visited many Buddhist pilgrimage sites. However, the great caves which were excavated out of the hills at Barabar in Bihar, in his time and that of his grandson Dashratha, were for the ascetic sect of the Ajivikas.

We find from here onwards, for at least the next one thousand years, a fluid tradition in which members of the same family freely worshipped and patronized the stupas and temples of the Buddhist, Jain and Hindu faiths.

The earliest surviving Buddhist art of the world are the sculpted railings of stupas of the second century BCE. Ashoka's pillars had only images which were common to all faiths, such as the *Chakra*, which stands for cosmic order. The Bharhut stupa railings, originally in Central India, bring us for the first time specific Buddhist themes, including Jataka stories. These were made under the rule of Sunga kings, who personally worshipped Hindu deities.

Similarly, at Sanchi, also in Central India, sculpted railings were made around a stupa, in the 2nd century BCE. They present Buddhist themes and were made under the rule of benevolent Sunga kings who worshipped Hindu deities.

In the 1st century CE, under the rule of the Satavahana kings, great entrance gateways were made to the large stupa at Sanchi. These continued Buddhist themes. Inscriptions show that the Satavahana rulers followed Hindu deities and were fully generous to the Buddhist *Sangha*.

It is significant that at least the first six hundred years of surviving Buddhist art was all created under the rule of kings who worshipped Hindu deities.

The first formalized deity seen in Buddhist and Jain art is Gajalakshmi—Lakshmi with elephants who shower water upon her. Like the *yakshi*, she also represents the bountiful abundance of nature. Lakshmi continues till today in Hindu worship and in Buddhist worship in Japan and other countries.

In Western India, the 2nd century BCE ushered in one of the greatest periods of the entire art of Buddhism. Over a period of about a 1,000 years, more than 1,200 caves were hewn out of the mountains of the Western Ghats. Most of them were profusely sculpted and painted in the Buddhist tradition.

The first phase of prolific excavation was from the 2nd century BCE till the 3rd century CE. Great Buddhist prayer halls and *Viharas* for the residence of monks were made under the rule of the Satavahanas and the Kshatrapas. Though these kings revered Hindu deities, they patronized all religious establishments.

The Buddhist cave number 18 at Bhaja of the 2nd century BCE brings us some of the earliest-known representations of the Hindu deities Indra and Surya. They continue in worship till today in Hinduism and in Buddhist temples in Japan. A 'gana' of the 2nd century BCE made at the Buddhist site of Pitalkhora carries an inscription which states that he was the donation of a goldsmith Kanhadasa, which means 'servant of Krishna', a Hindu deity.

There is an inscription dated around 150 CE at Nasik Caves issued by one Gautami Balashree, who was the mother of a Satavahana ruler Gautamiputra. She praises Lord Krishna, but the purpose of the inscription is to donate an excavated cave to the Buddhist monastic order. There are hundreds of inscriptions in the Western ghats, issued during the Satavahana rule, which record donations of people from all walks of life to the Buddhist monastic order. So, it is obvious that though the rulers had their own religious preferences, there was no pressure on the population to follow the faith of the ruler.

According to the inscriptions, the Kushana Kings worshipped Hindu deities themselves. However, in keeping with Indic traditions, they were fully benevolent to Buddhist and Jain establishments.

The fertile valley of the Krishna River was the cradle of civilisation in the Eastern Deccan. This area became one of the greatest centres of Buddhism and over 140 early Buddhist sites have been listed in this region.

The exquisite phase of the art of the Amravati Stupa was under the rule of the Satavahana rulers. They were devoted to Hindu deities and were fully benevolent to the Buddhist Sangha.

The Ikshvakus came to power in the Krishna Valley in the second quarter of the 3rd century. A large number of monastic establishments were founded at Nagarjunakonda for the residence, study and worship of at least four different sects of Buddhists.

As in the case of all major Buddhist monuments since the 2nd century BCE, these at Nagarjunakonda were made under the rule of kings who worshipped Hindu deities themselves. As was often the case, some female members of the royal family were devoted to Buddhism and made personal donations to the monasteries.

The period of Gupta rule in North India brings some of the finest and best-known Buddhist, Hindu and Jain art. It is significant to note that many of the kings personally followed Hindu practices. However, some of the greatest Buddhist art of the world was made in their benevolent rule. Records also show that these kings gave very generous grants for Buddhist establishments. In fact, the most vibrant and important centres of Buddhist thought and worship reached their height during Gupta rule. These were the wondrous university of Nalanda and the Mahabodhi temple at Bodh Gaya.

We also find wonderful Jain images whose inscriptions state that they were made under the rule of Hindu kings, such as Ramagupta, named after the Hindu deity Rama. Some of the finest Hindu art, at Eran and other sites, was made under the rule of a king named Buddhagupta.

At the magnificent site of Ajanta, in the horseshoe-shaped gorge of the Waghora River, great shrines and monasteries had been carved out of the heart of the mountain in the second century BCE. This was in the rule of the Hindu Satavahana kings. In the mid 5th century, under the rule of the Hindu Vakataka kings, it saw renewed activity.

As in the Indic tradition seen earlier in the Western and Eastern Deccan, feudatories, ministers of the king and even queens freely followed the Buddhist faith. They also patronized Buddhist caves and art. There were no religious divisions and the patrons of the Buddhist caves sometimes proclaim their descent from Hindu deities.[56]

It is not surprising then that many Hindus believe that Buddha was the last incarnation of Vishnu. This is not illustrative of any desire to obliterate Buddhism in favour of Hinduism, but as an acknowledgement of the continuity-in-separation it represented.

There is possibly some truth in the view that Buddhism ultimately spread far more widely beyond the shores of India, than in India itself, because the Hindu faith, from which it (partially) rebelled, did not consider such rebellions as heresy. Within India, Buddhism faced the genuine possibility of assimilation, whereas abroad its presence marked a new departure, and undivided followers. 'The fate of Buddhism affords us a highly instructive instance of India's efforts to assimilate its own rebellious and intractable elements.'[57] Thus, Hinduism predated Buddhism, coexisted with it and outlived it. In spite or the rise of heterodox faiths, for millennia, 'India was really Hindustan, almost completely Hindu; even Buddhist heterodoxy went through a long process of integration with the parent faith before it was finally assimilated ... the deepest foundation of India's Great Tradition is also largely Hindu.'[58]

Interestingly, Explanation II of Article 25 of the Constitution, and judicial pronouncements at the highest level after 1947 have affirmed the organic interconnectivity between Hinduism, Buddhism and Jainism, and also Sikhism, which emerged in the medieval period as a highly enlightened and powerful new religion. Pronouncing on the Hindu Marriage Act (1955), the Supreme Court upheld its premise that any reference to Hindus shall be construed as including 'any person who is a Buddhist, Jain or Sikh by religion'. It reiterated this umbrella-like characteristic of inclusion in Hinduism in 1966, when followers of the Swaminarayan sect sought recognition as a separate religion. Such judicial verdicts should not be interpreted as an act of religious expansion by legal means, but a pragmatic realisation of the essential nature of Hinduism, and its foundational interface with the Indic faiths that emanated from it.

If Hindus were conscious of their identity, created a civilisation on that basis and that civilisation was Hindu in essence, what could be the next line of attack of Hindu-phobic critics? Their next argument is that there was no such thing as Hinduism, a unified religion in the singular. If Hinduism as a religion as we know it today did not exist in the past, how could our foundational history be called Hindu? The remarkable civilisational ecosystem that Hinduism spawned would be valid only if Hinduism, and even more importantly its world view, could be identified as a coherent set of beliefs and practices. If it can be proved that this was not the case, then the case of a Hindu period in our history would fall flat.

The naysayers argue that Hinduism never had a unified core. No one god, no one religious text, no one supreme temple, no one pope and no one set of prescribed rituals made it just a collation of diversities which cannot qualify to be a 'coherent' religion in the way Abrahamic faiths are. To give a 'random' way of life—where practice is not universally codified and divinity is not unrelentingly singular— the pedestal of a religion is an act of post facto creative reconstruction, with the sole aim of historical aggrandisement. In other words, the existence of 'excessive' diversity within the practice of the Hindu way is the reason why it must be denied the label of a rationally consistent religion.

The dramatis personae of this kind of thinking are familiar. Wendy Doniger writes: 'For the past few decades, scholars have raised several and strong objections to the use of any single term to denote one of the world's major and most ancient faiths. … "Hinduism" (dare I use the "H" word, and may I stop holding up my hands for mercy with quotation marks?) is, like the armadillo, part hedgehog, part tortoise. Yet, there *are* armadillos, and they were there before they had names. I would like to suggest some ways in which the disparate parts of what we call Hinduism have in fact existed for centuries, cheek by jowl, in a kind of fluid suspension.'[59]

The academic ease with which Doniger conflates diversity with disparity is amusing. And, because of this basic misinterpretation, the whole, for her, cannot cohere; it can only be disparate, somehow hanging together in 'fluid suspension'. What is quite clearly in evidence is a yearning for the sanitised and clear-cut structures of her own faith, Christianity, and other Abrahamic faiths. The cerebrally calibrated but—for the foreigner—bewildering plurality of Hinduism perplexes Doniger. 'There is, after all, no Hindu canon; ideas about all the major issues of faith and lifestyle—vegetarianism, non-violence, belief in rebirth, even caste—*are subjects of debate not dogma* [emphasis mine].'[60] She, therefore, goes about trying to make a Venn diagram, 'a set of intersecting circles of concept and beliefs and practices, some of which are held and done by some Hindus but also by members of South Asian religions, such as Buddhism and Jainism'.[61] The exercise is superficial and mechanical, because the attempt to make a menu of a religion like Hinduism is ridiculous. Her conclusion is, however, predictable. 'But since there is no single central quality that all Hindus must have, the emptiness in the centre suggests that the figure might better be named a Zen diagram, a Venn diagram that has no central ring.'[62]

There is a certain superciliousness with which Doniger writes, and which she hopes to get away with it. Her book, *The Hindus: An Alternative History*, created outrage in a section of Hindus for the literal interpretation of the Shivalinga as simplistically—and titillatingly—a symbol for the penis. While Hindus, who have taken many such deliberate distortions of their religion over the centuries, should perhaps have let it pass, Doniger's response to the protest was most revealing. 'I had written all my other books for an American audience, primarily for my students. That was one reason why I was totally blindsided by the passionate Hindu response to my book, *The Hindus*: it hadn't occurred to me that Hindus would read it.'[63]

Really, Ms Doniger? If a leading scholar on Hinduism in America writes a 779-page book on Hindus, why should she presume that Hindus would not read it? Are they illiterate? Can none of them read English? Are they totally indifferent to the conclusion others draw about them and their faith? Do they still behave like the 'natives' in colonial times, passively accepting the arbitrary generalisations made about them by their 'masters'? What would Ms Doniger think if an Indian scholar wrote as voluminous a book on the practice of Christianity by Americans, with sweeping generalisations about their faith and its practice, with only the defence, when questioned, that he or she never thought the Americans would read it? Can a book which claims academic credentials seriously be written on the assumption that no matter what it says, the 'natives' would neither know nor read nor mind? The whole thing smacks of a new form of Orientalism, wherein people like Doniger feel that, ensconced in the citadel of Western Indology, they have the right to cavalierly pronounce judgement on one of the oldest and most refined religions of the world, and get away with it. And, in any case, if challenged, their reflex defence can always be—and, indeed, Doniger resorts to it—that this is evidence of the rise of Hindu fundamentalism in India.

It is this kind of Orientalism that allows Doniger to casually compare Hinduism to a hybrid between a hedgehog and a tortoise, and to believe that this is a scholarly assessment. But an examination of her methodology would show why her conclusions are wrong. Doniger's 'study' of Hinduism is to trawl through the countless texts that constitutes the enormous corpus of Hinduism, focus deliberately on the peripheral rather than the obvious central theme, dig out the odd factoid for quixotic or titillating affect, mechanically highlight the differences between varying traditions and practices, and then conclude that the diversities are so great that Hinduism cannot be written with a capital 'H'. What she refuses to understand is that the diversity that mesmerises her into believing that there in not one but many Hinduisms, is *precisely* what Hinduism is about. In evolving over millennia, instead of congealing into a brittle set of absolutes, Hinduism fully enabled both diversity of opinion and local variations of key themes, *without* losing the centrality of its narrative. That diversity of practice and thought is puzzling for people like Doniger, who retain a nostalgia for the 'system' and 'order' of simpler-to-comprehend Abrahamic faiths. The problem is that she is so overawed by this diversity that she misses the wood for the trees. The coherence of the central theme, so obvious to practitioners of Hinduism, eludes her, or is deliberately overlooked. Her conclusion is that a religion that refuses to cohere in more predictable ways from a Western standpoint cannot be a singular religion at all.

Doniger cannot find 'the central ring' in Hinduism because she is not looking for it. To prove her scholarly credentials, she expends a great deal of energy in focusing on the innumerable spokes in Hindu belief and practice, without understanding that they are all a part of a central wheel. If Hinduism can be likened to a massive river, Doniger's eyes are on its countless tributaries. Unfortunately, her conclusion is not that there is a majestic river which they ultimately join, but that the tributaries are proof that there is no one river at all. For instance, there are six systems—not one—of Hindu philosophy. All of them differ with each other, but all of them are united in their search not for divinity but for the ultimate truth. The inspiration for the search of this ultimate truth comes from the remarkable metaphysical insights of the Upanishads. But there is no one Upanishad, nor is it known who wrote them. To understand that truth, there is not one but several ways, through jnana (knowledge), karma (action) or devotion (surrender). The paths differ, but their goal is the same. The Hindu pantheon has no one absolute God. There are thousands of gods, starting with the supreme Trinity of Brahma, Vishnu and Shiva, and their powerful consorts, and even children and avatars, including local variations that allow even a piece of rock to be venerated, but all of them essentially reflect the one truth of an all-pervasive, omniscient, omnipotent, pulsating consciousness called Brahman. At one level, Hindus extravagantly humanise their gods, celebrate their birth and marriages and life events; but at another level they are, like harmonious schizophrenics, aware that this is the pageantry of devotion that in no way undermines the higher spiritual truth that all gods represent that one Ultimate. The Vedas are considered by some as revealed texts, but there are Hindu schools that question their validity, such as the Charvakas. Religious practice is diverse, including the esoteric Tantric school, but Hinduism accepts that at the level of apara vidya, preparatory knowledge—a spiritual aspirant has the freedom to choose any form of religious of spiritual practice.

No wonder then that Doniger is flummoxed. Paradoxically, she herself provides the uniting reason behind this kaleidoscope—Hindu philosophy and practice, she writes, *are subjects of debate not dogma* [emphasis mine]'. If a religion allows for debate, and eschews dogma—which many Abrahamic faiths insist upon—must it, for this cardinal 'taint', cease to be seen as a unified religion, and become an armadillo, a hedgehog crossed with a tortoise?

Perhaps, Doniger, as a non-Hindu foreigner writing for American audiences, can be forgiven for her inability to understand Hinduism's unity in diversity. But the views of Indians like Amartya Sen—who once told me that he could not give up his Indian passport because of his love for Sanskrit—are more difficult to comprehend. Sen argues that 'seeing Hinduism as a unified religion is a comparatively recent development. The term "Hindu" was traditionally used mainly as a signifier of location and country, rather than of any homogenous belief.'[64] As evidence, Sen states that 'Sanskrit not only has a larger body of religious literature than exists in any other classical language, it also has a larger volume of agnostic and atheistic writings than in any other classical language.'[65] In saying this, Sen does not understand—or deliberately ignores—the contradictory nature of his stance. When he wants to prove the diversity of Indian civilisation, he quotes—as I shall examine later—the practice of tolerance to different points of view within Hinduism. But, this very tolerance becomes, in another context, a reason for him to doubt whether Hinduism was a unified religion at all. Expectedly, Romila Thapar concurs with Sen. 'The multiplicity of reasonably independent sects has led some scholars to speak of the Hindu traditions (in the plural). The term "Hindu" to describe a religious identity came into currency as late as the second millennium AD.'[66]

Hinduism may have, like all religions, taken time to evolve into an identifiable unity. The date when this was achieved—and there can be no final date, since religions like Hinduism continue to evolve—can be debated, but Hinduism had certainly become a unified religion for its practitioners in ancient India itself. On the question of its singularity, the scholar, linguist and translator, A.K. Ramanujan, has an effective rebuttal. Ramanujan famously wrote the essay on 'three hundred Ramayanas', an acknowledgement of the variations to the theme permitted within Hinduism. He also dwelt on the great and the little traditions in Hindu belief and practice. His conclusion was the recognition of diversity, not the negation of Hinduism. His wry comment on those who thought otherwise was: 'One way of defining diversity for India is to say what the Irishman is said to have said about trousers. When asked whether trousers were singular or plural, he said, "Singular at the top and plural at the bottom." Another way of talking about a culture like the Indian is through the analogy of a hologram — that is to say that any section is a cross-section, any piece of it is a true representation of the whole, as any cell of the body is supposed to be a true sample of the whole body.'[67]

Interestingly, as a youth, Ramanujan, was perplexed at his father's belief in both astrology and astronomy. By Western standards, astrology is at best speculative, while astronomy is a scientific study of the precise movement of planets. However, Ramanujan, a sophisticated student of Hinduism, soon realised that this was not a question of irreconcilable disparity, nor was such surface 'inconsistency' about 'inadequate education or lack of logical rigour'.[68] He understood that the Hindu mind is like a toolbox or a chest of drawers. You can pick up one tool, or open one drawer, but the tool is a part of a single toolbox, and the drawer is part of one chest of drawers.

To conclude that Hinduism encourages and nurtures a diversity of thought and practice is one thing. To infer that because of this inherent eclecticism it is not a religion at all, is quite another. For those mesmerised into negativity by the surface multiplicity of Hinduism, Professor Rajiv Malhotra has a telling phrase, 'anxiety over chaos'. Bewilderment over Hinduism's effortless diversity is typical for those more comfortable with linear Abrahamic faiths like Christianity and Islam. 'But Dharmic civilizations are more relaxed and comfortable with multiplicity and ambiguity than the West. Chaos is seen as a source of creativity and dynamism. Since the ultimate reality is an integrally unified coherence, chaos is a relative phenomenon that cannot threaten or disrupt the underlying coherence of the cosmos.'[69] The room for philosophical speculation that Hinduism permits is the validation for a search and an exploration of what this cosmos is about. But for this reason 'Indian metaphysical flexibility is not to be confused with randomness, duplicity, or lack of rigour ... The Nyaya Shastra rigorously demands five steps to establish a thesis; Mimamsha has seven principles for framing a problem; there are techniques known as "tantr-yuktis" for writing scientific texts in Sanskrit; and there are various established methodologies for debating opponents'.[70] Malhotra makes an apt comparison between Hinduism and the banyan tree. 'The banyan is unique among trees in that the branches sprout first and eventually bow down to the ground and become the roots of a new tree, each providing nourishment and stability to the entire tree. The tree is a single structure but functions like a complex, decentralized organization ... Its multiple roots and branches represent multiple origins and sources—all parts of the same living organism, even if the whole cannot be comprehended at one glance. Each of the separate roots feeds every trunk, and hence every leaf is connected to the entire root system.'[71] Thus, Hinduism 'is a network ... an open architecture intertwined internally and externally. It is naturally assimilative, and this makes it a highly efficient system for adaptation and for the fostering of diversity.'[72]

There is, of course, a basic irony in Hinduism's derogation by some 'liberals'. One would have thought that liberal opinion would be appreciative of a religion that relies less on dogma and more on debate. It would make a virtue of the fact that Hinduism enables diversity to thrive when many other faiths are prescriptive and rely on diktat. However, instead of lauding this eclecticism, they conclude that Hinduism is only about diversity ad infinitum. In doing so, they not only betray their liberal credentials, but also do injury to a religion that revels in differences of opinion and practices within its identifiable central narrative. Heterogeneity in expression then becomes a reason to question homogeneity in substance. In a curious endorsement of the hedgehog–tortoise parallel, Sen, who otherwise expresses pride at the level of heterogeneity in Hindu thought, concludes that 'the Hindu traditions do not constitute a melting pot in any way whatsoever'.[73] The truth is that Hinduism is *both* a salad bowl and a melting pot. It is—and was—a great religion not because it was linear or prescriptive, but because, self-assured in its central narrative, it was not intimidated by diversity. 'It is perfectly acceptable in Hinduism to be a polytheist, monotheist, monist, pantheist, agnostic, atheistic, animist or any combination thereof'.[74] This is proof of its deeply eclectic spirit, not a reason to devalue its coherence. As Rabindranath Tagore says: 'To experience unity in diversity and to establish unity amongst variety—this is the inherent dharma (the spirit) of Bharat. Bharatvarsha never interpreted diversities as hostility.'[75]

If Hindus created a civilisation, how old is it? Does it have an antiquity that places it among the oldest civilisations of the world, comparable to Egypt, Mesopotamia, Greece and China, or is it possibly older than all of them? This may sound an innocuous question of establishing chronological coordinates, but it is deeply enmeshed in an ideological debate, where there is a prominent school of historians which strongly opposes any such claim. I shall discuss, on broad but specific lines, the mass of scientific and textual evidence available to substantially predate the hitherto conventional theories of the antiquity of the Hindu civilisation. But first we need to go into the reasons why such evidence is rejected offhand by some people.

In June 2020, the vice chancellor of the prestigious Jawaharlal Nehru University in New Delhi issued an invitation to a webinar on 'The Saraswati Civilization: A Paradigm Shift in Indian History'. No sooner was this done, a storm of protest broke out. Senior faculty members of the Centre of Historical Studies, where the webinar was organised, wrote to the vice chancellor expressing 'grave concern and misgivings'. The ostensible reason was that they were not consulted before the invitation was issued. But, the real reason, which was also responsible for the protest of the leftist student associations, was something quite different. It was the belief that such webinars are a conspiracy by the Hindu right to falsely 'glorify' Hindu civilisation by giving it an antiquity it did not possess. Some of them dubbed it as yet another attempt to give a platform to right-wing speakers, an attack on liberal values and secular progressive history, an incentive to communalism.

This reflex opposition to a substantial corpus of recently discovered historically verifiable evidence to re-examine the date of origin of ancient India, is once again proof of the reflexive Hindu phobia that has become the hallmark of left-leaning historians since 1947. They are, unfortunately, supported by many well-meaning 'secularists' who are afraid that this may strengthen the cause of Hindu fundamentalism.

Let us assume that there are, indeed, some overenthusiastic Hindus who seek to blindly glorify ancient India. Does that mean that all substantive research on Indian civilisation's antiquity, cutting across a spectrum of disciplines, must also be rejected outright? Is there no scope for objectively examining the data and the reasoning, and allow for rational debate? Even if we accept that there is a need to fight Hindu chauvinism today, must the historical evaluation of the past be perennially held hostage to this apprehension? Do independent scholars, both Indian and foreign, seeking to interrogate India's civilisational origins using cutting-edge technology automatically become Hindu fundamentalists? Is there always a hidden agenda in any research that may shed positive light on the antiquity and refinements of our ancient past?

These questions need to be sensibly debated, but that is rarely done. There is an entire mass of scholarly work on the antiquity of ancient India, and it is not my intention to even remotely detail it. However, is will suffice the purpose to give a broad outline. For a considerable period, the established view was that the Aryans invaded India sometime around 1500 BCE, overran the pre-existing Harappan civilisation, and settled largely along the Gangetic plains, to commence the Vedic period. As a result of this invasion, the Harappans, who spoke Dravidian, were driven towards south India, and the Sanskrit-speaking Aryans established their hegemony in the north. This was a theory long favoured by the British. The Aryans were presumed to be of European origin. Hence, they were migrants from the West, thus allowing the British to claim ownership, indirectly, of ancient India, and deny at the same time the possibility of the indigenous roots of Indian history. The theory then said that, in time, the Western-origin Aryans, by mixing with the indigenous population, lost their civilisational vitality, and it was for the British, millennia later, to resurrect that original civilisation by the benediction of their colonial rule.

It was a convenient theory, except that it has been roundly rubbished by almost every serious historian. The Aryan Invasion Theory (AIT) has now been consigned to the historical dustbin. As Dr Upinder Singh says: 'One of the most popular explanations of the decline of the Harappan civilization is one for which there is least evidence. There is, actually, no evidence of any kind of any military assault or conflict at any Harappan site.'[76] Romila Thapar endorses this conclusion. 'The archaeological picture of the second and first millennium BCE (or even earlier for that matter) provide little or no support for a large scale invasion or a displacement of peoples and culture.'[77] What has been overwhelmingly accepted is that the Indo-Aryans were migrants who came to the subcontinent over a period of time (as, indeed, all the inhabitants of the subcontinent—and indeed of all Europe too—must have been migrants at some point of time since the common ancestor of the entire human race came from Africa). The question is *when* did the Indo-Aryans come, and *what* was their interface with the Harappan culture? The answer to this provides the key to the antiquity of Indian civilisation.

The answer lies in the swirling waters of that mysterious river, Sarasvati. The oldest ancient Indian text, the *Rig Veda*, which shows great knowledge about the geography of north-west India, speaks about the Sarasvati as a mighty river flowing from the mountains to the sea. Moreover, it mentions this river repeatedly. 'In forty-five of its hymns, the *Rig Veda* showers praise on the Sarasvati; her name appears seventy-two times, and three hymns are wholly dedicated to her. ... Sarasvati's waters are lauded as a "great flood", she is "great among the great, the most impetuous of rivers", and was "created vast". "Limitless, unbroken, swift moving", she "surpasses in majesty and might all other waters" or of rivers. At least one of the Vedic clans, the Purus, is said to dwell "on her grassy banks".'[78] The Mahabharata too has lengthy descriptions of the river, including of the ashrams and tirthas on its banks.

This textual evidence for the existence of a mighty river that once flowed from the Himalayas to the ocean, between the Yamuna in the east and the Sutlej in the west, has been rigorously examined by independent research cutting across a wide matrix of scientific instrumentalities. The Department of Space of the Government of India used remote sensing satellite data, along with the digital elevation model, to identify the Sarasvati. Using historical maps, archaeological sites, hydrogeological and drilling data, it came to the conclusion that the paleochannel along the current, mostly dry, Ghagra River was, indeed, the course of the mighty Sarasvati River. Sometime around the end of the third millennium BCE, the Sarasvati dried up. Most experts accept the theory that between 2500 BCE and 1900 BCE, there were tectonic disturbances which caused a tilt in topography of north-western India, resulting in the migration of rivers. This affected the directional flow of two of the major tributaries of the Sarasvati, the Sutlej and the Yamuna. The Sutlej moved westward and became a tributary of the Indus, and the Yamuna moved eastward to become a tributary of the Ganga. The resultant water loss led the Sarasvati to dry up in the Thar Desert in the third millennium BCE. Indeed, centuries *after* the *Rig Veda*, the Brahmanas refer to the drying up of the river.

It is important to bear in mind that such inferences today are not only based on the surmises of historians and the subjective interpretation of textual material. An entire stable of scientific tools, not available until the recent past, such as those mentioned in the preceding paragraph, together with oceanography, hydrology, morpho-dynamics, geology and historical data are deployed. To put it simply, if a mighty river once flowed, its existence leaves behind objective evidence verifiable by scientific methodologies, and the same evidence can also indicate the timeline when that river ceased to exist, or dwindled to just a seasonal flow.

If, therefore, the Sarasvati did exist as a major river and the *Rig Veda* testifies to that in very specific words, not once but repeatedly, it follows that the authors of this text must have been on Indian soil at a time when the river existed in its original form. Since the process of the drying up of the river has been dated to around 2500 to 1900 BCE, they must have been in India, not in 1500 BCE as assumed earlier, but at least a millennium—if not more—before that.

Michel Danino, in his meticulously researched and fascinating book *The Lost River*, makes it clear why, in the light of current data, the earlier theories stand refuted: 'Yet, following Max Müller, all conventional history books and encyclopaedias tell us that the *Rig Veda*'s hymns were composed by "Aryans" who entered the sub-continent around 1500 BCE and pushed on towards the Yamuna–Ganges region, crossing sometime between 1200 and 1000 BCE. Whatever the countless dates proposed (there are countless variations of this scenario), the said "Aryans" could have only settled in the Sarasvati region after 1400 or 1300 BCE—centuries after the river had totally dried up. We are, therefore, asked to believe that the Aryans crossed at least five large rivers—the Indus and its four tributaries—to settle down on the banks of a long, dry river, which they went on to extol as "mighty", "impetuous", "best of rivers", etc. The proposition is incongruous in the extreme.'[79] The only plausible explanation he says is that 'the hymns that praise the Sarasvati—and some of them are found in the oldest books of the *Rig Veda*—must have been composed while the river was still flowing, which can be no later than the third millennium BCE.'[80]

Some historians still question this conclusion, and their objections need to be examined. Romila Thapar reiterates an earlier theory propounded in 1833 by Indologist Edward Thomas. Thomas argued that the Sarasvati was actually the Helmand River in southern Afghanistan. In the Avestan language of ancient Iran, the name of the chief tributary of this river is Harahvati, linguistically similar to Sarasvati. The migrating Aryans on their arrival in north-west India, so Thomas argued, transferred their memory of this river to another river in India, a small stream Sarsuti, flowing into the Indus. A second objection is that the word 'samudra' should not be taken to mean the sea. It was necessary to assert this, since the Helmand, instead of flowing into the sea, ends in a swamp in Afghanistan. Hence, if the *Rig Veda* specifically says that the Sarasvati flowed 'from the mountains to the sea' (giribhya a samudra), it is necessary to argue that samudra does not mean the sea, but any collection of water, such as a lake.

Danino and many other scholars strongly rebut this rather unconvincing theory. Danino says, 'If the migrating Aryans were so attached to a Sarasvati left behind in Afghanistan, it is unclear what prevented them from transferring its name to the Indus—the first river they encountered after descending into its vast plains—or to any of its respectable tributaries, from the Jhelum to the Sutlej. … It stretches the imagination to picture them having a sudden afterthought some 200 or 300 years after they left Afghanistan, and lauding the bygone Sarasvati by transferring its hallowed name to a petty seasonal stream.'[81] On the samudra matter, Danino relies, inter alia, on historian and Sanskritist P.L. Bhargava, whose majestic book, *Geography of Rigvedic India*, clearly brings out the knowledge the Vedic Indians had of the sea and of maritime warfare. The word 'samudra', plainly meaning the sea, occurs some 160 times in the *Rig Veda*. 'In none of these occurrences,' Danino emphasises, 'can the word Samudra stand for a swampy Afghan lake.'[82]

It must be conceded that there is still no unanimity among scholars on the Sarasvati. While some experts like Danino marshal impressive evidence to support the theory of a mighty Sarasvati that once flowed along the current Ghaggar Valley, there are others who question this inference. Tony Joseph, in his comprehensively researched book,

Early Indians, surveys the entire corpus of contemporary research, and concludes: 'The overwhelming evidence today, therefore, is that what shrunk the Ghaggar–Hakra was not a tectonic event that stole its waters and gave it to the Ganga and the Indus, but a mega drought that had global impact. To reiterate, the Ghaggar was a monsoon-fed river that was weakened by monsoon failure, and not a mighty, snowmelt-fed river that was used to "breaking mountaintops" as migration denialists insist'.[83] Scholars are entitled to their opinions; perhaps, instead of tectonic shifts, it was a mega drought that dried the Sarasvati. Yet, it is my view that the manner and frequency with which the Sarasvati is lauded in the *Rig Veda* (and other texts) could not only be a flight of imagination. The 'mighty' and 'tempestuous' river flowing 'from the mountains to the sea' could hardly be the description of a rain-fed, seasonal, mostly dry Ghaggar, originating not in snow-capped mountains but in the foothills of the Shivalik Hills.

If, therefore, we proceed on the theory that the Aryans were in the subcontinent more than a millennium earlier than what was their supposed date of migration, there is still one missing link that needs resolution. This theory makes the Aryans a part of Indian soil coterminous with the Harappan civilisation. What then was the interface between the two? Until recently, conventional history was divided between 'pre-Aryan' and 'post-Aryan'. The two phases were seen as an irreconcilable binary, with almost nothing in common. However, a great deal of recent research is radically changing this mechanically polarised view. The overwhelming evidence now points to an interface between the two as the part of a process that was both assimilative and transformative. This is particularly so since many of the principal sites of the Harappan civilisation—Kalibangan (Rajasthan), Banawati and Rakhigarhi (Haryana), Dholavira and Lothal (Gujarat)—are situated along the banks of the Sarasvati. If the Aryans too were in this region, how can it be that there was no interface whatsoever between the people who together inhabited this region?

The evidence that there was such an interface is overwhelming. Danino and other scholars have examined the data at great length, and it would suffice to highlight their main findings. The continuities are both tangible and intangible. Earlier analysts placed considerable emphasis on the fact that while the Harappan civilisation was urban, the Vedic civilisation was rural. However, this absolute divide is artificial. As Dr Upinder Singh says: 'City and village are not two opposite poles but interdependent and interacting parts of a larger cultural and ecological system.'[84] Thus, we find that later cities like Mathura, Kaushambhi, Rajgir and Vaishali reproduce, almost identically, the architectural features of fortresses and moats found in the Harappan cities. Even more remarkable is the fact that the famous practice of standardisation found in Harappan cities is repeated in later historical cities, and is recommended in precisely the same ratios by Kautilya in his *Arthashastra*, as well as the Vastu Shastra architectural manuals (both recommend the 5:4 ratio for the construction of major buildings, which was precisely what the Harappans used). The discernible continuity is easily seen also in the emulation of the Harappan wells built with trapezoid bricks, and in pillared halls, house plans and even construction techniques used in later times.

The weights and measures used by the Harappans provide another striking example of continuity. The Harappan weight system, starting at just below a gram and going up to 10 kg, and the geometric progression by which the measure increases, clearly inspired the weight system described in the *Arthashastra*, and is exactly the same as that used in the later kingdoms of the Gangetic plain.

This replication of Harappan practices can be seen in the area of technology and crafts as well, be it bangle- and bead-making or shell and ivory artefacts. The bronze casting method, also known as 'lost wax casting', used by the Harappans to make, for instance, the famous dancing girl statue, was subsequently used throughout the subcontinent, including, most famously, for the Chola bronzes in the thirteenth century CE.

'Even the married Hindu woman's custom of applying vermilion at the parting of the hair has Harappan origins: figurines found at Nausharo and elsewhere show traces of red pigment at the same spot. Some orthodox Hindu men continue to wear an amulet tied to the upper-right arm, exactly where the so-called "priest king" (as seen in Harappan seals) displays one.'[85] The noted art historian Stella Kramrisch rightly concludes that the Harappan 'tradition remains unbroken, for the themes and the forms of the Indus Valley during the second and third millennium BCE are continued in Indian art when it re-emerges in the third century BCE.'[86]

Intangible heritage also shows some striking continuities. A great many seals of the Harappan civilisation were discovered and their iconography provides rich material in support of this. Thus, common Harappan forms such as the swastika, the unicorn looking like a single-horned bull, the eight-shaped endless knot, the pipal leaf and the fire-worshipping altars are common symbols that persist even today. Of great interest is the most well-known Harappan seal, known as the Pashupati seal. It shows a dominant figure seated in a yogic posture with a tricorn headdress and three faces, surrounded by beasts—hence the name 'Pashupati'. Since many seals depict the same figure, it is reasonable to presume that he was an object of special reverence. Leading scholars concur that the depiction is strikingly reminiscent of Shiva. The tricorn headdress recalls the trimurti in Hindu religious practice, as also the trishul (depicted independently on many seals and recurring frequently in the still-undeciphered Harappan script), which is the symbol of Shiva. Such a correlation becomes stronger due to the presence of many seals showing a majestic humped bull, quite identical to Nandi, Shiva's bull. We also find lingas that are startlingly similar to later—and current—Shaivite iconography. 'Altogether, the evidence of the cult of a Shiva-like ("proto" or not) deity in the Indus-Saraswati civilization does build up into a consistent whole.'[87]

There are also a great many seals dedicated to what appears to be a mother goddess, and their ubiquity is proof of their special importance. John Stratton Hawley and Donna Marie Wulff, who have written an important book, *Devi: The Goddesses of India*, assert that 'the styles of modelling they display were carried forward into subsequent ages. Female sculptures from the Mauryan period (fourth to second century BCE) and even later often look very much like their Indus prototypes.'[88] To this, if we add seals depicting yogic postures (for instance, there are some showing a man seated cross-legged with his hands together in the traditional greeting of a namaste), there is more than a reasonable basis to agree with John Marshall's categorical conclusion: 'Taken as a whole, [the Indus Valley's peoples religion] is so characteristically Indian as hardly to be distinguished from still living Hinduism.'[89]

Thus, instead of seeing the Indus and the subsequent Gangetic civilisations as two separate phenomena, it would be far more accurate to view them as a part of a cultural continuum. An oft-cited argument to emphasise their separateness is that one was urban and the other was rural or pastoral. However, Dr Upinder Singh argues that the Harappan civilisation underwent a gradual process of deurbanisation, leading to an eastward and southward migration. It did not come to a sudden end, and the late Harappan phase was marked by the decline in urban features and the diversification of agriculture. In this phase, 'even if there were several waves of Indo-Aryan migrations in the pre-Vedic period, the migrants constructed their civilizational world view on Indian soil, and also assimilated elements of the Harappan culture'.[90] In support of this view, she cites the fact that there are about 300 clearly non-Sanskrit words in the *Rig Veda*. These 'loan words' indicate that the Rig Vedic people were interacting with those of the Harappan civilisation. 'There are many tribes with non-Indo-Aryan names in the *Rig Veda*, such as Chumuri, Dhuni, Pipru and Shambara. The text also refers to Aryan chieftains with non-Indo-Aryan names, e.g., Balbuta and Bribu. All this is indicative of processes of cultural interaction.'[91] Romila Thapar accepts that the genius of cultures is found in the intermixture of peoples and ideas, and endorses this reasoning: 'The attempt to see Vedic culture as Aryan, and radically different in race and language from that of the

Indus Valley, is discounted today. The theory most accepted today is less of a separate Aryan race that invaded India and displaced existing cultures, and more of a composite "Indo-Aryan speaking peoples", and this takes back by at least a millennium the antiquity of ancient India.'[92]

Some scholars are still unconvinced, citing, for instance, the absence of the image of the horse in Harappan iconography. This is, indeed, rather curious, since the horse was known in India in much earlier times as testified to by the Stone Age rock paintings of Bhimbetka. Perhaps, as Sanjeev Sanyal says, 'the answer lies in the hundreds of unexcavated sites littered across India and Pakistan or in the thousands of bags of animal bones from earlier excavations that have not been examined for decades.'[93] The fact that the Harappan culture knew writing, and the Vedic culture did not, is also proffered as proof of the unbridgeable difference between the two cultures. However, the overwhelming evidence clearly points to overlapping continuities, and there is remarkable research underway to assign the real antiquity of this indigenous Indian civilisation, through new applications of astronomy, genetics, genealogy and anthropology. The veteran historian R.C. Majumdar had come to this conclusion as far back as 1952: 'There is enough evidence to indicate that some of the fundamental conceptions of Hinduism are derived from this culture. ... On the whole it is now being gradually realized that the present civilization of India is not merely a development of the Aryan civilization, as has so long been generally held, but that it is a composite product resulting from the fusion of several cultures in which the contribution of the Sindhu Valley Civilization must be regarded as an important factor.'[94]

But all this is anathema to left-leaning historians. The doyen of this school, Professor Irfan Habib, wrote a paper in 2001 titled 'Imagining River Sarasvati: A Defence of Common Sense'. The principal thrust of his arguments was that the mighty Sarasvati as lauded in the *Rig Veda* is an imaginary river, a river in the abstract. A small tributary of the Sutlej, the Sirsa, could have been mistaken for it. Or else, the link between the Ghaggar and the Sarasvati could have been the result of a canal built by Firoz Shah Tughlaq in the fourteenth century CE. Both these arguments appear highly contrived and are easily countered. The minor river Sirsa hardly matches the textual description of the Sarasvati; and the canal theory, as Danino says, is both factually untenable, and is, frankly, 'irrelevant to the issue of the lost river'.[95] Habib's conclusion is that 'all claims built upon the greatness of River Sarasvati are, accordingly, nothing but castles in the air, however much froth may be blown over them'. Danino's scathing response is: 'Should we assume that the rishis, having perhaps consumed an overdose of Soma, hallucinated on the banks of a skimpy Sarsuti? ... If Sarasvati were "the river in the abstract" why place it specifically after the Ganga and the Yamuna and before the Sutlej ...'[96]

The real reason behind Habib's animated—if untenable— attempt to demolish the evidence for the Sarasvati is, however, entirely different. It is, as he himself says in the conclusion of his paper, merely to privilege the Vedic civilisation over the Harappan, a case of 'false patriotism'. This is his real concern—that the entire body of research and study in this matter is nothing but a conspiracy by those who, for political reasons, want to give greater antiquity to ancient India, and—even more dangerously—to Hindu India. In response to such an ingrained apprehension, he is willing to support the colonial theory of Aryan invasion, and to discount completely the possibility that there could have been an interface between the Harappan and Vedic cultures. To postulate such an interface would be to legitimise Vedic appropriation of the past, and thus further the 'cultural paranoia' of proponents of Hindutva.

The motivation of Marxist historians is stated with complete clarity in a book consisting of essays dedicated to Irfan Habib. 'The efforts since independence at identification of the Indus Civilisation with the Vedic Aryans seem to aim at the glorification of the Vedic culture for several reasons: first, the identity of the Indus civilization with the Rig Vedic culture helps not only to establish a much greater antiquity for the Vedic Dharma and culture than hitherto recognized but also to give them the credit for producing one of the oldest civilizations of the world, at least as old as the Mesopotamian civilization. Secondly, it bestows its "original home to the Rigvedic Aryans within the Indian sub-continent" and gives them the credit of exceeding in extent all other contemporary civilizations of the ancient world. ... Why after all do these scholars want to glorify the Vedic culture? Here lies the ideological underpinning of archaeology for two reasons: the Vedas are considered to be the "source of Hindu social, political and economic institutions" and Hindu culture is actually, "The Indian Culture". The construction of history of their vision, they think, will help homogenize Indian culture and the nation.'[97]

The purpose behind the critique thus becomes quite transparent. The emphasis is not on objective historical evaluation, but to somehow stall Hindu 'aggrandisement'. Any claim, howsoever reasonably argued, about the antiquity of Indian civilisation, and its indigenous origins, must be opposed because it *must* be an attempt to rewrite history for 'Hindu glorification'. India must not be counted among the most ancient civilisations of the world—even if this has been accepted by the overwhelming majority of historians—because to do so would feed 'Hindu xenophobia'. It is the clearest illustration of a closed mind, driven only by the ideological opposition to the possible prefix of 'Hindu' to new historical and scientific data. The a priori assumption that greater Indian antiquity automatically conflates to a more ancient 'Hindu' India is the sole ideological motivator.

If the obsession is with Hindutva politics, and seeing its undesirable fingerprints on all historical research, including by foreign scientists— geologists, climatologists, environmentalists and historians who have nothing to do with a right-wing Hindu agenda—then the conclusions will be dictated not by the data and views presented but by that obsession. Amartya Sen's reaction is an apt example. 'Thus, in the Hindutva theory, much hangs on the genesis of the Vedas. In particular who composed them (it would be best for Hindutva theory if they were native Indians, settled in India for thousands of years, rather than

Indo-Europeans coming from abroad)? Were they composed later than the Indus valley civilization (it would be best if they were not later, in sharp contrast with the accepted knowledge)? How ancient were the alleged Vedic sciences and mathematics (could they not be earlier than Greek and Babylonian contributions, putting Hindu India ahead of them)? There were attempts by the Hindutva champions to rewrite history in such a way that these disparate difficulties are simultaneously removed through a simple device of "making" the Vedas also the very same people who created the Indus civilization!'[98]

Clearly, the obsession here is with Hindutva and Hindu India. All new research is thus ab initio suspect, for it is bound to further these goals. Conversely, old and outdated theories, many of them clearly the design of colonial rule, must be preserved, for to interrogate them might unleash the genie of Hindutva! This is the self-defeating dialectic of those who analyse the past solely in terms of how it serves ideological imperatives of the present. If some overzealous Hindutva votaries are guilty of this approach, so are the left-oriented historians. The truth lies between both extremes, and the only sustainable conclusion is that ancient India—even if migrations of people were a part of it—was largely indigenous and of far greater antiquity than was supposed earlier. Tony Joseph, who relies heavily on path-breaking genetic research of recent years, writes in his book, *Early Indians*, that while the Aryans may have been migrants over a period of time from Central Asia's steppes, it would be wrong to believe that the 'Vedas or "Sanskrit" or the "Aryan" culture was imported flat-packed and then reassembled here. "Aryan" culture was most likely the result of interaction, adoption and adaptation among those who brought Indo-European languages to India and those who were already well settled inhabitants of the region.'[99] Alas, much more could be known if the Harappan script had been deciphered. Whenever it is, it could well put the final seal on the historical evidence cited.

Marxist historians devalue the civilisational tag of ancient India by analysing it exclusively in class and economic terms. Certainly, this is also one way of studying the past, but the problem is twofold. Firstly, this approach excludes all other dimensions, and insists that this is the only way to evaluate history. Secondly, the tools used are highly derivative, an almost complete transplant of Marx's outdated, uninformed and stereotypical analytical framework in the Indian context. Marx never visited India, nor did he, from all accounts, expend much energy in studying or analysing India. But having elaborated a path-breaking theory of class conflict in the European context, he felt he was entitled to comment upon the historical evolution of all societies. Unfortunately, very few Marxist or left historians questioned the validity or applicability of his sweeping generalisations about ancient India. The consequence was an entire school of Indian historians parroting Marxist categories of historical analysis as the gospel truth with doctrinaire zeal.

Marx's imagination about India was overwhelmingly coloured by his notion of 'Oriental despotism' in which little else happened except the oppression of a passive people by absolute rulers. Any civilisational impulses were thus stagnant, as ossified villagers were caught in the 'Asiatic Mode of Production'. As he wrote: 'Indian society has no history at all, at least no known history. What we call its history, is but the history of the successive intruders who founded their empires on the basis of that unresisting and unchanging society.'[100] Just as his unidimensional view of Indian history, as only one of 'successive intruders' was ridiculously inaccurate, so was his elaboration of the 'Asiatic Mode of Production'. This mode 'envisaged despotism and stagnancy as key characteristics which nullified movements towards change, parallel to that of Europe. In the absence of private property there were no intermediary groups between king and peasant, nor classes or class conflict of a kind that would lead to dialectical change. This was further nullified by the absence of commercial centres and cities specializing in production for a market which, if they had existed, might have encouraged economic change.'[101]

The analysis is so patently unhistorical as to hardly merit a response. The assumption that in ancient India there was no private property, or no other structures of power except king and peasant, and no commercial centres or cities specialising in the production of specific products, betrays a lack of knowledge of our history which is, frankly, unpardonable. We did have powerful kings, but their powers were rarely absolute; treatises like the *Arthashastra*, among many others, speak specifically of the limitation to royal prerogatives. The matrix of society was complex and multilayered, mediated by caste, local leadership, religious centres and other foci of influence. Powerful trade guilds were in existence. Cities produced not only for internal consumption, but also for export. Even the peasantry, although economically vulnerable, was a part of a larger societal matrix, empowered by notions of praja. A reading of Chanakya, or of Ashoka's edicts, clearly brings this out.

But, for Marx's followers in India, none of this was important. The complex yet delicate filigree of Indian civilisation was ideologically trampled upon by the dialectical prism of class conflict, and analysed solely from the point of view of whether there was a 'feudal mode of production' or slavery or serfdom in India. While it is nobody's case that there was no economic inequality in India—as there is in any society—and that this can be an area of legitimate study, it is certainly not the only lens from which the past can be evaluated, especially when the tools to do so are mechanically transplanted from Europe's historical evolution, with which alone Marx was familiar. The ideological and academic mimicry of Marxist historians, therefore, needs to be called out.

Historians like Dr Upinder Singh have done so. Marxist historiography, she says, played an 'extremely influential' role in the construction of the history of ancient and medieval India from the 1950s onwards. She acknowledges that the achievement of Marxist historians was to shift the focus to agrarian relations, and class and economic structures. But, in her gentle way, she also chides the insularity of the Marxist school. 'Indian historians have often tended to treat religious cults and traditions primarily as ideologies reflecting social and political power structures of the time. It must be recognized that the many different strands of religious thought and practice are an important aspect of history in their own right and need thorough investigation.'[102]

An important consequence of the need to study the history of societies and culture from the bottom upwards, and not only from the top to bottom, was the rise of the subaltern school of history. It widened the canvas of historical study and brought out micro examinations which shed useful light on how the economic, social and political structures affected the ordinary person. However, the problem with micro emphasis was that it often became a reason to deliberately ignore the macro picture. The narrative of history then became a series of microscopic studies, with no attempt to create a larger picture from the mass of localised data. In particular, there was a tendency—probably inspired from Marxist historiography— to focus entirely on economic deprivations, validating Dr Upinder Singh's critique of such an approach. For instance, in an appreciation of Socrates or Plato, the evaluation does not necessarily have to be based on how they would have interacted with a peasant. This is not to devalue the peasant, but to accept that a balanced evaluation of any historical period cannot be circumscribed by such a unilinear approach. Even Amartya Sen, who is resolutely opposed to the concept of a Hindu civilisation, or even a coherent civilisation that was dominantly Hindu, accepts that the academic binary pursued by subaltern studies—the micro or nothing else—can be a distortion: 'There is, in fact, no basic contradiction in choosing the subaltern perspective of history and taking systematic note of the scholarly accomplishments of the elite.'[103] Of course, in saying so, he is himself proposing a binary—either a subaltern examination of only social and economic deprivation, or the accomplishments of the elite. Ancient India was much more than such extremes.

There are other arguments used to diminish the achievements of Hindu civilisation, such as to view it only from the prism of caste hierarchies, or to argue that one of its principal vehicles for ideas, Sanskrit, was impermeably elitist and, therefore, so was this civilisation. I shall deal with such criticisms—and much more—in the overall evaluation of this civilisation in the proceeding chapters.

2

THE AUDACITY OF THOUGHT

Why did a civilisation, with Hinduism, or Hindu Dharma, or the Hindu way of life at its core, survive from millennia before to the present, when most ancient civilisations elsewhere exist today only as archaeological artefacts, museum relics or historical memories? Ancient Mesopotamia, Egypt, Greece and China were great civilisations of their times, broadly contemporaneous with the Indian civilisation, but have ceased to exist as a living tradition, whereas the Hindu civilisation, in spite of so many vicissitudes, has survived, and continues to shape the lives of its followers. It is true that Hindu civilisation too may not exist in exactly the same way as in the past—in some ways that is good, and in others unfortunate. But most of its central tenets and beliefs are a part of the lives of Hindus, and essentially constitute a living tradition.

To pose this question is not to propound a case for Hindu superiority, or downplay the achievements of the other foundational civilisations, great in their own time. The purport behind this question is to try and understand, without prejudice of any kind, why Hindu civilisation showed the resilience to survive. The attempt to answer this question goes to the core of what that Hindu civilisation was, how it was conceived, how it evolved and why it did not become confined to the walls of a museum. As Mahatma Gandhi says: 'I believe that the civilization India has evolved is not to be beaten in the world. Nothing can equal the seed sown by our ancestors. Rome went, Greece shared the same fate, the might of the Pharaohs was broken, Japan has become westernized, of China nothing can be said, but India is still, somehow or the other, sound at the foundation.'[1]

Gandhi wrote these words in 1909 in his first book, *Hind Swaraj*. At that time he was agitated by British attempts to downplay India's ancient heritage and claim the Western civilisational model as the most superior. The contextual background to what he wrote notwithstanding, the basic thought he voiced needs to be further probed. Was this survival just happenstance, a quirk of evolution, a historical coincidence, a luck of the draw played by time? Or, was there more to it, and if so, what? What were those factors that coalesced in such a way so as to enable this survival? Was there something intrinsically different in the way this civilisation was structured ab initio that prevented it from fading away into oblivion? Were there elements within it, so constituted from the very beginning, that gave it the resilience to withstand direct and indirect attempts to vanquish it? Were the strengths that enabled it to persist random, or the result of a conscious application of mind? These are questions to which we must seek answers, not in terms of definitive or absolute truths, but in the nature of a deliberation, a contemplative examination, leaving enough room for other views and opinions.

I will argue that the great strength of this civilisation was that it began its journey in overwhelmingly *cerebral* terms. It grappled first with ideas, processes of thought and the realm of concepts, before it created the civilisation associated with it. The compressed cerebral energy—with few parallels in the world—that shaped its foundations played a deeply influential role in the material superstructure that followed. The depth and insight of the original ideation influenced all aspects of the civilisation. It was internalised as thought, before it actualised as artefact or secular construct. The dialectic between idea and form, concept and practice, enabled the ideological world view to survive even if the form was destroyed, and the form to persist even when ideation momentarily ebbed.

In other words, the Hindu civilisation was founded, first and foremost, on the audacity of thought. There were, undoubtedly, derogations and distortions of that thought in subsequent times. But even so, the intensity of that initial application of mind, and the fact that over time it percolated down in a myriad forms to the level of the ordinary person, provided a protective shield to ensure survival. Civilisations die when their animating thought impulses wither or are overwhelmed. The Hindu civilisation's thought processes were never overwhelmed, even when its people were conquered. This is important, because monuments can be destroyed, but the fortress of ideas is imperishable.

The core of this thought process was spiritual, as distinguished from simply religious practice. The spiritual vision both transcended and guided religious rituals, and spilled over into the secular realm. This did not make it a religious civilisation. The spirituality was more about ultimate truths, an exploration of the world of ideas, and not a manual only for religious worship. This spiritual churning could have a religious counterpart, but would survive even without it. As Rabindranath Tagore says: 'In reality, our history had deeply serene and *contemplative* phases—for the longest period of time—periods not without war or turmoil, but *essentially grappling with pivotal concepts in the realm of thought* [emphasis mine].'[2] Sri Aurobindo also speaks about 'an ingrained and dominant spirituality, an exhaustive vital creativeness and ... *a powerful, penetrating and scrupulous intelligence* ... each at a high intensity of action ... the stamp put on her by that beginning she has never lost [emphasis mine]'.[3]

Travellers from abroad—from Huan Tseng to Fa Hein to Al Beruni—also noticed this vital quality. This has also been observed by insightful foreign observers even in our times. For instance, Lin Yutang, a Chinese who escaped Communist China to settle in America, and Octavio Paz, a diplomat from Mexico who was posted in India in the 1950s, allude to much the same thing. Lin Yutang spent a lifetime studying ancient Chinese culture; but when he wrote a book on the wisdom of India he openly spoke—not realising the political ramifications this would have in some circles in India now—about 'the fabulous Hindu mind'.[4] Octavio Paz wrote that India's ancient culture displayed 'in its highest moments, the incarnation of a totality that is plenitude and emptiness, the transfiguration of a body into form that, without abandoning sensation and the flesh, is spiritual'.[5]

To understand the reasons for the resilience of Hindu civilisation we must explore what this 'realm of thought' which Rabindranath Tagore mentioned was about.

The *Rig Veda*, composed sometime perhaps in the third millennium BCE, has this remarkable hymn (*Nasadiya Sukta*) on creation:

> There was neither non-existence nor existence then; there was neither the realm of space nor the sky which is beyond. What stirred? Where? In whose protection? Was there water, bottomlessly deep?
>
> There was neither death nor immortality then. There was no distinguishing sign of night or day. That one breathed, windless, by its own impulse. Other than that there was nothing beyond.
>
> Who really knows? Who will here proclaim it? Whence was it produced? Whence is this creation? The gods came afterwards with the creation of this universe? Who then knows whence it has arisen?
>
> Whence this creation has arisen—perhaps it formed itself, or perhaps it did not—the one who looks down on it, in the highest heaven, only he knows—or perhaps he does not know.[6]

This hymn, perhaps the first recorded rumination in Hindu philosophy on the origins of the universe, is remarkable for its eclectic tone and tenor. There are no certitudes; no injunctions for obeisance; no religious commands, or call to ritual. There is awe, there is wonderment, but, above all, there is enquiry, an emphasis on the need to ask, to probe, to go beyond conventional categories of thought to the realm of speculation, and an invitation to ideation. The questions signify an impassioned yearning for truth, but this yearning is willing to accept that the answers may need to embrace negation even as they seek to find the right assertion, and that, in this process, the path to truth can be many things but not simplistic or dogmatic.

The etymological meaning of Veda is sacred knowledge or wisdom. There are four Vedas—*Rig, Yajur, Sama* and *Atharva.* Together they constitute the Samhitas that are the textual basis of the Hindu religious system. To these Samhitas were attached three other kinds of texts. These are, first, the Brahmanas, which are essentially a detailed description of rituals, a kind of manual for the priestly class, the Brahmans. The second are the Aranyakas. Aranya means forest, and these 'forest manuals' move away from rituals and incantations and magic spells to the larger speculations of spirituality, a kind of compendium of the contemplations of those who have renounced the world. The third, leading from the Aranyakas, are the Upanishads, which, for their sheer loftiness of thought, are the foundational texts of Hindu philosophy and metaphysics. Because they come at the very end of the corpus of the Vedas, they are also collectively called 'Vedanta', or the end of the Vedas, expounding the uncompromisingly non-dual nature of the cosmos—Advaita.

An important point needs to be noted here. From the very beginning, Hindu religion had two distinct strands. The first was preoccupied with ritual and prayer and gods and goddesses, and at a baser level with superstition and magic potions and spells and the like. Very early on in the Vedic age, we come upon an endless array of deities or quasi-deities, many of them representing, quite understandably, the dramatic forces of nature that were looked upon by early humans with wonderment and reverence. Hence, we had gods like Indra, who controlled the elements; or Agni, fire; or Aditi, who is an early version of the mother goddess, symbolising the mysterious powers of procreation.

But, as the Aranyakas and Upanishads show, as does the hymn on creation from the *Rig Veda* referred earlier, there was, also from the very beginning, a stronger strand that sought to understand the origins and meanings and purpose of life, and to explore what could be the one unifying force underlying the bewildering complexity of the universe. This strand was less taken up with ritual and divinities and the *practice* of religion and more with the philosophical substratum underlying the practice. In comparison with the other great religions of the world, Hinduism was probably not unique in nurturing two such divergent approaches, but it is almost certain that no other religious tradition so far back in time had such a pronounced emphasis on the pursuit of knowledge as an end in itself, largely divorced from the ritual of religion.

The Upanishads, composed centuries before the Common Era, constitute one of the foundational texts of Hinduism. The authors of the Upanishads are not known, nor do we have their exact chronology or date. It is certain that initially they were, like all Hindu texts, orally transmitted from generation to generation, and only reduced to text in classical Sanskrit sometime around 600 to 400 BCE. The Upanishads do not constitute a single volume compiled separately. The exact number of Upanishads is not known either, but by common consensus there are about twelve principal Upanishads attached to the *Rig, Sama, Yajur* and *Atharva Vedas*.

In keeping with the contemplation that marked the foundational period of Hinduism, the Upanishads are metaphysical poems, at once mystical and evocative. They resonate with a wisdom that is transparently a product of the deepest meditative insight, unhindered by structured presentation but robust, with a clarity of vision that is borne of unquestioned personal anubhav or experience. There is a Self, Atman, a pulsating, all-pervasive cosmic consciousness, beyond definition and name and form or attribute because any attribute would only circumscribe its limitlessness. This Self is the highest reality. It encompasses all of creation. We are all a part of it and its manifestation—Tat Tvam Asi or That Thou Art. The Self is the same as Brahman—Ayam Atma Brahman or the Self is Brahman. These utterances are two of the four Mahavakyas or Great Sentences of the Upanishads. The Upanishads use 'Atman' and 'Brahman' interchangeably. The apparent multiplicity of the world is an illusion. Once the ego and the senses are stilled through deep meditation, we realise our true Self, beyond all sorrow and pain, and realise that our true reality is 'That'. All human differentiation then becomes false, a product of the illusion of Maya. In that non-dual, or Advaita identification with Brahman, we partake of a bliss that is beyond mortal comprehension.

The *Mundaka Upanishad* says: 'The universe comes forth from Brahman and will return to Brahman. Verily, all is Brahman.' The *Katha Upanishad* elaborates:

Above the senses is the mind,
Above the mind is the intellect,
Above that is the ego, and above the ego
Is the unmanifested Cause
And beyond is Brahman, omnipresent,
Attributeless. Realizing him one is released
From the cycle of birth and death.[7]

The *Mundaka Upanishad* also categorically proclaims the supremacy of the Atman or the Self:

The effulgent Self, who is beyond thought,
Shines in the greatest, shines in the smallest,
Shines in the farthest, shines in the nearest,
Shines in the secret chamber of the heart.
The flowing river is lost in the sea;
The illumined sage is lost in the Self
The flowing river has become the sea;
The illumined sage has become the Self

Brahman and Atman are used interchangeably, but are essentially one. In the grandeur of one famous sentence—Ayam Atma Brahman: Brahman is all and the Self is Brahman—the *Mandukya Upanishad* unequivocally asserts the unity between Atman or the inner Self, and Brahman, the Cosmic Cause. The assertion of this unity, and indeed the unity of all things existent, is a repeated refrain in the Upanishads. The *Chandogya Upanishad* explicates this beautifully in the story of Shvetaketu who asks Uddalaka, his father: 'What is wisdom?' And, Uddalaka says to Shvetaketu:

As by knowing one lump of clay, dear one,
We come to know all things made out of clay:
That they differ only in name and form,
While the stuff of which all are made is clay;
As by knowing one gold nugget, dear one,
We come to know all things made out of gold:

That they differ only in name and form,
While the stuff of which all are made is gold;
As by knowing one tool of iron, dear one,
We come to know all things made out of iron:
That they differ only in name and form,
While the stuff of which all are made is iron—
So through that spiritual wisdom, dear one,
We come to know that all life is one.

Having explained the unity of all things, the *Chandogya Upanishad* sublimely puts an end to all notions of all duality, by pronouncing the foundational concept—Tat Tvam Asi: That Thou Art—in the following manner:

In the beginning was only Being,
One without a second.
Out of himself he brought forth the cosmos
And entered into everything in it.
There is nothing that does not come from him.
Of everything he is the inmost Self.
He is the truth; he is the Self Supreme.
You are that, Shvetaketu; you are that.

Realisation brings freedom and infinite joy. The Upanishads are categorical that once an individual understands the pervasive omniscience of Brahman, and overcomes the sense of separateness created by the ego and the senses, the consequence is supreme bliss. As the *Taittiriya Upanishad* says: 'Realizing That from which all words turn back, and thoughts can never reach, they know the bliss of Brahman and fear no more.' There is, then, the feeling of unblemished plenitude that is actually the characteristic of our real Self. This sense of abundance is breathtakingly captured by the beginning shloka of the *Isha Upanishad*, about which Mahatma Gandhi is believed to have said that he would happily give up every scripture in Hinduism if he could keep just this one shloka:

All this is full. All that is full.
From fullness, fullness comes.
When fullness is taken from fullness,
Fullness still remains.

It is nothing short of amazing that these sermons on what constitutes ontological reality were taking place in forest academies thousands of years ago when most religious explorations elsewhere at that time were restricted to the deification of natural phenomena or simplistic magical incantations. The notion of the Absolute as nirguna, devoid of attributes, was in itself nothing short of audacious, because in most other civilisations of this time, energies were largely focused on the visualisation of a conventional deity, corresponding to human categories of thought.

The most valiant part—and the keystone—of the Upanishadic philosophy was the conceptualisation of Brahman as the all-pervasive and the only Absolute force permeating the universe. This became the basis of the powerful Advaita school of philosophy, of which Adi Shankaracharya in the eighth century CE became the legendary spokesperson. Brahman is urja or infinite energy, pure, pervasive cosmic consciousness, and unsullied awareness. It is intelligence personified—as can be inferred by the absolute order in the universe, both at the micro and macro level. The embodiment of perfect knowledge, Brahman is beyond knowledge, the knower or the known. It has no beginning, for it is eternal; it has no cause, for it is beyond the categories of time, space and causality; it has no end, for it always was and will always be. Its powers are unlimited; it is omnipresent, omnipotent and omniscient, a singular, indivisible, purna (complete in itself) and universal force—ekam eka sarvavyapi. Everything in the cosmos is an emanation of Brahman, but Brahman itself is beyond all activity and purpose as per our finite ways of thinking. Unchanging, it has no need to evolve or develop, grow or diminish. In its passivity, it is potentiality itself; in its aloofness it is omnipotent; in its apparent purposelessness it is infinite intelligence; and, in its indefinability it is definitiveness itself. It is. Nothing without it, is. Its ekarasa (uniformity) has no parts; its identity is akhanda (division-less). In this sense, it is self-luminous, without the need of predication, conditionality or qualification.

Having posited the absolute immanence of Brahman as the only Reality in the universe, the Advaita school asserted that Brahman and Atman (the Self) are the same. When we peel away the empirically manifest—mind, body, ego and senses—what is left is nirvisheshachinmatram or undifferentiated consciousness that is the characteristic of both Brahman and Atman. The objective and the subjective then become the same. Atma ca Brahma: Atman is Brahman, say the Upanishads.

But, if there is One, Unchanging, Eternal and All-pervasive Consciousness and nothing else, both at the cosmic level and in our individual selves, what is this visible, pulsating plurality of the universe? This phenomenal world, Advaita says, is real at one level, but Brahman is the only reality at the ontological level. The One remains the One, while the many proliferate as its reflection, as it were, without changing the essential nature of that One. If the difference between the finite and the infinite is so stark, so unmistakable and crystal clear, why do we mistake one for the other? Advaita's answer is that it is due to avidya or nescience. Avidya creates an error of perception that blurs the distinction between the real and the unreal, the eternal and the transient. The limitations of our sensory perceptions, the instability of our mind, and the false sense of ego that becomes a permanent adjunct to our lives, cumulatively create a Jiva that revels in its own finitude oblivious to its real nature. Once, when through correct knowledge that veil of ignorance is removed, we see what our real Self is; the experiential inference of the realisation of unity with Brahman is unblemished joy and bliss.

Over a period of time (the next 2,000 years), apart from Advaita, also called the Uttar Mimamsa, five other principal systems of philosophy developed in Hinduism. This, in itself, is illustrative of the fact that there was no attempt to straitjacket intellectual exploration. On the contrary, there was both an invitation and a sanction for it.

The five other schools of philosophy were the Nyaya, Vaisheshika, Sankhya, Yoga and Purva Mimamsa. All these schools were essentially guided by two fundamental tenets—investigation or mimamsa, and reflection or vichara. The investigation and reflection were about the ultimate nature of the world and the consequential purposes of life. The schools had overlapping concepts and reasoning in some respects, but their differences were equally marked and, in this sense, provide definitive proof of the eclectic milieu of those times, and the independence and robustness of thought they nurtured.

The *Nyaya Sutra* dates back to the third century BCE and is attributed to the sage Gautama. This school's principal preoccupation is with logic and dialectics, analysis and reasoning. For the nature of reality to be accurately comprehended, we must employ a methodology of observation and inference. To this end, the Nyaya relied primarily on four sources of knowledge—pratyaksha (evident manifestation), anumana (estimation), upamana (analogy) and shabda (verbal testimony). Such tools were essential, the Nyaya stressed, to establish whether that which is presumed or believed in actually exists or not. In other words, the importance of Nyaya lies in the fact that it sets out the analytical framework for enquiry, and refuses to accept anything only on face value or assertion.

The Vaisheshika school of the sage Kanada (third century BCE) relied closely on the tools of reasoning expounded upon by Nyaya, but went beyond them to formulate what must arguably be the first philosophical doctrine based on the recognition of the atom. All material objects, it asserts, are ultimately the product of four basic atoms found in earth, water, fire or air. Amazingly, for its times, the doctrine concludes that all finite objects can be broken down into parts and finally reduced to that one infinitesimal, indestructible and indivisible atom. A combination of atoms produces different products, which could, in their final form, be different from their constituent parts. The doctrine admits that in the evolutionary process from the atom to a finite whole, the end result could be based on a dominant characteristic or visesha, but essentially the world view of the Vaisheshika is pluralistic.

While foundationally realistic in its approach, the Vaisheshika recognises that not all substances are materials. The non-material aspects of cosmology include space, time, akasha (ether), mind and soul. At this point, somewhat reluctantly, Kanada accepts the possibility of a God or Ishwara who combined the four kinds of atoms and five non-material substances into an ordered universe. The essential tone of the philosophy, however, remains atheistic, since even while conceding the presence of God, it limits his role to the ordering of the universe, and not to the creation of the elements that constitute it.

The Sankhya school was initiated by sage Kapila in the seventh century BCE, and is one of the oldest systematised structure of thought in Hindu philosophy. In essence, the Sankhya assigns a cosmic duality to the universe, consisting of Prakriti and Purusha. Prakriti, unlike the pluralistic atomistic view of the Vaisheshika, is a pervasive singularity, eternal and independent, from which the universe evolves. But this evolution happens only when Prakriti comes under the influence of Purusha, which stands for awareness or the sentient principle.

Until the influence of Purusha, Prakriti, representing the 'potentiality of nature',[8] lies latent, its three constituents—sattva, rajas and tamas—in equilibrium. Sattva stands for that which is pure; rajas signifies energy and activity; and tamas connotes inertia and stolidity. This equilibrium is disturbed when Purusha interfaces with Prakriti, and evolution commences with all its manifest diversities. The emergence of the five cognitive organs—taste, touch, sight, sound and smell—and the five motor organs of movement, are a part of this evolution, as is the emergence of buddhi (intellect) and the ahamkara (ego). According to the Sankhya, this evolution is cyclical, with shrishti (creation) followed by pralaya (dissolution), and shrishti again followed by pralaya. For a human being, liberation consists in understanding the distinction between the material Prakriti and the sentient Purusha. This understanding comes by lifting the veil of ignorance through the pursuit of jnana or knowledge. For sheer conceptualisation, there is an awe-inspiring grandeur to the cosmic architecture profiled by the Sankhya. What is especially interesting is that in the self-evolving cosmic drama that it structures, there is no place for God.

The Yoga school broadly accepts the world view of the Sankhya but fleshes out the physical discipline and meditational regimen required by an individual to realise the separation (kaivalya) of Purusha, pure consciousness, from the non-sentient Prakriti. The *Yoga Sutra* is attributed to Patanjali and is dated to sometime before 400 BCE. Several scholars believe it to be of much greater antiquity, and it is very likely that even if composed later, the *Sutra* codifies a tradition and practice from several centuries earlier.

The *Yoga Sutra* begins with this aphorism—Yoga citti vritti nirodhah: Yoga is restraining the mind from discursive thought. This restraint, it believes, can be brought about by physical and mental discipline. Discipline is outlined as an eightfold path, starting from yama (self-restraint), niyama (virtuous observances), asana (posture), pranayama (consciously controlling breath), pratyahara (withdrawal of the senses), dharana (concentrating the mind), dhyana (meditation) and samadhi (a trance-like state in which there is complete union with the subject of meditation). Yoga literally translates to 'union', and the purpose of the entire regimen of the eightfold path is to prepare the disciple for this union with pure consciousness, the Purusha. Unlike the Vedantic system, which believes that enlightenment, based on jnana, can come to anybody at any time through direct anubhava or communion, Yoga provides to Sankhya a carefully structured complementary system of exercises of the body and mind that it believes is a necessary precondition to moksha or salvation. The physical Yoga exercises (Hatha Yoga) were more comprehensively codified between the ninth and the eleventh century, and today have acquired great popularity worldwide as a holistic and healing physical regimen. On one essential point, however, Yoga differs from Sankhya, and that is its acceptance of a personal God, who directs the cyclical evolutionary process from creation to dissolution.

The practice of dharma, through ritual action sanctified by the

Vedas, is the principal focus of the Purva Mimamsa. Jaimini (c. 400 BCE) was its chief theoretician. This doctrine believes in karma or action and not jnana as the path to salvation. Its preoccupation is with the practice and interpretation of Vedic rites and rituals, which are to be performed out of a sense of duty, and in the manner prescribed by the orthodox texts associated with the Vedas such as the Brahmanas. This school believes that performing the obligatory rituals, and abstaining from those that are proscribed, will lead by itself to the elimination of evil and the attainment, through the purification of the soul, of moksha.

The depth and range of philosophical churning that marked the growth and evolution of Indic thought in its formative years must have few parallels anywhere else in the world. This churning was characterised by a remarkable intellectual curiosity that refused to take anything for granted or to be confined to simplistic theism or conventional categories of personal prosperity and well-being. The concerns here were larger, about causes and origins, the nature of things, the secrets of the universe, the exactitudes of logic and inference, and the relationship between mind, the senses and the body—a collective rumination that soared beyond the finitude of the known into the infinities beyond. The rishis and sages who founded these systems did not grapple very much with faith and Godhood. In fact, most of the six systems, including Vedanta, were at the level of pure philosophy, atheistic in tone, seeking instead to carry out a corrosive enquiry into the ultimate nature of substance and spirit. In this process, the emphasis was not on what dogmatically is, or what emphatically must be, or what necessarily should be, but what *possibly could be*. The felicity and energy with which these thinkers volitionally left familiar—and more comprehensible—shores to plumb the depths of the unknown is nothing short of amazing.

A necessary consequence of the fact that Hindu civilisation welcomed ideation from its very inception was that it was dialogic. It consciously chose not to proceed on fiats, issued by one supreme authority, but on an exchange of views. Hence, the Upanishads were a dialogue between a guru and a shishya or disciple. The word Upanishad literally means 'to sit down near' at the feet of a master or teacher who shares with the pupils spiritual truths or wisdom. One has to imagine a setting in a forest sometime as far back as 2000 BCE or earlier, where a sage, who has spent decades perhaps in the search for truth and wisdom, shares thoughts, most often elliptically, with a group of students eager to begin their own journey in unravelling the mysteries of life. The conversation is not in the form of a formal dialogue, but through parable and suggestion, story and allusion, or statements of deep penetrative insight into what constitutes the transcendent reality underlying our lives and this universe. What is significant is that while obviously having the role of a mentor, the guru is open to questions being asked and instead of delivering a monologue from a pedestal, is willing to have a conversation which is guided as much by what the guru has to say as by what is being asked by the shishya. Significant too is that what the sage says is not in the nature of a command, but more in the format of an insight, inviting discussion and interrogation. Considering the fact that for many Hindus (including Adi Shankaracharya), even though the Upanishads are seen as shruti or revealed texts, the fact that they were dialogic, and not prescriptive, set the tone for the further evolution of Hinduism itself.

Other foundational texts of Hinduism carry forward this dialogic tradition. One of these is the *Brahma Sutra* by Badarayana written sometime around 450 BCE. In Indian tradition, Badarayana is identified with the legendary Vyasa who compiled the Vedas. The *Brahma Sutra* is known by many names—*Nyaya Prasthana*, because it puts the teachings of the Upanishads in a structured order; *Vedanta Sutra*, since it is a text on the Vedanta; *Sariraka Sutra*, since it deals with the nature and evolution of the embodied soul; and *Uttara Mimamsa Sutra*, since it deals with the final section of the Vedas, unlike the Purva Mimamsa which deals with the earlier sections.

A sutra 'is a short sentence or aphorism, shorn of all verbiage and designed to convey the essence of a religious or philosophical idea in the smallest space'.[9] In terms of the brevity of expression, and the intensity of thought compressed within it, it probably has no parallel in literary or philosophical discourse. For instance, the first sutra in the *Brahma Sutra* simply says—Athato Brahma Jigyasa: Hence now a deliberation on Brahma. Max Müller quotes Patanjali (the great grammarian) in stressing that sutra writers derived greater joy in reducing an aphorism by a word or a syllable than in the birth of a child! The *Brahma Sutra* has 550 sutras, each not more than a word or two, which cumulatively constitute a systematic investigation into the world view of the Upanishads, but are near impossible to understand in isolation. On this chiselled and ruthlessly attenuated allusion of thought, pregnant with meaning, commentaries were written running into hundreds of pages and thousands of shlokas.

The first chapter is on samanvaya or harmony. The purpose here is to take the many disparate statements in the Upanishads and harmonise them in order to grasp their one indisputable message— Brahman is the only, pervasive and supreme reality, characterised by sat chit ananda or being, awareness and bliss. The second chapter brings out in full measure the great scope for democratic dialogue in the Hindu methodology of discourse. It is titled 'Avirodha' or non-conflict, and takes on board *objections* to the Vedantic assertion of the non-dual supremacy of Brahman. These objections emanate from other schools of Hindu philosophy as also from Buddhism and Jainism. That these objections were considered important to record and answer is proof of the validation of dialogue as a means of finding the truth. It is also indicative of the fact that the notion of harmony in Hinduism is about taking on board viewpoints that are opposed to the thesis being presented. The conclusion is thus a synthesis of several views or, at the least, an outcome of actively acknowledging the contra-perspective. The extensive tikas or tippanis, that is, commentaries, on the original text are further evidence of the freedom to freely pursue interpretations of what the truth could be.

Along with the Upanishads and the *Brahma Sutra*, the Bhagwad Gita completes the triad of the three foundational texts of Hinduism.

Not surprisingly, like the first two, the Bhagwad Gita too is in the nature of a dialogue. The Gita (and I shall discuss this work later too) consists of 700 shlokas in eighteen chapters. It is embedded in the Mahabharata, a voluminous literary epic eight times the length of the Odyssey and Iliad combined. The epic was probably written around 500 BCE, and since it makes no reference to Buddhism, most scholars consider it to have been composed before the advent of Buddha.

When the Great War—Mahabharata—was about to begin, Arjuna, the most accomplished warrior among the Pandavas, refused to fight. Arraigned opposite him were his own kinsmen—uncles, brothers, teachers, elders, companions, and his resolve faltered. 'I desire not victory, nor kingdom, nor pleasures,' he told Krishna, 'if these are to be won at the cost of so much bloodshed.' Krishna, who was his sarathi or charioteer, then counselled him; and, in the end, Arjuna, his mental equilibrium restored and his sense of confusion removed, picked up his bow and arrow and boldly entered the battle. But the important thing is that this final outcome was not the result of a one-sided sermon by Krishna. He may have been God incarnate, but Arjuna does not hesitate to have a dialogue with him, asking him pointed questions, seeking clarifications, arguing his own point of view and interrogating even the Almighty's logic.

From its very early validation in the foundational texts, the tradition of a sabhya samvad, or civilised discourse, seems to have persisted all along as can be seen from the Great Debate between Adi Shankaracharya and Mandana Mishra in as late as the eighth century CE. Shankaracharya (788–820 CE) was a great votary of the jnana marga or path of knowledge as the way to achieve moksha or salvation. His motto was Satyam jnanam, anantam Brahman: Knowledge is truth; Brahman is eternal. Mandana Mishra, on the other hand, was a staunch believer in the Karma Kanda marga, wherein the scrupulous performance of rituals as sanctified in the Vedas was the path to moksha. The ideological gap between them was wide, and their commitment to their separate viewpoints was passionate. Both were exceptionally learned scholars too. If Shankaracharya was arguably Hinduism's greatest thinker, Mandana Mishra was a formidable opponent, and looked upon as an avatar of Brahma by his disciples.

Their methodology of dealing with their opposing points of view was shastrartha, or dialogue and debate. When Shankara walked into Mandana's home on the banks of the river Narbada in Mahishmati (modern Madhya Pradesh),[10] the latter was not pleased to see him. He was busy with the rituals of his father's shraddha or death anniversary, and the sight of a celibate sanyasi was considered inauspicious for those of his belief, in which leading the life of a householder while performing the prescribed Vedic rituals was the correct choice to make. Apparently, he was rude to Shankara, who did not, however, rise to the bait. Finally, it was agreed that the debate between the two scholars would commence the next day. Mandana Mishra asked Shankara to choose an umpire, and was surprised when he said that Ubhaya Bharati, Mandana's wife,[11] would be the arbiter. The learned lady agreed, and put a garland of flowers around the neck of the two contestants, declaring that the person whose garland withered first would be considered defeated. It was also decided that whoever lost would become the follower of the other, and adopt the rules of life of his opponent.

The debate went on for anything between seventeen days to six months, as per different accounts of the event. In the end, the garland worn by Mandana Mishra withered away, and it was clear that Shankara had won the argument. But Ubhaya Bharati was not willing to concede defeat. She said that, as the wife of Mishra, she was one-half of his person, and this had sanction in the acceptance of the androgynous concept of ardhanarishwara in Hindu thought. Therefore, she would like to debate with Shankara. Shankara was reluctant to do so, for under the rules that he followed, a sanyasi debating with a woman was not permissible. But Ubhaya Bharati was insistent, and Shankara agreed.

This remarkable narrative has to be assessed beyond merely the colourful details added later by imaginative biographers. What the dialogue actually represented—and that is the reason why it was projected as such an important part of Shankara's life—was to assert the primacy of thought over ritual, at a time when precisely the opposite seemed to be given more importance by Hindus. The sixth and the seventh centuries CE saw a revival of Hinduism, and the relative decline of Buddhism. However, a part of this revival was excessively focused on Puranic mythology, and the mechanical performance of Vedic ritualism. Somewhere in all of this, there was a divorce from the loftiness of thought that was the essential substratum of the Hindu vision. In the pursuit of how exactly to perform a ritual as per precise Vedic injunctions, the glorious mystical insights of the Upanishads had been overwhelmed. Temples were flourishing, but there was a disconnect between the motions of worship and the philosophical foundations underlying it. There was the need to once again reassert the jnana marga to salvation, to relink Hinduism to its metaphysical insights, and restore to it the grandeur of thought and contemplation. That was the manifest purpose of Shankara, and there could be no better metaphor to project it than his victory in a debate over Mandana Mishra. Indeed, there is little doubt that Mishra's defeat must have made a major impact on the beliefs and practice of Hinduism across India. Even without modern means of communication, the progress of the debate and the intricacies of the arguments, witnessed by thousands of people, would have spread by word of mouth to tens of thousands more across the length and breadth of the country. The debate, when seen in the historical context of the evolution of Hinduism, further institutionalised, at the highest level of learning, the importance of dialogue, discussion and discourse—not coercion, violence or acrimony.

The exploration of thought requires openness to opposing points of view. Given Hinduism's foundational emphasis on intellectual deliberation, it could not but be broad-based in its intellectual approach. The Upanishads lay down this dictum unequivocally—Ekam sat vipra bahudha vadanti: The truth is one, the wise call it by different names. At a time when most civilisations elsewhere were asserting that they alone have the monopoly of truth, the Upanishads were admitting that the one truth can have differing interpretations. Another Upanishadic injunction says—Udar charitanam, vasudhaiva kutumbukam: The world is one family for the magnanimous. Once again, at the beginning of recorded history, when most human endeavours were occupied with building walls around their own belief systems, our seers were emphasising that, in spite of differences, if one is large-hearted—as one should be—the entire world is one family. A *Rig Vedic* mantra endorses this broad and tolerant way of thinking—Anno bhadra kritavo yantu vishvataha: Let good thoughts flow to us from all directions. This saying is engraved at the entrance of India's modern-day Parliament. It signifies the shunning of insularity of thought and the porousness to different points of view, even an invitation to non-conformity.

It is not surprising then that Hinduism's philosophical heritage is unique for the remarkable range of heterogeneity it enables within its overall central narrative. I have already spoken about the six principal systems of Hindu philosophy. But there were other schools of thought too, with their own committed followers and reasoning, often in direct, even flamboyant, opposition to more mainstream Hindu thought. One of these was the Charvaka Lokayatika school. It provides a fascinating insight into the intellectual diversity of those times, and the degree of deviation from conventional thinking that was tolerated.

While it is true that several of the major schools of Hindu philosophy were less preoccupied with a personal God, and built their ideological structures on an atheistic template, the Charvakas openly denied the existence of God or of any supernatural forces whatsoever, and argued a well-thought-out case for materialism. Typically, they *argued* their case and did not only resort to blind opposition. The external world, they asserted, exists objectively and is governed by verifiable laws and not by any supranatural force. Our only valid source of inference is pratyaksha (direct perception), and what cannot be perceived does not exist. The material substances that we can infer through direct perception are earth, water, fire and air. The world consists of varying combinations of these four mahabhuta (fundamental elements). Consciousness is not anything transcendental, but a product of the combination of these elements in a specific form and under specific conditions. There is no soul that survives death. The body returns to the four basic elements that constituted it. Nothing remains to transmigrate or be reborn. *The Vedas are bereft of all sanctity* since they suffer from the three errors — internal contradiction, untruth and meaningless repetition.

It is said that Brihaspati, who founded the Charvaka school around the seventh century BCE, was a proponent of materialist hedonism. Since there was nothing before, and there will be nothing beyond the life that we have, it must be enjoyed to the full without inhibition or thought of extraneous forces:

> While life is yours, live joyously
> None can escape death's searching eye;
> When once this frame of ours they burn
> How shall it e'er again return?[12]

However, it can be argued equally well that the real purpose of the Charvakas was to make individuals responsible for their own life without the crutches of an external deity or agency. This assumption of responsibility conferred a much-valued freedom. Essentially, Brihaspati was a rebel. He was against superstition, ritualism, caste, scriptural authority, Brahmanism and the stranglehold of the priestly class. Religion, he said, was an instrument in the hands of the priests to exploit the common person, and God is only the invention of the rich. It is this injustice and oppression that we need to fight in our present lives, instead of condoning matters by believing — as the priests would want us — that our miseries are due to deeds done in past lives. In this sense, Brihaspati and the Charvaka school predated Marx — who famously said that 'religion is the opiate of the masses' — by over a millennium and a half.

Another interesting strand of philosophy is related to the sanctity of sound, concretised through shabda (the word). Sometime between the sixth and the fourth century BCE, the great grammarian Panini wrote the *Ashtadhyayi*, the foundational treatise on Sanskrit grammar. In the second century BCE, Patanjali wrote his *Mahabhashya* or 'Great Commentary' on the *Ashtadhyayi*. It is a matter of speculation whether this Patanjali was the same as the Patanjali who wrote the *Yoga Sutra*. This being as it may, the *Mahabhashya*, which dwells extensively on shiksha (accent), vyakarana (morphology) and nirukta (etymology), is the earliest work on the philosophy underlying Hindu grammar. Bhartrihari, in the fifth century CE, wrote the *Vakyapadiya*, elaborating further on this linguistic philosophy. His theory of sphota theorised that the act of speech consisted of three stages—pashyanti (conceptualisation), madhyama (the speech itself) and vaikhari (the comprehension of the listener), thus revealing the 'consciousness' of the speaker. The cumulative impact of such penetrative speculations by grammarians saw the emergence of another entity—dhvani or universal sound—and a varying philosophy—Shabda Advaita—which considered, in contrast to Brahman, vaka shakti to be the eternal, omnipresent and indivisible principle uniting the cosmos.

There were influential esoteric schools of thought and practice too. One branch that is of special interest is that of Shakti, which involved the worship of the feminine principle, as embodied in Durga, the consort of Shiva. The practitioners of this form of devotion, who believed that Shiva's real power was sourced in, or incomplete without, his feminine consort Shakti, developed a complex system of secretive and mystical rites and mantras. This gradually evolved into the esoteric Tantric philosophy, which is codified and elaborated upon in the Samhita or Aagama texts. In general, the cult of the Devi or female Goddess (about which I shall talk later), had great popularity, and was practised on a pan-India scale, and although some aspects of it were nonconformist, they too were embraced within the capacious folds of Hinduism.

Apart from these numerous schools of different strands of thought and practice in Hinduism, there were two major religions, Buddhism and Jainism, which emerged around the same time, and in some manner posed a challenge to the entire spectrum of Hindu philosophy. Buddha was born in Lumbini in around the sixth century BCE in the royal kingdom of Kapilavastu, and lived to the age of eighty. As a young prince he was deeply influenced by the human suffering he saw around him. This suffering, he was convinced, was inevitable in a life that was both transient and unfulfilling, and meaningless beyond the superficial cycle of happiness followed by sorrow, joy followed by grief. He decided then to renounce life and search for the truth that would lead to nirvana or liberation from the cycle of birth and death.

Buddha's enduring concern was with dukkha or suffering inherent in incarnate life. On receiving enlightenment while meditating under the Bodhi tree in Bodh Gaya, he enunciated the Four Noble Truths and the Eightfold Path to liberation. The four truths, simply put, were that there is suffering, there is a cause of suffering, there can be cessation of suffering and there is a way or a path to end the suffering. The Eightfold Path is the way to the cessation of suffering. The eight steps, or the middle way, which he enunciated were right view, right intention, right speech, right action, right livelihood, right effort, right mindfulness and right concentration.

Up to this point, there was nothing in what the Buddha preached that was either entirely original or in conflict either with Hinduism as a whole or with the Advaita philosophy of the Upanishads and Shankara's elaboration of it. However, the metaphysical reasoning underpinning Buddha's preoccupation with sorrow, and the way out of it, was, in many respects, directly at variance with the Upanishadic doctrine. There is nothing like an enduring Self, Brahman or Atman, said the Buddha; in this state of anatta (non-self) what exists is only the rupa (body) and the nama (mind). Everything that we see is samghata (an aggregate); all is inherently nairatmaya (unsubstantial). Moreover, even the self, at the level of body and mind, is anityatva (eternally transient and impermanent). The reality that we see around us has no svabhava (transcendental substratum); it is samtana (in constant flux), and all experience is kshana bhanga vada (a series of impressions, conceived and extinguished in the same instance), so that no one can ever step into the same river twice. Nirvana, or liberation from sorrow, is literally the realisation of the emptiness of the notion of self, a process of blowing out and extinguishing oneself from the binding shackles of the web of life, samsara.

This kernel of Buddha's philosophy was taken to new extremes by later Buddhist thinkers. The Yogachara school of Mahayana Buddhism asserted that only thought, in its ever-changing flux, is real, and there is no external reality whatsoever. This exclusive emphasis on the ephemeral mind as the only identifiable reality to the exclusion of all else took subjectivism to another level, and was called Vijnanavada. Another school, whose chief proponent was Nagarjuna (c. 150–250 CE), was the Madhaymika school of Mahayana Buddhism. Nagarjuna postulated the theory of Sunyata or Emptiness, in which he denied not only the existence of external objects but also the perceiving self. Since there is nothing like a Self, and all things are transient and pratityasamputapada (a product of dependent origination), the entire world, mind and matter, is illusory. Nirvana is the outcome of the understanding of this nihilistic Void.

The denial of the Self, or of the ontological reality of Brahman, was a negation of the grand cosmic design of the Upanishads. Equally, the later evolution of Buddhist thought, that either completely denied external reality or even the mind, signified a new subjectivism and nihilism. Buddha was more concerned with human suffering per se, and the ways to overcome it in the here and now, than with the metaphysical assertions of Atman and Brahman. His was a revolt also against the ritualistic aspects of Hinduism. But his teachings ended up repudiating the philosophical underpinnings of Upanishadic thought as well.

Perhaps the most significant difference between Buddhist thought and Vedanta was on the emphasis each placed on dukkha or suffering, and ananda or joy. The Upanishads defined the ultimate realisation of Brahman as indescribable bliss. Buddha defined nirvana as the cessation of sorrow, not the benediction of bliss. Nirvana, in the Buddhist sense, is an emptiness where all cravings and aversions have ceased. Vedanta, in contrast, is where, after one has transcended the limitations of body and mind, what is left is the union with Brahman and the rekindling of the flame of unalloyed joy. Nagarjuna's Sunyata was nihilistic; it essayed an exhilarating emptiness that stilled the normal turbulence and agitations of the mind. But Nagarjuna would not make the quantum leap to describe Sunyata in positive terms as bliss.

But, this notwithstanding, there were many similarities between Buddhism and Hinduism, especially Vedanta. The devaluation of the external world was common to both. The need to find a way out of sorrow was an imperative for both. Ways to still the sterile agitations of the mind was something both agreed upon. And, both Buddhism and Vedanta were convinced about the end goal of philosophy as liberation, moksha or nirvana.

Between the certainties of Advaita, which asserted the pervasive presence of Brahman signifying Sat chit anand: Being, awareness and bliss, and the certainties of Buddhism, which denied the existence of anything permanent amidst an ocean of impermanence and sorrow, was the deliberate ambivalence of Jainism. Although twenty-four Tirthankars or spiritual teachers had preceded him, Mahavira is accepted as the principal icon of the Jain faith. Like the Buddha, he was born in a royal family. Though there is no unanimity on dates, it is generally believed that he was born in the Muzzafarpur district of Bihar in 599 BCE, and died at Pawapuri in 527 BCE. Around the age of thirty, he too, like the young prince of Kapilavastu, left home to search for truth. After twelve years of intense penance and meditation, he acquired Kevala Jnana, or infinite knowledge.

As against the assertions of absolute truth, Jainism consciously postulates a doctrine of uncertainty. The significant point is that it does so not by simplistic rejection, but in keeping with the intellectual rigour of those times, through a considered theoretical structure of thought. Reality, Jainism says, is complex and admits a plurality and multiplicity of viewpoints—anekantavada; the search for truth must eschew absolutisms and accept the validity of partial standpoints— nayavada; no postulate can be made in such a manner that it denies the possibility of conditional predications—syadavada.

In support of such a deliberate doctrine of relativity, Jainism cites the parable of seven blind men examining an elephant, and depending on what part they touch, coming to a different conclusion of what it is. More formally, Jainism sought to debunk the proponents of 'one-sidedness' by its sapatabhangi or seven-step theory, whose purpose is to establish that knowledge of reality is relative. The seven possibilities that the saptabhangi doctrine outlines are—maybe, it is; maybe, it is not; maybe, it is and is not; maybe, it is inexpressible; maybe, it is and is inexpressible; maybe, it is not and is inexpressible; maybe it is and is not and is inexpressible. The one word that is common to all seven viewpoints is 'maybe'. In Jainism, 'maybe' is the antidote to dogmatism, in particular, that of Hindu and Buddhist metaphysics. Jainism brought to the ideological debate a freshness of view that is invigorating for its sheer audacity to question the propensity of other systems of philosophy to believe that they alone are right. And, in many ways, the relativism that it outlined deeply influenced the future evolution of Indic thought.

The important thing is that neither Buddhism nor Jainism were looked upon with inherent or irreconcilable antagonism by Hinduism. Some hostility might have prevailed in the early phase of the rise of the new faiths, but this subsided over time, and I have shown in the previous chapter how Hindu monarchs extensively patronised both. The reason for this larger tolerance was that Hinduism *allowed* for heterogeneity, even revolt from its mainstream beliefs, assured that this would not in any way dilute the overarching coherence of its belief system. Buddhism and Jainism were viewed not as antithetical to Hinduism, but as emanations from it, entirely in keeping with the diversity of thought sanctioned by it. If Brihaspati of the Charvaka school could say without fear that the Vedas have no sanctity, why would Hinduism have a problem if the Buddha denied the existence of a transcendent Atman? If the Nasidiya Sukta of the *Rig Veda* could ask who knows what the truth is, and speculate that even perhaps the creator may not, why would Hinduism take umbrage against the Jain belief in the relativity of truth? It is possible that, occasionally, 'ideological' differences may have led to friction, but these were of a minor nature, and never assumed, as some historians seem to think, a major confrontation with either of these heterogeneous faiths. Perhaps there were greater differences between Shaivites and Vaishnavites *within* Hinduism than with proponents of either Buddhism or Jainism. Hinduism's accommodative ethos enabled a multiplicity of viewpoints, sanctified by the acceptance of the basic premise that the pursuit of truth can have differing narratives.

It is surprising, therefore, that a leading American Sanskrit scholar like Sheldon Pollock argues that in the ancient shastras 'knowledge is by and large permanently fixed in its dimensions; knowledge, along with the practices that depend on it, does not change or grow, but is frozen for all times in a given set of texts that are continually made available to human beings in whole or even in part during the repeated cycles of cosmic creation'.[13] Perhaps, he was focusing on certain basic texts that are regarded by many as Shruti or revealed texts. However, the important thing to focus on is the diversity of thought permitted within them, and the degree of tolerance of heterodoxy against them. As I have already noted, there was no concept of heresy or blasphemy in Hinduism, nor was there one overriding dogma, church, pope, text or prescriptive ritual. Thus, in Valmiki's Ramayana, for instance, a pundit called Javali could question the divinity of Rama, and call his actions 'foolish' for an otherwise intelligent and wise man, asserting at the same time that 'there is no after-world, nor any practice for attaining that'.[14] Not uncharacteristically, there are hundreds of versions of the Ramayana, adding their own colour, emphasis and context, without any threat to the central narrative of the epic. In the Mahabharata, a hermit called Uttanka could castigate Krishna himself for not doing enough to prevent the war at Kurukshetra, thereby causing so many to suffer for no fault of theirs.[15] Adi Shankaracharya, who is credited with the revival of Hinduism, could fearlessly rubbish central tenets of Hindu faith with lyrical felicity. In his famous stotra, the *Nirvana Shatakam*, he states—Na dharmo, na chartho, na kamo, na moksha: None of the four purusharthas or goals of life in the Hindu world view have meaning. Indeed, he goes further to say—Na mantro, na teertham, na veda, na yajnah: Neither mantra, nor pilgrimage sites, nor consecrated ritual, not even the Vedas are of any value. All that matters is Chit-ananda rupam: Awareness and Bliss. In this context, he actually conflates himself with Shiva—Shivo ham, Shivo ham: I am Shiva, I am Shiva. In most other conventional religions, especially the Abrahamic faiths, this assumption of godhood would be considered blasphemy. Indeed, by contrast, we have the example of the great Sufi mystic, Al-Hallaj (858–922 CE), in Persia, almost contemporaneous with Shankaracharya, who was put to death for having had the temerity to say—Ana'l Haq: I am the Truth. In ancient Greece, Socrates, the great philosopher, in the fourth century BCE, was sentenced to be killed by drinking hemlock, accused of 'impiety' and for his espousal of what is now called the logic of Socrates. At that very time in India, many divergent schools of philosophy were revelling in the freedom given by their faith to explore the truth in the way they thought fit. In such a milieu, Buddhism was genuinely under threat of being assimilated within the larger diversified matrix of Hinduism; indeed, many Hindus still believe that Buddha was the last avatar of Vishnu. No wonder then, that Buddhism could flourish with much greater ease with its identity as separately preserved, outside the shores of India, than in the land where it was born.

Actually, Amartya Sen is right when he writes that Sanskrit has a larger volume of agnostic or atheist writings than any other classical language. Sheldon Pollock too is strongly rebutted by other reputed Western scholars. George Cardona, also a prominent Western Sanskrit scholar, emphasises 'the sharp critical thinking skills of early Sanskrit studies across various disciplines. ... At no point in early and medieval India was there an absolute, thoughtless acceptance of tradition, even by different followers of a single tradition. ... Nor are grammatical, exegetical, or logical systems made solely as maidservants to Vedic tradition.'[16]

Indeed, the ability of Hinduism to adapt and modify to changing needs shows conclusively that it could reinterpret its knowledge systems. An important—and even pivotal—illustration of this is the transition from nirguna (attribute-less) Brahman to a saguna (attribute-full) Ishvara. Of the six systems of Hindu philosophy, the one that was the most pervasively influential was the Advaita or Vedanta school, which believed, as we have seen, in an absolute monism—the nirguna, formless, all-pervasive cosmic consciousness, Brahman. While this was an exceptionally powerful concept, and is being validated by latest scientific discoveries in the areas of cosmology, quantum physics and neurology,[17] it was much too dry a concept for the ordinary devotee. There was a need, therefore, to unite the unrelenting non-dualism of Vedanta with a theism that was more appealing to ordinary people craving for the grace of a personal God in their search for solace and assurance.

It is to the lasting—but not uncharacteristic—credit of Hinduism, that it was able to respond to this need, not arbitrarily, nor by fiats or simplistic denial, but through the use of logic and reasoning anchored in a philosophical context. The imperative to bridge the notion of a persistently transcendent and aloof Brahman, to a theism more responsive to our daily lives, was the task at hand and it was taken up with systemic intellectual rigour. On the hard rock of Vedantic philosophical structure, there soon sprouted a lush undergrowth of what was, in emotional terms, a more fulfilling theism, where, essentially the focus moved from Brahma to Ishvara, and from logic to devotion.

Ramanuja was born in the year 1017 in Sriperumbudur, south India, some two hundred years after the death of Shankaracharya. Even as a child, he acquired a mastery of the Vedanta doctrine. Adopting the life of a sanyasi, he settled down in Srirangam. He wrote several highly regarded treatises on Vedanta, and seminal commentaries on the *Brahma Sutra* and the Bhagwad Gita. Although, he did not seek to consciously differ from Shankaracharya, he is ultimately associated with the doctrine of Vishist Advaita, or qualified non-dualism, which moulded Advaita towards a personalised theism.

Ramanuja did not contest Shankara's assertion that Brahman is supreme, all-knowing, omnipotent and omnipresent, characterised by the experience of sat (being), chit (consciousness or awareness) and ananda (bliss). However, he did not support the Vedantic assertion that Brahman is attribute-less. Pure consciousness, Ramanuja argued, is an untenable construct. A thing without any attributes is as good as being non-existent; and, if it has attributes, it cannot be pure consciousness. It is not possible 'for the mind to apprehend an undifferentiated object. What is known is necessarily known as characterized in some way.'[18] The interpretation that Brahman is 'nirguna' is, Ramanuja asserts, a misreading of the Upanishads. What the Upanishads actually intend to indicate is that 'some qualities are denied while there are still others characterizing it.'[19]

If Brahman, although supreme, is not without attributes, then it must be determinate, a whole, no doubt, but with verifiable elements. These, according to Ramanuja, are the individual souls, their bodies, inanimate matter and, overseeing them all, Ishvara or God. The Absolute, therefore, is not unqualified and indeterminate, but has svagatabheda (internal differences), which are chidachidvishishta (real and have separate autonomy). They may be dependent on Brahman, but are not subsumed into 'nothingness' by it. It follows then that the empirical world is not an illusion. To say that it is purely phenomenal, a product of the illusionary powers of Maya, is wrong. Nor can it be dismissed as a product of avidya or nescience. There is nothing logically inconsistent in accepting that the infinite can give rise to the finite, or that there can be diversity within unity, and a coherence between a whole and its parts.

On the foundations of his philosophical divergence with Vedanta, as especially propounded by his formidable intellectual predecessor, Shankaracharya, Ramanuja built an elaborate and appealing edifice of the art of prapatti (complete surrender) to the prasada (grace) of Ishvara. What is more, he invested considerable thought to elaborating what constituted bhakti. Ramanuja's greatest contribution thus was not the denial of Brahman, but the inclusion within its pervasive supremacy of the validity of devotion to a personal God, and in doing so, providing for ordinary mortals an alternative form of spirituality compared to the remote intellectual aloofness of nirguna Brahman. In the structure of Advaitic thought, he provided the philosophical key to open the gates of bhakti and gave philosophical backing to earlier traditions of theistic worship evidenced in the *Vishnu Purana*, the *Harivamsha* and the *Bhagwata Purana*, as also the later poet-saints called the Alvars in south India. Once he laid the intellectual framework for theism, his thought process was taken much further by later thinkers like Madhava, Nimbarkar, Vallabha and Chaitanya. The secret of this adaptational genius lay in the fact that Hinduism was neither brittle in thought, nor prescriptive in faith.

Indeed, the dialectic between Adi Shankaracharya's vigorous monism and Ramanuja's persuasive theism provides a telling illustration of the cerebration within Hinduism. Shankara's Brahman was, for lay devotees, much too intellectualised a construct. It did not provide the assurance that human insecurity and fulfilment seek in the here and now. Human beings require some tangible concept of the Absolute to identify with; they need to pray to a divinity that they can internalise in personal terms; they need the solidarity of faith, not in a concept but in a deity that is comprehensible and not merely the consequence, however compelling, of logic alone. Ramanuja understood the logic underpinning Shankara's notion of Brahman, but was keen to find a way to provide philosophical legitimacy to theism, with all its pageantry of worship and ritual and bhakti. The basic fact is that Ramanuja and the thinkers that followed him were guided by the need to make spirituality more religious, whereas Shankara was motivated by the desire to make religion more spiritual. In this sense, the Brahman of Advaita and the Ishvara of Ramanuja were two sides of the same coin of human yearning. One catered to human vulnerability and fulfilment in the life lived now, the other catered to the search of the human intellect for ultimate truths. Shankara, for all his fealty to the Upanishadic Brahman, was not unaware, one suspects, of the need to derogate his uncompromising monism. It was precisely for this reason that he segmented the jnana marga at two levels—para vidya or higher knowledge, where the primary concern was the metaphysical comprehension of the Absolute; and apara vidya or lower knowledge, where bhakti, worship, Yoga, prayer, surrender, ritual and devotion were given legitimacy, as a part of the preparatory steps to move from apara to para vidya.

If this remarkable application of mind provided philosophical legitimacy to the practice of theism, a similar intellectualism was behind the Hindu concept of divinity, and of bhakti or devotion. This may sound unconvincing to some people, who are overwhelmed by the number of gods and goddesses in the Hindu pantheon. But, if we pause for a moment to distil the overriding concept behind the multiplicity of deities and the infinite variations in worship, we will discover that almost nothing in the Hindu practice of devotion is random or purely ritualistic. This is not to deny that very often mechanical ritual finesses the intellectual construct behind the practice. However, the attempt here is to see whether, beyond the surface chaos of the practice of Hindu religion, there is a larger vision defining the notion of divinity and devotion.

As I have stated earlier, the earliest notions of divinity were related to the dramatic forces of nature, and the wonderment and awe they generated. Thus, there were gods like Indra, symbolising rain, thunder and lightning; Agni, venerating fire; or forms of the mother goddess in recognition of the miracle of procreation. These early notions of divinity, however, soon gave way to the pivotal notion of the Trinity—Brahma, Vishnu and Shiva, standing for creation, preservation and destruction, respectively. The Trinity corresponds to the Hindu notion of the cycle of time—everything comes into being, sustains for some time and then passes away. The three gods oversee this ordained cycle of time, and stand in contrast to the transience of manifest phenomena. As Ishvara, they are ultimate symbols of grace, power and benediction. But all three also represent that unchanging and eternal notion of nirguna cosmic consciousness—Brahman. The Trinity, thus, assumes form for the need of the devotees but, ultimately, in the perception of those very devotees, it is formless as well, a conscious act of planned divine derogation from the supremacy of Brahman.

This duality in the perception of divinity is the key to understanding both Hindu philosophy and Hindu religion. Assured of the primacy of the nirguna Infinite, which is formless, eternal, indivisible, omnipotent and present in everything, animate and inanimate, and of which the gods too are an emanation, Hindus have no inhibition in giving full play to the human imagination in embellishing, adorning and humanising their deities. This duality of approach to the divine is mostly beyond the comprehension of many foreigners, especially those from the Abrahamic faiths, where divinity is prescriptive and singular. What they do not understand is that for the Hindu mind, revelling in the plurality of the divine, representation is an act of devotional joy; it is plural in projection, and singular in belief, but that singularity is a matter of conceptual belief, not representational linearity.

Thus, the Infinite is One; the manifest is transient, a product of avidya, ignorance; and the gods are a divine means to lead us from ignorance to moksha, from the transient to the eternal. For this act of unlimited grace, our gods *deserve* to be venerated in full measure, without inhibition, in as many forms as possible, and with all that the human mind can creatively summon to show a sense of gratitude and surrender.

Since the Ultimate is infinite, its abundance must, at the manifest level, be given its full due. That due cannot be straitjacketed by conventional notions of scriptural correctness, as is the case in most other religions. The firm anchorage of the one Brahman legitimises the joyous variations in the depiction of Ishvara. Indeed, Hinduism provides ample, even exuberant, evidence of this. The pantheon of our gods, the range of attributes we give to them, the myriad ways we worship them, the uninhibited manner in which we portray them, the songs we compose for them, the art we create for them, the rituals with which we venerate them, the delight with which we humanise them, the personal rapport we build with them, is not a sign of mindless, primitive polytheism, but the joyous human depiction of a vision that is monotheistic in concept and plural in representation—the ability to see the One in the many, and the many in the One.

It is for this reason that Hindus can worship a stone, a rock, a tree, a mountain, a river, without comprising their monotheistic conviction. It is not the intention here to enumerate all the gods Hindus worship, or provide a description of all the attributes they confer on them, or narrate all the stories built around them. Suffice to state the principle—when the nirguna transcendent is unshakeably ensconced, the saguna becomes, for the joyous purposes of devotion, delightfully vibrant. Then, even the Trinity is depicted not as austere or unidimensional, but lovingly imbued with multiple attributes. The sheer grandeur of this devotional imagination is awe-inspiring.

This pervasive nirguna–saguna dialectic is amply illustrated in the intellectual conceptualisation of the presiding Trinity. Thus Brahma, the creator, is recognised to be the manifestation of Parabrahman, the very embodiment of the formless, nirguna Brahman. But, in his saguna form as Brahma, he is depicted with four faces and four arms, one holding the Vedas, the second the rosary or beads, the third a srura or ladle for the sacrificial fire, and the fourth a kamandal or utensil with water. He is usually portrayed as sitting on a lotus, dressed in white, with the swan as his vehicle.

Vishnu, the preserver, is also considered a manifestation of Parabrahman. The *Bhagwata Purana* specifically equates him with Brahman, beyond form, all-pervasive all-knowing consciousness. With this as his permanent attribute, he is lovingly adorned as Ishvara. He is depicted with four hands—the first holding a conch shell (symbolising spiralling cyclic existence); the second, the Surdarshana chakra, the discus used to restore dharma; the third, a gada or mace standing for power or authority; and the fourth, a lotus, conveying purity or transcendence. Adorning him is the Kaustabha gem in a necklace and Vaijayanti, a garland of flowers. The mystical Srivatsa mark is depicted on his chest in the form of a curl of hair. He wears yellow garments, and is shown standing or seated in a yogic posture, or reclining majestically on the coils of Shesha, the king of the Nagas or serpents. Devotees give him many names. The *Vishnu Sahasranama*, a lyrical enumeration of the thousand names of Vishnu, is a popular devotional recital.

Shiva, even more emphatically than Brahma and Vishnu, is perceived and internalised as the formless, limitless, unchanging, transcendent Brahman, and the Atman (Self) of the universe. But with this internalised as his essential nature, devotees depict him in endlessly endearing forms. A serpent adorns his neck, the crescent moon is elegantly poised on his head, the holy Ganga River flows from his matted locks, the third eye that opens to destroy Kama, the embodiment of desire, is resplendent on his forehead. His weapon is the trishul or trident; he meditates on a tiger skin; his throat is neelkantha (blue) because he drank the poison distilled from the primeval churning of the oceans, the Samudra Manthan; he carries a rosary made of rudraksha; his bare body is smeared with ash to remind us of the transience of existence; and the damru or drum signifying primeval sound is his accompaniment. As Ishvara, he is the eternal Yogi, the patron god of meditation and Yoga, living as an ascetic on the snowy heights of Mount Kailasha. But he is also the quintessential householder, with his wife Parvati, and sons Ganesha and Kartikeya. In his fierce aspect he is Rudra; in his benign aspect, Ashutosh; and, for his childlike simplicity, simply Bhola. He is also Nataraja, the lord of dance; and, he is Pashupati, the lord of animals. Like Vishnu, he too has a thousand names and more.

The conceptual hyphenation between nirguna and saguna, which is the enduring intellectual construct of the Ultimate in Hinduism, is seen not only in the presiding Trinity, but percolates down to all visualisations of divinity. It is also the philosophical substratum of all mythology. The Hindu mind compels the harmonisation between the non-dual spiritual unity of perception at the ontological level, and the profuse plurality of depiction at the level of devotional worship. It is not, especially for the foreign observer, an easy dialectic to comprehend, because the prolific surface multiplicity is often seen as such, in isolation, severed from the absence of that very multiplicity in terms of foundational cognition. In the case of Shiva, his depiction as lingam—that ultimate bridge between form and the formless—is, in particular, a reason for ignorant and simplistic commentaries.

Wendy Doniger, for instance, believes that the nirguna–saguna tension in Hinduism is not resolved. She is perplexed because the same text often refers to the divine in both nirguna and saguna ways. To her, this is a lack of consistency, or evidence of a conflict of viewpoint. 'The avatar,' she protests, 'is constantly bumping into his own nirguna image; the texts never fully accept this resolution of the nirguna–saguna tension.'[20] Such a comment would certainly bring a smile to Hindus. What Doniger finds contradictory is precisely the effortless conceptual synthesis Hindus take as normative and par for the course. If someone believes that for purposes of sanitised clarity, godhood can only be one or the other, then it is their inability to understand the cerebral suppleness of the Hindu spiritual vision.

Shankaracharya and Ramanuja put their philosophical imprimatur in bridging this apparent dichotomy centuries ago. For Doniger, the 'logical outcome of merging with a nirguna deity—moksha—would be the disappearance of bhakti, with no god to be the object of devotion'.[21] She has obviously not understood that in Hinduism, the acceptance of the nirguna Ultimate *sanctions* the legitimacy, for purposes of human devotion, of a saguna deity. Only this can explain why Adi Shankaracharya, arguably the greatest exponent of the nirguna Brahman, also wrote the most evocative devotional hymns to saguna deities. To understand the primacy of nirguna, saguna bhakti is a perfectly valid path.

In Advaita metaphysics, the human mind consists of three elements—buddhi or intellect; ahamkara or ego; and chit or the awareness of the silent, transcendent observer. The intellect, like a monkey jumping from one branch to another, is forever—and mostly sterilely—active; the ego creates the false obsession of the 'I', the perennial delusion that the transient personal world is the only reality. Both the intellect and the ego need to be stilled, for the chit to awaken. The overwhelming sense of atma samarpan, that is, the absolute surrender to a saguna Ishvara that bhakti invokes, helps in stilling the intellect and the ego. That opens the way to brahmananubhav, when the chit allows the Atman within each of us to merge with Brahman, since both are one limitless reservoir of bliss, held back from ourselves because we only live at the level of the intellect and the ego. Bhakti to a saguna Ishvara is thus a vital preparatory step—apara vidya as Shankaracharya called it—to the realisation of the nirguna Brahman. There is no contradiction, as Sheldon Pollock seems to believe, between the vyavaharik and the paramarthik levels of religio-spiritual experience. The worship of a deity at the vyavaharik or human level, and the experience of Brahman, the supreme consciousness, at the transcendental or paramarthik level, are seamless steps to the common goal of moksha. Nirguna and saguna are, therefore, not contradictory to each other, nor are they, as Doniger derisively says, 'a concoction that monistic Hindu philosophers imposed upon a saguna bhakti tradition',[22] but complementary phases in the unified process of self-realisation.

Doniger, and scholars like her, make the cardinal mistake of interpreting Hindu spirituality literally. They are, therefore, inadequate interpreters of the deeper unitary vision that transcends the apparent surface contradictions within Hinduism. Doniger's interpretation of the lingam in Hindu worship is a good example of this inadequacy. For her, if Hindus look upon the lingam in terms of its real meaning, which is a mark or sign or emblem, and not accept it as a phallic symbol, they are being prudish. This prudery, she argues, is due to the wrath of the Muslim conquerors who savagely destroyed lingams taking them to be a representation of the phallus, a form of obscene idolatry. Or else, they internalised the disgust of the British conquerors who were repelled at what they believed was the vulgar worship of the male organ. It is true that some members of the Hindu right wing, unacceptably ignorant about the remarkable way in which the Hindu world view includes the sensual in a balanced life—dharma, artha, *kama*, moksha—try to impose an alien Victorian morality on Hindu society and behaviour. But, what is far more important is to evaluate the overall evidence within Hinduism on what the lingam stands for.

Doniger is the mistress of the obscure Hindu religious or mythological texts. In isolating these, she is not coy about her motivation: 'The Sanskrit texts were written at a time of glorious sexual openness and insight, and I have often focused on precisely those parts of the text ...' If this provides her academic titillation, so be it. But it is quite another thing to use such material—mostly of a flimsy, scattered or non-generic nature—to argue a point of view without taking the overwhelming weight of evidence which leads to the contrary conclusions. If this balance is deliberately jettisoned, it becomes a new form of Orientalist insouciance camouflaged as academic learning. For instance, she will pick, in her own words, 'an obscene hymn in the *Rig Veda* about a sexual competition between a male donkey and the god Indra' to argue that 'Indra bequeaths to Shiva some aspects of his mythology, including myths of castration'.[23] Or she will choose another text in which 'Randy scratches her itch with a lingam of skin'.[24] Or she will visit a temple in Gudimallam in Andhra Pradesh, where the carving of the lingam is 'definitely' that of the male sexual organ. Even more amusingly, she will—after criticising the British for their unfair interpretation of the lingam exclusively as a phallus—quote a fictional character, Mr Bhoolabhoy, from Paul Scott's novel *Staying On*, who says that every erection he has reminds him of the Shiva lingam! With this in her armoury, she concludes that 'there is convincing textual evidence that people in ancient India associated the iconic form of the lingam with the male sexual organ'.[25]

Perhaps, in the remote past, some people did, and perhaps some people still have a similar conception of the lingam. The miracle of procreation is also a gift of God, and there is nothing wrong in associating Shiva with it. Hinduism permits such freedom of interpretation. But, as against the evidence Doniger cites, there is overwhelmingly greater evidence to believe that most Hindus see the lingam as an aniconic representation of Mahadeva, shorn of material features, a replica of the dome of the cosmos, the central sthambha or pillar in the holy yajna 'that connects the primal energy of the earth to the sky',[26] aloof and detached, a reminder of what Shiva himself is in his essence, ajanmam (unborn), akhandam (indivisible) and nirakar (formless). The Upanishads speak of the lingam as a sign of That; the *Atharva Veda* sees it as a column of light, without beginning or end, amatra (infinite), whose beginning and end even Brahma and Vishnu could not find. In two of the most revered sites for Shiva worship, Kedarnath in the Himalayas and the Vishvanath temple in Kashi, the lingam is almost nirguna in its features, a mere piece of undefinable rock jutting from the earth below. For the vast majority of Hindus, the lingam stands for the cosmic energy personified by Shiva; it is a symbol of the eternal ascetic that is Shiva; it is the sign of the destroyer of evil who is Shiva; it is a mark of the benediction that is Shiva; it is the eternally still icon to the ecstatic dance of Shiva.

The vast corpus of textual material in Hinduism can certainly enable a researcher to focus on the quixotic. But, that is the lazy option, good for sensation rather than insight. The far more difficult task is to infer the larger movements of thought which animate practice, locate the preponderant themes and identify the overarching holistic vision that informs great religions. It is then that we can elevate the literal to the philosophical, not reduce the philosophical to the literal. As U.R. Ananthamurthy rightly says: 'For us writing in India, it should never matter what is translatable in English and what would be acceptable to the literary ethos of the West. If we begin to think that what is good is that which is eminently translatable into the modern western ethos, we cannot be forgiven.'[27]

The imaginative grandeur of Shiva's real image comes through when in the Tandava dance he choreographs the cosmic cycle of creation, preservation and destruction. As immortalised in the Chola and Kurkihara bronzes, he is seen dynamically poised in the midst of his vigorously rhythmic portrayal of the endless swirl of the universe. Around him is a frame of fire, representing the pulsating energy permeating the universe; in his upper right hand is the damru, symbol of the primal sound of creation; in his upper left hand is a flame, pointing to the inevitability of destruction of all things transient; his lower right hand benevolently extends the promise of grace and redemption; and his lower left hand points downward to the demon below his feet, indicative of the ignorance that we must conquer. His movements, while in perfect harmony, are so fast and vigorous that the tongue of flame in his hand creates the illusion of a circle of fire, and the sound of the drum appears to emanate from all quarters. In the midst of this energetic dance, his face is the picture of calm, symbolic of his transcendence, where he is immanent in the dance of the cosmos but totally above it. As Nataraja he, therefore, represents srishti, creation; sthithi, preservation; samhara, destruction; tirobhava, illusion; and anugraha, grace.

The sheer loftiness of the spiritual imagination in creating such an image to represent the cosmic cycle of creation and destruction leaves one breathless. The great art historian and philosopher Ananda Coomaraswamy says unhesitatingly that such a depiction of primal rhythmic energy is 'the clearest image of the activity of God which any art or religion can boast of'.[28] Fritjof Capra, a scholar of considerable prominence of theoretical physics, concludes that Shiva's dance is the mythological counterpart of the dancing universe, representing the 'ceaseless flow of energy going through an infinite variety of patterns that melt into one another'. 'Modern physics has thus revealed that every sub-atomic particle not only performs an energy dance, but also is an energy dance; a pulsating process of creation and destruction'.[29] Shiva's cosmic dance is thus the choreography of the universe enabled by the omnipresent but nirguna Brahman. It is significant that because of the dance of energy it represents, a beautiful statue of Shiva as Nataraj has been installed at the European Organization for Nuclear Research (CERN).

Other depictions of divinity in Hinduism also show the remarkable combination of religious devotion and application of the mind. Rama and Krishna, the two most prominent avatars of Vishnu, provide a good example. The story of Rama was immortalised by Valmiki in the Ramayana, written in Sanskrit sometime between the fifth century BCE and the first century BCE. Since then, there have been countless local variations of the narrative, including the iconic *Ramcharitmanas* of Tulsidas, penned in the sixteenth century CE. The lore of Krishna has also been the subject of countless works, including the *Harivamsha*, the *Vishnu Purana* and the *Bhagwata Purana*.

It is not the intention here to elaborate on the narratives of these two gods who have for millennia effortlessly captured the minds of the devotees. The narratives are well known, not only in India but also abroad, and performed and recited the world over. For our purpose, what is important is to speak about the conceptualisation of the two divinities. Rama was conceived as maryada purushottam, the epitome of rectitude, the touchstone of impeccable behaviour and the role model of the perfect human being. He stands for order and stability, of equilibrium and equipoise in the working of the cosmos, where choices are determined not by whim but by the conscious thought of what is right, as an end in themselves, even when other choices could have been made. Krishna, on the other hand, is conceived as leela purushottam, the human incarnation of the playful, whimsy divine who is unconventional, nonconformist, lovingly mischievous, the very embodiment of God delightfully playing the fool for no other reason than the sheer joy of it. Thus, while Rama is the dutiful son, the caring brother, the devoted husband and the steadfast family man, Krishna is the adorable child who steals butter, the precocious adolescent who flirts with the gopis, the irresistible flute-playing lover who frolics with women, young and old, on the banks of the Yamuna, and the incorrigibly unfaithful companion to his beloved and supreme love, Radha.

There can be no two more contrasting profiles of arguably the two most popular gods in Hinduism. Why did the Hindu mind create these two beloved deities in such drastically different ways? Why did it not, for purposes of devotion, choose a monochromatic representation of divinity rather than this explosive kaleidoscope of differing attributes? The answer provides the key to the cerebral complexity of Hinduism, and its fearless resolve to uninhibitedly plumb the unusual in order to provide a glimpse of the plenteousness of divinity. If the Ultimate is beyond definition yet fulfilment personified, it cannot be portrayed in simplistic and predictable ways. While not all its infinite aspects can be captured, because it is both omnipresent and omnipotent, a glimpse can be provided of this very infinity by portraying it in myriads of ways, each only a fragment of the whole, and yet a window to that endless canvas. Maryada purushottam Rama is one aspect of the predictable grandeur of the universe; leela purushottam Krishna is another aspect of the playful energy of the cosmos. Both represent facets of the seamless benediction of Ishvara, and the omniscience of Brahman.

If maryada, at one end of the divine spectrum, stands for the assurance of conventional order, leela, at the other end, celebrates its subversion, since the physical universe, as modern science shows, is constantly assembling and dissembling in the same instant. Maryada and leela thus become two sides of the same divine coin. In the eternal cycle of creation, preservation and dissolution, order and disorder combine; the predictable interfaces with the unpredictable; the constructive overlaps with the destructive; form interacts with flux. The representation of the divine must take cognisance of this process, not be conjured as an entity unrelated to it. To jolt one into cognition of this, Krishna must defy all notions of conventional divinity and steal butter; he must forsake predictable morality and have a thousand lovers; he must not be the well-behaved but the rebellious child; he must be the unforgivably flirtatious adolescent; he must be the polygamous but consummate lover; he must be the sage who counsels Arjuna in the Bhagwad Gita; and he must be the crafty strategist who leads the Pandavas to victory in the Mahabharata. Divinity, if wished to be portrayed truthfully, cannot be straitjacketed.

If Rama symbolises the acceptable notion of divinity, Krishna—in substantial aspects of his persona—symbolises its antithesis. From these two polarities, equally loved by devotees, emerges the synthesis that the divine is endlessly multifaceted, indefinably beyond known human categories, and truly representative of the infinitude of the Supreme.

The concept of leela, in particular, is a remarkable aspect of Hinduism, and once again illustrative of the harmonious dynamics between saguna and nirguna. In the play of leela, godhood reduces itself lovingly to the level of the human. It does so for the benefit of devotees, in order to embellish the *accessibility* of the saguna svaroop (form) of Ishvara. Thus, Krishna, the Almighty personified, is scolded by his mother, Yashoda, for stealing butter; he is punished by Radha for his philandering; and he is admonished by the Kauravas for 'cheating' in the Mahabharata. Rama, the Supreme, gracefully yields to his mother's request at his birth that he shed his godly profile, and in one instance the all-powerful Lord becomes a newborn child wailing in the arms of his mother; he willingly succumbs to the conspiracy of being banished for fourteen years to the forest; and he, who is the remover of all sorrow, is bereft with grief when Sita is abducted by Ravana. The examples of these role plays are endless. But devotees know that all this is merely the enticingly benedictory leela of the divine. In reality, the one who is scolded, or the one who grieves for his missing wife, is the transcendent, all-knowing, all-powerful, all-pervasive nirguna Brahman. The nirguna is his essential nature; the saguna is the grace of his leela. Tulsidas puts it succinctly—Aguna, saguna dui brahma svarupa, akath agadha anadi anupa: The qualified saguna, and the unqualified nirguna, are two aspects of the same Brahman; both are unspeakable, unfathomable, without beginning and without parallel. He then compresses tomes of philosophical reasoning, and with remarkable brevity explains why the nirguna becomes the saguna—Aguna arupa alakha aja joi, bhagata prem basa saguna ho joi: That which is attribute-less, imperceptible, unborn and unqualified, becomes qualified under the influence of the devotee's love.

The resolve not to confine the representation of the divine in insularly singular terms also explains why, transcending traditional notions of gender dominance, Hinduism must be the only major religion to accord near equal space to the Devi or the Goddess in its devotional pantheon. This is not to minimise the patriarchal nature of Hindu society as it developed later, and the pervasive subordination of women. I shall discuss all this subsequently. My focus here is on the conceptual notion of divinity where, notwithstanding actual social practices, full play is given to the feminine principle. We have noted how evidence indicates that a mother goddess cult was widely prevalent in the Harappan civilisation. The early Vedic deities were also often feminine, for instance, Agni. Later, each member of the Trinity had his consort—Brahma and Sarasvati, Vishnu and Lakshmi, and Shiva and Parvati. In addition, Rama is incomplete without Sita, and Krishna is forever associated with Radha. Feminine divinity is ascribed to an entire range of things. The earth itself is a goddess, Bhudevi. The river Ganga is Ganga Ma. Temples exclusively devoted to the Devi dot the entire religious landscape of India. Vaishno Devi in Jammu gets record crowds. Festivals fully devoted to the Devi enjoy exceptional popularity, such as Durga Puja, a major religious event especially for Bengalis. 'Devi, the Goddess in India, is one of the guiding forces of Indian civilization. In the whole world, a more complete rhapsody on the divine feminine would be hard to conceive.'[30]

As always, behind this exuberant devotion to the Devi, there is a powerful cerebral construct. Devi stands for the incredible creativity of Maya, that elusive energy that both creates the illusion of the sensory world, and provides the path of redemption from it. She is also—as best elaborated in the Sankhya philosophy—the symbol of Prakriti, the potency of materiality, which coming into contact with the pure consciousness of Purusha, leads to creation. Finally, and as a result also of the first two, she is the Shakti or Energy that pervades all living things animate and inanimate. In a generic sense, this is well-illustrated in the metaphysical interpretation of creation in the context of Shiva. Brahman, as I have discussed, is omnipresent formless energy; but, if for human purposes, it is given form, Shiva is chit, the pure, attribute-less consciousness within all of us, and Shakti is chitrupini, the power inherent in that consciousness. Shakti is nought without Shiva, but equally, Shiva is powerless without Shakti. The two are complementary to the point that they are indistinguishable. They are equal in every respect, be it adhishtana (abode), anushtana (occupation), avastha (condition), rupa (form) and nama (name). Neither can exist without the other, and only together do they actualise this universe and transcend it. In the very first stanza of the *Soundarya Lahiri*, Shankara's passionate hymn to the Devi, he bows to this union:

> O Bhagwati,
> Only if Shiva is conjoined with You can He create
> Without You, O Shakti, He cannot even move
> O, Mother, Hari, Hara and Brahma worship You
> Only because of my virtuous deeds in the past
> Can I salute You!

In such a conceptualisation, Shiva is Brahman, the unmoving, changeless potentiality, and Shakti is the power latent within him. The analogy of one that is still in perfection and the other that can ruffle that stillness as part of an integrated cosmic design, is a part of the Shiva–Shakti construct. If Shiva is the still waters of the cosmic pool, Shakti is the ripple that emanates from it. That ripple, part of the cosmic unity signified by Brahman, but symbolising the energy within it, is personified for purposes of theism, in the form of the Devi.

It is significant that the four mathas that Adi Shankaracharya established in the eighth century CE are known as Shakti peeths, or the abode of the power of the Devi. In Sringeri, the first matha he established, there is a temple dedicated to the Devi in her form as Sharada. At the entrance of this temple is inscribed the Upanishadic mahavakya—Aham Brahmasmi: I am Brahman, thereby underlining the fact that Shakti, in her theistic form of the Devi, is a part of the non-dualistic omniscience of Brahman. 'Sharada who represents the saguna form of the Supreme Absolute is the great Matrix of the Universe displaying in her hands the symbol of the jar of nectar and immortality, a book signifying supreme knowledge, a rosary the beads of which signify the subtle aksharas or bijas from which the gross forms of the universe emanate, and the Chinmudra standing for the awareness of the Jiva with Brahman. She is the light of all Upanishadic knowledge and as such is Brahmvidya.'[31]

In tantric vidya, the Sri Chakra, which represents the deity in a geometrical design, is considered the highest form of compressed energy. The design is replete with symbolisms. The bindu stands for pure bliss and consciousness, representing the primordial divine being. When this pure consciousness seeks to manifest itself, there begins a process of vimarsha or contemplation. Shiva is the primordial undifferentiated consciousness, and Shakti the vimarsha that leads to creation. In the Sri Chakra, the triangles with the apex upward represent Shiva and the triangles with the apex downwards represent Shakti. A combination of the two depicts Brahman, both in its static and dynamic forms. In his Bhashya on the *Kena Upanishad*, Shankaracharya emphasises the complete identity between the all-knowing Atman and its chit, Shakti—Sa Atma sarva pratyaya darshi chit Shakti svarupa matraha. It is not surprising, therefore, that he made Shakti upasana compulsory in all his mathas.

In her saguna form, the Devi or Shakti is presented in as varied a range of representations as any male god. Her names are many— Durga, Amba, Gauri, Bhavani, Kali and so on. Once again, the attempt here is to capture as many possible facets of the divine. Sarasvati is the goddess of knowledge, music, art, speech, wisdom and learning. She is depicted dressed in white, holding a lotus and books, and playing the veena. Her vahana or mount is the swan or the peacock. Lakshmi is the goddess of good fortune, prosperity, wealth, fertility and all things luxurious. Her garments are usually in red, and she is seen holding a lotus. Parvati represents, as we have seen, the

Shakti of Shiva. She is portrayed as fair and beautiful, usually dressed in red, and gentle in demeanour. Sita is the symbol of the ideal wife, and Radha—much like Krishna is to Rama—quite the opposite, the parakiya, or extramarital love of Krishna. Perhaps the most dramatic form of the Devi is Kali, another form of Parvati. Unlike the demure Parvati, she is depicted as dancing wildly on the prostrate but calm body of Shiva. Black in colour, her eyes are red with intoxication, her hair dishevelled and her tongue sticks out of her mouth; she is shown wearing a garland of human skulls, and in her many hands is a scimitar, a severed head and a kapala (skullcap) for collecting the blood of the severed head. Her abode is the cremation ground.

For many foreign observers, this is a bizarre representation of divinity, a form of unacceptable primitivism. Why would Hindus, for whom the Ultimate is the formless Brahman, simultaneously worship a deity of this kind? The reason is imbedded in the Hindu devotional imagination which, precisely because the divine is beyond definition, and more than what the human mind can ever conceive, must be portrayed in as many aspects that can capture some of its profusion. Kali is incomprehensible to those who wish to see divinity in predictable, linear terms. She is perfectly natural to those who see her as representing one facet of the divine, the unvanquished and fiery Mahakali—destroyer of evil, the goddess of Time and the symbol of invincible might. Never for a moment does her deliberately dramatic iconography distract the devotee from what she stands for—as the most powerful personification of Shakti. The devotee sees in her terrible form the force of divine protection, love and kindness. As a perceptive foreign scholar writes: 'In confronting her, we are not only horrified but potentially saved: a vision of Kali takes us beyond the constraints through which and within which we live. Kali releases.'[32]

Of significance is the fact that Kali dances wildly *on* the prone body of Shiva. In the presence of her passion and power, Shiva is happily rendered like a shava or corpse. The Devi is then supreme. Indeed, the important sixth-century CE text, the *Devi Mahatmya* (glorification of the goddess), equates her with the sole ultimate reality, superseding the gods. A millennium later, in Tulsidas's *Ramcharitmanas*, Sita hails Girija (another name for Parvati), in these words—Nahim tava aadi madhya avasana, amita prabhau Bedu nahin jaana, bhava, bhava, bibhava parabhava karini, bisva bihomani svabhasa biharini: You, O goddess, have no beginning, middle or end, and hence you are eternal; your infinite glory is a mystery even to the Vedas; you create, maintain and destroy the universe; you enchant the cosmos, and sport independently.

In portraying divinity, Hinduism often deliberately uses the intellectual construct of discordant juxtaposition. Kali, the visibly grotesque, serves the purpose of pole-vaulting the routine imagination to a new level of insight, a state of mind best attuned to realising the suprahuman powers of the divine. The portrayal of divinity must be the outcome of unfettered imagination. Hence, it is also depicted as androgynous, ardhanarishwara, both male and female.

Other key gods in the Hindu pantheon are conceived of in the same idiom. The beloved Ganesha is depicted as half-human, half-elephant. This can be derisively dismissed as the primitive 'elephant god', or become a means of driving home the point that conventional human categories cannot apply to visualising that which is beyond these categories. When divinity is presented in such improbable juxtapositions, it jolts the mind away from known constraints of thought. The experience is one of transcendence as, indeed, Ganesha invokes. He stands for Vighneshvara, the remover of obstacles, the lord of intellect and hence of letters and learning, and is identified with the mantra 'Om'. Another most revered deity is Hanuman, called by foreigners as the 'monkey god'. However, it requires the Hindu spiritual imagination to illustrate the principle that the divine must be seen in all things, including in the animal world. In his visible form, Hanuman is a monkey. In his essence, and as worshipped, he is the eternal symbol of devotion to Rama, the quintessential brahmachari or celibate, the yogi incarnate, a symbol of great strength and valour, and gyan, guna sagar—the embodiment of knowledge and scholarship.

Beyond the concepts of formlessness and form, and the dialectics of image and construct, representation and meaning, ordinary mortals also seek an ideological framework to find meaning and purpose in the real world of life's everyday tasks and obligations. Spirituality and religion provide solace and hope, but there is also the need of a credo of life, applicable not in worship or philosophical rumination, but in life as actually lived. Once again, the intellectual wellsprings of Hinduism come to the rescue, through the message of the Bhagwad Gita. We have already seen that the text is in the nature of a dialogue between Krishna and Arjuna, where Arjuna is despondent and refuses to take up arms against the Kauravas who are his kinsmen. Krishna then counsels him, and that is the essence of the Gita.

The greatness of the Gita lies not on its philosophical chastity to any one school of thought, but to the solace it provides to the existential dilemma that often confronts human beings—one is born, one lives and one dies, and in between there could be joy but there is also sorrow and grief. There is no redemption from the starkness of this sterile, predictable charade, and often the purport of ambition and achievement, of causes and goals, becomes opaque. In this sense, Arjuna's futility and weariness was symbolic of a common person. He could not comprehend an imperative for action in a phenomenal world that was stubbornly inexplicable. The greatness of the Gita is that it enabled Krishna, through his discourse, to give purpose and meaning to the existential predicament of people like Arjuna.

The most important concept that the Gita enunciated was that of nishkama karma, of action, without attachment or thought of reward, as a consecration, done without selfish desire in a spirit of surrender. Krishna says:

> Hear my truth about the surrender of works, Arjuna. Surrender, O best of men, is of three kinds.
>
> Works of sacrifice, gift, and self-harmony should not be abandoned, but should indeed be performed; for these are works of purification.
>
> But even these works, Arjuna, should be done in the freedom of a pure offering, and without expectation of a reward. This is my

final word.

It's not right to leave undone the holy work which ought to be done. Such a surrender of action would be a delusion of darkness.

And he who abandons his duty because he has fear of pain his surrender is of Rajas, impure, and in truth he has no reward.

But he who does holy work, Arjuna, because it ought to be done, and surrenders selfishness and thought of reward, his work is pure, and is peace.

This man sees and has no doubts: he surrenders, he is pure and has peace. Work, pleasant or painful, is for him joy.

For there is no man on earth who can fully renounce living work, but he who renounces the reward of his work, is in truth a man of renunciation.

When work is done for a reward, the work brings pleasure, or pain, or both, in its time; but when a man does work in Eternity, then Eternity is his reward.[33]

Nishkam karma is thus the Gita's practical formula for a person to maintain equipoise and equanimity in taking the actions and choices the mundane world demands. The Upanishads asserted that we are That—Tat Tvam Asi—but they did not elaborate on how, given this reality, we negotiate life at the empirical level on a daily basis. The Gita provides the answer to these questions by stating that no one in this world can live by completely renouncing action. However, we can rid ourselves of the negative emotions produced by our actions if we act without thought of reward, with detachment and in the spirit of surrender. Such an attitude is entirely consistent with the Gita's reiteration that Brahman is the transcendent reality permeating and sustaining the universe. In fact, says the Gita, it is precisely the individual who has understood what the essential reality is who can best practise nishkama karma:

The man who sees Brahman abides in Brahman; his reason is steady, gone is his delusion. When pleasure comes he is not shaken, and when pain comes he trembles not.

He is not bound by things without, and within he finds inner gladness. His soul is one in Brahman and he attains everlasting joy.

For the pleasures that come from the world, bear in them sorrows to come. They come and they go, they are transient: not in them do the wise find joy.

But he on this earth, before his departure, can endure the storms of desire and wrath, this man is a Yogi, this man has joy.

This man has inner joy, he has inner gladness, and he has found inner Light. This Yogi attains the Nirvana of Brahman: he is one with God and goes unto God.

Holy men reach the Nirvana of Brahman: their sins are no more, their doubts are gone, their soul is in harmony, their joy is in the good of all.

Following the Upanishads, the Gita affirms that the inner Spirit in each individual—Atman—is identical with the cosmic energy of Brahman. Your doubts and grief are misplaced, Krishna tells Arjuna, because as part of Brahman, your essential nature is beyond death. Only the physical body decays and dies, while you yourself are a part of the unchanging Eternal:

He is never born, and he never dies. He is in Eternity: he is for evermore. Never born and eternal, beyond times gone or to come, he does not die when the body dies.

But Arjuna, like any mortal, was not content with only metaphysical assertions. He wanted the assurance of a divinity that he could identify with, a personal god, far more accessible than the attribute-less Brahman. 'In thy mercy thou hast told me the secret supreme of thy Spirit, and thy words have dispelled my delusion,' he beseeches Krishna, 'but show me, O God of Yoga, the glory of thine own Supreme Being.' And, Krishna grants him his desire, revealing to Arjuna his celestial form in all its copiousness:

And Arjuna saw in that form countless visions of wonder: eyes from innumerable faces, numerous celestial ornaments, numberless heavenly weapons;

Celestial garlands and vestures, forms anointed with heavenly perfumes. The Infinite Divinity was facing all sides, all marvels in him containing.

If the light of a thousand suns suddenly arose in the sky, that splendour might be compared to the radiance of the Supreme Spirit.

And Arjuna saw in that radiance the whole universe in its variety, standing in a vast unity in the body of the God of gods.

Trembling with awe and wonder, Arjuna bowed his head, and joining his hands in adoration he thus spoke to his God:

I see in thee all the gods, O my God; and the infinity of the beings of thy creation. I see God Brahmana on his throne of lotus, and all the seers and serpents of light.

In this one act of divine revelation, the Gita executes a remarkable task by transmuting the indefinable Brahman–Atman of the Upanishads into a personal god. In a reiteration of the nirguna–saguna construct, the Gita too harmonises the nirguna Brahma into a devotional theism in response to the human urge to see divinity in a personalised form, but without denying the ultimate supremacy of Brahman. In counselling Arjuna, Krishna synthesised several paths to moksha, all sanctioned by Hindu tradition — jnana marga, the path of knowledge; karma marga, the path of selfless activity; and bhakti marga, the path of devotion to a personal god.

In the foundational millennia of our history, empires rose and fell, armies won and lost, kings came and went, and cities flourished and dwindled, but the philosophical academies of the mind never ebbed. The preoccupation about who we are, what the universe is about and what are the end goals of human existence, remained a vibrant continuum. Systems of thought, once articulated, never died out. Some, like Buddhism in particular, received extensive royal patronage, and reached out to shores far beyond India. Others, even without being adopted by emperors, had a band of dedicated followers who continued to codify, discuss and elaborate upon the original teachings of their founders. The Indic system of explicatory bhashyas or commentaries ensured that thought structures did not fade away. At the same time, the tradition of argumentation and debate, often even a trifle acrimonious, preserved the activism of both critics and defenders. The important thing was that all these argumentations were not confined to hermitages or monasteries or to a handful of disciples at the feet of a remote sage, but acquired a larger momentum and popularity that permeated to people at large who, even if not involved in the finer metaphysical nuances, were more than aware of the broad contours. The depth, robustness of argument, courage of conviction and sanction to dissent and, where necessary, synthesise, is what made the philosophical canvas of Hindu civilisation different. It was an amazing mosaic of philosophical enquiry, spiritual quest, religious practice and metaphysical analysis, with a unified coherence underlying its great diversity.

I shall now examine how this tradition of cognitive thinking impacted other aspects of this civilisation, in the areas of art and creativity, science, society and politics.

3

THE REALM OF IDEAS

The spiritual quest of Hindu civilisation, and the deep thought that went into its structuring, could not but spill over into other areas of human endeavour. Art and culture was one such area. It is not my intention here to provide an account of the range of its creative canvas, be it in dance, music, theatre, literature, sculpture or architecture. There are countless books that deal with each of these subjects. The aim here is to focus on the approach to aesthetics, the cerebral rumination on what constitutes beauty and qualifies to be art. This is the unique aspect that deserves careful study in order to understand the distinguishing feature of the foundational period of our civilisation. In accordance with the contemplative philosophy that preceded the creation of artefacts, creativity was not a pursuit of excellence alone, but the definition of excellence itself was a consequence of a seminal reflection on what excellence should be.

Around 200 BCE, and possibly earlier, there lived an individual called Bharat Muni. As the word 'muni' connotes, he was a sage. Bharat wrote the *Natya Shastra*, consisting of thirty-six chapters and six thousand shlokas. At one level, the *Natya Shastra* was a compendium for the performing arts with a detailed manual of instructions. Its subjects included dramatic composition, structures of a play, construction of a stage, genres of acting, body movements, make-up, costumes, role and goals of an art director, musical scales, musical instruments and the integration of music with art performances. Such a comprehensive treatise was remarkable for its times even at the level of a manual. It is concrete evidence of the degree of sophistication of the performing arts so far back in our history. But the *Natya Shastra*'s real genius lay in what it outlined in chapters six and seven. This was the theory of rasa, spelling out the philosophy of aesthetics relating to art. This intellectual meditation on what the anubhav or artistic experience should be, both for the creator and the observer, and as an end in itself, was unknown to the world then, and still remains a remarkable contribution of India to the world of creativity.

I am talking here of a highly sophisticated and developed concept of the artistic experience at a time in human evolution when in many parts of the world people had not yet come down from trees. However, if you accept the Western understanding of the origin of aesthetics as a philosophy, you are likely to be told that it began with a series of articles on 'The Pleasures of the Imagination' by the journalist Joseph Addison in the magazine *The Spectator* in 1712! The word 'aesthetics' is derived from the Greek 'aesthetikos', but a quick search on internet will tell you that aesthetics as a branch of philosophy began only post 1712. There is very little appreciation in Western and even Indian academia of the fact that this subject was fully elaborated upon in India some two thousand years earlier. That, of course, is the burden of ignorance colonised countries must bear, and live with even today in the cultural asymmetries of a globalising world. It is understandable too that while from the eighteenth century onwards there was a spirited discussion in the West on different facets of aesthetics, in India, where it all began, there was the frozen peace of intellectual inertness under colonial rule, the past forgotten, or excavated only as a museum relic.

But let's return to Bharat Muni and his theory of rasa. Rasa, Bharat says, is the essence, the very sap, the inner feeling, of the experience of art. The nature of this experience cannot but be related to the basic premises of Hinduism's spirituality which encompasses all creation and is inherent in all things. While Brahman itself is nirguna or attribute-less, for those who experience it, brahmanubhav, the overwhelming and unmistakable inferential, is a feeling of chit or total awareness, and ananda or absolute bliss. Ananda, or unalloyed joy, is the beej word of Hinduism. The essential nature of our Self or Atman is joy; Brahman, is joy; the world is joy. We are from joy, and we return to joy, which is our sole essence, prior to birth, during life, and on death. For reasons that I have discussed earlier, the joy which is the nature of our real Being, is pushed to the margins because the buddhi (mind), ever active and never still, and the ahamkara (ego), the futile sense of 'I'-ness, dominate our lives. The spiritual purpose of life then is to quieten the mind and vanquish the ego, so that the chit or the Atman, the silent and joyful observer within us, awakens and makes us aware of who we really are—purnta or unblemished joy and fulfilment. As Stella Kramrisch, one of the first Western observers to understand the linkage in Hindu art between the creative and the sublime, writes: 'Art originates in Mahat (The Great Consciousness) and evolves in buddhi. Subsequently, the ego apprehends and according to its limitations, modifies the work in progress, but it has no part in the creative process.'[1]

The purpose of art, then, must be to take us closer to anand. It must, in some way, jolt us away from our routine and mundane preoccupations, and transform our consciousness so that we are more predisposed to discover who we really are. The beautiful must be liberating. As a verse of the *Natya Shastra* says: 'Let Natya be the fifth Vedic scripture ... leading to joy and spiritual freedom.' The Upanishadic dictum is—Raso vai saha: He is rasa. The 'He' is Brahman. Brahman is joy. Therefore, the rasa, or the essence or relish or flavour of artistic experience, has to be joyous, or such as to prepare us to experience the transcendent. 'The Hindu mind views the creative process as a means of suggesting or re-creating a vision, however fleeting, of a divine truth; and regards art as a means of experiencing a state of bliss akin to the absolute state of Ananda or jivanmukti.'[2] The aesthetic experience is then meaningful if it is, in some form, liberating from the contours that constrain our normal perceptions. The spiritual—and equally secular—notion of joy in Hindu spirituality frees us, even if momentarily, from our self-imposed shackles of routine existence. It is in this sense that we must understand what the *Vastu Sutra Upanishad* says: 'From the knowledge of art arises divine knowledge, and such knowledge leads to liberation.' The linkage of the creative to the spiritual transforms the artistic vision. Beauty then becomes 'less a property of things, art or otherwise, and more an experience and a state of being'.[3]

While the divine is juxtaposed with rasa, it should not be—and was never intended to be—seen exclusively in a religious sense. However, the spiritual notion of joy, which is dominant in Hindu philosophy, is relevant. The ananda of the experience of Brahman is used as a touchstone, a measure or definition, of the joy that art has the potential to create. The artist endeavours, through form, word, melody or dance, to pursue this potential. Yet, dissonance is not ruled out. Obviously, art cannot be only about positive emotions of happiness. Sometimes, good art is also about discordance, about the less-than-happy things that abound in life. This is all, as I shall explain, factored in. But the theory of rasa still believes that the ultimate impact of art should be to elevate our consciousness. This can be done by what is inherently joyous, and also by portraying the derogations from that joyousness. Both should lead to a sense of artistic fulfilment that, through the change in consciousness, makes us aware of what our true nature and that of the cosmos is— ananda.

Harsha Dehejia has a beautiful passage about the attraction of the Ananda–Brahman. 'In the ultimate analysis it is the ananda-brahman which holds the many and diverse manifestations of the Indian mind together, it is the ocean where all rivers meet, it is the still centre where all movement ends, it is the silent nada where all sounds end, this is the mind of the Buddha which understands all questions but does not need to provide an answer, this is the Krishna at the centre of the rasa-mandala who holds everything together and Vishnu on the adishesha, it is the formless vishranti that Shiva experiences when he is dancing the Ananda Tandava, it is the resting point beyond all forms. It is also the citta-vritti nirodha of Patanjali. ... This is the moment of perfect beauty beyond the beautiful.'[4] According to the theory of rasa, the artist is motivated by the search for the ananda within, although the artist expresses it without. 'The Indian artist sees the world with open eyes and the inner world with his eyes closed. ... God is the Nama (name), and a work of art is the body and the house in which the Formless, the Beyond Form, the Goal of Release and

Source of all Forms, reveals itself. ... In Indian art the figures are, as it were, modelled by breath, which dilates the chest and is felt to carry the pulse of life through the body to the tips of the fingers. This inner awareness was given permanent shape in art.'[5]

In the invocation of rasa, Bharat identifies eight dominant bhavas or emotions. These are sringara (the sensual and the romatic), hasya (the comic), karuna (the pathetic and the sorrowful), raudra (the furious), vira (the heroic), bhayanak (the terrifying), vibhatsa (the disgustful or the odious) and adbhuta (the marvellous). Later commentators added a ninth, shantam (the quiescent). These bhavas act as vibhava (determinants), anubhava (consequents) and vyabhichari (transitory states of feelings) in the internalisation of rasa. As can be seen, the list of bhavas include those that are not simplistically about joy, such as the terrifying , the furious, the disgusting and the pathetic. But sorrow is only a temporary abeyance of joy, as disgust is of reverence, anger is of serenity and the ugly is of beauty. Taken together, in isolation or in any sequence of combination, the purpose of good art, Bharat believes, should be to alter, through these emotions, the consciousness of the viewer. It should trigger a disjunct from the mundane world, create a state of wonder and, ultimately, in that state of altered consciousness, bring the viewers closer to a confrontation with themselves, and what their real being is, which cannot but be the ability to see, even in the non-joyous, the possibility of ultimate joy.

Aesthetics then for Bharat is as much about the work of art as it is about the state of mind and the perception of the viewer, the drishta. This involves the manner in which, at a secondary level of perception, he becomes an observer–participant in the act of seeing, drishti. While darshana is the surface act of seeing, drishti, derived from the noun 'drishya', is not just seeing or listening but internalising the seen and heard through perception, feeling and enlightened insight. The *Natya Shastra*'s concern is whether the drishta of beautiful art is in the frame of mind to undergo a transforming experience. For this, first and foremost, the observer has to have control over the mind. If the mind is preoccupied with an endless array of extraneous thoughts, or is in the grip of the ego, the ability to participate in the artistic experience is diminished, if not vitiated. It then becomes a superficial experience, where our indriyas, or sensory perceptions, are superficially active and obstruct a non-subjective awareness. This devaluation of the communication between art and the viewer leads to the devaluation of the experience of rasa.

The complete aesthetic experience for the participant in art is possible only when the mind is stilled. The tranquil mind is conducive to the internalisation of the creative experience. Only a mind which realises the joy within can seek the true measure of the beauty without. This is the mental discipline which Hindu aesthetics demands of the viewer. When the creator of art is inspired by ananda, and the viewer's mind is both tranquil and in contemplative alertness, the appreciation of the beautiful takes place at another level of consciousness. 'In the antara hradaya akasha (internal space of the heart) is the realization of beauty in perfect form, where a perfect concord exists between viewer and viewed.'[6] In this conceptual sense, aesthetics links the spiritual with the creative. As the *Aitreya Brahmana* says: 'Now (He) glorifies the arts; the arts are refinement of the Self; with these the worshipper recreates the Self.'

Several seminal works were written elaborating the *Natya Shastra*'s theory of rasa. In the eighth century, Udbhata is credited with adding a ninth bhava to the eight mentioned by Bharat, namely, shantam, or tranquillity. Rudrata, a contemporary, added a tenth—affection. Lollata (early ninth century) and Dandin argued that bhavas could be many more; any heightened emotion could qualify to be a rasa. Nayaka (late tenth century) was of the view that rasa was experienced when the viewer overcomes unpleasant and worldly emotions.

However, the most influential commentator on rasa was Abhinavagupta (c. 950–1020 CE), a Shaivite philosopher from Kashmir, whose work, the *Abhinavbharti*, is a classic. Abhinavagupta referred to the *Natya Shastra* as *Natya Veda*. His focus was on perception—how is an art performance viewed? Does it represent tattva or a higher truth or plane of reality, or is it just aropa or a surface superimposition? Rasa, according to him, is a state of total transcendence, experienced by one who has rasikatva, the cultivated ability to discern aesthetic constituents. It requires sahradayatva or an aesthetic susceptibility to focus on the art or artistic performance. This aesthetic predisposition is enabled by a heightened capacity of visualisation, which in its highest form is called pratibha. The spectator is then transported to a state of pure contemplation, where he or she goes beyond their subjective perceptions and attains a level of undifferentiated concentration which is akin to ananda. In that moment of ananda, 'the very language of "name and form" (nama and rupa) evoke that beyond form (pararupa and arupa)',[7] recalling the Upanishadic dictum—Ekam rupam bahudya yeh karoti: All forms are in the end the reproductions of one form. The vyakta, that which is expressed, is inspired by the avyakta, that which is unarticulated. Form becomes the expression of the formless, and the formless becomes the source of form. The need, Abhinavagupta emphasised, is to have rasiks or aesthetically oriented personalities, who are capable of experiencing such an emotion, and have the utsah (energy) and the exposure to pursue it.

The ancient and widely used expression 'Satyam Shivam Sundaram' is also related to a viewpoint on aesthetics. Satyam stands for the eternal truth. That truth is Brahman, the ultimate and unchanging reality, beyond attributes, but experienced as ananda or unalloyed bliss. Shiv is the saguna embodiment of Brahman. He is thus saubhagyakari (auspicious), for he is the harbinger of the abundance of joy. That which is representative of the truth and is auspicious, is sundar or beautiful. A link is thus established between joy and beauty. One leads to the other, and connects the viewer of art with the art itself. The medium is Shiva. He presides over the panchakritya— creation, protection, destruction, removal of Maya and moksha. Art moves likewise from creation to liberation, destroying ignorance and the distortions of the ego, along the way.

The ananda, which Hindu aesthetics links to beauty, is not fragmented. On the contrary, it is overwhelmingly holistic, representing an indivisible wholeness that must infuse the entire canvas of artistic imagination. It follows that all artistic expression and experience has to be interlinked. The various branches of art may appear to be different, representing separate skills and training, but essentially the same notion of beauty permeates all forms of creativity. No one artistic endeavour can be viewed in isolation and, no one branch of art is complete without a knowledge of the others. The ancient treatise *Vishnudharmottara* (mid-fifth century) 'opens with a conversation between a king and a sage. The king desires to learn the whole meaning of art, but is told that he must know the theory of dancing. To this he agrees because the laws of dancing imply the principles that govern painting. But the sage further insists that the king shall begin by studying music and song, for without a knowledge of the arts, their effort in space and time cannot be fully understood, nor their purpose be achieved.'[8]

The common spiritual inspiration for art shows in different mediums. The *Natya Shastra* enumerates 108 postures in Bharatnatyam dance. These can be seen in dance performances, as also in the magnificent Chola bronzes and in the stunning stone rendering of the entire set of stances in the Chidambaram temple. The Kathakali dance of Kerala comes alive in the wooden panels that depict its movements, or the wooden panels come alive in the dance performances they portray. The 108 types of movements of the *Natya Shastra* are brought alive in all sculptural forms—Hindu, Buddhist and Jain. The beatitude on the faces of the ladies in the Ajanta frescoes mirrors the serenity of the magnificent Gandhara stone portrayals of the Buddha. Classical musical ragas sung in a temple at specific times of the day seem to have been composed to effortlessly enhance the worship of the deities. The poetry eulogising women finds expression in the seductively fulsome depictions of goddesses and apsaras carved in stone or sandstone. The same stillness, form and flux sets the tone of all art forms of ancient India, making it 'an organic whole where all dimensions of life are considered together in their essential relationship of interconnectedness and interdependence and overlapping'. This 'multi-layered concurrence', this 'unitary vision', is sourced in the theory of rasa, which is 'the ultimate experience of the creator, the spectator and the hearer alike … so that, even if for a brief moment, the transcendental experience of beatitude or bliss (ananda) can be evoked.'[9]

The Hindu theory of rasa, therefore, primarily establishes the ideal touchstone of beauty. This is the unchanging factor of all art. Having outlined the first principle, it sanctions a profusion of instructions, manuals and injunctions which are specific to any one particular form of art. Unity and multiplicity thus become part of a singular discussion. This corresponds with the nirguna–saguna interface. Nirguna Brahman is the eternal and constant truth. Once the singularity of this ultimate truth is accepted, the saguna is free to encompass endless variations of that one truth. Kapila Vatsyayan has a remarkable analogy to illustrate this unified duality. She compares the Hindu vision with that of a double-reed flute: 'One reed is a perennial strain, a tonic, immutable trans-space and time; the other reed plays the tune of immediate time and space. The one is repetitive but stable; the other changing. The two together create the music that sounds different at different times.'[10] The unchanging reed is what is called sashvat and sanatan. The changing is parampara or specific tradition. The dialogue between the unconditioned and the conditioned, the unqualified and the qualified, and the unchanging and the contingent, is a continuum in both the spiritual and the creative realm.

A great deal of thought went into devising specific rules for each area of artistic expression. Let us look at some examples to illustrate this enormous application of mind. Apart from the *Natya Shastra* and the *Vishnudharmottara*, there were innumerable shastras on different aspects of art, with detailed instructions on conceptualisation, iconography, proportion, preparation of materials, mediums, skill development and training. The canons of architecture were codified in more than one treatise, the most famous being the *Mayamatam* and the *Mansara*, compiled during the Chola period, over a thousand years ago. Maya, the divine architect, is said to have authored the 3,300 verses and 36 chapters of the *Mayamatam* which deal extensively with the choice of sites, the form of construction and iconography. The *Mansara*, similar in nature, is even longer, counting 5,400 verses and 70 chapters. Predating both of these by at least another thousand years is the Vastu Shastra, or the science of architecture, which was already well-known in Vedic times. Many of these texts are no longer extant, but those that are, provide evidence through cross-citing of the long tradition of this scholarship. For instance, the *Samarangana Sutradhara* written by Maharaja Bhoja of Dhara (c. 1010–1055 CE) is a complete manual on all arts. Although it has a special focus on architecture, it deals—illustrating the interdisciplinary relationship of such texts—with painting as well. A painting, says the text, should have six limbs—pramana: appropriate size; rupabheda: variations in form; sadrishya: reflections of reality; bhava yojana: the ability to evoke the desired mood; lavanya yojana: a glimpse of the beautiful; and varnikabhanga: the choice of the right colour.

Rang or colour provides a fascinating example of the contemplation that was invested in linking art to emotion. The word 'rang' is etymologically derived from the word 'ranj', which connotes a state of mind, for example, manoranjana, which means the experience of happiness. The inner states of our mind are called 'antarang', or the inner colours of our psyche.[11] It is not surprising, therefore, that different colours depict different objects or emotions. The colour blue is that of Vishnu. It carries the bhava of the limitless sky and evokes a sense of infinitude. Krishna, and his variable moods, is captured by the colour of the deep monsoon clouds that bring succour to the parched earth. Shiva, the eternal ascetic, is portrayed in the colour of camphor. Red stands for passion, but equally that of auspiciousness and well-being. Lakshmi, who is the harbinger of plenty and good fortune, is depicted in red. Green is a symbol of the fecundity of nature, of spring, and of a sense of contentment with Prakriti or the environment. Saffron is the colour to show bravery and heroism, but also detachment and spirituality. Texts like the *Vishnudharmottara* and the *Chitrasutra* discuss in detail the choice of colours and the emotions that they are meant to evoke. Few people are aware that Vatsyayan's *Kamasutra*, written around the third century, is not only about the art of lovemaking, but also contains a detailed account of the techniques of painting.

Sculpture was one of the great artistic achievements of Hindu India. The remarkable Chola and Kurkihara bronzes are immortal examples of this. There were innumerable Shilpa shastras on the canonical requirements of good sculpture. Thus, 'the sculptor had to master six essentials according to sage Pippalada: the knowledge of stones; the compositional diagram; the carving and the dressing of stone; the arrangement of the various elements of a sculpture; the representation of the mood of a piece; and the final integration of all its component parts.'[12] It should not be inferred from this that such detailed instructions left little space for the intrinsic talent of the artist. Such canonical works were meant as guidelines and for training. They were used by master craftsmen for pedagogical purposes in artistic guilds all over the land. However, they allowed the talented artist full freedom in conceptualisation and execution.

According to the shastras, the sthapati or architect was the incarnation of Brahma, the creator himself, in the form of Vishvakarma. The purpose behind this was not to make architecture religious, but to imbue architecture with a gravitas which was akin to the divine. The sthapati's team included the sutragrahi (the draughtsman), the vardhaki (the painter) and the taksaka (stonemason). The Vedic texts refer to forts and citadels, and the *Rig Veda* speaks convincingly of a palace of a thousand doors and as many columns. The Mauryan Empire (321–232 BCE) saw Indian craftsmen build stupas and chaityas and vast and complex shrines from natural rock, as well as sophisticated secular buildings as can be seen in the remains of the palace at Pataliputra (modern Patna). The grammarian Panini (520–460 BCE) refers to well-developed Hindu temples, and later these evolved into the northern Nagara style with its stepped pyramid roofing structures, and the southern Dravida style.

The designing of the Hindu temple followed a certain pattern. Its location was carefully chosen, for it had to represent the axis of the world, axis mundi, and radiate spiritual energy. The entrance was often grand, consisting of a richly decorated crowning tower, followed by a courtyard or a series of pillared halls. These, in turn, led to a corridor leading up to the sanctum sanctorum, garbagriha, literally the womb, a small enclosed area deep in the recesses of the temple, where the deity or the lingam was placed. The design was meant to illustrate the imperative that the spiritual journey needs to be directed inwards. To reach the spiritual core, one has to travel through the distractions of the material world, and as one proceeds further, prepare oneself for the physically unembellished but emotionally personal—almost secretive—spiritual encounter. Suddenly, the noise and bustle of the outside word recedes and gives way, through the contouring of architectural space, to the possibility of personal communion. The deity itself is often unostentatious, and in Shiva temples like Kedarnath and Vishvanathji in Kashi, almost without form, harmonising the nirguna principle within the paraphernalia of saguna worship. The shikhara or pinnacle soaring to the sky directly above the garbagriha demonstrates the power of the deity in the garbagriha below to confer the possibility of redemption beyond the confines of material space.

A.K. Ramanujan has said that the Hindu temple is designed to represent the human body. 'The ritual for building a temple begins with digging in the earth, and planting a seed. The temple is said to rise from the implanted seed, like a human. The different parts of a temple are named after body parts. The two sides are called the hands or wings, the hasta; a pillar is called a foot, pada. The top of the temple is the head, the shikhara. The shrine, the innermost and the darkest sanctum of the temple, is a garbagriha, the womb-house. The temple thus carries out in brick and stone the primordial blueprint of the human body.'[13] This constructional pattern can be clearly seen at the great Lingaraja Temple in Bhubaneshwar, the Jagannath Temple in Puri and the temples at Tanjhavur and Kanchipuram, to name just a few, as also in the thirty-five exquisite Buddhist, Jain and Hindu temples carved out of the vertical face of the Charanadri Hills between the fifth and the tenth century CE. The multistoreyed Kailash Temple at Ellora, designed to recall Shiva's abode at Mount Kailash, is an architectural wonder. Covering an area twice the size of the Parthenon in Athens, it is carved top-down out of a single rock to precise geometrical symmetry, requiring the excavation of 200,000 tonnes of rock. As Stella Kramrisch says: 'Indian temple architecture, in the fullness of its development, establishes in spatial terms an intellectual and actual approach to the Supreme Principle of which the deity is symbolic.'[14]

The preparation of Yajnas, or the ritual consecration ceremonies, were also the result of precise mathematical design. Considerable thought went into the choice of the consecrated space, the erection of the yupa or central pole and the construction of the altar. 'The unit for constructing the altars is the brick. But these bricks must conform to exact measurements and specified shapes, the rectangular (adhyardha), the triangular (adhyardhardha), or the square (panchami). Each brick represents a unit of time, and the 360 bricks are the 360 days of the year. ... The five layers of the brick are the five seasons, and each is consecrated on a different day.'[15] The entire ceremony is 'carried out to the accompaniment of recited verse which consecrates these items and gives them cosmic significance. Bhuh, bhuvah svaha is earth, sky and heaven. The recited verse in precise measure (i.e., the vak of the *Rig Veda*) is the methodology of this consecration.'[16]

The bubble shape of the Buddhist stupa too was purposely designed to convey the cosmos, the anda or 'world egg', 'symbolically transformed into the mythical Mount Meru around which are slung like garlands the heaven and the earth'.[17] There was a free exchange of symbols, motifs and designing between Hindu and Buddhist art. At Gandhara and at Mathura, there developed a remarkable school of art which showed how Greek influence in sculptures was assimilated within the indigenous artistic tradition. Gandhara, comprising the Kabul valley and adjacent areas in current Afghanistan, came under the rule of the Central Asian Kushanas from about the first century BCE to the fifth century CE. The writ of the Kushanas extended to Mathura too, which was at the centre of several trade routes, and became an important centre for the arts. The Central Asian influence changed the iconography of the depiction of the Buddha. The school of sculpture under the earlier Mauryan dynasty was reticent about the sculptural representation of the Buddha since, as per Buddhist philosophy, he had passed into the nothingness of nirvana, and was better depicted through symbols. But this changed under the influence of the Kushanas. Beautifully detailed, three-dimensional and full-bodied sculptures of the Buddha, and later of Vishnu and Shiva, began to be made, which were an inspiration for the flowering of the art of sculpture under the subsequent Gupta dynasty.

This kind of assimilation and exchange was not coincidental. It was possible only in a civilisation where a great degree of contemplation had already been invested in the theory of aesthetics. So long as the bhava of rasa was pursued, peaceful assimilation of 'outside' influences could only be enrichening.

Although Gandhara and Mathura provide visual proof of the uninhibited sculptural detailing of the human form, the body itself was very much a focal part of Hindu aesthetics. It was the medium for the creation of rasa, and of experiencing it, the shariram yajna (vital link) between the material and the spiritual, the micro and the macro, the sensory and the transcendent, and the sensual and the ascetic. Every aspect of it, therefore, needed to be studied, both in dynamic motion and at rest. Shiva is called Nataraja, the Lord of Dance. So is Krishna—Natwar. I have referred to the Ananda Tandava of Shiva, with its remarkable harmony of movement and stillness. In the *Natya Shastra*, Bharat devised 108 postures of dance, each depicting the sheer flexibility, beauty and poise of the body. The human form in arts was celebrated in Hindu aesthetics, because it was filled with rasa, as a gift of the divine. That rasa is in evidence when the body is adorned, but also in the luminosity of the fasting Buddha, or the majestic detachment of Mahavira clad only by digambara, the sky.

In sculpture, we see the body frozen in bronze or stone, and yet it appears to be moving. In dance, we see it moving, but within that movement there is also stillness. This remarkable interaction between poise and counterpoise was the great achievement of the artist. Once it was accepted that the body was a canvas for the depiction of rasa, there was no inhibition in portraying it in all its splendour. Thus, women in sculpture and in painting have full breasts, swaying hips and narrow waists, and this absence of reticence applies equally to the laywomen as well as apsaras and goddesses. The human form is depicted in all its myriad glory, including the erotic (more on this later) and the androgynous. Thus, in Hindu art iconography, we have the depiction of the ardhanarishwara, part man and part woman, brought out with great finesse and skill by the artist, one half of the body displaying male features and the other female. What is interesting—but not surprising—is that the ardhanari was not a random display of artistic imagination. It was the actualisation of the philosophical concept of the coming together of Purusha and Prakriti, as delineated in the Sankhya philosophy, and of Shiva and Parvati, representing the eternally hyphenated play of the formless Brahman and the Shakti within it.

There are seven recognised forms of classical dance in India—Bharatanatyam, Kuchipudi, Odissi, Mohiniyattam, Manipuri, Sattariya and Kathak. It is not my intention to describe all of these, so I will examine, from the point of view of the foundational rasa theory, the Bharatanatyam dance, which is the oldest classical dance tradition of India. Its developed existence is noted in the second-century Tamil epic *Sillapattikaram*, and its postures are found in ancient temples all over India, especially in the south. A Bharatanatyam performance is a carefully structured symphony of rhythm, movement, metre and meaning, with the purpose of arousing in the audience the deeply emotional and fulfilling experience of rasa.

This can be clearly inferenced from the sequential flow of a traditional Bharatanatyam performance. It begins with the alarippu, a burst of pure rhythm, where the dancer captures the attention of the audience by the sophistry of his or her dance movements solely to the beat of the mrindagam and cymbal. Then follows the jatisvaram, where melody is introduced to the metre, and draws the audience to a higher level of involvement in the performance. Once this is secured, meaning is added to the melody and metre in the shabdam. By now the audience should have transcended the normal distractions of the mind, and increasingly become absorbed in the emotional intensity of the concert. In the varnam that comes next, the dancer has the freedom to improvise and explore the full emotive canvas of the chosen song or lyric. At this point, the artist and the audience should be in communion with each other as common participants in the evocation of rasa. The next stage, the padam, deliberately introduces a contemplative pause, where to more subdued music, the artist performs abhinaya, or dance-drama, and a hushed atmosphere of quietude and reverence embraces the viewers. This lull is followed by the tillana, the climax, where to the full accompaniment of music and metre, the dancer breaks into pure dance, taking the audience to a feeling of unalloyed joy, the aim of rasa.

If the performance is structured to lead the viewer towards the possibility of the anubhava of rasa, it must achieve the same goal for the artist as well. The dancer has a formidable repertory at command. The first is the sheer geometry of body movement, the fixed upper torso, the gracefully bent legs, the elegant flexing of the knee and the spectacular footwork. At least twenty of the postures the dancer assumes are asanas from Yoga. The second is the sophisticated vocabulary of sign language—the mudras or gestures of the hand, the movement of the eyes, the artful twitching of the facial muscles. The third is the music, the rhythmic patterns and the emotion of the words being set to dance. The fourth is the dancer's resplendent attire and the special make-up used. The fifth is the stage and settings for the performance. Acquiring excellence in all these areas requires years and decades of sadhana under a guru. But ultimately, the dancer's performance, to invoke the rasa within themselves, has to be more than merely the sum of these skills and accomplishments. In Hindu aesthetic theory, the artist must lose himself or herself in the very emotions they are trying to convey. They must rise above the moment and achieve a higher level of personal consciousness. Their performance has to go beyond technical virtuosity and reach transcendence. Their movements to music and metre have to be embellished with an inner rhythm and soul melody. Then alone do they become the embodiment of rasa as prescribed by the *Natya Shastra*.

It is for this reason that rasa has a sacred quality to it. The great Bharatanatyam exponent Balasaraswati says: 'The Bharatanatyam recital is structured like a Great Temple: we enter the outer tower of alarippu, cross the half-way hall of jatisvaram, then the great hall of shabdam, and enter the holy precinct of the deity in the varnam. ... The expanse and brilliance of the outer corridors disappear in the dark inner sanctorum; and the rhythmic virtuosities of the varnam yield to the soul stirring music and abhinaya of the padam. ... Then the tillana breaks into movement like the final burning of incense.'[18] The conflation of the experience of rasa with the sacred is not a prescriptive requirement of the *Natya Shastra*. It is the extraordinary, pure, uplifting and joyous feeling that makes it acquire a sacred quality. Given the intensity and fulfilment of the experience, the dancer and the audience, the raseshvari and the rasik, both participate in what appears to be a spiritual experience. In this sense, classical Indian dance 'reflects a being at the highest order of spiritual discipline, sadhana, and is considered a Yoga. Its performance is a ritual act or yajna, a sacrifice of the personal self to a higher transcendental order. It is a medium which evokes the supreme state of bliss, ananda, and the vehicle of release, moksha.'[19]

The rasa theory is based on three pillars—one, the setting of a transcendental ideal in terms of emotional experience; two, the devising of objective rules to acquire the skills to pursue that ideal; and three, the subjective freedom within those rules for personalised expression.

Like dance, Indian classical music too provides a fascinating illustration of this triad. The origins of our classical music lies in the

Vedas and, in particular, the *Sama* and the *Rig Veda*. The melodic chanting of shlokas of the *Rig Veda* enabled the *Sama Veda* to encrypt twelve different swaras, and their innumerable combinations, for the intonation of shlokas. This encryption indicated the melody, the rhythm and metric organisation. The *Natya Shastra* has four separate chapters on stringed instruments (chordophones), hollow instruments (aerophones), solid instruments (idiophones) and covered instruments (membrophones). The later Puranas—*Bhagwata*, *Markandeya*, *Vayu* and *Linga*—and *Vishnudharmottara* also have large chapters on musical instruments and theory. There were a great many other texts too, showing prodigious scholarship on music. They are no longer extant, but we know that they existed because of the reference to them in texts which still exist. It is evident, therefore, that music was a matter of serious study in ancient India.

My purpose here is to show the convergence of the theory of rasa and the conceptualisation of music. Perhaps more than any other discipline of art, Indian classical music is overwhelmingly devoted to the creation of the right mood for the evocation of rasa. Certainly, no other organised school of music in the world is so specifically tailored. The beginnings of this approach can be seen in Dhrupad music, which is described in the *Natya Shastra*. The word 'Dhrupad' comes from the word 'Dhruva', which means immovable and permanent. Dhrupad sangeet has a deeply soulful quality to it, a robust yet infinitely delicate feel, which enhances its invocatory abilities to evoke the desired mood. From the Dhruva of its primary note, fixed and unchanging, it reverberates outward in ever expanding circles of melody, building the mood of the chosen raga.

The raga is at the centre of the tradition of our classical music. Each raga consists of a fixed set of notes, an arrangement of swaras, that are immutable. In English, 'swara' would translate as a note, whereas 'there is no western equivalent of swara, because swara includes not just the basic note, but also a kind of melodic eco-system which surrounds it'.[20] The swara structure of a particular raga is inexorably fixed; but its presentation by a musician is infinitely flexible. This combination of iron-cast fixity and complete freedom of improvisation is one of the key defining features of a raga. Of course, the improvisation takes place, just as in dance, within a performance sequence. Thus, a Dhrupad recital will normally go through the four phases of sthayi, where the essential note structure of the raga is established in slow tempo, antara, where the raga is further elaborated upon, the sanchari, where numerous permutations and combinations of the notes of the raga are dexterously demonstrated, and the abhoga, the sombre concluding segment. The same pattern can be seen in khayal, which came as a later development during the medieval period as a result of Islamic influence. In khayal, the raga goes through an initial vilambit, where the mood of the raga is unhurriedly delineated, to an antara, and finally to a drut or fast tempo conclusion. Carnatic music, based on the raga system, but with its own unique style and usage of metre, does the same.

These sequential phases in a performance have been structured so as to allow the artist to optimally create the mood or rasa of a particular raga. Each raga is in itself the embodiment of a mood. Thus, a raga can stand for the mood of the time of the day—early morning, afternoon, dusk or late evening. It can also represent the mood of the changing season, for instance, the raga Malhar evokes the mood of the monsoons. A raga can also portray different emotional moods—of love, languor, separation, joy, contemplation, detachment, devotion and so on. One has to marvel at the degree of study that must have gone into the selection of varying structures of notes to create a distinct melody, and then identify the melody with the corresponding mood it evokes. Over time, different gharanas, or schools of music, came up with their own way of delineating or rendering a raga. Later, a remarkable series of paintings were made—the Ragamala Paintings—which gave visual form to the moods of different ragas.

The amazing thing is that the artist—whether vocal or instrumental—has no notation of notes before him or her, but can perform a raga for hours. The structure of the raga is etched in the mind from long years of practice and learning. Without straying from that structure, the artist has the fullest individual freedom to elaborate upon the raga in accordance with his or her own genius, but always guided by the unchanging primary goal of the creation of rasa. 'We have to accept that our music is indeed the most sophisticated, oldest and developed in the world. Nowhere can we come across a system … where each note is lively because it is applied according to the required frequency of the particular raga. On a chronometer scale we have twelve notes but in our music there are 22 shrutis (microtones), and each shruti has its own phase of application for a particular note in a particular raga. Our raga system is a melodic concept and is only one of its kind in the world.'[21]

Rhythm was at the core of both music and dance, and a part of every branch of creative expression. It is not coincidental that Shiva is shown with a damru or percussion drum in his hand as a symbol of the play of cosmic rhythm. Anahata naad, also called Omkar dhvani, is the unstruck mythical sound that occurs spontaneously in deep meditation. Depending on the intensity of a seeker's concentration, and the level of his or her mental purity, this sound itself can take the seeker to the highest level of consciousness, where the incessant activity of the mind ceases, leading to turiya, a state in which a person is so intoxicated by joy that they become oblivious even to their surroundings. When sound is married to music and dance in the right tala or metre, the outcome is rasa. For Hindu aesthetics, primeval sound and primeval rhythm combine to create the arts. The *Natya Shastra* devotes an entire chapter to tala or metre. Thus, the study of rhythmic patterns of beat and metre achieved an incredible level of sophistication in ancient times.

All music and dance has some kind of beat to it. But in India, the belief was that beat and metre are the very essence of the rhythm of the universe. The working of this vast cosmos has a unity and symmetry to it. The ebb and flow of seasons, birth, life and death, the revolution of planets, the movement of galaxies—everything reverberates to an ethereal rhythm. It is this rhythm that must find reflection in our creative expression. 'There are two key ideas in Indian aesthetics and art-making: chhandomaya and ananda. Chhandomaya is the rhythm, balance, proportion and harmony that is the essence of all nature and life.'[22]

The word 'tala' is said to originate from the two words—ta from the tandava of Shiva, and la from the lasya of Parvati. Lasya connotes the cadence of rhythm, the languorous unfolding of beat to a pattern. Ta stands for the beat itself.

Broadly, all talas are divided, in accordance with the pace of life itself, into three main categories—vilambit (slow laya), madhya (medium laya) and drut (fast laya). Within this broad framework, there are an incredible number of permutations and combinations. Well-known talas of north Indian music are Dadra, Rupak, Kaharwa, Jhaptala, Chautala, Ektala, Deepchandi, Jhumra and Dhamar. The talas of Carnatic music vary slightly, and are highly scientific. In the north, the most popular percussion instrument is the tabla, while in the south it is the mridangam. All talas are bound by a specific time structure based on precise mathematical calculations, which is cyclical and ends in the sama, which marks the end of the cycle, only for it to begin again. This corresponds to the Hindu philosophical concept of time which is also cyclical—creation, maintenance and destruction, and then the cycle of time begins again, anadi, anant. The sama marks the explosive coming together of melody and metre, in an act of marvellous symmetry, indicating the order and precision of the universe in spite of its vast network of moving parts. Both the musician and the percussionist delight in that moment of ecstatic synchronisation, while the audience feels a tangible emotion of joy and liberation. Interestingly, there is also the notion of the khali, when there is, as a part of the complex structure of the laya, one moment where there is an *absence* of beat. This moment of silence in the unfolding of metre, brings in a tantalising stillness in the performance. It stands for the larger principle of movement and stillness, sound and silence, that go hand in hand in a performance of dance and music. The vast cosmos has a melody underpinning it. That melody has a rhythm. When this melody and rhythm conjoin with the right expertise, rasa is the outcome.

Ancient Indian literature, which was prodigious in output and genre, also saw a great deal of deep examination and analysis of the correlation between rasa and the written word. This study permeated everything, from agama (religious texts) to shastra (scholarly treatises), itihasa (tradition), purana (history and mythology) and akhyana (epics). But, it was particularly noticeable in kavya (poetic works) and kavita (poetry). The two epics, the Mahabharata and the Ramayana, are well known. Both can also qualify as kavyas. The basic point is that 'kavya literature as it developed from about the fifth century BCE becomes highly organized in form, richly adorned with figures of speech, taut in style, profuse in metres, and above all aimed at producing methodically a defined aesthetic experience in an audience, hearer or reader.'[23] *Natya Shastra* discusses in length the emotional quotient of a dramatic performance, and this depended on the extent to which it evoked the eight basic bhavas that I have discussed earlier.

Later, an entire array of scholars extended the *Natya Shastra* rasa theory to the entire literary canvas—poetry, prose and fiction. Bhamaha, sometime prior to the fifth century, argued that literary expression is best able to produce the desired rasa if it has a kind of vakrata (curvature) in the nature of obliqueness, the deconstruction of reality and figurativeness. The description of the purely empirical acquires aesthetic value if it is embellished both by the alankara (stylistic usage of words)—and he identifies some three dozen ways in which this can be done—and the 'curvature' that can, in a transformative manner, absorb the attention of the reader. Dandin, in the seventh century CE meticulously analysed ten qualities of style that contribute to the making of good literature. Vamana took this analysis further, as did Rudrata, who added several forms of figurative speech but also stressed the need for auchitya (harmony) between form and content. Anandavardhan, in the eleventh century, stressed the importance of vyangya or satire, where the surface meaning may be substantially different from the intent of what is said. His contemporary, Kuntaka elaborated upon Bhamaha's curvature theory, and identified six types of expression that bring this out the best—phonetic, lexical, grammatical, sentential, contextual and the work taken as a whole. In parallel, literary scholars, like Udbhata (eighth century CE), Lollata (early ninth century CE), Nayaka (late ninth century CE), Dhananjaya (c. 1000 CE) and Bhoja (eleventh century CE), wrote learned treatises on the linkage between bhava and literature, adding new emotions like shantam or calmness, and affection. Bhoja argued that the 'sensitive' is the queen of all rasas, for it encapsulates the essence of rasa.

It was recognised that rasa was the output not only of a sensitivity to emotion, but equally to literary techniques. Thus, a careful analysis was made of several instruments that could go into writing, such as bhranti or the conjuring of delusion, rupaka or metaphor, ullekha or deliberate emphasis, samasokti or allusion and the invocation of a different image by allusion, slesha or the use of puns, purayokta or paraphrasing, asambhava or the creation of awe or wonder, visama or deliberate inconsistency, adhika or hyperbole and yukti or the expression of covert meaning. Clearly, in the early period of our history, a great amount of scholarly work was done on analysing literature. More importantly, amidst the multiplicity of opinions and the vigour of debate based on extensive study, there was an essential theoretical unity in the understanding that, like with other areas of art, good literature must be able to produce the requisite level of rasa.

Sanskrit was the language for much of this remarkable literary output. Its grammar was the subject of rigorous study and refinement. The great grammarian, Panini (somewhere between the fourth and the sixth century BCE) wrote the foundational *Ashtadhyayi*, which is arguably the most scientific and detailed lexicon on grammar composed before the nineteenth century in any part of the world. Amazingly, in spite of its antiquity, it was not the first treatise of its kind and was only continuing an already long-established tradition of linguistic study. Panini acknowledges the seminal contributions of Sanskrit scholars before him such as Kashyapa, Gargya, Galava, Charkravarman, Bhardvaja, Sakatyana, Sakalya, Seneca and

Sphotayana. Katyayana wrote a valuable commentary, *Varttika*, on the *Ashtadhyayi*; this was followed in the second century BCE by Patanjali's pathbreaking *Mahabhashya*, and in the fifth century BCE by Bhartrihari's *Vakapadiya*. In keeping with the cerebral nature of the times, these works were as much about grammar as about the philosophy of grammar.

Over this period, Sanskrit evolved from its restrictive Vedic structure to become a more homogenous language. Vernacular offshoots like Pali and Prakrit took it to the masses. Sanskrit works were also translated into many other languages. For instance, a Tamil translation of the Mahabharata and the *Skanda Purana* was done in the eighth century. In the eleventh century, Kamban produced the first Tamil Ramayana. Kannada translations of the Mahabharata and Ramayana came out in the tenth and twelfth centuries and a Telugu translation a little later. Sanskrit also became the language of various Buddhist and Jain traditions. Undoubtedly, it was the dominant lingua franca of ancient India, and along with a Sanskritisation process (as described by the sociologist M.N. Srinivas in 1952), in which the content of Sanskrit seeped into popular traditions and thought processes, there was also an opposite 'Deshification' process, by which ideas embedded in diverse local traditions made their way into Sanskrit. Thus, we see that in ancient India, 'Sanskrit and local traditions flow back and forth, producing a constant infusion of lower class words and ideas into the Brahmin world, and vice-versa.'[24]

However, scholars like Sheldon Pollock argue that Sanskrit was essentially an elitist language and an instrument of political and cultural hegemony. It is true that like with many classical languages, the use of Sanskrit was more prevalent among the elite. For instance, this is true of Latin too, which is still taught in elitist educational institutions in the United Kingdom, like Eton and Harrow. Yet, notwithstanding this, Latin is respected as a language of culture, refinement and ideas. The content of Latin has survived in a host of European languages it gave rise to, such as Italian, French, Portuguese, Spanish and English. Until as late as the eighteenth century, Latin was the language of science, technology, medicine and law, apart from, of course, classical literature. It was also the language in Europe of international communication, scholarship and diplomacy. Since some of those countries which speak languages derived from Latin and value it as an ancient and classical language and the repository of much wisdom, were also ruthless colonisers, does that make Latin *only* a language of exploitation? Are the Vatican and the Pope only 'colonisers', since Latin is still the official language of the Holy See?

It is a moot point whether Sheldon Pollock would agree to see Latin only from such a narrow perspective. Why then does he not have the same approach to Sanskrit? Rajiv Malhotra makes a spirited critique of these kinds of double standards, and confuses it with a new Orientalism in some sections of American Indology. He accepts that Sanskrit was more a preserve of the elite and that some sections of its corpus do contain prescriptions for social and gender exclusion. But, it is essential that, as with other classical languages, a narrow dismissal is tempered with the right balance and judicious appraisal. Sanskrit, Rajiv Malhotra strongly argues, was also the 'repository of philosophy, art, architecture, popular song, classical music, dance, theatre, sculpture, painting, literature, pilgrimage, ritual and religious narratives. It also incorporates all branches of natural science and technology—medicine, botany, mathematics, engineering, dietetics etc.'[25] More than anything else, it was the vehicle of the great spiritual, philosophical and creative wisdoms distilled over millennia. Malhotra adds that it was not just a communication tool, but also a vehicle for 'enduring sacredness, aesthetic powers, metaphysical acuity, and ability to generate knowledge in many domains'.[26] And, finally, it represented one of the finest achievements in linguistic structuring, incorporating deep thought and the study of grammar and phonology.

It is essential, therefore, to see Hindu India in holistic terms where sanskriti—a word derived from Sanskrit—or culture is concerned. The cerebral rumination on key aspects of creativity should not be seen only as the preserve of cloistered or elitist scholars working in isolation, but as the leitmotif of an entire civilisational epoch.

Not surprisingly, the amount of sheer thought and ideas generated in this area permeated to all levels of society through the network of artisans and craftspeople and the innumerable regional and localised adaptations of the central narrative, leading to a vibrant folk-art tradition. If ordinary people acquired a knowledge of theoretical constructs in the practical making of artefacts, or understood the concept of rasa in the way it manifested itself in their daily lives and emotions, royal patronage based on genuine knowledge also enlarged the circle of general familiarity. In the Gupta period (300–600 CE), which has been described as the golden age for the fruition of much of the creative ideation of the preceding centuries, scholars have identified that 'an exceptionally fine aesthetic ideal is apparent in many parts of the sub-continent. Art and literature both reveal parallels in their ideals of beauty,' indicating that the Guptas 'may have been responsible more for the spread of a common artistic idiom … imbued with a strong intellectual flavour, displaying a fine balance between representational credibility and abstracting tendencies'.[27] It cannot be a coincidence that King Samudra Gupta (335–375 CE), whose empire extended from the river Ravi in the west to the Brahmaputra in the east, and from the Himalayas in the north to the Vindhyas in the south, with several tributary states further south, issued a series of exquisitely crafted gold coins in which he is depicted as both a conqueror *and* a musician. Nor could it be happenstance that his successor, Chandragupta II, who ruled at the height of Gupta ascendancy, was a great patron of poets, philosophers, scientists, musicians and sculptors.

When ideation on the intricacies and substance of creativity has been incubated for millennia, it is bound to find reflection in the pursuit of the aesthetic ideal. Kings aspired to be seen as cultured because that was *expected* of them by the people at large. Royal patronage reinforced popular aspirations among the populace for cultural knowledge, and provided institutional venues for their aesthetic fulfilment and enjoyment. Thus, a few centuries after the Gupta age, we have the remarkable example of Raja Bhoja (c. 1010–

1055 CE), who ruled over an extensive kingdom in the Malwa region, with his capital at Dhara, near present-day Bhopal. Although his conquests were not insignificant, Bhoja is best remembered as a patron of the arts, literature and the sciences. As a scholar-king, he was the role model of later Hindu monarchs like Krishnadevaraya of the Vijayanagara dynasty, who chose to call himself 'Abhinava Bhoja', the new or modern Bhoja. Under Bhoja, his capital Dhara became a renowned intellectual centre. It is said that in his kingdom even humble weavers could compose metrical Sanskrit kavyas. Bhoja wrote as many as eighty-four books on subjects as diverse as astrology, lexicography, Sanskrit grammar, poetics, dramaturgy and a commentary on Patanjali's *Yoga Shastras*. He was also a great poet himself—the work *Shringara Prakash* is one of his notable works— and a well-known musician.

There was, in the Hindu period of our history, a proclivity to allow ideas, concepts and abstractions to be a part of a ceaseless intellectual journey in order to consciously enlarge creative horizons. It is for this reason, for example, that while our epics, the Ramayana and the Mahabharata, are at their core narratives of battles, they incorporate long, contemplative stanzas on aspects of existence that have no direct connect with victory and defeat in the battle. In the Mahabharata, for instance, there is a fascinating dialogue between the Yaksha and Yudhishtara, the eldest of the Pandavas. The five Pandava brothers and Draupadi are in exile in the forest of Dwaitavana, when they go to look for water to quench their thirst. Each of the younger brothers ventures to the shores of a pond, but before they can drink, the Yaksha of the pool asks them to desist and first answer his questions. All four ignore the Yaksha's injunction and fall dead. Yudhishtara is the last to go, and unlike his siblings, agrees to answer the Yaksha's questions. Throughout the night, the Yaksha asks him questions on birth and death, joy and pain, success and failure, love and fulfilment, purpose and motive, myth and reality—the bewildering mosaic that constitutes the phenomenon of living. Here are some examples of that fascinating dialogue:

*What is more fleeting than the wind? asked the Yaksha, and what is
more numerous than grass?*

> The mind, O Yaksha, is more fleeting than the wind.
> Thoughts are like grass, fecund, undetermined.

*And say, O Yudhishtar, who is the best friend of one whom death has
just beckoned?*

> A prayer beyond want, reaching the open sky.
> Charity is the best friend of one about to die.

O wisest of all of Kunti's progeny, tell me who is truly happy?

> That man is happy who does not stir from home,
> Cooks his own meal, isn't in debt and is happy to be alone.

*O Arya, in your speech so careful, tell me now, what in this world is
most wonderful?*

> Millions pass on, yet the living think they won't die.
> What can be more wonderful than this wonderful lie?[28]

It is these moments of pause and reflection, of the sheer joy of
ideation, not only in literature but in every branch of art, that marks
the creativity of the foundational period of our history. The exploration
of the mind has no barriers, and the intense spirit of cerebral enquiry,
exploration and interrogation that we saw in the area of spirituality
and metaphysics was bound to spill over in the cultural field as well.
The theory of rasa was a result of this template of mind; it both ignited
the remarkable achievements in culture, and was also its outcome.

When the pursuit of culture acquires such an intensity and
lineage, it is bound to create an impact beyond its normal territorial
boundaries. The impact of Indian culture for over a thousand years in
South and South-east Asia proves this, and must count as perhaps the
world's only example in the ancient and medieval period of significant
cultural export without military conquest. From the sixth century BCE
onwards, the tenets of Buddhism were taken abroad not only in the
original Sanskrit but also in Pali to China and much of South-east Asia.
From the Amaravati period in the second century CE, through the

Gupta, Pallava, Pala and Chola dynasties in the succeeding centuries right up to the twelfth century CE, Hindu culture spread across all of South and South-east Asia. The largest Hindu temple in the world, and one of only two dedicated to Brahma, is at Angkor Wat in Cambodia. The story of the Ramayana has immensely popular local variations in Cambodia, Laos, Thailand and Myanmar. The Champa dynasty, which ruled for over a thousand years in what is present-day Vietnam, was Hindu and followed the cultural mores and practices of India, including the Sakya calendar. Tamil is an officially recognised language in Malaysia and Singapore. In Thailand, which is officially Buddhist today, the names of people and places are derivatives of Sanskrit. Archaeological findings across the region, right up to the Philippines, show that Sanskrit, and its most important religious and secular texts, were part of local cultures. The Borobudur temple in Indonesia is a monumental example of the influence of Hindu philosophy and architectural principles; and Bali is still a Hindu enclave in an otherwise overwhelmingly Islamic nation, and remains the only place I have seen (India included), where a huge statue of Bheema dominates a prominent city square.

Unfortunately, there has been a tendency among some historians to ignore, neglect or devalue the cultural achievements of ancient India. For them, such achievements were avoidable obiter dicta, an unimportant side to show more important things like determining the modes of production, or deciding whether society was feudal or primitive or something in-between. I am tempted to conclude that this cavalier undermining of historical reality was an unforgivable distortion. Romila Thapar only reluctantly—and partially—agrees with this. 'The focus on culture, beliefs and ideologies could be a necessary addition to the earlier historical emphasis on politics and the economy, but it is not definitive history since history requires a correlation between the reading of a text and its multi-layered contexts.'[29] There is, indeed, no harm in making this correlation. However, that does not dilute the autonomous nature of cultural refinements and their assessment as something of importance in itself. As Dr Upinder Singh says: 'Marxist writings often tended to work with unilinear historical models derived from Western historical and anthropological writings. ... Religion and culture were often side lined or mechanically presented as reflections of socio-economic structures. ... This also applies to the history of ideas and the aesthetic dimensions of the Indian past reflected in literature, art, and architecture.'[30]

It is this sidelining that I wish to correct. Hindu India must be given due recognition for the amazing calibre of its cultural canvas, the cerebral energy, originality and innovation that infused it, and the unique correspondence it achieved between aesthetic theory and practice. The tragedy is that not enough people are aware of this. For instance, in his widely read recent book, A *History of Civilizations*,[31] Western historian Fernand Braudel writes: 'Centuries later, (after Ashoka 264–226 BCE) ... a new classical India took shape under the victorious insignia of Hinduism, or what is known as the Hindu "Renaissance", since this was the time of its artistic greatness, *when India mastered all that it had learned from elsewhere. This included, in particular the art of Greece, brought through Alexander the Great's conquest in the Indus area, 327–325 BCE* [emphasis mine].'[32] The mindset is still one of evaluating India's aesthetic legacy from the prism of Greek influence, rather that understanding that it was only a peripheral intervention in an intense artistic journey begun thousands of years earlier. Only when someone is unaware of this basic fact, can they conclude, in a book claiming to have knowledge of world civilisations, that Hindu India's cultural renaissance occurred when 'India mastered all that it had learnt from *elsewhere.*' The time has come to accept that in the areas of art, culture and aesthetics, ancient India was probably the most advanced and refined civilisation in the world, and this was a product of the intellect on its own soil, not the result of what may have been assimilated from outside.

Ancient civilisations develop complex social systems. These systems are the result of how a given set of people choose to adopt certain kinds of behavioural patterns, taking into account their external ecosystem and their internal world vision of what should matter in life. As with culture, it is not the intention here to give an extensive account of the entire canvas of social practices of this period. The focus would be to examine certain key aspects that reflect the same excogitation that characterises Hindu civilisation in the areas of spirituality and culture.

The way human beings organise themselves and structure their value systems often have similarities or overlaps with all societies in a certain historical phase. And yet, there are some social practices and some ways of responding to human situations that are unique to every civilisation. Collectively, they represent both practice and philosophy, concept and construct, choices and priorities, ethics and institutions. Not all of this is unblemished. Societies often become the platform to initiate or perpetuate social inequities and in this sense reflect the unjust aspects of organised human behaviour. These also must be considered in an overall assessment of the social milieu of this period.

Hindu India was notable for the way it saw life going through four ashrams or stages. Brahmacharya, consisting of the early years, were most profitably devoted to the acquisition of knowledge and pursuing a celibate life; the next phase, grihasta, was that of the householder, who must pursue a livelihood and experience the joys of physical pleasure; vanaprastha was the intermediate stage, when the responsibilities of a householder ceased, and a person prepared to gracefully withdraw from a direct involvement in the daily vicissitudes of life; and, finally, the last years were meant to be devoted to the bliss of salvation through sanyasa, the complete cessation of desire.

Life has a beginning and an end. All human beings have to go through childhood, adulthood, old age and death. To this inevitable linearity, our ancient texts matched corresponding pursuits or priorities. The assumption was that if a human life had a span of a hundred years, the first twenty-five would be devoted to study and the practice of celibacy, the second twenty-five to the life of a householder, the third twenty-five to preparation for a withdrawal from life and its transitory pleasures and the last quarter to the realisation of spiritual liberation. It was a remarkably balanced way to look at the commencement and fruition of human life, marked by an acceptance of the fact that behaviour and priorities must evolve and change with the passage of time, in accordance with the changing capacities and needs of both the human body and the mind. In this acceptance lay redemption.

It is important to emphasise that the four ashrams were neither prescriptive nor universally mandatory. The division of a life into four quarters was meant to be indicative, and there could be variations as to when a person felt that he or she should move from one to the next. There was no compulsion, too, in the sequential phasing. Persons were free to choose if they wished to lead their entire life as a celibate absorbed in the pursuit of knowledge, or to become a renunciate straight after the completion of their studies, or to never opt to become a householder, or to persist much longer in the pursuit of worldly preoccupations and forego altogether the solitude and detachment of the final years of their life. Equally, the focus of each ashram could overlap with the others. Thus, a householder could display traits of renunciation as befitted the vanaprastha stage; similarly, a person devoted to the acquisition of knowledge, as conjoined for the brahmachari, could become a householder while still primarily absorbed in the pursuit of knowledge.

The ashrams represented a world view based on observation of life. What a person can do, or wishes to do, is different when he or she is young and different when they are older. To fight against this physical, hormonal and mental truth is the choice of every human being. But to flow with it, and accept it with equanimity and joy, is to impart a grace to living that opens the gates to an even more complete happiness, albeit of another kind, as one ages and nears the inevitability of death. In such an approach, there is not the denial of the vibrancy of life, and the joys that it offers, but a deep understanding that the definition of both the vibrant and the joyous changes with time. The joys of youth and adult life may be more passionate and fulfilling and absorbing at the time when they unfold, but could, perhaps, appear transient and ephemeral, even futile, for a person who is looking for more enduring peace, contentment, stillness, calm and unconditioned joy in later life.

The four ashrams, and the phases of life they delineate, are not about the constricting of happiness but about redefining it. Change is the eternal marker of empirical existence. To see life as a gift of the Almighty, and to enjoy it fully, does not mean that we become oblivious to our changing capacities of enjoying it, or our need to explore different ways of doing so. When we are young, the possibilities life offers seem to be infinite in terms of physical time. When we are older, there is the realisation that time is not perennially elastic. There is a spiritual elegance in adjusting to this gracefully.

The Hindu world view offers the hope of greater joy towards the culmination of life, than at its commencement. The four ashrams are, thus, not pessimistic or melancholic but optimistic. This may sound paradoxical, since the capacity to enjoy conventional joys is biologically and physically greater when younger. But such conventional joys could be short-lived, or less enduring than what we would want, whereas the joy that could be ours in the later years of our lives could be far more permanent because it is less dependent on external conditionalities and more on an inner and autonomous transformation. To be a part of the effervescent mountain river is one kind of joy; to be a part of the mellow river, deeper and more quiescent and content, as it nears its merger with the ocean, is another kind of joy. The Hindu attitude asks us to make the transition, in keeping with the parameters of life, from one kind of joy to another, even greater joy.

Attachment brings momentary joy, and also the guarantee of pain. To transcend attachment is to ensure lasting joy and an insulation from pain. When one has no compulsion to seek, one is happy with what one has. This is not defeatism, but a highly exalted pragmatism.

In this sense, the concept of the four ashrams is inextricably linked to Hindu spirituality and the message of the Bhagwad Gita. Moksha, or the liberation from the stranglehold of the three gunas—rajas (activity, passion), tamas (chaos, destructiveness, darkness) and sattva (goodness, harmony)—that collectively constitute empirical life, is the ultimate goal of life. The three gunas constitute our personality, and are an instrument in the hands of Maya to keep us prisoners of illusion. To reach a stage when illusion is eclipsed, and we are joyous without cause, in tune with Brahman, which is unalloyed bliss and peace, is the greatest benediction life can shower. A life is an instrument to achieve that goal. The means for it must include the ability to transcend the transient and move to the eternal. If we succeed, the joy that is guaranteed is far greater than when we mistook the transient for the eternal. An enlightened life must teach us, in the course of its unfolding, to distinguish between the transient and the eternal. If the first two phases of our life make an allowance for us to be more absorbed with the transient, the last two provide us the opportunity to evolve to the eternal.

Does this mean that our normal happiness when we are younger should always be tinged with the sadness that it is transient? Such a disconsolate approach is far from the intent of those who conceived the four ashrams. But Hindu spirituality does demand a life that is not completely blinded by attachments. The Bhagwad Gita's message of nishkama karma, of pursuing the ends of life with a sense of detachment, of working with dedication and energy but not hankering for the reward, is a prescription, as I have discussed earlier, for peace of mind. The Bhagwad Gita does not necessarily prescribe renunciation of life. As individuals, we have to acquire skills, use them productively, have a family, acquire wealth—in short, be a part of the legitimate pageantry of life. But our enjoyment of all of these will be enhanced and not diminished if, in the midst of them, we also inculcate a sense of detachment, of distance from the results that we seek and are so dependent upon. Such an approach fosters equilibrium and equipoise, a more enlightened ability to take the ups and downs of life in our stride and to better absorb setbacks so as to achieve our aims even more effectively.

This detachment—not from joy but from the addiction to joy—must progressively increase as life progresses, because only then can we achieve the paramount goal of self-realisation. The four ashrams in the Hindu world view are a unique and gentle way to take us towards that goal without denying the normal pursuits of life. In that sense, they represent not the exact physical demarcations of time, but emotional evolutions of attitude, in a manner that life resembles an infinitely fulfilling arc, from the ecstasy of dawn to the bliss of sunset.

'The organization of the four Orders is a unique feature of Indian society. Though the historian is mostly concerned with one of them alone, viz. that of the householder, he cannot ignore the influence that the other three must have exercised upon it.'[33] Essentially, the ashrams in Hindu society, were a means to integrate the spiritual vision with the trajectory of the ordinary life. To call it, as some historians like Wendy Doniger do, a Brahmanical conspiracy, is to deliberately undermine the grandeur of the concept in order to somehow discover a baser, ulterior motive. According to her, the concept of the ashrams was 'an attempt, on the part of Brahmins who inclined to renunciation, to integrate that way of life with the other major path, that of the householder'.[34] Many of the practices espoused by Brahmins were, indeed, oppressive and intended to perpetuate an inequitable hierarchy in their own favour. But to see this motivation in concepts such as that of the ashrams is a far-fetched and even mischievous interpretation. Not all Brahmins sought to live a renunciate's life. They were part of society, like those of other classes. Moreover, the ashrams do not represent a simple polarity— renunciation versus the life of a householder. The concept was a holistic one, where both polarities were reconciled as a part of the evolution of a balanced life. It was the Hindu way of seeing the value of life in its entirety, recognising the changes that must occur in it, and providing a schema where these changes can be understood, and dealt with, without diminishing the possibility of joy and fulfilment.

Another institution of great importance in Hindu life was of the four purusharthas, the goals of life. These were dharma, artha, kama and moksha. I shall discuss each of them separately, but collectively they essay the possibility of a balanced life, based not on arbitrary or unrealistic exclusion, but of inclusion in proportion so that, ultimately, an individual could attain, after living a full life, the benediction of enduring peace and happiness, which is moksha. Typical of Hindu processes of thought, none of the goals are simplistic injunctions. Each involves great complexity of thought, with the general tendency to refrain from prescriptive or mandatory commands, allowing full space to each person for internalising the goal and reacting to it in the contextual circumstances of his or her own situation.

Perhaps, the most tantalisingly complex is the concept of dharma, derived from the root word 'dhr', which means to support, to uphold, and to sustain. The easily accessible meaning of the word is variably a code of conduct, duty, virtue, goodness, right action, piety, law and custom. But none of these appellations convey the full meaning of the term. The word occurs frequently from the time of the *Rig Veda*, in almost every text of importance. The Dharmashastras (c. 600–300 BCE) and the Dharmasutras (c. 200 BCE to 900 CE) were special texts dealing with dharma. These claimed to be based on shruti (Vedic texts), smriti (commentaries on shruti texts) and a general notion of shishtachara, good custom or correct behaviour. The most famous of these was the *Manusmriti* (c. second century CE).

Dharma is at the core of the Hindu notion of ethics. What is right conduct? Is there an infallible touchstone to judge what is right? Who has the authority to pronounce what is correct behaviour? Is there a set of unchanging rules which are universally applicable? Does ethical conduct vary with context and circumstance, or is it absolute for all situations? Most civilisations have chosen to believe that certain things are absolutely right or absolutely wrong. In the Biblical tradition, for instance, we have the Ten Commandments. Islam also categorically lays down what is permissible and what is not. The Hindu approach, on the other hand, is highly nuanced and complex, both emphasising certain virtues which should be followed, and simultaneously providing derogations from that ideal, based on context, situation and circumstance.

Many observers have inferred from this calibrated ambiguity a debilitating moral relativism. Hindu society, they argue, was tainted by the absence of an iron-cast moral framework and a clear and prescriptive set of do's and don'ts, while accommodating a convenient set of alibis to avoid moral responsibility. The truth is that Hinduism hesitates to endorse certitudes which are not universally validated. What is right in one set of circumstances may be wrong in another. The purposes of morality are best served by an indicative framework of ethical conduct without the rigid and absolute condemnation of all deviations. This lack of judgemental diktats was influenced by the fact that all rules in the Hindu world view fall into two broad categories. There is the paramarthik reality, where a person, in the realisation of brahmanubhav, has spiritually evolved to a level where he or she is beyond strictly conventional categories of right and wrong. In this state, their mind is above punyam and paapam, saukhyam and dukkham, good and evil, pleasure and pain, to use the words of Shankaracharya. They are recognised for their wisdom and contemplative transcendence, nivritthilakshana dharma. No absolute code of ethics can be prescribed for such a level of consciousness. The second level is vyavaharik, the empirical world of everyday life, where privritthilakshana dharma prevails, prescribing a code of moral behaviour. In this world, laws are made by humans for humans. Religious sanction could often be invoked to ensure compliance, but there was equally the pragmatic recognition that definitions of ethicality at the empirical plane could be neither infallible nor universal. Even a cursory examination of societies would show variations in custom and social usage, differing norms of acceptable behaviour and disparities in ritual and community practice. What was considered ethical conduct for one set of people, was considered unethical by another. Given this, the Hindu mind was reluctant to accept an unequivocal set of moral imperatives which claimed unanimity. 'Since all empirical phenomena are transient they can have no decisive significance or axiomatic moral value. There is no such thing as sin in Indian ethics, only errors of cognition—avidya, or ignorance.'[35]

This does not, of course, mean that Hindu society lacked all moral compass, or countenanced immorality. While it had the courage to challenge simplistic moral certitudes, the Hindu texts are replete with recommendations for what should constitute ethical conduct. The *Manusmriti*, an otherwise controversial text, lays down ten elements of dharma—Dhritih kshama damo steyam, shauchamindriyanigraha, dhirvidya satyamakrodho, dashakam dharmalakshanan: Steadiness, forgiveness, self-control, abstention from unrighteous appropriation, purity, control of the sense organs, discrimination, knowledge, truthfulness and absence of anger. These are the tenfold forms of dharma. Other texts stress on the three d's—dana, charity and giving what is owed to others; daya, empathy for all fellow creatures; and dama, restraining one's passions. In a luminous stanza, the Mahabharata says: 'Anger must be controlled by forgiveness; fear by vigilance; inclination and aversion by patience; confusion and doubt and laziness by practice; greed by contentment; adharma by generosity; dharma with careful thought; attachment to objects by meditation on their passing nature; the tendency to talk too much by periods of silence; pride by compassion; all ill-effects of material prosperity and wealth by sharing.'[36] The Mahabharata repeatedly emphasises ahimsa paramo dharmah, the paramount importance of non-violence. In the epic, Bhishma makes the pronouncement: 'Whatever has its beginning in justice that alone is called dharma; whatever is unjust and oppressive, is adharma. This is the rule settled by those who can be respected.'[37] Significantly, he adds that 'if one dharma is destructive of another dharma, then it is wickedness in the garb of dharma, and not dharma. Only that is dharma truly, which is established without denigrating and opposing another dharma.'[38] The Buddhist ideology of dhamma (the Pali word for dharma), which was widely disseminated by Emperor Ashoka through his rock edicts, highlighted non-violence, toleration, kindness and compassion towards others.

Thus, the normative framework of ethical conduct was not lacking. But, while accepting such virtues as ideals to aspire to, Hindu thinking persists with the foundational question—are ethical values the same for all people in all manners, or does ethical conduct, at the human level, also have to take into account the *context* of the dramatis personae: who acted thus, with whom, in what manner, in which situation, under what compulsions and for what goals? Idealism was not jettisoned; it was vehemently endorsed. But it was also tempered by realism, taking on board the basic fact that howsoever noble the ideal may be, human behaviour will be influenced by contingent circumstances that may not be mala fide but are factors in evaluating the extent to which ethical conduct deviated from an inflexible—and impractical—absolutism.

In practice, therefore, dharma may be influenced by several factors. These could include the correct behaviour according to a person's desh dharma or conduct in different regions, ashram dharma or stage of life, kula dharma or family and community fealties, jati dharma or caste considerations, svabhava dharma or personal nature, svadharma or choices of conscience, and appadharma or action taken in times of dire emergency. While ideal ethical conduct is desirable, numerous factors operate in the choices human beings make, and it is a moot point whether, regardless of the situation *as it exists*, people should have behaved differently. It follows then, that human behaviour must be judged, not by one normative yardstick, but several contingent factors. That is why, Yudhishtara, who is also known as Dharmaraja, the epitome of dharma, is unable to answer the question posed by the Yaksha—What is dharma? 'Reason is of limited use for it is unconvincing, without tarka or foundation,' he answers the Yaksha. 'Neither are the sacred texts helpful as they are at odds with one another; nor is there a single sage whose opinion could be considered authoritative'. Throwing up his hands in despair, Dharmaraja's final answer is: 'The truth about dharma is hidden in a cave.'[39]

The uniqueness of the Hindu notion of ethics is that it refuses to be blindly prescriptive or to deal with human beings as though they were schoolchildren and must, in all circumstances, follow an absolute canon of conduct imposed from above as a fiat. Ethical absolutism leads to absolute hypocrisy. It is better, therefore, to define ethics in generally desirable ideals, while also taking into account circumstances in which it may not always be possible to follow them. In other words, Hinduism, without depriving itself of an ethical framework, puts the onus far more on the choices individuals make, often in difficult situations. In doing so, it does not encourage unethical behaviour, but only recognises that every human being must decide, within the matrix of his or her own situation, what is the right thing to do in a given set of coordinates. That is why, Yudhishtara, when accused by Draupadi of contravening dharma in allowing her to be shared by all the five Pandava brothers, says: 'Dharma is sukshma (subtle), O Draupadi. Who has defined it? This pleases me, so it must be right.'

The Mahabharata is, as Gurcharan Das argues, the ultimate book which tests ethical choices confronting human beings. Almost every character in it is caught in the conundrum of what is right and what is wrong, and innumerable compromises are made along the way to illustrate that human beings have to make choices while trying to balance principles which are ideal with situations which are not. No one is entirely unblemished, nor is anyone fully evil. Dharmaraja Yudhishtara, who prides himself for his devotion to dharma, is addicted to gambling, and even gambles away his wife, Draupadi. Those who are considered good sometimes countenance wrong, and those who are considered bad occasionally behave honourably.

It is far easier to confidently define morality in simple and doctrinaire terms. It requires courage to acknowledge that such confidence may be misplaced, and final judgements may need to be more circumspect. For instance, in a situation of appadharma, where life and limb are in danger, a person can act in whatever manner he or she deems best in self-defence, including the use of violence, in spite of the injunction against it. Resorting to violence would also be necessary in times of war. Modern jurisprudence also recognises extenuating circumstances under which responses, otherwise culpable, need to be condoned due to the nature of the grave and sudden provocation. If a person is dying of starvation, would it be wrong for him or her to steal an apple from a rich person's abundant orchard, or can this act be condoned due to extenuating factors? Is a lie damnable in all situations, or is it justified if it saves lives that need to be saved? The Hindu view of ethics is compelled to grapple with such dilemmas before it passes final judgement on the moral quotient of an action.

It would be wrong, therefore, to accuse the Hindu world view of moral relativism. Like other civilisations and societies, Hinduism recognises an ethical code of conduct—and emphasises this repeatedly—but is also mature enough to understand that such a code will be implemented by people who will need to take the call as per their viveka. This is the human predicament, where what should be done is known, and yet there are derogations or deviations necessitated by the context of a given situation. Only rasa, moksha, sanyasa, sphota and bhakti are, as A.K. Ramanujan says, beyond contextuality.[40] Hence, some choices, even if not strictly ethical, are understandable if not entirely condonable in context, and the person concerned must bear their consequences. Ultimately, we are dealing with people and not devas or gods. Who then can say what is right or wrong in all cases and situations? A guide can be provided, but each of us have to make the choice of acting as per our conscience and the situation we find ourselves in. The ethical system of the Hindus sought to simultaneously delineate ideals of ethical behaviour, and dwell on the underlying fallibility of the basic human situation, which is finite, vulnerable, contingent, conditioned and, in ontological terms, ephemeral. As Yudhishtara says to the Yaksha: 'In this cauldron fashioned from delusion, with the sun as fire and day and night as kindling wood, the months and seasons as the ladle for stirring, Time (or Death) cooks all beings: this is the simple truth.'[41]

In the Mahabharata, the actions of Krishna himself illustrate the difference between textual rectitude and practical choices. There are at least six incidents in the epic, crucial to the outcome of the war between the Kauravas and the Pandavas, which call into question the ethicality of his actions in terms of the prevailing code of fair play, or at least in terms of the *expectation* of fair play from him.

On the eve of the war, Krishna's attempt was to wean away the mighty warrior Karna from the Kauravas. This he did not by appealing to Karna's sense of rectitude, or by persuading him to see the legitimacy of the Pandavas' claims. His strategy instead was to use a crucial nugget of information about Karna's personal life to break his pledge of unwavering loyalty to his childhood friend and benefactor—Duryodhana. In reality, Karna was the firstborn of Kunti, from an unintended liaison, before her marriage, with Surya, the sun god. Krishna was aware of this, and chose this moment to reveal the truth to Karna. The news had a traumatic impact on the young warrior. At one stroke, the Pandavas, whom he regarded as his most implacable foes, were revealed to be his brothers. Krishna did not stop there. He went on to outline in detail the advantages that would accrue to Karna were he to betray his old loyalties:

> 'You know that a son born to a woman when she was a maiden, becomes, by law, the son of the man she marries. Accordingly, you are a Pandava. You are the eldest of the Pandavas. You are a Pandava on your father's side. You are a Vrishni, my cousin, my relative, on your mother's side. Come with me now. I am going to Yudhishthira. Your brothers will fall at your feet. All the kings who have assembled to help the Pandavas will honour you as the eldest Pandava. You will be crowned by them as their king. You will be the king and Yudhishthira will be the Yuvaraja. He will lead the white horses of your chariot to your presence and lift you to your seat. The dark and beautiful Draupadi will belong to you, since you are a Pandava. Yudhishthira will get into the chariot after you. The mighty Bheema will hold the umbrella over your head. Your younger brother Arjuna will be your charioteer. He will hold the reins over your horses. Nakula, Sahadeva and I will be walking behind your chariot.'[42]

Krishna's mission did not succeed because Karna, in spite of the enticements blatantly outlined to him, refused to give up his friendship with Duryodhana, who had stood by him when he needed support most. But Krishna's request was not a complete failure either. Karna's emotional equipoise was shattered. His animosity to the Pandavas was weakened. His hitherto resolute morale for battle was shaken. Krishna had prepared the ground for him to concede a boon of the greatest significance to Kunti, who met him a few days later. Kunti too was unable to persuade him to forsake Duryodhana; however, not wanting to completely disappoint his mother, he promised her that he would not attack Yudhishtara, Bheema, Nakul and Sahadeva. The duel with Arjuna was something to which he was irrevocably pledged, but, at all times, he assured Kunti, at least five of her sons would remain alive.

During the war, the Pandavas, at the explicit urging of Krishna, managed to kill the top warriors on the Kaurava side by means which were, at best, expedient, and at worst, deceitful and unfair. Bhishma was more than a match for anyone on the Pandava side. His arrows were wreaking havoc on the Pandava army. In consultation with Krishna, the Pandavas decided to meet Bhishma and ask him how he could be defeated. Even though he was duty-bound to fight on the side of Dhritarashtra, Bhishma, at a personal level, had the greatest love for the Pandavas. Krishna's clear reasoning was that if Yudhishtara posed the question to Bhishma, the grand old man would certainly reveal the answer. The plan worked. 'Place the warrior Shikhandi before me,' Bhishma said, 'and I will have to put down my bow.' Bhishma had sworn never to fight against a woman, and that included even a man who had once been a woman. Shikhandi was a man only in appearance. In reality, he was an incarnation of Princess Amba of Kashi. Amba had wanted to marry Bhishma, but the latter, wedded to his oath of celibacy, had spurned her advances. The princess had then sworn to avenge this humiliation. Born again as Shikhandi, she led the attack on the venerable warrior. Bhishma relinquished his arms, and Arjuna's arrows were quick to pin him down.

Drona, the towering guru of the Kuru clan, was another formidable foe whose depredations were taking a heavy toll on the Pandava forces. Krishna's plan to kill him was ingenious. It was well known that Drona was extremely fond of his son, Ashwathamma. If he was told that Ashwathamma had died, Drona would, Krishna said, lose all desire to fight. But Drona would believe this news only if Yudhishtara, who never spoke an untruth, conveyed it to him. Yudhishtara baulked at being told of his role; Arjuna too was disapproving. But Krishna's exhortations were totally persuasive. 'If Drona lives for but half a day, the Pandava army will be wiped out,' he said. 'A lie to save lives is not immoral. In fact, in certain situations a lie is permissible.'

The plan was implemented with Machiavellian skill. Bheema had killed an elephant called Ashwathamma. Yudhishtara, the reluctant conspirator, did not tell a complete lie when he told Drona, 'Ashwathamma is dead!' adding in an inaudible whisper, 'the elephant called Ashwathamma'. The shattered Drona, unquestioningly believing Yudhishtara, lost his will to fight. A few caustic words from Bheema on the inappropriateness of a Brahmin indulging in wanton killing were enough to make him dispiritedly put down his arms, and Dhrishtadyumna, son of Dhrupad, swiftly cut off his head.

Karna was killed when, during his fight with Arjuna, he got down from his chariot to lift its wheel which had sunk into the ground. It was against the rules of war to attack a man when he was unarmed, and Karna asked Arjuna to respect this code of conduct. But Krishna was quick to intervene. Fair play in war had no application, he said, to those who had scant respect for it themselves. By supporting Duryodhana's unjust cause, Karna had forfeited his right to be dealt with fairly. Eyes flaming with anger, Krishna recounted the inhuman and unscrupulous manner in which, just a few days earlier, Karna had ganged up with other Kaurava luminaries to kill Abhimanyu, Arjuna's young son. 'Kill Karna now, before he returns to his chariot,' Krishna pressed Arjuna, and the next moment, Karna, his head severed from his body, lay dead on the battlefield.

Jayadratha, the ruler of Sindhu and the son-in-law of Dhritarashtra, was killed, if not by a tampering of temporal laws, then by divine manipulation. Jayadratha had been instrumental in the death of Abhimanyu. Arjuna had sworn to either avenge his son's death by killing Jayadratha before sunset the next day, or to immolate himself. Having heard of Arjuna's oath, Jayadratha, protected by the entire might of the Kaurava army, remained effectively elusive. At the end of an exhausting day of fighting, he was still beyond the reach of Arjuna. The horizon was darkening with the imminent sunset. Krishna was worried. Jayadratha emerged triumphantly from hiding, only after he was very sure that the sun had set. But just as he did so, the sun inexplicably peeped out from the darkness to shine again. This time Arjuna did not let the opportunity slip by. One arrow from his bow and the exultant Jayadratha was dead. Krishna had saved Arjuna from his vow of self-immolation by creating a false sunset to lure Jayadratha from his hideout.

Duryodhana was the last of the Kaurava brothers to be killed. With honourable magnanimity, Yudhishtara had offered him a duel with any of the Pandavas using a weapon of his choosing. Krishna was quick to chide Yudhishtara for such foolhardy generosity. Duryodhana was too good a fighter, he said, to be defeated by anybody except perhaps Bheema. Fortunately, Bheema himself challenged Duryodhana to fight him with the mace, and the latter readily accepted. The fight was long and bitter. The two opponents were evenly matched. But, after a while, it became clear that even though Bheema was the heavier of the two, Duryodhana was more agile and the better fighter. Krishna, who was watching the duel intently, confided to Arjuna that Bheema would never be able to win in a fair fight. He had to be defeated by unfair means. 'Has Bheema forgotten his vow to break Duryodhana's thighs?' Krishna asked Arjuna in a voice loud enough for Bheema to hear. Arjuna, quickly grasping Krishna's intent, smacked his own thighs as a signal to Bheema. Bheema got the message. In one forceful blow, his mace smashed Duryodhana's thighs, leaving him prostrate and writhing in agony. It was against the rules of war to hit below the navel. Duryodhana was thus not expecting to be hit on his thighs. Bheema too would not have broken the rules of war but for Krishna's unambiguous urging. Balarama, who was observing the fight, was furious at the unfair means adopted. He was ready to attack Bheema, but was restrained by Krishna. Then Duryodhana, who was in his death throes but still mentally alert, spoke. His last words were a damning indictment of the means adopted by Krishna during the war. The fallen warrior recounted each incident—the disarming of Bhishma, the killing of Drona and Karna and, of course, the use of duplicitous means for his own defeat. There was unconcealed contempt in his voice; and, the heavens themselves seemed to endorse his stand by raining flowers on his head when he died.

Krishna's response to the accusations of Duryodhana is extremely interesting. First, he admitted that he had resorted to unfair means. The Kauravas, 'who were the very flowers of Kshatriya prowess', could not, he said, have been killed by fair means. The vow he had made to Draupadi at Kamyaka forest could thus be fulfilled only by the pursuit of deceitful means. Deception, Krishna said, is acceptable when the enemy is stronger. 'The gods themselves are not above it; we have only followed their example,' he said. The Kauravas symbolised adharma. They had to be defeated. In such a situation, 'the end,' he said, 'justifies the means.' In the prevailing times, 'unsullied righteousness' could not be practised. The fourth age, the Kalyug age, had begun. In this age, absolute morality would be at a discount.

The working of fate and destiny did not allow right and wrong to retain their sharply distinctive focus. 'It is the rule of time. You must not try and change the course of Destiny. She will have her way. She is unrighteous too, and she fulfils herself in many ways, mostly unrighteous.' Krishna's final argument was that in his human avatar, he had to play the game as a mortal would. 'When I am living as a god, I act like a god; when my form is that of a gandharva or a naga, my actions and behaviour are in conformity with such a status; now, as one born of human parents, I must act and behave as human beings would.'[43]

The truth probably is that Krishna's conduct in war reflected the code of ethics of the theories on war and statecraft prevalent in those times. Dandaniti, the use of force in politics, and rajaniti, the conduct of kings, were well-developed fields in ancient India. It is beyond doubt that more than one treatise on these subjects existed. Even though such texts are no longer extant, there is enough evidence in Vedic and Pali literature to point to the great importance given to these areas. Perhaps, the most important work specifically dealing with statecraft was Kautilya's *Arthashastra*, written during the reign of Chandragupta Maurya (r. 324–313 BCE). 'The *Arthashastra* says nothing about fair play in battle, and evidently looks on conquest of the demoniac variety as the most profitable and advisable. ... The rules of war could only be maintained strictly by a king certain of victory, or certain of defeat. Where chances were narrow, the claims of self-preservation inevitably made themselves felt.'[44]

Dharma, therefore, was not—indeed could not be—a universal moral writ written in stone. Hindu civilisation was both bold and pragmatic enough to understand this, without diluting the autonomous importance of ethical values. Dharma was sukshma, elusive and subtle; artha, or the pursuit of material well-being, on the other hand, was sthula, concrete and tangible. For a civilisation that remained so preoccupied with matters of spirituality and philosophy, the unhesitating ideological acceptance of the importance of material pursuits would come as a surprise to many. However, the Hindu world view never proposed the spiritual and the material against each other. Each had their own importance as a part of a balanced life.

Indeed, Hinduism must be the only religion that expressly includes the fulfilment of physical desires and the pursuit of prosperity as among the supreme goals of life. Chanakya in his *Arthashastra* privileges artha over both dharma and kama. '(Some teachers say that) the three objectives of human endeavour (dharma, artha and kama) are interdependent and should be pursued equally. Excessive importance given to any one brings harm not only to that objective but to others as well. Chanakya, however, says: artha is the most important for dharma and kama are both dependent on it.'[45]

Material well-being was never seen as an obstacle to moksha;

on the contrary, only persons with a livelihood could be expected to properly devote themselves to the pursuit of salvation. Hindu society's sanction to the balanced acceptance of wealth differs dramatically from the Biblical injunction that a rich person will find it next to impossible to enter the portals of heaven. The Valmiki Ramayana has this nugget of advice—Dhanam arjaya kakuthstha idam jagat, antaran nabhijamn nirdhanasya mrtasya cha: Acquire wealth. The world has for its roots wealth. There is no difference between a poor man and a dead one. The Mahabharata too argues that 'the perception that one should give up all possessions whatever, and cultivate disdain for wealth is no less a disorder: disorder, because such an attitude goes against human reality. It says: there is neither freedom in poverty, nor is there bondage in wealth.'[46] Thiruvalluvar, in his *Thirukkural*, which was written in Tamil some two thousand years ago and is considered the very repository of wisdom, echoes this sentiment— 'Pini imai selvam vilaivinbam emam aniyemba nattirkiv vainthu: Important elements constituting a nation are: being disease free; *wealth*; *high productivity*; harmonious living and strong defence [emphasis mine].'

It is not surprising, therefore, that two of the most important deities in a Hindu's life are Lakshmi and Ganesha. Lakshmi, as we have seen earlier, is the goddess of good fortune, wealth and prosperity. She is an ubiquitous presence even now in homes across the country, in cities and villages alike. Expectedly, she is of special importance for traders, offices and business establishments, and her blessings are sought to keep the account books in the black, and to shower her followers with gold, horses, cattle and all the worldly riches they desire. Ganesha, too, is the god of material wealth, and especially of commercial success. No other Hindu icon is found so pervasively at the entrance of shops, offices and homes as an omen of good fortune, obviously a continuation of a long-established tradition. Moreover, his portly figure, with an ample and well-fed stomach, has nothing to do with the self-denying asceticism that is often wrongly associated with Hindu spirituality. Nor is Lakshmi an emaciated recluse. She is beauty personified, emerging from a sea of milk, the radiant harbinger of plenty.

It was the endorsement of material pursuit as a valid goal of life that accounts perhaps for the early development in ancient India of a vibrant merchant class. We have evidence that traders in the Harappan civilisation sold and bought from as far as Mesopotamia, and those of the Vedic period were as intrepid. The textile industry was particularly well developed; trade guilds flourished; vardushikas (moneylenders) were well established; vriddhi (commercial rates of interest) were prevalent; and prayojakas (investors) competed with one another for profit. It is interesting that although usury was common, moneylending was not considered as bad as it was in Christianity and Islam.

The foundations of the Indian civilisation were, therefore, most enlightened in accepting the position of worldly wealth in the desired scheme of things. The only caveat was that wealth should be earned without doing violence to others, and that prosperity should always remember the importance of charity. Professor A.L. Basham, who has written one of the most comprehensive treatises on ancient India, sums it up well:

> It has been often said that ancient society was not an acquisitive one. ... Poverty, it is more than once said, is living death. ... From the time of the *Rig Veda*, which contains many prayers for riches, worldly wealth was looked upon as morally desirable for the ordinary man, and indeed essential to a full and civilized life. The ascetic who voluntarily abandoned his wealth performed an act of renunciation, which entitled him to the utmost respect—(but) the ascetic's life was not that of an ordinary man, and the theoretical classification of the four stages of life gave ample scope in the second stage to the householder, who was indeed encouraged to build up the family fortunes, and to spend part of them at least on the pleasure of the senses. Thus the ideals of ancient India, while not perhaps the same as that of the West, by no means excluded money-making. India had not only a class of luxury-loving and pleasure-seeking dilettanti, but also one of wealth-seeking merchants and prosperous craftsmen,

who, if less respected than the brahmans and the warriors, had an honourable place in society.[47]

The same intellectual pragmatism that sanctions the pursuit of artha, also gives legitimacy to the relevance of desire among the four highest goals in the Hindu scheme of things. At a philosophical level, the attempt was to integrate desire and the sexual urge in a spiritual framework, with eroticism as its natural attribute, even as there was in equal measure the emphasis on the need to overcome desire, with asceticism as its deviational attribute. The *Rig Veda* says that desire was the first movement that arose in the One after it had come into being through the power of abstraction. 'Desire arose first in It, which was the primal germ of mind; (and which) sages, searching with their intellect have discovered in their heart to be the bond which connects entity with non-entity.'[49] The very strength of the urge made it useful to use as a metaphor to convey or explicate a metaphysical point. The *Brihadaranyaka Upanishad* says: 'Just as a man, closely embraced by his loving wife, knows nothing without, nothing within, so does this "person", closely embraced by the Self that consists of wisdom, knows nothing without nothing within.'[50] The same Upanishad also has this passage where a woman's genitals are used as symbols to describe a sacrificial fire: 'Woman is a fire, Gautama: the phallus is her fuel; the hairs are her smoke; the vulva is her flame; when a man penetrates her, that is her coal; the ecstasy is her sparks.'[51] As I have discussed, the major gods in the Hindu faith have all got consorts. They are rarely described as celibate recluses; they may be said to be beyond passion in an ontological sense, but in their incarnate form they are explicit in the demonstrative attraction of the opposite sex. The goddesses do not lag behind. Their love for their husbands or lovers is often portrayed in an assertively earthy and sensual manner. Gods and goddesses represent a conscious duality, Purusha and Prakriti, complementing each other.

The inclusion of desire in the larger religious and spiritual vision gave it both sanctity and philosophical legitimacy. Kama, the God of

Love, akin to the Greek Eros, or the Roman Cupid or Amor, has been exalted in a hymn of the *Atharva Veda* as a supreme god and creator. 'Kama was born the first. Him neither gods, nor fathers, nor men have equalled. Thou art superior to these and for ever great.'[52] The *Rig Veda* pays similar homage to him, commending him for worship since he is unequalled by the gods. 'May Kama, having well directed the arrow, which is winged with pain, barbed with longing, and has desire for its shaft, pierce thee in the heart.'[53] According to the *Taittiriya Brahmana*, Kama is the son of Dharma, the god of justice, and Shraddha, the goddess of faith. By another account, he sprang from the heart of Brahma, and there are other texts which assert that he is Atma-bhu or self-existent. The *Harivamsha* states that Kama is the son of Vishnu and Lakshmi, and this appears to be the most accepted view.

According to Hindu mythology, it was only Kama who was able to distract Shiva from his deep meditation by arousing in him amorous thoughts for Parvati. He did this at the bidding of Brahma himself for the great demon Taraka could only be destroyed by a son of Shiva, and Shiva could not have a son until he broke his meditation. The *Saura Purana* says that when Brahma asked Kama to perform the deed, the latter declared: 'There is no hero, no proud woman, no learned man too powerful for me. I pervade the whole universe, moving and still, beginning with Brahma the Creator.'[54] In Tulsidas's *Ramcharitmanas*, there is a description of the impact of Kama on everything around him as he made his way to Shiva. Restraint, fortitude, knowledge, renunciation, devotion and wisdom ran helter-skelter as Kama approached; the scriptures hid in the crevices of the mountains; all creation—animate and inanimate—awakened to his touch; rivers swelled to reach the ocean; rivulets, ponds, creeks sought to merge with each other, trees bent towards each other; birds and animals swayed under his magic; even the sanyasis and yogis could not resist his influence.

The story goes that Shiva, angered by the disruption in his meditation, burnt Kama to ashes. He then requested Parvati to ask for a boon, and she answered: 'Now that Kama has been killed, what can I do for a boon from you today? For, without Kama there can be no emotion between man and woman which is like ten million suns. When emotion is destroyed, how can happiness be attained?' Shiva repeated his offer of a boon and Parvati asked that Kama be brought to life again to heat the world, for without him she did not wish to request anything at all. And so, Kama was reborn, this time, according to the *Bhagwata Purana*, as Pradhyumna, son of Krishna and Rukmini. Another version of the story is that Shiva said that he could not revive Kama in the same form that he was in before his destruction. He agreed, however, that he could be revived in spirit, formless, but still ubiquitous in his influence.

The cosmological acceptance of Kamadeva as a primal force of attraction, almost of gravitation, led to the emotions he personified — desire, love, sexuality—to be given a place among the four highest purusharthas of human life. Dharma and kama now came to be viewed not as antithetical pursuits but as valid elements coexisting harmoniously in conjunction with each other as a part of a balanced life. In the Mahabharata, Bheema argues emphatically that kama is superior to both dharma and artha, for without kama there can be no desire either for artha or dharma; even a sage absorbed in meditation is moved by kama; kama is the best because it provides happiness. However, the emergent consensus was the espousal of dharma, artha and kama is of equal importance in the multicoloured mosaic of life. The *Manusmriti* speaks of the trivarga, the three ends of life: 'It is said that dharma and artha are together the best, or that kama and artha are the best combination, or that dharma alone is the best, or that artha is the highest, but the best is to follow the trivarga, looking to all three together.'[55]

The *Kamasutra*, Vatsyayana's famous treatise on the art of love (c. first century to fifth century CE), reiterates this balanced view. Vastyayana writes: 'Man, the period of whose life is one hundred years, should practise dharma, artha and kama at different times and in such a manner that they may *harmonize* together and not clash in any way … a man practicing dharma, artha and kama enjoys happiness in this world and in the world to come. ... Any action which conduces to practice of dharma, artha and kama together, or of any two, or even one of them, should be performed, *but an action which conduces to the practice of one of them at the expense of the remaining two should not be performed* [emphasis mine].'[56] This is an extremely important point if we are to understand the Hindu thinking behind the formulation of the four purusharthas. Dharma, artha and kama should be pursued in harmonious combination, and none in exclusion; each goal is valid in itself, but must be followed in conjunction with the other two, in proportion, so as to lead to the ultimate goal of a balanced life.

Kama is, therefore, not a sanction for hedonism. It is not a licence for uncontrolled licentiousness. The genius of the Hindu vision lay in the inclusion of both the material and the sensual among the four highest goals of life. This was in response to the pivotal role they play in human life and the sheer potency of their attraction. To say that they do not matter, or should not matter, would be unrealistic and spawn a great deal of hypocrisy. But, having given sanction, the injunction is that none of them should be pursued in exclusion, and that the three only guarantee a balanced life if pursued in proportion. This interfaces with the four stages of life—there is a time and moment for privileging certain priorities; this is not mandatory, but a legitimate inference based on empirical observation. These priorities could reflect the four purusharthas, and if each is practiced in harmony and balance, they lead to both fulfilment and prepare the way towards the final goal of moksha.

The *Kamasutra* states that kama is the enjoyment of appropriate objects by the five senses of hearing, feeling, seeing, tasting, and smelling, assisted by the mind together with the soul. Desire to be truly fulfilling had to be elevated beyond the merely physical. Ideally, it was meant to be a total experience in which passion harmonised with sentiment, ambience and aesthetics. It was then that one could capture that elusive mood, the rasa, the very taste, the essence, the hidden flavour of the pleasurable moment. Krishna, the lover, was the ultimate rasik (that is, one who knows of rasa, is immersed in it, and can arouse it in others). Krishna's loveplay with the gopis on the banks of the Yamuna in Vrindavan—as is described by the *Bhagwata Purana*, the *Vishnu Purana* and the *Harivamsha*—was one in which the physical was interwoven with melody, grace, madhurya (sweetness), a sense of the moment, the setting and the resplendence of nature. Sringara rasa, or the sensual mood, was the outcome of this heady mix. While the texts show no squeamishness in fulsomely depicting Krishna's rasa with the gopis, it is not without import that once he leaves Vrindavan, he—so goes the lore—never returns. His definitive departure is meant to convey one integrated message—Kama has validity, but not exclusive validity; desire is a window to the divine, but not the only window; the sensual is joyous, but so can be the non-sensual.

The Hindu view of life was always shaped by two parallel themes—one emphasised the legitimacy of desire, the other stressed the joys of transcending such desire. Shiva gambolled in sensual play with Parvati for such an extended period that the other gods began to worry; but the same Shiva remained for years immersed in the most sublime meditation, totally oblivious to the senses. The dialectics of Hinduism were not either/or. It was not that one path was right, and the other wrong. Both were valid, for the ultimate premise was that there was more than one avenue to experience the bliss of the infinite. Mythology became a tool to correct the exclusivity of just one approach.

The almost Confucian stress on a balanced life, in which kama has its legitimate role to play, led to a considerable degree of unabashed and scintillating sensuality in the arts. In literature, Kalidasa, who adorned the court of Chandragupta Maurya II in the fourth century CE and is considered one of the greatest playwrights of Indian literature, had a great deal of sensuality in his works. He was particularly elaborate in the description of the physical features of his heroines, whether Shakuntala or Urvashi or others. For him, the eyebrows of one were like ripples of water, the breasts of another were like bunches of flowers, the thighs of another like the trunk of an elephant and the lower lip of a fourth like the red bimba fruit. Such descriptions also flowed from his pen where goddesses were concerned. In one of his plays, *Kumar Sambhava*, the description of Parvati was so explicitly sensual that even the gods, it is said, were scandalised and in retribution, Kalidasa was struck by leprosy. This apocryphal punishment did not, however, deter other great poets of the time. The verses of Bhartrihari, the philosopher-poet of the fifth century CE, were uninhibitedly erotic, as were those of Bilhana, who served at the court of the Chalukyan king, Vikramaditya VI (r. 1076–1127 CE). The love lore of Krishna, and his ethereal and passionate romance with Radha, was the subject of decidedly carnal poetic outpourings triggered by Jayadeva's *Gita Govinda* in the twelfth century CE. But, what is significant that even Adi Shankaracharya's outpouring of deep obeisance to Parvati as the mother goddess, the Soundarya Lahiri, has decidedly erotic overtones.

The same interface between spirituality and sensuality is seen in many Hindu temples, and most famously in Khajuraho and Konark. Most of the Khajuraho group of temples in Madhya Pradesh were built between 885 CE and 1050 CE during the rule of the Chandela dynasty. The majority of them are dedicated to Shiva and Vishnu, but some also to Jain tirhthankars. These temples are partially decorated with explicit sexual imagery, including couples in coital postures. The Konark Temple near Puri was built in the thirteenth century during the rule of King Narasimhan of the Eastern Ganga dynasty. It is dedicated to Surya, the sun god. Here, too, we see a profusion of carnal images. The presence of such carvings without the slightest inhibition in a public space is proof of the acceptance in Hinduism of the philosophical legitimacy of kama. However, the erotic sculptures are but a fraction of the overall ornamentation of the temple. They are shown as a part of the many varied pursuits of a complete and fulfilling life. The validity of desire, and the need to pursue it in enlightened proportion, is thus clearly brought out. Moreover, the fact that the erotic is displayed on the walls of a temple is proof that desire was considered a part of the profusion of divinity. In Hinduism, there is no dichotomy between the sacred and the profane. The so-called profane is a part of the sacred. The sacred is not brittle; it is not circumscribed; it is not finite; it is all-inclusive and pervasive. 'Only the vital sensuous awareness which the art stimulates can provide the fuel which is consumed in the transcendental fire.'[57] When desire is imbued with such a vision, it both encompasses and elevates the profane. Desire, tempered by dharma, and as part of a harmonious life, becomes a means of achieving aikya or oneness with the Ultimate, tanmayate or a state of blissful absorption in God, overcoming the false duality between desire and the object of desire. A life lived well and in the correct manner, replenished by all that life has to offer, prepares us for the final experience of moksha, where the sheer intensity of unconditional, unsullied joy transcends the preparatory categories of dharma, artha and kama. As Adi Shankaracharya says in his *Nirvana Shatakam*—Na dharmo, na chartho, na kamo, na moksha, chidanandarupah shivo ham shivo ham: Neither dharma, nor artha, nor kama nor moksha matter, for I am eternal bliss and awareness, I am Shiva! I am Shiva!

The openness to observe, explore and analyse life in all its many facets and to view it holistically created a predisposition to investigate the realm of knowledge. Centuries before the first universities came up in other parts of the world, India had developed advanced centres of learning spread across the country. In the north-west, at Gandhara, the famed university of Takshila was established as early as the sixth century BCE. Other important learning hubs were at Vikramshila, Shravasti, Kashi, Pataliputra, Somapuri and Tamluk, in what are now the states of Uttar Pradesh, Bihar and Bengal. Ujjain, Padmavati, Vanavasi, Vallabhi and Palitana were the main educational centres in central and western India. In the south, students congregated at Madurai, Kanchipuram, Nagarjuna Vidyapeeth and the Kanthaloor University, also called 'the Nalanda of the south'.

Undoubtedly, the most famous university was Nalanda in present-day Bihar. There is evidence that it may have been set up as early as the fifth century BCE, but it was certainly at its apogee during the

Gupta period. More than ten thousand students, who could gain admission only after a tough entrance exam, were in residence there, and they were taught by the best teachers. No expense was spared for the upkeep of the university; apart from royal patronage, both of Hindu and Buddhist kings, the revenues from about a hundred villages was earmarked for this purpose. Students came to Nalanda from as far off as China, Japan, Korea and Tibet. All students were provided with clothes, food, lodging and medical attention. Nalanda had a hundred lecture halls, and three separate buildings for the housing of manuscripts in a separate library quarter known as the 'mart of knowledge'. The atmosphere of the university was one of query and interrogation. Students were encouraged to go beyond merely the accumulation of knowledge to the acquisition of wisdom. This was vouched for by the Chinese-Buddhist scholar, Hieun Tsang, who spent five years at Nalanda. 'The day is not sufficient for asking and answering profound questions,' he wrote. 'From morning till night they engage in discussions; the old and the young mutually help each other.'[58]

The importance given to education, and the encouragement to the study of disciplines with an interrogatory frame of mind rather than learning by rote, was bound to lead to original—even pathbreaking— results. I have touched upon the pioneering work done in the areas of logic, philosophy, linguistics and grammar. Very high standards of excellence were reached also in mathematics, astronomy and technology. The predisposition to interrogate and question phenomena nurtured scientific research. 'Scepticism is an indispensable foundation of what is called "science". The fundamental premise of scientific inquiry is that an unknown truth can be learnt through iterative experimentation and exploration. A school of thought that is dogmatic cannot profess to be scientific'.[59] The Harappan civilisation was notable for its geometrical town planning, its well-fired bricks of a standard size and its methodical system of weights and measures that followed precise ratios—something unique in the ancient world. In Vedic times, the building of altars required detailed arithmetical and geometrical calculations. The *Shulba Sutras*, 'geometrical appendices to the manuals of ritual (*Shrauta Sutras*), include the oldest known formulation of the theorem named after Pythagoras, developed in the context of Vedic altar-building.'[60] The *Surya Siddhanta*, a Sanskrit treatise written sometime around the beginning of the Common Era, calculated that the earth is spherical, and gave near accurate measurements of the earth's and the moon's diameters. According to Carl Sagan, 'Hindu cosmology gives a time-scale for the earth and the universe which is consonant to that of modern scientific cosmology.'[61] The most well-known Hindu astronomer–mathematicians were Aryabhata I (499 CE), his pupil Latadev (505 CE), Varahamihira (550 CE), Brahmagupta (sixth century CE) and Aryabhata II (950 CE). Brahmagupta is credited with developing a symbol for the operation of 'zero', which is a dot underneath numbers. Aryabhata II then used it extensively in the decimal system. What is interesting, and in consonance with the spirit of philosophical enquiry of these times, is that Hindu mathematicians seemed to have 'an intuitive insight into numbers, and their arrangements into patterns and series, from which may be perceived inductive generalizations', and this led to the origin of analytical methods, leading to 'the perfection of the decimal system and … the solution of certain indeterminate equations'.[62]

Charaka, who is believed to have been the court physician to Kanishka around the first century CE, devised the system of Ayurveda (the science of longevity), which was remarkable for its insights into the functioning of the human body and its treatment as a holistic organism, combining both physiological and psychological factors. Several centuries earlier, Patanjali's *Yoga Sutra*, apart from its philosophical content, also devised the science of Hatha Yoga, which was a series of asanas or postures for holistic mental and physical well-being. Sushruta, who wrote the *Sushruta Samhita* (c. 800 BCE), is regarded as the first surgeon of the world. Evidence of his contribution can be gauged by the fact that by the first century CE, specialised surgical equipment in common use 'consisted of twenty types of knives and needles (shastra), thirty probes (shalaka), twenty tubular instruments, and twenty-six articles of dressing (upayantra)'.[63] The important point to note is that scientific achievements did not happen in silos; the urge to explore and expand the horizons of knowledge led to a multiple, simultaneous and multisectoral impact. For instance, anyone who has seen the copper Buddha at Sultanganj in Bihar, or the Iron Pillar now in Delhi, cannot but be amazed at the technological advances made so early in the field of metallurgy.

It is significant that many Hindu constructs and philosophical concepts are finding validation by science today. The notion of Brahman, as the infinite, eternal, nirguna consciousness pervading the cosmos, is being endorsed by the latest discoveries in cosmology, quantum physics and neurology. Cosmologists accept today that the universe is amatra (infinite); that it is anant (eternal), where a Big Bang can be followed by a Big Crunch in an unending cycle of creation, existence and destruction (Kaala); and that it is supremely intelligent, as Brahman is sarvapratyayadarshinin. Quantum physics has established that the empirical reality we take to be real is not what it seems, and following Einstein, even time and space are relative, and matter and energy interchangeable (Maya); and that the universe is inexplicable unless we assume that nirviseshchinmatram (consciousness) is primary and matter is derivative. The latest research in neurology shows that the mind, when in deep meditation, experiences brahmanubhav (unalloyed joy and bliss), which is the nature of the Atman (Self) and Brahman, in complete conformity with the assertions of Advaita. (This subject has been dealt with in great detail in the chapter, 'The Remarkable Validation of Science', in my book, *Adi Shankaracharya: Hinduism's Greatest Thinker*.)

The current preoccupation with ecology and the imperative need to preserve the environment also resonate deeply with the emphasis given by Hindu civilisation to nature. The Shanti Mantra of the Upanishads says: May the heavens be at peace, may the sky be at peace; may the earth be at peace; peace to the water; peace to the trees and nature; may the gods be at peace. The Hindu view treats all matter—animate or inanimate—as the manifestation of the divine. The elements of nature are given special reverence. All life is constituted by the panchabhutas or the five elements of space, earth, fire, water and air. These elements then assumed a divinity of their own. The earth is a goddess, bhumi devi; rivers, as the repositories of water, are also goddesses; fire, agni, is worshipped. The early hymns of *Rig Veda* exalt nature. In the theory of Ayurveda, all vegetation has medicinal value. Vastu Shastra, the science of architecture, emphasises the importance of building in conformity with nature. Pristine forests and mountains are seen as the natural abode of sages. Trees like the tulsi and the peepal are objects of worship. A great number of animals are directly seen as the vahanas or divine vehicles of deities and respected and worshipped. The Sanskrit word for nature, 'Prakriti', connotes primal energy.

Many colonial commentators, and later-day modernists, have ridiculed the Hindu concept of time, according to which the process of creation moves in cycles, and each cycle has four great periods or yugas—satya yuga, dwapara yuga, treta yuga and kali yuga. The Hindu units of time range from microseconds, to trillions of years. The two basic takeaways from Hindu time calculations are one, that time is not linear but cyclical—it begins to end and ends to begin; and two, that conventional time is relative. Both these theses are being validated by science today. As regards the enormous lengths of time associated with yugas, which run into billions of years, and where Pauranic mythology, astronomical calculations and mathematical surmises interface, cosmology today is urging us to relook at our conventional time categories. For instance, the age now scientifically ascribed to the universe makes our human time horizons literally less than in the blink of an eye.

We have been used to measuring time in multiples of thousands of years. The division between before Christ (BC), and after Christ, Anno Domini (AD), may have been replaced by the more secular labels of Common Era (CE) or Before Common Era (BCE), but our imagination of time and antiquity is still in thousands. The age of the universe has been estimated at around 13.7 billion years. The sun, which is the centre of our solar system, has been dated to be about 4.6 billion years old. The sun, and the planets that circle it, make one revolution of the Milky Way in 220 million years. The galaxy closest to ours is Andromeda, some 2.5 million light years away. The galaxy that we can observe as being the most distant from us is about 45 billion light years away. It would take some 13 billion years for light from this distant galaxy to reach us. Why should it be so incoherent if according to our ancient notion of time, a kalpa, or the time between the creation and recreation of a universe, was calculated at 4.32 billion years? Our ancient calculations may on occasions have been close approximations, but they still demonstrate the ability of moving away from the conventional human categories of time to a scale that is remarkably in consonance with what we are discovering about our universe today.

Political science could not be an exception to this spectrum of original thinking. There is a view that, unlike in Greece for instance, ancient India did not develop a well-thought-out political philosophy. In more recent times, colonial theorists and leftist historians—a curious combination—have sought to tarbrush kingdoms and empires of the past under the denigrative rubric of 'oriental despotism'. I think it is time to move away from such hasty generalisations, and examine objectively the evidence at hand.

The Hindu mind believed in rta, which stood for order, custom, dharma, institutions and the rule of law, not necessarily in democratic terms as we interpret them today, but in the nature of an established framework of rules of conduct to enable people to function in an organised society. The converse of rta could only be anarchy, where the law of the jungle prevailed and might alone was right. The description used in ancient texts for such a state of affairs was 'Matsya Nyaya', where the big fish eat the small fish. The institution of kingship was essential to uphold rta and prevent anarchy. The philosophical sanction for the existence of a ruler was thus quite akin, as some historians argue, to Locke's Social Contract theory propounded some two thousand years later, wherein people themselves, in their own self-interest, concur in one among them assuming the power of a ruler to end anarchy and enforce custom and law. As Valmiki's Ramayana says: 'Where the land is kingless the rich are unprotected, and shepherds and peasants sleep with bolted doors.' The Mahabharata also says that people suffering from anarchy chose Manu to be their king, and paid him taxes; in return, kings pledged themselves to maintain the safety and security of their praja or citizens.

In due course, and as a consequence of this need, the institution of monarchy became the central pillar of the state. A state was supposed to have saptanga, the seven elements. These consisted of a king, a council of ministers, a capital city, territory, a treasury, an army and a foreign ally. The need for a more nuanced and elaborate political philosophy became progressively greater as major kingdoms arose. The Mauryan empire was the first near pan-Indian power, as was that of the Guptas later. The king assumed impressive imperial titles like 'chakravartin' or 'digvijaya', conqueror of the world. Works on political theory and practice were composed in parallel with this development. For a civilisation that placed so much stress on ideation and construct, it was hardly likely that this would not happen. The most important texts on political science were Kautilya's *Arthashastra*, the Shanti Parva passage in the Mahabharata, sections of the Ramayana, the Dharmashastras, Thiruvalluvar's *Thirukkural* and later, during the Gupta period, the *Nitisara* (Essence of Politics) of Kamandaka and the *Nitivakyamrita* (Nectar of Aphorisms on Politics) of the Jain scholar, Somadeva Suri. Kautilya mentions that there were at least five schools of political science that predated his work, and names as many as thirteen authors prior to him who had contributed to them.

Broadly, the Hindu view of statecraft reflected two aspects, both diametrically opposed to each other when seen in isolation, but in harmony when taken together. The first focused on the imperative of preserving the state, strengthening the king and keeping enemies, both within and without, at bay. In securing these objectives, statecraft could be cynically unsentimental, ruthless and amoral. Both the

Arthashastra and the Shanti Parva list a series of measures which are entirely devoted to the perpetuation of kingly power, and by extension, of the kingdom. The state was expected to be almost totalitarian, with the theoretical right to interfere in all areas of society, including family matters. To prevent subversion or the possibility of rebellion, espionage was recommended, and elaborate instructions are given in the *Arthashastra* on how to use it effectively. Deception, in order to confuse malcontents, was considered an efficacious tool. This could be taken to extremes by standards of conventional morality. The Shanti Parva, as expounded by the smitten Bhishma lying on a bed of arrows, states: 'When wishing to smite, (the king) should speak gently; after smiting he should be gentler still; after striking off the head with his sword, he should grieve and shed tears.'[64]

Dandaniti, or the power of exemplary punishment, was essential to preserve the supremacy of the state and the maintenance of social order. The *Manusmriti* is categorical on this: 'Punishment alone governs all created beings, punishment alone protects them, punishment watches over them while they sleep; the wise declare punishment to be identical to the law. ... The whole world is kept in order by punishment, for a guileless man is hard to find; through fear of punishment the whole world yields the enjoyment which it owes.'[65] The state must proceed on the assumption that if they can, people will be corrupt. Kautilya says that to find out when a government official is cheating the state is as difficult as knowing when a fish is drinking water.

To protect and promote the interests of the kingdom, the *Arthashastra* sanctions the use of the four upayas or tools—sama (conciliation by negotiation), dama (the use of gifts or inducements), danda (force or punishment) and bheda (creation of dissension). It also speaks of asana, the art of deliberately postponing a decision by sitting on the fence. In moments of crisis, the king was entitled to resort to any means to safeguard the state. According to the Shanti Parva, appadharma, the dharma of dire necessity (to which I have referred earlier), was the right of the state, just as in modern times democratic governments can suspend personal liberties in moments of national emergency. 'The section (of the Shanti Parva) dealing with periods of disaster contains some of the most cold-blooded realism in the history of political theory.'[66]

While one part of political theory was obsessed with power, the other, quite characteristically of the Hindu mind, prescribed the opposite, viz., limits to the use of that power. The king, although all-powerful, was conjoined, for the sake of the power that he wished to retain, to work in conformity with dharma, respect established customs which were considered inviolable, and devote all his energy to the welfare of the people by approximating to the ideal of a rajarishi or a sage–philosopher. The Mahabharata outlines the basic guiding principles for enlightened kingship: 'Let the king first discipline himself. Only then must he discipline his subordinates and his subjects, for that is the proper order of discipline. The king who tries to discipline his subjects without first disciplining himself becomes an object of ridicule in not being able to see his own defects. The interest of his subjects is his sole interest, their well-being his well-being, what is pleasing to them is pleasing to him, and in their good lies his own good. Everything that he has is for their sake, for his own sake he has nothing.'[67]

The *Arthashastra* is equally categorical: 'The king's pious vow is readiness in action, his sacrifice, the discharge of his duty. In the happiness of his subjects lies the king's happiness, in the welfare of his subjects, his welfare. The king's good is not that which pleases him, but that which pleases his subjects.'[68] It is for this reason that the *Arthashastra* prescribes a very exacting regimen for the training of the king, and for the schedule to follow on assuming power. The schedule is so demanding, that if followed literally, the king would be left with less than four-and-a-half hours for sleep and three hours for eating and recreation.

The epics also candidly lay down clearly the vices that a good king must avoid. These include falsehood, uncontrolled temper, carelessness, procrastination, lack of discrimination, laziness, addiction to the senses, taking wrong counsel, inability to keep state secrets and trying to do too much at once. Conversely, the virtues that a king must have are also categorically laid down by Lord Buddha himself. These are dana (liberality, charity and generosity), sila (morality), pariccaga (self-sacrifice for the good of the people), ajjava (integrity, honesty and sincerity), maddava (kindness), tapa (austerity and self-control), akkoda (non-anger and freedom from hatred), ahimsa (non-violence), khanti (forbearance, patience) and avirodha (ruling in harmony).[69]

The king was advised to choose the ministers on merit; the ministers were also advised to state their views fearlessly. The state was expected to be sensitive to public opinion; the people were not to be excessively taxed, and cesses were to be collected, as the *Manusmriti* rather picturesquely puts it, only as a bee would suck honey, or a calf gently drink milk or as a leech sucked blood drop by drop. During the imperial rule of King Ashoka (c. 268–232 BCE), his rock edicts clearly show the ruler's profile as a benevolent patron devoted to the welfare of his people. He believed in lokasamgraha or universal welfare, and one of his edicts says: 'I am not satisfied with hard work or carrying out affairs of state, for I consider my work to be the welfare of the whole world.' A king acquired political legitimacy by winning the approbation of the ruled. Kalidasa defines a ruler's rajadharma as pravartatam prakritihitaya parthivah (working for the welfare of all his people). The *Arthashastra* bluntly says that it is *unrighteous* for a king to do an act which excites popular fury. 'The Mahabharata explicitly sanctions revolt against a king who is oppressive or fails in his function of protection, saying that such a ruler is no king at all, and should be killed like a mad dog'.[70] The epic also says that an undeserving heir, even if he or she is the only child, should never ascend the throne.

Political texts, most notably the *Arthashastra*, provide evidence of an elaborate administrative structure that extended up to the village. Great attention was given to the affairs of the treasury, the readiness of the army and to foreign policy. Realpolitik was the essence of diplomacy. Kings were to assume that neighbouring kingdoms were natural enemies, while neighbours beyond neighbours were natural allies. There is detailed consideration on how to deal with foreign kingdoms depending on an assessment of their armed strength and the state of their internal stability. For instance, it was considered strategically expedient for a weak king to defer to a stronger neighbour; if a king is defeated in battle, the aim should be to retain the kingdom by paying due homage to the conqueror. In victory, there was consensus that vanquished kings should be made vassals but reinstated in their kingdoms, and respect given to the customs and traditions of the conquered people.

Along with the rise of kingdoms there were also 'republics' ruled by an assembly of elders, where decisions were taken by consensus rather than a royal fiat. The judgement is out on how far such republics were actually democratic in their functioning, but there is little doubt that non-monarchical states existed, and that rule by consent rather than command was their strength. The most well-known of these was the Vrijjian confederacy of which the Licchavi tribe was a part. Lord Buddha himself is said to have been an admirer of the Licchavis, advising his disciples to study the working of the assembly of the Licchavis. So long as they retained their traditions, they could not be defeated, he told the Mauryan king Ajatashatru, who was seeking to conquer them. There was, obviously, conflict between the rapidly growing kingdoms and the independently minded confederacies. In the *Arthashastra*, Kautilya, who supported monarchy and the further expansion of centralised imperial kingdoms, strongly supported their destruction. On the other hand, the Shanti Parva supported these states, and sought their preservation. It seems quite clear that at one time these relatively more democratic polities were a significant factor in politics. Coins and inscriptions indicate that they continued to survive, and even flourish, especially in western India, until the fifth century CE.

The deeply ugly factor amidst this brilliant multisectoral canvas of ideas, constructs and concepts was the disfiguring institution of caste discrimination. Its origins are supposedly traced to the Purusha-sukta or the Purusha hymn of the *Rig Veda*. The operative lines are: 'When they divided Purush, into how many parts did they apportion him? What do they call his mouth, his two arms, and thigh and feet? His mouth became the Brahmana; his arms were made into the Rajanya; his thighs the Vaishya; and from his feet the Shudras were born.'[71] At the time when this was composed, it did not mandate a prescriptive hierarchy. 'It is expressly stated in the (complete) text that no part of the whole may claim exclusive importance and superiority over the others; collaboration and exchange of services are the essence of this organismic theory, the various organs of the projected Purusha body-image are related in structural consistency'.[72] It is likely that in the initial centuries that followed, caste was not exclusionist; it was—as Lord Krishna states in the Mahabharata—the creation of four varnas on functional grounds and in accordance with guna or attributes; birth as the assumption of caste is not mentioned.

Recent scientific studies in genetics seem to support this view. Tony Joseph, who has extensively studied DNA-related historical evidence, says categorically: 'The caste system in India is *not* coterminous with the arrival of the "Aryans" in the sub-continent. It fell in place around the ankles of Indian society only about two millennia later. And by the time it came about, intermingling had already taken place to varying degrees.'[73] Nor was the initial functioning of the varna system so discriminatory. For instance, both the Ramayana and the Mahabharata were written by rishis who were not born of Brahmin parents—Valmiki's father was a Shudra and Ved Vyas was born to a fisherwoman. In the Mahabharata, there are passages which expressly repudiate caste barriers. When Bhrigu tells Bharadvaja 'that caste divisions relate to differences in physical attributes of different human beings, reflected in skin colour, Bharadvaja responds not only by pointing to the considerable variations in skin colour *within* every caste, but also by the more profound question: "We all seem to be affected by desire, anger, fear, sorrow, worry, hunger and labour; how do we have caste differences then?" There is also a genealogical scepticism expressed in another ancient document, the *Bhavishya*

Purana: "Since members of all the four castes are children of God, they all belong to the same caste.'"[74] Amish Tripathi also points out that even a shruti text like the *Jabali Upanishad* was written by Jabali, who is said to have been born to an unwed Shudra mother and his father's name was unknown.[75]

The caste system acquired its oppressive features around the first century CE, when the Dharmashastras were misused by vested interests to enforce an iron-cast social hierarchy. Certain passages in the *Manusmriti* were used to give dharmic sanction to exclusion, exploitation and subjugation, although the smriti itself neither stands for religious sanction, nor is it a consistent text. Possibly because of its textual variations we have examples, even later, of the bending of strictly endogamous rules. 'So many kings were of Shudra or Brahmin origin rather than Kshatriyas that by the time the Muslim rulers reached India they found it difficult to make a correct identification of either a class or a caste among their opposite numbers.'[76] Romila Thapar also accepts that 'the actual working of the caste in Indian society permitted of variations, in accordance with local conditions,'[77] which could not be inferred from a literal reading of the Dharmashastras. At the philosophical level too, it was but natural that proponents of the powerful Advaita school like Adi Shankaracharya would oppose caste discrimination. If Brahman is pervasive in all things—animate and inanimate—then how could human beings be of different categories? This is why Shankara in his *Manishapanchakam*, said to have been composed on the spot when he encountered a chandala (or person of the lowest caste) in Kashi, exclaims: Chandalo stu sa tu dvijo stu gururityesa manisha mama: Whosoever has the knowledge of the supreme Brahman, is the preceptor, be he a chandala or a Brahmin.

However, in spite of such high-minded protestations, there is no denying that the working of caste in actual social practice was a pervasive evil. It was—and is—an indelible blot on the civilisational legacy of India; it kept large parts of the populace institutionally cut-off from the many achievements of Hindu India, and also unleashed inhuman suffering for no other reason than the accident of birth.

The same gulf between theory and practice can be seen with regard to the status and respect accorded to women. At the level of philosophy, Hinduism, as I have discussed, gave great importance to Devi, the representative of the cosmic powers of Shakti. Women as the symbols of that Shakti should likewise have been held in great esteem. It would seem that in the early period of ancient India, this indeed was the case. The *Brihadarayanka Upanishad* recounts the episode where in a large assembly of learned men called by King Janaka of Vidheha, the lady Gargi openly debates with the most prominent scholar and sage, Yajnavalkya. Her questions irk the venerable teacher at one point, but Gargi persists, and stops only when her questions are answered. Yajnavalkya's wife, Maitreyi, is also cited for her profoundly important question to her husband. Contemplating retiring to the forests, Yajnavalkya wants to make a settlement between Maitreyi and his second wife, Katyayani. At this point, Maitreyi, asks him whether wealth can guarantee immortality. Yajnavalkya says no, it cannot, to which Maitreyi asks him to tell her what she can do to achieve immortality, and the sage obliges by speaking at length about the Atman and the Jiva. Quite clearly, women were accepted interlocutors in such matters, at a level of equality.

The Mahabharata too has strong women who follow what they think is right. Draupadi may have been put at stake and lost by Yudhishtara in the famous dice game, but she is hardly the reticent or abashed woman when she is brought into the assembly of men to be gambled away. She questions the morality of the proceedings, and asks the fundamental question—did Yudhishtara have the right to put her on stake? If he had lost his own freedom first, how could he decide what to do with her? For a woman to speak with such freedom and assertion in an assembly of men is an indication that women were not mere doormats. Draupadi was, of course, a member of the royal family, but the inference can be drawn that there was social sanction for women to voice their views fearlessly even when an attempt was being made to humiliate them. The epic also records how Draupadi strongly argues with Yudhishtara to take to arms to avenge the injustice meted out to the Pandavas by the Kauravas.

There are other early texts too which provide evidence of the relatively equal status of women. The *Satpatha Brahmana* states that a woman is half her husband. This is in conformity with the concept of ardhanarishwara, where divinity is physically depicted as androgynous, half male and half female. We find injunctions in some texts on the need to honour and worship women; the gods themselves are displeased if women are not accorded due respect, and retribution for violation of this injunction is assured. The *Arthashastra*, one of the most comprehensive texts on contemporary practices of the period, records that in Mauryan times, women could be bodyguards to the king, serve in the administration, choose an ascetic's life and donate to temples or monasteries out of their free will and using their own money.

However, there is little doubt that by the time the *Manusmriti* was written around the second century CE, the position of women had considerably eroded, and the sway of a patriarchal society fully established. The *Manusmriti* says: 'A girl, a young woman, or even an old woman, should not do anything independently, even in her own house. In childhood a woman should be under her father's control, in youth under her husband's, and when her husband is dead, under her son's. She should not have independence.'[78] It also has injunctions such as this: 'A virtuous wife should constantly serve her husband like a god, even if he behaves badly, freely indulges his lust and is devoid of any good qualities.'[79] However, the *Manusmriti* itself is not a homogenous text, and contradicts itself often, indicating that it had more than one author. For instance, the text at one point says that a dvija man and a Shudra woman should not marry. But it also sanctions property to be given to a Shudra wife married to a 'higher' caste. Similarly, it forbids widow remarriage, while at the same time fixing a length of time that a widow must wait for a husband who is missing, before she remarries. Notwithstanding such contradictions, there was, starting around the beginning of the Common Era, an organised attempt to sanctify through social sanction, the complete subjugation of women. This was a condemnable derogation from the earlier freedom, respect and equality that they seemed to have enjoyed.

An objective evaluation of Hindu civilisation must accept such failings, and any attempt to gloss over them, or whitewash them, are retrograde and unforgiveable. These faults have been used by critics to discredit the other achievements of this epoch, and quite rightly so. The need to bring about much delayed and imperative social reform within Hindu society is further discussed later. Yet, in spite of such unforgiveable failings, the overall achievements of this period of our history are truly remarkable, and are crying out for a much delayed recognition. What we need to realise is that across the length and breadth of Bharatvarsha, there evolved, over millennia, a civilisation that showed a profound application of mind to every aspect of organised as well as abstract human behaviour. It demonstrated the capacity of great and courageous divergent thinking, refusing to restrict itself to simplistic certitudes, and a willingness to wade deep into concepts and constructs that challenged conventional thought. The canvas of ideas it grappled with, and synthesised and internalised, was vast — metaphysics, philosophy, religion, creativity, aesthetics, sociology, ethics, science, political theory, foreign policy, war-planning, economics, commerce — and the conduct of human life itself. What was notable was the spirit of eclecticism that characterised it, and its openness to dialogue, debate and dissent. In the next chapters, I shall examine what was the impact on this civilisation of the Turkic invasion, and later of British colonisation.

4

THE ISLAMIC CONQUEST

The conquest of India by foreigners, starting with the seventeen invasions of Mahmud Ghazni (r. 1001–1025 CE), and the subsequent establishment of the Ghurid empire in Delhi under Mohammad Ghori in 1202 CE, left Hindu India physically destroyed and psychologically traumatised. Earlier, invaders like the Greeks led by Alexander conquered the northernmost areas in the fourth century BCE, and following his death, a series of subsidiary Greek invasions continued for the next 400 years. In 57 BCE, the Sakas, a foreign tribe from Central Asia, also made their entry, albeit briefly. These invasions and conquests saw subjugation and loss of lives. But the Hindu civilisation had never seen conquerors like the Islamic Turkic invaders, who were so blindly committed to the destruction of a culture, so fanatically driven by a belief in the superiority of their religion, so unrelenting in their hatred for those not belonging to it and so passionate about the need to convert the unbelievers.

The purpose in saying this is not to excavate history to create acrimonies in the present, but to be truthful to history. There has been, especially after 1947, a concerted, organised and deceitful attempt to gloss over the facts of history in the false belief that this will be in the interest of preserving secularism in India. However, we are now seeing a backlash against this dishonesty. The truth about what actually happened needs to be accepted in order to go beyond it, towards the imperatives of strengthening our multireligious and plural republic.

It would be useful to examine some of the arguments given to falsely underplay the magnitude of destruction and violence of the Islamic conquerors. Marxist historians have asserted that Muslims did not wreak havoc and plunder, but that Hindus themselves preferred the egalitarianism guaranteed by the Shariat to the social discrimination of the Smritis. This is simply untenable. There was no question of a democratic choice being given to the conquered Hindus. The invaders believed that they were the chosen ones, the believers, and that those who were not were kafirs, unbelievers, beyond the pale. The territory of the kafirs was dubbed Dar-al-Harb, a place that needed to be conquered by the sword to make it Dar-al-Islam, the land of Islam. There was, indeed, social oppression in Hindu society in the form of the caste system, and I have acknowledged this earlier, but it is an absurd quantum jump of illogic to conclude from this that Hindus were willing to en masse and happily convert to Islam, or volitionally choose to support those who broke their temples, pillaged their homes, ruthlessly killed them and destroyed their culture.

Motivated apologists have other unconvincing theories also. One of these, propounded by the late Professor Mohammad Habib of the Aligarh Muslim University, sought to extenuate the extent of savagery by arguing that it was motivated by the 'lust for plunder', which any conqueror would display. In his book, *Sultan Mahmud of Ghaznin*, first published in 1924, he discounted, therefore, the repeated destruction of Hindu temples. It could be true that temples were attacked because they were also the repositories of great wealth; but it is stretching the imagination to believe that fanatical hostility against non-believers was not a motivation. The unfortunate fact is that this attempt to downplay Islamic religious bigotry was sanctified by people of intellectual eminence and erudition like Jawaharlal Nehru. In his book *Glimpses of World History*, Nehru writes in a letter to his daughter Indira, that Mahmud Ghazni was 'hardly a religious man', and that he admired the architecture of Hindu temples.[1] However, he omits to mention what Professor Habib himself acknowledges, that Mahmud gave instructions to burn down hundreds of temples.

It is also argued that the Turkic invaders cannot be singled out for attacking those of another faith; Hindus too destroyed Buddhist and Jain places of worship. However, I do not believe that Hindus ever attempted the destruction of Buddhist and Jain religious sites anywhere near the level of desecration wrought by the Muslim conquerors. There may have been some cases of violence between the Indic faiths, but—as I have painstakingly argued earlier—the overwhelming historical evidence establishes beyond the slightest doubt that Buddhism and Jainism flourished in India within the overall broad-based world view of Hinduism, and that Hindu kings—far from being hostile to these two faiths—were both patrons of their viharas and monasteries, and even professed believers in their doctrine. In any case, citing one 'wrong'—for which there is very little evidence—as exculpation for another, is hardly an argument worth countenancing.

The most popular theory among 'secularists' is that the level of atrocities, and the targeted attack against Hindu culture, civilisation and religion, consists largely of 'poetic exaggeration' since evidence of this has come from Muslim court chroniclers whose job was to extol the ruler and magnify the glories of his conquering prowess. Even if we admit that some part of the testimonies of this nature allowed for hyperbole, no objective historian can deny the extent of destructive iconoclasm that is inferable from the accounts. A.K. Warder, Professor of Sanskrit and Indian Studies, University of Toronto, who has no interest in whitewashing either side of the conflict, writes: 'The Turkish conquests of more than half India between 900 and 1300 were perhaps the most destructive in human history. As Muslims, the conquerors aimed not only to destroy all other religions but also abolish secular culture.'[2] Will Durant, the well-known chronicler of civilisations, is as categorical: 'The Mohammedan conquest of India is probably the bloodiest story in history ... its evident moral is that civilization is a precious thing whose delicate complex of order and liberty, culture and peace may at any time be overthrown by barbarians.'[3] The degree of physical destruction is vouched for by noted art historian Heinrich Zimmer too, who laments that in north India 'very little survives of the ancient edifices that were there prior to the Muslim conquest: only a few mutilated religious sites remain.'[4]

Amartya Sen concedes that 'the slash and burn culture of the Muslim invaders ... devastated several cities and ruined many temples, including particularly famous ones in Mathura, Kanauj, and (Somnath).'[5] He also acknowledges the account of the Arab–Iranian traveller Alberuni who accompanied Mahmud to India, of this carnage. 'Mahmud utterly ruined the prosperity of the country, and performed these wonderful exploits, by which Hindus became like atoms of dust scattered in all directions.'[6] However, he believes that the Hindutva movement is deliberately highlighting Muslim destruction 'through motivated selection and purposefully designed emphases as well as frequent exaggeration'.[7] He is in a hurry to move away from the barbarism of the Muslim invasion to the undeniable and welcome syncretic elements of Hindu–Muslim culture that developed much later and over time.

It is possible that some politically affiliated sections of Hindu society are seeking to deliberately dwell on Muslim atrocities of the past in order to create religious divisions and exploit them for their own benefit. Such an approach is wrong and needs to be countered. However, it is equally wrong to gloss over history and falsify it for present-day 'secular' imperatives. The suppression of historical truth, which was part of a planned design by a combination of politicians, historians and commentators for decades after 1947, is leading now to a backlash among Hindus which is far more inimical to the preservation of secularism. However laudable the end goal may be, historical truths cannot be erased or denied or glossed over, because evasion and suppression creates an equal and more dangerous counter-reaction, especially when incontrovertible proof of what was sought to be hidden begins to surface. Reconciliation with history is best done through acceptance, not by evasion or supression.

Today, a mass of evidence has been collected on the relentless cultural and physical decimation carried out, not only by the initial invaders, but for centuries afterwards under the empires they set up in India. Sita Ram Goel catalogues this in his two-volume work, *Hindu Temples: What Happened to Them*.[8] The evidence—archeological, literary and epigraphic—hardly leaves any room for doubt on this score. As mentioned earlier, Muslim rulers were fond of court historians keeping a record of their rule. These records, even if one discounts the flowery language and the need to glorify the patron, recount in great and specific detail the relentless destruction of temples, libraries and cultural artefacts that were the living heartbeat of the civilisation that existed before. Temples in their thousands were razed to the ground; deities were mutilated; exquisite sculptures both in stone and metal were smashed; knowledge centres were demolished. Maulana Minhaj-us-Siraj, the thirteenth-century historian, recounts in his *Tabaqat-i-Naziri* that Mahmud's 'illustrious deeds became manifest unto all mankind within the pale of Islam when he converted so many thousands of idol-temples into masjids'.[9] According to him, Mahmud took away the idol from Somnath and had it broken in four parts; one of these was interred at the entrance of the main mosque in Ghaznin and another at the gateway to the Sultan's palace. The Quwwat-al-Islam mosque, built in Delhi at the Qutub Minar by Qutubuddin Aibak, still has a plaque that says: 'This fort was conquered and the Jami Masjid built in the year 587 (1192 CE) by the Amir (Aibak) … may Allah strengthen his helpers. The debris of 27 idol temples … were used in the construction of the mosque.' In the early thirteenth century, Bakhtiyar Khilji destroyed the universities of Odantapuri, Vikramshila and Nalanda in Bihar. Nalanda was among the most prestigious learning centres of the world, and the world's first entirely residential university. It had ten thousand students and two thousand teachers. An entire generation of scholarship was wiped out when Khilji massacred the students and the teachers. The library at Nalanda, which is said to have contained nine million valuable manuscripts and represented the institutional wisdom of centuries, was put on fire and continued to burn for months after his attack. Many more recorded examples can be provided of this religious fanaticism and vandalism, but suffice to say that the collective impact of this onslaught nearly destroyed Hindu civilisation, and if it has continued to survive, the credit must go to the reservoirs of resilience and adaptation within it, and not to any lack of effort on the part of the new rulers.

Falsified history nurtures its own mythologies. A breed of writers and intellectuals still persist in trying to portray the Islamic invasion as some kind of great syncretic carnival, where the invaders came and partook of the local sweetmeats, and the conquered had a happy morsel of biryani, while both sat down to work out the Ganga-Jamuni tehzeeb that we so value today. The bathos of this imagined utopia works only on the ignorance of facts or deliberate distortion. The case of Amir Khusrau (1253–1325 CE) is instructive. Many people believe that he was a mystic, a Sufi poet, the spiritual disciple of his contemporary, the great Sufi saint Nizamuddin Auliya; he is regarded as the progenitor of Hindavi, a language that moved away from Persian and dipped liberally into Braj Bhasha, the language of the common masses; he is seen as having enabled Khari Boli, the precursor to the Hindi spoken today; he is also widely known as the 'father' of Urdu and the qawwali, and possibly the inventor of the sitar and the tabla; his admirers have given him the title of 'Tuti-e-Hind' or the Parrot of India; his love for India has been extolled; and his qawwalis are still very popular across India.

But there is another aspect to Amir Khusrau. He was a prominent member of the court of five Sultans who ruled from Delhi, the most important among whom was Allauddin Khilji. In this capacity, he wrote extensively about their conquests and victories and their destruction of the temples of the infidels. In his book, *Khaizan ul Futuh*, he describes how 'the kick of Islam' destroyed the beautiful temple of the dancing Shiva at Chidambaran. When Malik Kafur, Allauddin's general, attacked the Chidambaran temple—to exactly quote Amir Khusrau's triumphant language—'the heads of brahmans and idolators danced from their necks and fell to the ground at their feet, and blood flowed in torrents. The stone idols called Ling Mahadeo, which had been established a long time at the place and on which the women of the infidels rubbed their vaginas for satisfaction, these, up to this time, the kick of Islam had not managed to break. The Musalmans destroyed all the lings and Deo Narain fell down, and other gods who had fixed their seats there raised their feet and jumped so high that at one leap they reached the fort of Lanka.'[10]

The same tone and language is there in his descriptions of other such desecrations.

Amir Khusrau is an interesting case study. Undoubtedly, his creative output shows that he had assimilated some aspects of Hindu civilisation (his mother was a Hindu), especially in the areas of language and music. At the same time, he provides sufficient proof of his approval of the destruction of Hindu temples and his hostility to the faith of the infidels. Unfortunately, those who seek to whitewash history, dwell only on his contribution to the composite 'secular' culture of India. This distortion of history through deliberate amnesia is wrong and needs correction, because it is becoming increasingly futile to hide the truth. The correct appraisal would be to appreciate his cultural contributions to the ultimate development of a syncretic culture, while accepting that this did not change his hostility to the Hindu religion, nor did it represent any reduction or mitigation in the continued destruction by Muslim rulers of Hindu religious and cultural artefacts.

The great Mughal emperor Akbar (1556–1605 CE) is frequently cited as the example of the tolerance and intermingling of Hindu and Islamic culture. It is true that he showed an eclectic side to Islamic rule hitherto not in evidence. He abolished the jiziya tax on Hindus, was married to the Hindu princess of Amber, had Hindus like Birbal and Todar Mal as key ministers in his court, celebrated Hindu festivals like Diwali and Dussehra, allowed Hindus to have their own judicial courts and personal laws, was a follower of the more inclusive Chishti school of Sufism and was fond of open religious discourse between scholars of different faiths under a platform he created, the Din-i-Ilahi. His religious liberalism can be gauged from his pronouncement that the wisdom of Vedanta is the wisdom of Sufism, and his belief that all religions are either equally true or equally illusionary.

However, selecting him as the emblem of the nature of Islamic rule in India requires caution. More than three centuries after the advent of the Muslim invasion, a dilution of the ferocious iconoclasm that marked the original Turkic invaders could be expected, especially since Akbar's wife was Hindu. However, there is recorded evidence that in spite of this, Akbar converted temples to mosques and demolished temples such as at Nagarkot in Himachal Pradesh. Moreover, his religious broadmindedness was staunchly opposed by the powerful orthodox Islamic clergy, the ulama, who declared him a heretic, and issued a fatwa for all Muslims to revolt against him. This certainly indicates that his personal tolerance in matters of religious faith was not shared by other members of the ruling Muslim elite, which may have been kept at bay by the emperor, but was far from being emasculated, as the rule of subsequent Mughal emperors clearly brings out.

Akbar's successor, Jahangir, already showed signs that his father's broadmindedness was more personal than an institutionalised policy. Jahangir had little appreciation for Hinduism, or for inter-religious dialogue. Historical records show that he reverted to the practice of destroying temples—a Durga temple at Kangra and a Vishnu temple at Ajmer are notable examples. He also ordered that no new Hindu temples were to be built. His son and emperor, Shah Jahan, was openly intolerant. 'He discriminated against non-Muslims and destroyed many Hindu temples, seventy in Varanasi alone. In Kashmir, he demolished the ancient temple at Anantnag ("The Serpent of Infinity"), a name of the cosmic cobra that Vishnu rests upon, and renamed the town Islamabad. ... When he built the great Jami Masjid, in Delhi, he included a rather miscellaneous arcade made of disparate columns from twenty-seven demolished Hindu temples.'[11]

Aurangzeb (1605–1707 CE), the next emperor, was viciously hostile to Hindus and Hinduism. He reimposed the jiziya tax on Hindus, restored the levy on Hindu pilgrims, increased taxes on Hindu merchants, cancelled the few existing endowments to Hindu temples, destroyed Hindu temples with impunity (sixty-nine in Rajasthan alone), demolished Hindu gurukuls, actively encouraged conversions, murdered the Sikh Guru Tegh Bahadur for blasphemy, and deliberately built mosques at some of the holiest Hindu sites, such as the Vishvanath Temple at Varanasi and the Keshava Deo Temple at

Mathura. Not only religion, but culture was also at the receiving end of his narrow Islamic vision. Curbs were put on poetry, music, dancers and musicians, dealing another body blow to the creative resources of the Hindu civilisation and the emerging Hindu–Muslim cultural interaction.

Given this record, it is rather surprising that Dr Amartya Sen claims that Akbar 'laid the formal foundations of a secular legal structure, and of religious neutrality of the state'.[12] Firstly, such a sweeping statement ignores the fact that tolerance for other religions, and state neutrality to people's religious choices, was the practice for centuries during the Hindu period of our history. Hindu empires professed respect for all faiths, were patrons of Buddhism and Jainism and remained largely neutral in the religious choices of their subjects—something which Sen himself cites often. On what basis then does he anoint Akbar as the 'founder' of this tradition? Akbar's laudable religious tolerance was more representative of individual proclivity, and hardly laid the foundations of a 'secular legal structure', as the records of his own successors amply shows. Sen himself acknowledges the historical fact that Akbar's son, Jahangir, revolted against his father for abandoning Islam. It is also true that Abdul Haqq Dehlavi, the most well-known Islamic theologian of that time, dismissed the Din-i-Ilahi as merely an 'innovation' and proudly asserted Akbar's staunch Muslim credentials. Abdul Qadir Badauni, the historian of that age, was also openly hostile to such experimentations.

The interesting question is, why do knowledgeable commentators then resort to this kind of historical selectivity, or make such categorical conclusions from transparently inadequate evidence? In the case of Sen, he makes no secret of his reasons. 'Hindutva critics have sometimes focused particularly on the intolerance of Aurangzeb. ... Indeed, some Hindutva sectarians see historical justice in discriminating against Muslims precisely because Aurangzeb is said to have done the opposite—discriminating against Hindus—in the late seventeenth century.'[13] He is right, of course—history should not be excavated to use the past for violence in the present. But, if

'Hindutva sectarians'—to use Sen's description—excessively highlight Aurangzeb's bigotry, well-intentioned votaries of secularism, like Sen, err on the other side of the extreme, disproportionately valorising Akbar as the template of Muslim rule as a whole. In between these two extremes, truth is the casualty. The aim of both sides becomes not to profile what actually happened in the past, but to give to historical narrative an ideological spin. Neither side is able to convince the other, each side doubts the bona fides of the other, and none of them comes close to constructively moving forward beyond distorted historical reconstruction.

The late Nobel Laureate, V.S. Naipaul, wrote his book *Among the Believers* after extensive travels in the Islamic world. Unlike Amartya Sen, who downplays the destructive religious evangelism of Muslim rule in India, he minces no words about what kind of impact it had. In an interview to the newspaper *The Hindu* in 1998, he said: 'I think when you see so many Hindu temples of the tenth century or earlier disfigured, defaced, you realize that something terrible happened. I feel that the civilization of that world was mortally wounded by those invasions. The Old World was destroyed. Ancient Hindu India was destroyed.'[14] Next year, he reiterated his views in an interaction with the magazine *Outlook*: 'The millennium began with the Muslim invasions and the grinding down of the Hindu-Buddhist culture of the north. This is such a big and bad event that people have to find polite, destiny defying ways of speaking about it. In art books and history books, people write of the Muslims "arriving" in India, as though the Muslims came in a tourist bus and went away again. The Muslim view of their conquest of India is a truer one. They speak of the triumph of the faith, the destruction of the idols and the temples, the loot, the carting away of the local people as slaves. ... The architectural evidence—the absence of Hindu monuments in the north—is convincing enough. The conquest was unlike any that had gone before. There are no Hindu records of this period. Defeated people never write their history.'[15]

In the same interview, Naipaul argues that the Muslim conquerors succeeded in 'the grinding down of Hindu India'. The loot and plunder and destruction, and their religious hostility to non-believers, was not restricted to the original foreign invaders, but a feature of the entire period of Islamic rule. He cites the example of Vijayanagara in this context. 'Let us consider two last dates. In 1565, a year after the birth of Shakespeare, Vijayanagara in the south is destroyed and its great capital city (Hampi) laid waste. In 1592, the terrible Akbar ravages Orissa in the east. This means that while a country like England is preparing for greatness under its great Queen, old India in its sixth century of retreat, is still being reduced to non-entity. The wealth and creativity, the artisans and architecture of the kingdom of Vijayanagara and Orissa must have been destroyed, their lights put out.'[16] Naipaul's larger point is that such depredations dealt a body blow to the creative impulses of the Hindu civilisation. 'This is where we come face to face with the Indian calamity. When places like Vijayanagara and Orissa were laid low, all the creative talent would also have been destroyed. The current was broken. We have no means of knowing what architecture existed in the north before the Muslims. We can only be certain that there would have been splendours like Konark and Kanchipuram.'[17]

In an article in the UK newspaper, the *Guardian*, writer-historian William Dalrymple attempts to rebut Naipaul's outspoken views. Naipaul's 'jaundiced' view, he argues, was due to the influence of the 'imperial historiography of Victorian Britain', where the British sought to paint the Muslims as plunderers to bring out their own 'civilizing mission'. Vijayanagara, he says, was 'heavily Islamicised by the sixteenth century'. This can be inferred by the fact that 'the Hindu kings of Vijayanagara appeared in public audience, not bare-chested as had been the tradition in Hindu India, but dressed in quasi-Islamic court costume', symbolic, according to him—on the authority of American Sanskrit scholar, Philip Wagner—'of their participation in the more universal culture of Islam'. Vijayanagara had adopted 'many of the administrative, tax-collecting, and military methods of the Muslim sultans that surrounded it—namely, stirrups, horseshoes, horse armour, and a new type of saddle'. Its architecture also showed evidence of the use 'of the arch and the dome of the Islamic north'.[15] Reciprocally, Hindu influences were also discernible in the Islamic sultanates, with whom the Vijayanagara kingdom on occasion entered into strategic alliances.

I am not, however, clear what these arguments prove. Because the kings of Vijayanagara did not appear bare-chested in public, or because they used stirrups or horseshoes, and because, where they felt politically necessary, they aligned themselves with one Muslim sultanate to finesse the other, was Vijayanagara not a Hindu kingdom? Or that, when it was defeated, the Muslim sultans did not savagely destroy the city and, in particular, attack its remarkable temples? To quote a few instances of Hindu–Muslim syncretism in architecture, in dress or in administrative practices, is more an acknowledgement of the unavoidable fusions wrought over centuries, and not a change in the mindset of Muslim conquerors against kafirs and their practice of destroying Hindu cultural and religious artefacts.

It is a moot point too whether the Vijayanagara kings, on conquering a Muslim sultanate, would have as relentlessly destroyed mosques. Historical records clearly bring out that Krishnadevaraya (1509–1528 CE)—the most illustrious ruler of Vijayanagara and among the greatest kings India has seen—respected all faiths. He was himself a Vaishnavite, but extended wholehearted patronage to Shaiva, Jain and other sects. He employed Muslims in his army, encouraged them to settle in the capital city and erected a mosque in 1439 for them to pray. For the Muslim officers in his court, he placed a copy of the Koran before his throne so that they could perform the ceremony of obeisance before him without sinning against their religious injunctions, even though the Vijayanagara kingdom was formed with the aim of protecting Hindus and Hindu culture from Muslim attacks. Christian Portuguese also found residence in the capital. The Portuguese traveller, Barbosa, who visited Hampi during Krishnadevaraya's rule, wrote: 'The king allows such freedom that every man may come and go and live according to his own creed, without suffering any annoyance and without enquiry whether he is a Christian, Jew, Moor or Heathen.'

The fact of the matter is that for Muslim rulers to pursue a policy of violent religious intolerance towards the Hindu faith was more a matter of norm than an exception. By contrast, in the Hindu civilisation that preceded their coming, and in the actions of Hindu rulers who survived their onslaught, this kind of destruction of religious sites was more an exception than the norm. I have cited the example of Krishnadevaraya, and the same can be said about, for instance, Shivaji, who founded his kingdom in Maharashtra in 1647 CE. Shivaji captured Bijapur, one of the Muslim sultanates which waged war against Vijayanagara. He took over its treasury, horses and elephants, but did not, as his Muslim chronicler Khafi Khan writes, violate his policy of not desecrating mosques or seizing women.[18]

Sufism, which within the bounds of religious orthodoxy, sought to reinterpret Islam in mystic terms, emphasising the search for truth and advocating spiritual communion over religious ritual, was greatly influenced by Hindu metaphysics and the Bhakti movement that flowered in the centuries following the establishment of Muslim rule. The Sufi movement, whose saints spoke in the language of the common people, enlarged the footprint of Islam in India, especially in rural areas. But the Sufi faith never rejected Islam, and many of its leading figures were vocal supporters—as in the case of Amir Khusrau—of the religious iconoclasm practised by Muslim rulers. Some like Shaikh Ahmad Sirhindi (1564–1624 CE), a prominent representative of the Naqshbandi school of Sufism, strongly protested against Akbar's revocation of the jiziya tax, accused him of sullying the purity of Islam and condemned Guru Nanak and Kabir for not following the Sharia. Sufism, while projecting the gentler face of Islam, was very often—though not always—the other side of the coin of Islamic evangelism. The Sultan's sword, and the Sufi's sermon worked in tandem; the aim of both was the propagation of Islam. When William Dalrymple says that 'Islam in India was spread much less by the sword than by the Sufis,'[19] he is making the mistake of presenting the two as polarities. Firstly, he is overestimating the role of Sufism, which increased its outreach and strengthened its mystic ideology only much later, largely also as a result of the influence of Hindu metaphysics and the Bhakti movement. Secondly, he is underestimating the role of the sword, which—as historical records show—continued its destructive depredations till Aurangzeb, and in periods coterminous with the height of the Sufi movement, which it frequently patronised.

The purpose here is not to denigrate the Sufi movement in India, but to stress the need for balance in appraising its role during the period of Muslim rule. Sufism had many redeeming features, including the emphasis on the primacy of devotion, surrender and the ecstasy of communion with the Almighty. It generally displayed a greater tolerance in religious matters, and the accessibility for people of all faiths to its pirs, aulias and dargahs often tempered the destructive aspect of Muslim rule. But it would be incorrect to argue that it substituted—wholly or even partially—the approach of Muslim rulers to the Hindu faith. In the area of spirituality and philosophy, it did represent the relative fusion of Hindu and Islamic thought, and this cultural exchange was undeniably a definitive outcome in many other areas as well. In over half a dozen centuries of Islamic rule in India, Hindu and Muslim cultures enriched each other in music, poetry, architecture, painting, food, social behaviour, customs and even religious practices. This is the foundation of the Ganga–Jamuni tehzeeb we speak of today, which also makes India unique.

The mistake is to presuppose this cultural exchange as the dominant feature of the Muslim conquest in India with the deliberate aim of glossing over its documented destructiveness, its religious intolerance and the massive damage it caused to Hindu temples and civilisation. The narrative of history is not a binary—one or the other. There was, indeed, a gradual syncretism, as there was, in spite of this, the continuity of a relentless attack based on religious intolerance. Naipaul is right in unambiguously pointing this out. We are talking about telling history as it was, not creating a present where the past is falsely recreated, either by Hindus or by Muslims, or of penalising current-day Muslims for what happened in the past. I don't believe that was the intention of Naipaul either. In his only novel, *A Bend in the River*, the principal protagonist is Salim, a Muslim. His wife, Nadira, is also a Muslim.

The noted writer and film personality, the late Girish Karnad, was however a staunch critic of Naipaul, accusing him of regurgitating Orientalist ideas about Muslims and displaying 'a rabid antipathy to the Indian Muslim'.[20] The argument that an honest appraisal of Muslim rule is 'Orientalist' and influenced by British perspectives, as Dalrymple also argues, holds little water. Are Indians incapable on their own of examining the evidence on record of what transpired during this period? The British have come and gone. Their colonial biases and attempts to see themselves as the civilising power have been thoroughly exposed. They were as destructive of Hindu civilisation as of Muslim rulers. Indians are now attempting to see their history as it was, on the basis of evidence available, and without putting a gloss on historical facts. That gloss cannot be perpetuated by privileging syncretism over destruction, but by trying to see both in perspective.

The 'syncretists', however, often become emotional. 'This is one problem with Mr Naipaul's analysis of Indian culture,' Karnad says. 'He has no music and therefore no conception of what Muslims contributed to our history. If you don't respond to music, then you can't respond to Indian history because the real development of Indian culture has been through music.'[21] We can quibble with Karnad for believing that music is the only prism to record history. However, even if we accept that he uses music as a metaphor to illustrate the contribution of Islamic rule to Indian culture, it does not negate the fact that it was coterminous with a great deal of cultural and religious barbarism. We can express our unconditional appreciation for the qawwali, the khayal style of classical music, the innovation of the tabla and the sitar, the beauty of Urdu, but also need to accept that a great part of the cultural repository of Hindu India was irretrievably lost as a result of Muslim rule. What, after all, is the weighing scale one uses in evaluating history? Do we put the destruction of exquisite temples, Nalanda and the attack on Hindu cultures of learning and art on one side of the scale, and the eventual evolution of khayal classical music on the other? If the later Indo-Islamic architecture had noticeable Hindu motifs, does it mean that temples were not destroyed? If Dara Shikoh, the unfortunate prince who could not succeed to the throne after Shahjahan, expressed genuine appreciation for the Upanishads and had them translated into Persian, does that mean that Aurangzeb, his brother who became emperor and beheaded Dara, was not a bigot? The need is to see both sides of the picture and sensibly conclude that while a great deal of valuable cultural interaction did take place, it unfolded in parallel with a great deal of religious intolerance and wanton savagery.

The well-intentioned desire to see Muslim rule predominantly as a period of cultural synthesis cannot be achieved at the cost of whitewashing history. Such an attempt actually weakens the cause of genuine religious reconciliation. Dalrymple quotes foreign scholars David Gilmartin and Bruce Lawrence who, in their book, *Beyond Turk and Hindu*, assert that medieval Indian civilisation 'was the direct result of its multi-religious character, and the inspired interplay of cross-fertilization of Hindu and Islamic civilization that thereby took place'.[22] True, the period was multireligious, but there is little doubt that Hinduism survived *in spite* of the religious fanaticism of Islam, and that in addition to the 'cross-fertilization of Hindu and Islamic civilization', there was destruction on an unprecedented scale of the Hindu culture that preceded medieval India. The argument of cross-fertilisation becomes a trifle bizarre when Dalrymple goes to the extent of saying that even temples were hardly destroyed. He approvingly quotes Richard Eaton, another contributor to the book *Beyond Turk and Hindu*, who argues that on the basis of 'historicity that seems reasonably certain', only some eighty temples were destroyed during Muslim rule. That too happened only in cases of 'outright military defeat of Hindu rulers', or when 'Hindu patrons of prominent temples committed acts of disloyalty to the Indo-Muslim states they served. Otherwise, temples lying within Indo-Muslim sovereign domains, viewed as protected state property, were left unmolested.'[23]

It is this kind of falsehood, masquerading as historical scholarship, that creates the problem. The untenable claim that in six hundred years of Islamic rule only eighty temples were destroyed mocks the mass of evidence to the contrary—documented, archaeological, epigraphical. One excess leads to another, and votaries of the other extreme depict Muslim rule as only one of devastation and destruction, completely devaluing the significant cultural exchange that was also partly its consequence. Both sides then deliberately discount historical truth, and shadow-box with the fictions they want to live with. The sane alternative is to accept history as it happened, acknowledge the traumatising impact of the Muslim destruction of Hindu civilisation, recognise the inestimable loss that it caused to the collective assets—physical and intellectual—of a very significant part of our history, and accept that a great deal of that destruction was due to the religious fanaticism of the Islamic rulers. Hindus were ruthlessly subjugated and institutionally discriminated against by the Muslim state. The advent of Islamic rule broke the continuity and evolution of a great civilisation; it disrupted the creative rhythm of that remarkable period of history; it destroyed a great deal of its cultural artefacts; and, it provided the first example in Indian history until then, of such widespread and violent religious intolerance. True secularism can only arise from a reconciliation with history, not suppression of truth, for that only serves to strengthen the extremism of the counter narrative. As Amish Tripathi argues: 'Denial invariably leads to repressed truth finding expression in the ugliness of hatred and anger, as we see in some parts of India today. It's healthier in the long run for societies to accept, confront and then learn to handle the truth.'[24]

How did Hinduism survive the onslaught of the proselytising Turkic invaders? This is an important question, since the Islamic rule that followed used the powers of the state to propagate the superiority of Islam and believed in converting as many infidels as possible into its faith. There are examples, like that of Indonesia, where an overwhelmingly Hindu and Buddhist population almost entirely converted to Islam in the space of three centuries after Islamic sultanates were established there at the beginning of the thirteenth century. What was it that happened in India that gave it relative immunity from the proselytising prowess of Islamic rulers who ruled almost the entire country for over six centuries?

The simple answer to this is that Hinduism reinvented itself through the Bhakti movement, enabling a democratic decentralisation of the Hindu faith, so widespread in nature, and so full of ardour and conviction, that it has few parallels in history. Many Hindu temples—which played a pivotal role in the preservation and dissemination of religion—were razed; there did occur a fundamental discontinuity in the cerebral conversations that allowed Hindu civilisation to evolve and rejuvenate itself; centres of learning and repositories of scriptures and commentaries were, indeed, destroyed; the practice of Hinduism in structures hitherto taken for granted received a serious setback; Hindus were discriminated against through instrumentalities like the jiziya and pilgrim taxes. But, Hinduism escaped the confining cage intended to contain it by simply slipping through the crevices. It rediscovered itself, not through the institutional support that it had earlier enjoyed through the patronage of kings, or on the basis of the injunctions of the Brahmanical class, but by embracing the masses of its followers directly. In this process, faith and its perpetuation became part of an inner world of devotion, surrender and personal belief; the formal apparatus of religion became largely superfluous; the priestly class was relatively marginalised; and formal rituals were seen as mostly unnecessary. The net outcome was the reinvention of Hinduism through a powerful reform movement which looked inward rather than outward, and drew its sustenance from the people at large rather than the dictates of a rarefied elite at the top. A rainbow-coloured butterfly of this nature—combining devotional fervour, individual autonomy and social irreverence could hardly be killed by the conqueror's sword.

Hinduism had always been a way of life—it did not have only one book, nor one god, nor one church, nor one set of prescriptive rituals. Such a religion was structured to evade destruction because of the variable nature of its belief systems and practices, and the absence of any one central pillar which, if demolished, could endanger the entire edifice. At the same time, Hinduism had also developed very strong foundations of thought and practice in the millennia prior to the Islamic invasion. An important aspect of this strength was the ability to evolve and adapt. We have seen in detail how the nirguna aspect of divinity transitioned to the philosophical sanction for saguna practice. The foundations of devotional theism were laid by Ramanuja in the eleventh century. In creating space for the devotion to a personal god, Ramanuja, and the philosophers who followed him, were responding to a felt need. The *Bhagwata Purana*, dated to the eighth century, narrated the delightful exploits of Krishna as a child, and his irresistible attractions as a lover. The Krishna of the Bhagwad Gita, written centuries earlier—who had asked for personal surrender from his devotees—now descended from the pedestal of exalted divinity to a god ready for appropriation at a personal level. Jayadeva's *Gita Govinda* (twelfth century), which immortalised the love lore of Radha and Krishna, took this process further. Around the same time as the *Bhagwata Purana*—and even earlier—the sects of the Nayanars and Alvars in the south were propagating a new form of bhakti for Shiva and Vishnu respectively, which dispensed with ritual and formal rites of worship. These developments prior to the Islamic invasion had prepared Hindus for the democratisation and decentralisation of their religion. The *Bhagwata Purana* was translated from the original Sanskrit to almost all the regional languages. There were forty translations in Bengali alone.

The linguistic appropriation by vernacular languages of a religious tradition that was earlier largely propagated through Sanskrit, played a very significant role in ensuring the pan-Indian spread of the Bhakti movement. One of the earliest manifestations of this renaissance was seen in Maharashtra. Jnaneshvara (1271–1296 CE) wrote the *Bhavarthapadika*, also called the *Jnaneshvari*, which was a long commentary on the Bhagwad Gita. Written in Marathi, it soon acquired huge popularity, especially since it was written to a rhyme and metre that could be sung and chanted; its appeal was enhanced by examples and analogies that related to the ordinary life of its lay readers. Jnaneshvara, also known as Jnanadeva, was a member of the Varkari sect which commenced regular, popular pilgrimages to the Vithoba Temple in Pandharpur dedicated to Vishnu. The pilgrims, drawn from all sections of society, participated in spontaneous kirtans during their journey, giving to their faith a new and increasingly popular mass base.

Namadeva (1270–1350 CE), who was born around the same time as Jnaneshvar but lived for five decades more, was also a great devotee of Vithoba. Namadeva's hymns, expressed in commonly understood language, are characterised by a deep and intense devotion that was internalised by Hindus at large.

> I die unless Thou succor bring,
> O haste and come, my God and King!
> To help me is a trifle thing,
> Yet Thou must haste, my God and King!
> O come (how Nama's clamours ring)
> O haste and come, my God and King![25]

Breaking new ground, Namadeva showed scant regard to the hierarchies of caste. His inner circle included a barber, a gardener, a potter, a woman (Janabai, the maid), and even Chokha, an 'untouchable'. His simple but powerful message was that where there was devotion, social hierarchies or ritualistic purity did not matter.

The Muslims razed the temple at Pandharpur, but could not destroy the Bhakti movement. The movement received a new impetus from Eknath (1533–1599 CE), who republished the *Jnaneshvari* and wrote learned commentaries on Valmiki's Ramayana, and the *Bhagwata Purana*. 'But Eknath did more. He invented, as it were, a new form of deep religious life that needed no institutions or monasteries, no resignation from the world. He was a family man, devoted, austere, whose life was regulated around his hearth and his manuscripts, and yet he was a mystic. He showed how, whatever obstacles the Muslims put in the way, the Hindu could aspire to the deepest experience of his religion within the ordinary framework of life. Every day he practiced kirtan, and his songs are part of the Marathi heritage. They have a strong moral basis, are concerned with the simplest aspects of life, yet often soar to great heights of personal mysticism.'[26]

If Namadeva was a Brahmin, Tukaram (1598–1650 CE), arguably the greatest of the Bhakti poets of Maharashtra, came from a humble rural family of grain traders. His hymns, expressed an irresistible longing for the ecstasy of the highest spiritual experience, in the face of which the ritualism and ceremony of organised religion mattered little. In writing of his personal yearning for the union with the Absolute, he transported his audience to a new level of personal interface with religion.

> As on the bank the poor fish lies
> And gasps and writhes in pain,
> Or as a man with anxious eyes
> Seeks hidden gold in vain—
> So is my heart distressed and cries
> To come to thee again
>
> Thou knowest, Lord, the agony
> Of the lost infant's wail,
> Yearning his mother's face to see.
> (How oft I tell this tale!)
> O, at Thy feet the mystery
> Of the dark world unveil![27]

Bengal too was an important centre for the rise and spread of the Bhakti movement. Chandidasa, who lived at the confluence of the fourteenth and fifteenth centuries, wrote in his native Bengali and is regarded by many as the founder of modern Bengali literature. His poetry had an intensity borne out of personal experience. He was the village priest but was deeply in love with a washerwoman named Ramini. It was a liaison deeply frowned upon by the village community, but in keeping with the irreverence towards caste shown by many leading figures of the Bhakti movement, Chandidasa was not willing to disown it. On the contrary, he derived sustenance and inspiration from the story of the love between Radha and Krishna.

Indeed, Krishna and Radha were the focus of other writers too of the Bhakti school. Vidyapati (1352–1448 CE), a younger contemporary of Chandidasa, lived in Mithila, Bihar, and wrote in the language he knew best—Maithili. Surdas (1483–1563 CE) wrote in Braj, the language of the region around Mathura. Braj was also the choice of expression for Bihari (1595–1664 CE), court-poet of Jayasimha, the ruler of the kingdom of Amber in Rajasthan. Govindadasa, in the sixteenth century CE, wrote in Brajaboli, a local dialect having elements of both Bengali and Maithili.

All these poets acquired immense popularity. Their compositions had a sensuous simplicity, deriving strength from being based on the local idiom and turn of phrase. To the masses they provided a scripture that could be comprehended without effort and was thoroughly enjoyable for its lyrical informality. There was a directness of appeal in their writings that invoked an immediacy of response. Their lines sat easily on the tongue of the worshipper. Not surprisingly, the development of kirtans—the fast tempo, community singing of devotional songs—had a direct correlation with the popularity of these works. By this time, Jayadeva's *Gita Govinda* and Bilvamangala's *Krishnalilamrita* (eleventh century CE) had also been translated into other regional languages. The cumulative result was that the worship of Krishna, and especially his love lore with Radha, shifted from the sanctum sanctorum of the temple to the dust and din of daily life. Krishna's sensual love-play made a transition from the refined if passionate milieu of Sanskrit poetics to the earthy and seductive medium of the lingua franca of the masses. Radha and Krishna, humanised by Jayadeva, were now depicted in as many situations as it was possible for human lovers to find themselves in. It was a case of the divine imitating the human, and the human being enriched by the divine. The Lord and his consort were removed from the rarefied atmosphere of lotus-leaved arbours and ethereal jungle thickets, and placed with poetic adroitness in more familiar settings. Their rasa leela continued with unabated ardour, but in new situations that were inspired by—and related to—the humdrum routine of ordinary people. Thus, Chandidasa's Krishna saw Radha as she emerged from the river in the village, twisting her sari to dry like any village belle would do:

Who was that girl?
Friend, who was that girl
Inflaming the river
With her fair skin?
The gold necklace
On the peak of her breasts
Shone as the moon on the mountain snow,
The darkness in tears,
The shadows of the moon,
A flood of black hair rolled up on her hips.
She rose from the river
Like a slice of the moon,
Glistening in twilight dark.
As I stood watching
And losing myself,
She walked away wringing and twisting my soul
Together with her sari—dripping, blue.
My heart still shivers in a fever of love.[28]

Bihari's eyes saw Krishna and Radha exchange secret messages as Radha sat in a gathering of elders:

When he saw Radha
Sitting among the elders
You know what the wily Krishna did?
He brushed his forehead with a lily
Implying
'Say yes, dear beloved,
See, I'm even falling at your feet!'
Clever Radha
Consenting,
Flashed her mirrored ring
At the sun
And hid away her hand
In the mounds of her breasts
As though to say:
'When the sun sets under the hills
Lover, I will come to you.'[29]

In the popular psyche, Krishna and Radha became the universal symbol for the lover and the beloved. Krishna was the ideal nayak, hero, and Radha the ideal nayika, heroine. As a genre, the poetry about them came to be known as riti-kala or sringara-kala. The furtively ecstatic world of Radha, the woman in love, is of particular interest to these poets. Her transition from adolescence to womanhood, her inner turmoil, her uncertainties, the simplicity and intensity of her feelings, the shadow play between desire and her innate shyness—these themes fascinated them. Surdas described Radha's first meeting with Krishna—the burning sensual denouement under the as yet opaque surface of innocence:

'Who are you, my fair one?' the Dark One asks,
'And where is your family, your house?
You've never been seen in Braj lanes.'
'Never you mind—I stay in my yard
And play behind my gate, never venture out
Where, I've heard Nanda's boy is bound
To steal our butter and curd.'

'Now what of yours could I possibly steal?
Come on, let's both of us play.'
The gourmet of love, Sur's Lord, with his words
Disarms poor Radha, simple girl.[30]

What we are seeing here is the appropriation of divinity to a personal level of devotion that is quite beyond formal structures of religion. Surdas was the foremost disciple of Vallabhacharya, or Vallabha (1471–1531 CE), a Telugu philosopher who propounded the Shuddha Advaita doctrine, and founded the Krishna sect of Vaishnavism in the Braj region of northern India. Vishambhar Mitra, universally known as Chaitanya (1486–1534 CE), was the Bengali mystic who took Vaishnava bhakti to new heights. For his followers, he was Shri Krishna Chaitanya Mahaprabhu, the very incarnation of Krishna. Chaitanya argued that divinity was characterised by several shaktis, the three principal ones being jiva shakti, maya shakti and svarupa shakti. Individual souls were the emanation of the Lord's jiva shakti; the manifest world was a creation of the Lord's maya shakti; the expression of the Lord's own bliss was svarupa shakti. The relation between these shaktis was one of achintyabhedabheda or inconceivable oneness and difference, wherein each was different, but all were one with Krishna. For Chaitanya, Krishna was not only the avatar of Vishnu, but the highest manifestation of the divine, its supreme rasa. In this aspect, when he unites with Radha, the highest Shakti, the result is an irresistible experience of madhurya or sweetness, which is what the devotee must aspire to. It is said that for the evolution of his philosophy, Chaitanya sent six Goswamins, or theologians, to Vrindavan, to actually experience this madhurya. His form of worship required not temples or abstruse scriptures, but ecstatic singing and dancing, and the chanting of the Hare Krishna Maha mantra, the essence of the Gaudiya Vaishnava sect he founded. While his focus was not expressly on social reform, his practice of bhakti rejected the distinctions of caste, and promoted a devotional egalitarianism that greatly increased its attraction.

The many-splendored personality of Krishna, the butter-stealing adorable child and the passionate lover, lent itself easily to the rise of the Bhakti cult around him. But *maryada purushottam* Rama was also included in a very significant way. Ramananda (1400–1470 CE) was probably born in south India, where he was a follower of the Vaishnava order set up by the philosopher Ramanuja. Later he migrated to Varanasi and established his own sect, the Ramanandis. Notwithstanding the popularity of Valmiki's Ramayana and other works based on the epic, there is no proof of a cult exclusively devoted to Rama prior to this. Ramananda looked upon Rama as the supreme God; Sita, his shakti, and Hanuman, his faithful devotee, were part of this devotional triad. 'Ramananda was strongly opposed to the restrictions and injustices of caste. He threw his sect open to all, and his twelve personal disciples are said to have included women, an "outcaste", and even a Muslim. This frank egalitarian basis and the exclusive use of the vernacular set the sect apart from many others.'[31] Unfortunately, like much other valuable Hindu heritage lost following the Muslim invasion, only one hymn of Ramananda is extant.

The person who let loose a tidal wave of bhakti for Rama was Goswami Tulsidas (1532–1623 CE). His magnum opus, the *Ramcharitmanas*, which literally translates into 'the splendid lake of Rama's exploits', is arguably the greatest ode to Lord Rama. Like other writers of the Bhakti movement, Tulsidas, although well-versed in Sanskrit, chose to write in Awadhi, the language of the masses in northern India. Following the basic narrative of Valmiki, Tulsidas's *Ramcharitmanas* was an epic in itself—12,800 lines divided into 1,073 stanzas and seven kandas or sections. It also ranks among the greatest works of literature in the world, using a scintillating rhyme and metre that could be memorised and chanted with ease by the common devotee. Its soaring popularity has led it to be compared to the Bible for most Hindus, especially in north India. Mahatma Gandhi regarded it 'as the greatest book in all devotional literature'.

Tulsidas was, indeed, partial to the Brahman class, to which he himself belonged. However, his main contribution was to provide a philosophical argument which, overarching the dichotomy between nirguna and saguna, rendered the redeeming powers of bhakti to Rama as the sole and only fulfilling spiritual pursuit—Aguna saguna dui Brahma sarupa, akath, agaath, anaadi anoop: Nirguna and saguna are two aspects of the same Brahman—unspeakable, unfathomable, eternal and unparalleled. But unalloyed bhakti to Rama is greater than both, because even the mere recital of his name is a guarantor of salvation. There is no need, therefore, to waste time on the philosophical quibble over nirguna or saguna—Binu pada chalai sunai binu kana, kara binu karam karai bidhi nana, anana rahita sakal rasa bhogi, binu bani bakata bada jogi: The devotee immersed in pure devotion can walk without feet, hear without ears, perform tasks without hands, enjoy all taste without a sense of taste and speak eloquently without a tongue. Tulsidas does not negate the nirguna Brahman. But his argument is—Aguna, aroopa, alakh aj joi, bhagata prema bas saguna so joi: Even Brahman—attribute-less, formless, imperceptible and unborn—takes the form of Rama due to the bhakt's devotion.

Tulsidas is in his element explaining the power of bhakti which, for him, is the greatest and easiest path to redemption for an ordinary mortal. It is a complete and independent path to salvation; it is above the dialectics of jnana and vijnana, above knowledge and reasoning. Indeed, knowledge is subordinate to bhakti. The path of bhakti is easily accessible, where the grace of the Lord is effortlessly obtained. Bhakti creates detachment to worldly things, and fills the devotee with divine love. In a beautiful chaupai or quartet, Tulsidas says that when a devotee's body vibrates with joy in singing the praises of Rama, when the speech quivers with ecstasy, and the eyes brim over with tears in surrendering to Rama, and he or she is completely free from pride, desire and ego, then Rama is entirely accessible to the devotee. In the face of this joy, nothing else matters. Rama, in the words of Tulsidas, says exactly this to Shabri, who belonged to the lowest scale of the social ladder but had spent her entire life in selfless devotion to him—Jati paati kula dharma badhai, dhana bala parijana guna chaturai, bhagati heena nara sohai kaisa, binu jala barid dekhia jaisa: Caste, kinship, lineage, dharma, reputation, wealth, family, accomplishments and ability mean nothing for a person lacking in bhakti who is of no more worth than a cloud without water. Interestingly, while certainly qualifying to belong to the Vaishnava school of bhakti, Tulsidas effortlessly bridges the divide with the Shaivas—in his *Ramcharitmanas*, Ram pays fulsome tribute to Shiva, and Shiva is all praise for Rama.

In Punjab, the great Guru Nanak (1469–1539 CE), who founded the Sikh faith, was greatly influenced by the Bhakti movement. Sikhism, under Nanak, and the nine Gurus who followed him, the last being Guru Gobind Singh (1666–1708 CE), created a remarkably sublime and powerful monotheistic faith of nirguna bhakti. In clear Vedantic tones, its mul mantar or fundamental prayer—Ik Onkar: There is only one Supreme Being—made a powerful call of universal spiritual appeal. Like Brahman, the Sikh Absolute is nirankar (formless), akal (timeless), karta purakh (the Creator), agam agochar (incomprehensible and invisible) and is Waheguru (wonderous Teacher). The religion emphasised the non-duality of divinity—Ek noor te sab jag upja: From one luminous light the entire universe arose. In this one statement, it pole-vaulted above conventional religious orthodoxies.

Of great importance in the Sikh faith is mehar, kirpa, karam or the Grace of God. Guru Nanak taught that to obtain this, the most important form of worship is bhakti. Guru Arjan, in the *Sukhmani Sahib*, recommended that true religion is one of loving devotion to God. Selfless devotion and service can lead to Sach Khand or the Realm of Truth, which is the final union with the spirit of God, akin to the Advaita notion of brahmanubhav. Thus, Sikhism considers simran (the meditative remembrance) of God, and japna (chanting or kirtan of God's name) to be an essential part of religious practice. The singing of the Guru's hymns as contained in the Guru Granth Sahib—the only divine symbol of worship recognised by Sikhism—is practised through the shabad kirtans. The passages of the Guru Granth Sahib were poetically composed in rhyme, and lent themselves easily to exceptionally soulful musical compositions based on thirty-one ragas of classical music. Religious practice also strongly emphasised the importance of seva or service of humankind, and this included vand chakko or giving to the needy for the benefit of the community. Even today, the Sikhs are at the forefront of community service. Their Gurudwaras are now, as then, open to all, regardless of religion, background, caste or race. The langar or free vegetarian meals served there are also accessible to all, without recognising any distinctions of caste, creed or status.

Unlike other Bhakti movements of that period, the Sikh faith was forced to assume a military profile in order to resist and fight Muslim oppression. Two of the Sikh Gurus, Guru Arjan and Guru Tegh Bahadur, were brutally executed by Mughal emperors Jahangir and Aurangzeb respectively, and both for the same reason—refusal to convert to Islam. The tenor of Sikhism, however, was emphatically eclectic. Sikh scriptures refer to Hindu deities like Shiva, Brahma, Parvati, Lakshmi, Rama and Krishna, as also to Allah—not for purposes of worship but only to indicate alternate names of that One God. The Guru Granth Sahib, which was compiled by Guru Gobind Singh in 1678 CE, contains the hymns of not only the Sikh Gurus but also includes the traditions and teachings of thirteen Hindu Bhakti movement sants, including Ramananda and Namadeva. It also includes a Muslim Sufi, Sheikh Farid and Kabir, who states in the Guru Granth Sahib: 'I am not Hindu nor Muslim.'

Kabir (1440–1518 CE) was the most outspoken iconoclast of the Bhakti movement. He was born in Varanasi, and either born a Muslim or brought up by a Muslim weaver family. However, early in life, he became a disciple of Ramananda, imbibing not only his devotionalism but also his strong leaning towards Advaita philosophy. In earthy and colloquial language—Awadhi, Brij Bhasha, even Bhojpuri—easily understood by the masses, and expressed through pithy and earthy dohas called 'bani', he advocated the search for inner truth through humility, renunciation, detachment, meditation, solitude, kindness, love and bhakti. For him, God could be called Rama or Hari, or Allah or Khuda, but the spirit of Vedantic monism is clearly identifiable in his compositions, and his collection of lyrics is often called *Nirguni bhajans*:

> If God be within the mosque, then to whom does this world belong?
> If Ram be within the image which you find upon your pilgrimage
> Then who is there to know what happens without?
> Hari is in the East, Allah is in the West,
> Look within your heart, for there you will find both Karim and Ram
> All the men and women of the world are His living forms
> Kabir is the child of Allah and of Ram: He is my Guru, He is my Pir.[32]

Kabir was eloquent in his contempt for religious ritual, holy scriptures and hypocritical preachers:

> There is nothing but water at the holy bathing places;
> and I know that they are useless since I have bathed in them.
> The images are all lifeless, they cannot speak;
> I know, for I have cried aloud to them.
> The Puranas and the Koran are mere words;
> lifting up the curtain, I have seen.[33]

Belonging to a family of low-caste weavers, he had little time for the restrictions of caste or status:

> It is but folly to ask what the caste of a saint may be;
> The barber has sought God, the washerwoman, and the carpenter—
> Even Raidas was a seeker after God.
> The Rishi Svapacha was a tanner by caste.
> Hindus and Muslims alike have achieved that End, where
> remains no mark of distinction.[34]

It is said that when Kabir died, both Hindus and Muslims claimed his body. His teachings were preserved and propagated by a community of his followers called the Kabirpanthis. Kabir is emblematic of the organic unity of the Bhakti movement—he was the disciple of Ramananda and, in turn, Guru Nanak was greatly influenced by Kabir.

Something quite remarkable was afoot in south India too. The Nayanars and Alvars, whom I have mentioned earlier, can be called the founders of the Bhakti movement, and it is instructive to remember that many of the icons of the Bhakti movement in the north, like Vallabha or Ramananda, came from the south. The Nayanars were devotees of Shiva, and were led by a group of sixty-three Tamil saints during the sixth to eighth centuries CE. During the reign of the great king Raja Raja Chola I (947–1014 CE), the hymns of the Nayanars were compiled in a series of volumes called *Tirumurai*, also referred to as the *Tamil Veda*. The Alvars, literally meaning 'those immersed in meditation', were followers of Vishnu and of Krishna, led by twelve supreme saints who lived around the seventh to tenth century CE. The hymns of the Alvars were also collated in a volume, the *Nalayira Prabandhan*, a collection of 4,000 songs. Both the Nayanars and Alvars, while travelling from place to place, practised an intense mystical devotion bordering on ecstasy, which emphasised prapatti or complete surrender to the Lord. Their followers came from all classes, including those of the lowest castes; they shunned rituals and believed in direct, personal communion with the Absolute, in which there was no place for the intermediary role of the priestly class.

The powerful Virashaiva devotional movement in Karnataka had its roots in the Tamil Nayanar tradition. The Virashaivas were 'heroic worshippers of Shiva', and are also called the Lingayats. They rejected temple worship, rituals and Brahminical supremacy, replacing it with direct personalised worship of Shiva without gender, caste or class discrimination. Their only form of worship was the Isht-linga, a necklace with a pendant that contains the image of the Shivalinga. Basavanna (1105–1167 CE), who was the most towering figure of the Lingayat Virashaiva sect, is also called 'Bhakti Bhandari', literally 'the treasurer of devotion'. Basavanna's vachanas or hymns, intensely lyrical and devotional, movingly evoked the yearning for personal communion with Shiva, and railed against archaic social customs, taboos and superstitions, image worship, rituals like yajna and the sacrifice of animals, and the caste system. His Lord was Kudalasangamadeva, which stands for Shiva in the town of Kappadisangama in Karnataka, where three rivers meet—the Lord of the Meeting rivers:

> The rich
> will make temples for Shiva.
> What shall I,
> a poor man,
> do?
>
> My legs are pillars
> the body the shrine,
> the head a cupola
> of gold.
>
> Listen, O lord of the meeting rivers,
> things standing shall fall,
> but the moving ever shall stay.[35]

Stressing the importance of bhakti, he ridicules the paraphernalia of organised religion and temple worship:

> How can I feel right
> about a god who eats up lacquer and melts,
> who wilts when he sees fire?
>
> How can I feel right?
> about gods you sell in your need,
> and gods you bury for fear of thieves?
>
> The lord of the meeting rivers,
> self-born, one with himself,
>
> he alone is the true god.[36]

Allama Prabhu was a contemporary of Basavanna, and along with him (and Akka Mahadevi) is considered the patron saint of the Lingayat movement. The Kannanda poet Camarasa has written a powerful account of his life; given Allama's highly mystical vachanas, the book is appropriately titled *The Achievement of Nothingness*. The unitary consciousness of surrender and grace between a devotee and Shiva, unmediated by the externalities of religion, was the theme of Allama's writings also:

> With your alchemies,
> you achieve metals,
> but no essence.
>
> With all your manifold yogas,
> you achieve
> a body, but no spirit.
>
> With your speeches and arguments
> you build chains of words
> but cannot define the spirit.
>
> If you say
> you and I are one,
> you were me
> but I was not you.[37]

Along with bhakti, Basavanna and Allama Prabhu were powerful social reformers too. As in the Sikh tradition, they emphasised the importance of seva or service of humanity. 'Work is worship', Basavanna taught, and compassion the greatest virtue. 'Where is religion without loving-kindness?' is one of his most popular sayings in Kannada. His rejection of orthodoxy and ordained social hierarchies is borne out by his constructing—with the fullest help of Allama Prabhu—the Anubhav Mantapa or 'the hall of spiritual experience' in the city of Kalyan, where he was the chief minister in the court of King Bijjala II. Men and women from all social and economic backgrounds could come to the Mantapa to openly discuss spiritual questions, or any other matter of public importance. An institution like this, predating the Din-i-Ilahi of Akbar by centuries, could only be possible in the wake of the widespread social and religious reform ignited by the Bhakti movement. Even today, the Lingayats are a powerful sect in Karnataka, spearheading Shaivite bhakti, and often, given their numerical strength, determining who wins political power in the state.

Although Shiva was the dominant theme, Vaishnava literature also found place in Kannada Bhakti tradition. Madhava, the philosopher of qualified monism who followed in the footsteps of Ramanuja, was born in 1199 CE in a village near Udupi in Karnataka. A scholar, he wrote learned commentaries on the *Brahma Sutra*, the Gita and the Upanishads, and a gloss on the *Bhagwata Purana*. Unlike Ramanuja's Vishist Advaita, which was a qualified monism, Madhava was openly dualistic in his approach. For him, God, souls and the world were eternally three different entities. The Upanishadic statement 'Tat tvam asi' did not mean that the soul and Brahman are identical but only that the soul has qualities *similar* to Brahman. Madhava concedes that Brahma is the embodiment of supreme perfection, but asserts that Vishnu, as its embodiment, is unfettered in his powers as the creator, maintainer and destroyer of the world. Lakshmi, Vishnu's consort, is co-eternal with him and represents his creative energy. A devotee's only way to salvation is through uninhibited bhakti, for only devotion can move the Lord to extend his grace. Madhava takes Ramanuja's emphasis on bhakti to another level of fervour. The devotees are encouraged to brand their body with Vishnu's symbols, and carry out all the rites, pilgrimages and sacrifices, making worship, in thought and practice, the only means to moksha. The Vijayanagara kings provided further fillip to Vaishnava bhakti. They had the Mahabharata, the Ramayana and the *Bhagwata Purana* translated into Kannada, and spurred by their popularity, dasas or mendicant singers sang hymns in praise of Vishnu, Krishna and Rama. The visit of Chaitanya to the south in 1510 CE further strengthened this trend.

In current Andhra Pradesh, there was the influence of Nimbarka, a Telugu Brahmin who lived a little earlier than Madhava, and postulated a theory of dvaitadvaita, or dualistic non-dualism. This theory specifically refutes the predicateless character of Brahman, and breaks further from Adi Shankaracharya by arguing that Brahman, actually, undergoes parinama or actual change, while creating the dependent yet autonomous entities of Jiva and Prakriti. What is created is both different from Brahman, and yet not entirely different since its existence is dependent on Brahman. The material cause of creation is the power of Shakti inherent within Brahman. This interdependent world of similar yet different entities is governed by Ishvara, the supreme God, which Nimbarka, as part of the Vaishnava school, identifies with Krishna. As stressed by Ramanuja, and reiterated later by Madhava, Nimbarka also believes that bhakti and prapatti, total devotion and surrender infused with love, are the means for Brahmasakshatkara or the realisation of God.

On these philosophical foundations, the writer Nannaya (eleventh century CE) partially finished a popular translation of the Mahabharata into Telugu; the seminal work was completed by Tikkana (1220–1300 CE) and Yerrapragada (1280–1350 CE). Telugu versions of the Ramayana and the Puranas soon followed. Potana (1400–1475 CE), who lived an indigent life in the countryside, did a widely read translation of the *Bhagwata Purana*. Vemana, who belonged to a low caste, spread Shiva bhakti through his highly popular gnomic verses, which became famous for their ferocious attack on ritualistic orthodoxies and conventional religious practices:

> What are you the better for smearing your body with ashes?
> Your thoughts should be set on God alone;
> For the rest, an ass can wallow in dirt as well as you.

> The books that are called the Vedas are like courtesans,
> Deluding men, and wholly unfathomable;
> But the hidden knowledge of God is like an honourable wife.

> He that fast shall become (in his next birth) a village pig;
> He that embraces poverty shall become a beggar;
> And he that bows to a stone shall become like a lifeless image.[38]

An important aspect of the Bhakti movement was the rise of trail-blazing women devotees, who refused to be straitjacketed in the conventional stereotype of submission, subordination and inferiority to men. Aantaal, regarded as one of the twelve Alvar saint-poets, lived in the ninth century CE in Tamil Nadu. She was found abandoned under a tulsi tree by Periyalvar Timmoli, the great Alvar saint-poet, and he adopted her. She had no family of her own and never married. Mirabai was born in 1498 CE, daughter of a nobleman of the house of Mewar. It is said that as a child she was given an image of Krishna and grew so fond of it that her mother jokingly remarked that Krishna would one day be her bridegroom. Her childhood and youth were one of considerable grief and frustration. Her mother died when she was still very young. Her father was mostly away at war. In 1516, she was married to Prince Bhoja Raj, heir to the throne of Marwar. The marriage was childless and her husband died very soon after marriage. Mira spoke of herself as a celibate.

The significant common factor in Aantaal and Mira was that they looked upon Krishna as their husband. Both believed that in their previous lives they were gopis in Vrindavan. Mira considered herself to be an incarnation of the gopi Lalita, mentioned in the *Bhagwata Purana*. Aantaal decided to marry the Lord himself in the form of Ranganatha of Thiruvarangam (the reclining form of Vishnu).

Aantaal has left behind two basic works. In the *Tirupaavai*, a poem of thirty stanzas, she evokes Krishna by comparing him with the rainfall that produces fertility. Her second and longer work of 143 verses is much more explicitly sensuous. In a dream, she sees herself married to Vishnu, but Krishna remains elusive. Her burning desire for physical contact with him is the dominant theme here:

> He entered inside me and crushed me to pieces; he let
> my life escape and enjoys seeing me dance (in agony).
> My bones are melting, my eyes find no sleep
> for many days. I am whirling, and drown
> in the sea of suffering without the boat, the
> Lord of Venkata.

> I have lost the beauty of my breasts and my
> red lips, since Hrishikesha violated me.
> In the sole desire to be united with him my breasts grew large
> and jumped in joy. Now
> they make my life melt away and cause
> such agony.[39]

It is interesting that such impassioned and sensuous devotional writing has some parallels in the West as well. In the sixteenth century, Teresa of Avila fantasised about how a beautiful angel 'thrust a long dart of gold tipped with fire through my heart several times so that it reached my very entrails'. The pain, she wrote, was so real that she 'was forced to moan aloud, yet it was so surpassingly sweet that I would not wish to be delivered from it.'[40]

To return to Aantaal, the unredeemed intensity of her fantasies has an explosive and violent finale:

> Whether I weep or whether I worship him, he
> won't show his form to me.
> He does not come to embrace me, to hold me close,
> to enter me and wrap himself around me …
> Press down, flatten out, tie up tightly my breasts
> to remove the stain of dedicating them to His
> Beautiful strong arms…
> He did not enquire after me, did not bother that
> I was melting, crushed.
> I shall tear off with their very roots these
> breasts of mine,
> For they gained nothing from looking at Him
> who robs and plunders and is full of deceit.
> I shall throw them towards His chest to extinguish
> their burning.[41]

It was the ethos of the Bhakti movement, that notwithstanding such unabashed and transparently sensuous language to express her devotion for Krishna, Aantaal is counted among the most prominent and revered Alvar saints. She was considered an incarnation of Lakshmi. The great Vijayanagara king, Krishnadevaraya, composed an epic poem in Telugu, *Amuktamalyada,* dedicated to her and the *viraha* or suffering she experienced in being separated from Krishna or from Vishnu. Even today, many south Indian Vaishnava temples have a separate shrine for her.

Mirabai's songs, collectively known as her *Padavali,* are perhaps less sensual but no less intense. They profile a highly intimate and personal world in which nothing seems to exist except Krishna, the object of her desire. Like Aantaal, Mira too is wed to the Lord in a dream:

> Sister, the Lord of the Poor
> Came to wed me in a dream.
> Fifty-six crores of deities formed the bridal procession.
> And the bridegroom was the Lord of Braj.
> In my dream I saw the wedding-arch constructed
> And the Lord took my hand.
> In my dream
> I underwent a wedding ceremony
> And entered the married state.
> Giridhara has revealed himself to Mira:
> Her fortunes stem
> From good deeds in past births.[42]

Mira is consumed by her desire to give her all to Krishna:

> Giridhara is my true lover:
> On beholding His beauty, I long for him much.
> As night falls I set out to see him
> And at break of dawn I return.
> Day and night I sport in His company
> I please Him in any way I can.
> Whatever he clothes me in, that I wear.
> Whatever he offers, that I eat.
> My love for him is ancient and long-standing.

> Without Him I could not live.
> Wherever he places me, there I remain.
> If he sold me into slavery,
> I would acquiesce.
> Mira's Lord is the courtly Giridhara
> She offers herself in sacrifice again and again.[43]

Like Aantaal, Mira was a rebel. Her fanatical obsession with Krishna led her to become increasingly oblivious to the norms of conventional behaviour imposed on women in her conservative times. She began to receive sadhus, holy men, in the women's quarters, and travel to temples in the city all by herself. Her husband's family was not amused and, it is said, an attempt was made to poison her. Her involvement with Krishna was, however, unwavering:

> I donned anklets and danced
> The people said 'Mira is mad.'
> My mother-in-law declared
> That I had ruined the family's reputation.
> The king sent me a cup of poison
> Which I drank with a smile.
> I have offered body and mind
> To the feet of Hari
> And will drink the nectar of His holy sight.
> Mira's Lord is the courtly Giridhara:
> My Lord, to thee will I go for refuge.[44]

In addition to Aantaal and Mira, there was, in Kashmir, Lal Ded (1320–1392), also known as Lalleshwari, whose Shaivite bhakti mysticsm, expressed in Sanskrit poems called Vakhs, had a deep impact on the psyche of Kashmiris. Among the Nayanar saints was Karaikkal Ammaiyar. She left her husband, and after a pilgrimage to the Himalayas, settled in a cremation ground in the town of Alankatu, where she wrote hymns (included in the *Tirumurai*) describing how, oblivious to her feminine attributes, she just rejoiced in Shiva's divine dance among the dead:

> She has shrivelled breasts
> and bulging veins,
> in place of white teeth
> empty cavities gape.
> With ruddy hair on her belly
> a pair of fangs, knobbly ankles and long shins
> the demon woman wails at the desolate cremation ground
> where our Lord,
> whose hanging matted hair
> blows in all eight directions
> dances among the flames
> and refreshes his limbs
> His home is Alankatu.[45]

As remarkable was Mahadevi, known also as Akka or elder sister, who lived at the time of Basavanna. For her, Shiva was her beloved and husband, and she had no time for any worldly suitors, nor for her husband, Kaushika, the local chieftain. When Kaushika tried to force himself on her, she left her home and became a wandering mendicant, discarding even her garments, covered only by her tresses. In this state, she reached the Anubhav Mantapa in Kalyan, where followed a remarkable dialogue between her and Basavanna. When she was asked who her husband was, she simply said 'Chennamallikarjuna', meaning the 'Lord white as Jasmine'—the name of Shiva in the temple where as a child she fell in love with him. When asked why she was in the nude, her deeply evocative reply was:

> Till the fruit is ripe inside
> the skin will not fall off.
> I'd a feeling it would hurt you
> if I displayed the body's seals of love.
> O brother don't tease me
> needlessly. I'm given entire
> into the hands of my Lord
> white as Jasmine.[46]

The remarkable fact is that this wild-looking, completely unconventional woman was admitted into the Lingayat order. The vachanas she wrote constitute some of the most powerful poetry not only in the Virashaiva sect but in the entire corpus of the Bhakti movement:

> Like a silkworm weaving
> her house with love
> from her marrow,
> and dying
> in her body's threads
> winding tight, round
> and round
> I burn
> desiring what the heart desires.
>
> Cut through, O lord,
> my heart's greed,
> and show me
> your way out,
> O lord white as jasmine.[47]

What is most striking is the social iconoclasm of these women poets, their rebellion against conventional expectations and their sheer joy in revealing their devotion to the Lord irrespective of the consequences. Here, Mahadevi Akka expresses this irreverence with aplomb:

> I have Maya for mother-in-law;
> the world for father-in-law;
> three brothers-in-law like tigers;
>
> and the husband's thoughts
> are full of laughing women;
> no god, this man.
>
> And I cannot cross the sister-in-law
> But I will
> give this wench the slip
> and go cuckold my husband with Hara, my lord.[48]

The women icons of the Bhakti movement posed a challenge to gender orthodoxies and traditional notions of male superiority sanctioned by texts like the *Manusmriti*. The intense passion of these uninhibited female devotees led to a point of view that bhakti could be pursued best only if the devotees imagined themselves to be women. Many of the early hymns in Tamil and Telugu are by male poets writing in a woman's voice. Chaitanya was considered by many of his followers to be an incarnation of Radha, and his mystic–ecstatic form of worship openly encouraged male devotees to imagine themselves in the role of the gopis. We have it on record that several eminent saints experienced the loss of their manhood in moments of the deepest communion with Krishna. The Gujarati saint Narsi Mehta, born a century before Mira, wrote: 'I took the hand of that lover of the gopis in loving converse. ... I forgot all else. Even my manhood left me. I began to sing and dance like a woman. My body seemed to change and I became one of the gopis. ... At such moments I experienced moments of incomparable sweetness and joy.'[49] In the south, the eminent Vaishnava exponent, Vedanta Desika, used to wear the clothes of a woman while worshipping Krishna. An annual festival is still held in Chennai in memory of the saint in which his image, dressed as a woman, is taken out in a procession.

The Radha–Vallabhis emerged as a distinct group within the cult of Krishna bhakti in the sixteenth century CE. The founder of this movement was Hita Harivansh (1503–1553 CE). The most important of his works was the *Radha Sudha Nidhi* in which he lauded Radha; she was a veritable ocean of nectar, whereas Krishna was but a drop. The most extreme sect in the glorification of Radha was that of the Sakhi-bhavaks, which assumed the form of a separate grouping by the end of the eighteenth century, and derived its greatest strength from Bengal and the Mathura district. Its followers believed that they could worship Krishna *only* by imagining themselves to be gopis. Swami Ramakrishna Paramhamsa (1836–1886 CE), the towering Bengali saint also strongly believed that he could best achieve a vision of Krishna only if he approached him as a woman. 'As an adult, Ramakrishna undertook a systematic discipline of devotion as a woman of Krishna. ... For about six months (he) wore women's clothes and ornaments (sari, gauze scarf, bodice, artificial hair) and mimicked the movements, speech, smile, glance, and gestures of women.'[50]

The Bhakti movement was Hinduism's response to the violent and proselytising Islamic invasion. In this sense, it was as much about renewal as it was about self-preservation. If Hinduism had not shown the suppleness and energy to reinvent itself, and had remained brittle and fossilised as in earlier structures without the mass support enabled by the Bhakti movement, it may have suffered the same fate that befell it (and Buddhism) in Indonesia with the advent of Islam. Hinduism had existed for millennia before Islamic rule, but it was more a top-down model, although vibrant local adaptations even then enriched the overall tradition, and influenced those at the pinnacle. However, with the Bhakti movement, kirtans, hymns in the regional languages, and simplified and personal forms of worship and ardent devotion erupted from the bottom half of the social pyramid, and significantly expanded Hinduism's outreach to the masses where they were not only participants but initiators of religious and spiritual practice. 'The bhakti poet-saints were in dialogue with their own civilization, the Brahmanical part of it and its pretensions. Actually, they were in a passionate dialogue of the human soul with itself, yearning for union with God.'[51] In this process, it became a reform movement as well, as many orthodoxies, especially relating to caste and gender discrimination, were upended. As A.K. Ramanujan writes: 'In the lives of the bhakti saints "the last shall be first": men wish to renounce their masculinity and to become as women; upper caste males wish to renounce pride, privilege and wealth, seek dishonour and self-abasement, and learn from the untouchable devotee.'[52] Certainly, in great part, the Bhakti movement was an attack on rigid caste hierarchies, the supremacy of the Brahmanical order and the ritualistic paraphernalia of conventional religious orthodoxies. This does not mean that the subordination of women or the oppression of the lower castes was eliminated. But it did constitute a consistent and prolonged interrogation of these inequalities, and thus took Hinduism towards a much needed re-examination of some of its earlier sacrosanct dictums in religious practice and social interactions.

5

BRITISH RULE AND ITS AFTERMATH

The establishment of British rule in India deeply impacted Hindu civilisation and India as a whole, not only for the physical subjugation of its people and the humiliation this entailed, but for the *colonisation of the mind* that it achieved. While this is the goal of all colonising powers, the British were far more successful practitioners of this policy. It is my intention, therefore, to examine this process of the colonisation of the mind, and examine its consequences on Hindu and Indian sensibilities, rather than dwell on the political chronology of British conquest, and the enormous financial plunder that was a part of it. Suffice to say, that after the Battle of Plassey in 1757, where France, the competing colonising power, was routed, and the Battle of Buxar in 1764, where Bengal, Bihar and Orissa were ceded, the British East India Company became the supreme political power in India. After the defeat of the 1857 uprising against the colonisers, India as a whole came directly under British rule, and became the 'jewel in the crown' of the larger British Empire.

It has to be understood that the British aim was to prove to the natives that the rulers represented a superior civilisation whose ordained purpose was to civilisationally uplift the ruled. In the assertion and implementation of this project, there was a twofold goal. The first was to provide a *cultural* justification of the need for British rule. The second was to instil in the conquered a sense of inferiority with regard to their own civilisation, culture, history and traditions. In both these goals, the British succeeded beyond their wildest expectations. For the legatees of a highly refined, accomplished, cerebral, complex and nuanced civilisation that had existed—even if not without blemish—for millennia, the cumulative impact of the successful implementation of this dual strategy was disastrous, and its consequences are there to see even today, long after the British have packed up and left. Political freedom may be achieved on a fixed date; cultural colonisation leaves its footprint for decades thereafter.

In this chapter I shall endeavour to show—through important snapshots of key individuals and larger processes—how British colonialism worked to affect the *mindset* of the colonised, and what devastation it finally caused to the Hindu consciousness and self-esteem. Unlike other colonising powers, who often used brute force alone to consolidate their rule, the British played the game in a far more psychologically nuanced manner, engaging with the native culture in a manner so as to co-opt it into their civilisational ethos with the fullest cooperation of the victims.

Lord Thomas Babington Macaulay (1800–1859) arrived in India in 1834 to take up his assignment as a member of the Supreme Council to govern India, an offer he had accepted immediately because it would help him fulfil his cherished desire to give to the subject Indian people European knowledge so that 'they may in some future age, demand European institutions'. If this were to happen, it would be an enduring victory even if the sceptre were to pass away from the British Empire. For, as he said in a famous—and prophetic—speech in the House of Commons, 'There are triumphs which are followed by no reverse. There is an empire exempt from all natural causes of decay. Those triumphs are the pacific triumphs of reason over barbarism; that empire is the imperishable empire of our arts and our morals, our literature and our laws.'[1]

The future linguistic destiny of India fell into his lap almost immediately after his arrival in Calcutta. The Committee of Public Instruction set up by the British had been deadlocked for some time now because it was divided five against five. One set of five members wanted education in India to be essentially based on the heritage of its classical languages—Sanskrit, Persian and Arabic; the other wanted elementary education to be in the 'vernacular' languages, with English coming in at the higher levels. The Supreme Council made Macaulay the president of the committee in January 1835 to break the impasse, and he took little time to do so. On 2 February, he recorded his infamous 'Minute on Education', and in one rhetorical flourish, rubbished the entire civilisational heritage of all Indians.

In these amnesiac, postcolonial times, it is important to recall the mindset of the man. Macaulay argued the case of English because he believed fervently without the slightest iota of doubt that it was the product of a *superior* civilisation and culture. Whoever knows English, he wrote, 'has ready access to all the vast intellectual wealth which all the wisest nations of the earth have created and hoarded in the course of ninety generations. It may safely be said that the literature now extant in that language is of far greater value than all the literature which three hundred years ago was extant in all the languages of the world put together.'[2] Equally, and this was directly related to his notion of superiority, he was convinced that the culture of the natives was not only deficient, it was beyond redemption. How could they teach, at public expense, he asked, 'medical doctrines which would disgrace an English farrier—astronomy, which would move laughter in the girls at an English boarding school—history, abounding with kings thirty feet high and reigns thirty thousand years long—and geography made up of seas of treacle and seas of butter.'[3] Aware that his critics may point to the centuries of refinement and literary achievement each Indian language had behind it, he was blunt in his rebuttal: 'Does it matter in what grammar a man talks nonsense, with what purity of diction he tells us that the world is surrounded by a sea of butter, in what neat phrases he maintains that Mount Meru is the centre of the world?' He conceded that there could be some truth in Oriental sciences, but added dismissively: 'So there is in the Systems held by the rudest and most barbarous tribes of Caffrania and New Holland'.[4]

Macaulay was convinced that the sacred books of the 'Hindoos' were full of knowledge only of 'the uses of Cusa grass, and all the mysteries of absorption in the Deity'.[5] When the 'Hindoos' studied their texts, all that they learned was how 'to purify themselves after touching an ass, or what text of the Vedas they are to repeat to expiate the crime of killing a goat'.[6] There was no point thus in indulging the languages of the natives, whether classical or vernacular. English must be given primacy and propagated institutionally and immediately, and in doing so the long-term aim was utilitarian and crystal clear: 'We must at present do our best to form a class who may be interpreters between us and the millions we govern: a class of persons, Indians in blood and colour, but English in taste, in opinions, in morals, and in intellect'.[7] This class would in time become 'by degrees fit vehicles for conveying [our] knowledge to the great mass of the population'.[8]

Having stated his views without the slightest trace of ambivalence, Macaulay dramatically resigned, just in case his decision was not accepted, for he wanted to be no part of a system that gave encouragement to 'absurd history, absurd metaphysics, absurd physics, and absurd theology'.[9] He need not have worried. On 7 March 1835, Lord Bentinck, with whom he had spent some time in Ooty en route to Calcutta, gave his fullest approval to the ideas contained in the 'Minute'. All public funds would henceforth be used only for the teaching of English; no new students seeking to enter Oriental institutions would be provided stipends; professorships in such institutions would not be filled; no government money would be disbursed for printing anything in the native languages; and five schools for the teaching of English would be immediately opened in the major towns of Bengal.

The interesting thing about British colonialism was that while its goal was unalterably focussed, its practice was remarkably nuanced, conveying the impression that every decision had a deliberative side which allowed for debate, discussion and even dissent. Macaulay had his opponents among the British. The Orientalist lobby, opposed to his contemptuous dismissal of everything Indian and his arrogant espousal of English, was both vocal and powerful in the early years of British conquest. In 1781, William Hastings had founded the Calcutta Madrasa or Arabic college to enable Muslims to learn the principles and practices of Islamic law. A decade later, Jonathan Duncan, a scholar-administrator, set up the Sanskrit College at Banaras for the preservation and learning of the laws, literature and religion of the Hindus. In 1800, Lord Wellesley established the Fort William College in Calcutta. Here, the servants of the East India Company were required to learn Arabic, Persian and Sanskrit and six Indian vernacular languages. Interestingly, while they learnt English law and European history, they also had to study Hindu and Muslim law and Indian history. Fort William College was financed in part by small deductions from the salaries of all Company servants in India. In 1824, Lord Amherst inaugurated a Sanskrit College in Calcutta, and a year later, the Delhi College came up in Shahjahanabad, where though English made its debut, the medium of instruction remained either Arabic, Persian or Sanskrit.

The Company's goal was to rule India, and this would not be possible unless its employees learnt a little more about who they were going to rule. But in addition to this utilitarian logic, there was, in the initial phase, a genuine respect for, and curiosity about, the culture of the natives. Sir William Jones (1746–1794), who arrived in Calcutta in September 1783 to take up his assignment as a judge of the Supreme Court, was the most important figure of this scholarly interaction. Born in Westminster, he went to Harrow and Oxford, and was a linguistic genius who had learnt Greek, Latin, Arabic, Persian and a smattering of Chinese by the age of twenty-two. Unlike Macaulay, who purposefully reread Gibbon, Dante and Voltaire on his voyage to India, Jones spent his time journeying to Calcutta on board the frigate *Crocodile* to write a memorandum on what needed to be studied about Indian culture and civilisation. His list included Hindu and Muslim law, ancient scriptures, modern politics and geography of Hindustan, medicine, chemistry, surgery and anatomy of the Indians, and their poetry, rhetoric and music. Within four months of his arrival, on 15 January 1784, he had founded the Asiatic Society, which survives to this day and was in its time, the most vibrant institution on Indian heritage and antiquity.

In the Grand Jury Room of the Calcutta Supreme Court, thirty gentlemen of British and European descent met for the first meeting of the Society. They included Justice John Hyde, John Carnac, Henry

Vansittart, John Shore, Charles Wilkins, Francis Gladwin, Jonathan Duncan among others. William Jones spoke to them about how Asia was the 'nurse of sciences' and the 'inventress of delightful and useful art'.[10] Governor-General Warren Hastings was elected the first president of the Society and Jones the vice president. For the next several decades, the members of the Society did pioneering work in studying various aspects of Indian culture and translating its important treatises. William Jones learnt Sanskrit himself and translated Kalidasa's *Abhijnana Shakuntalam*, Jayadeva's *Gita Govinda* and the *Manusamhita* into English, and edited Kalidasa's *Ritusamhara*. He was also the first Westerner to analyse and write a paper on Indian classical music. It was his intention to bring out a compendium of Hindu and Muslim law, but he could not complete it. His *Institute of Hindu Law* was published in 1794 and his *Muhammedan Law of Inheritance* in 1792. In 1786, at the third meeting of the Asiatic Society, he made his famous observation that Sanskrit had perhaps common roots with Greek and Latin. 'The Sanskrit language,' he said, 'whatever be its antiquity, is of a wonderful structure; more perfect than Greek, more copious than Latin, and more exquisitely refined than either, yet bearing to both of them a stronger affinity, both in the roots of verbs and the forms of grammar, than could possibly have been produced by accident; so strong indeed, that no philosopher could examine them all three, without believing them to have sprung from some common source, which, perhaps, no longer exists'.[11]

Jones's attempt to link Sanskrit to Greek and Latin was undoubtedly motivated by a desire to somehow assimilate a language he so greatly admired within a European framework, for he was never in doubt about the primacy of Western culture. It must be remembered that he and his band of enthusiastic Indophiles were not questioning the superiority of British civilisation, or the right of the British to civilise the natives; they were only more open to the notion that the people they were ordained to govern had a cultural legacy which could not be dismissed and, indeed, in many areas, was worthy of respect.

Their aim was to rediscover India's glorious heritage for the Indians themselves, and their output towards this end was nothing short of astonishing. Sir Charles Wilkins (1750–1833) translated the Bhagwad Gita into English in 1785, and also published a translation of the *Hitopadesha*. H.T. Colebrooke, who was the president of the Society from 1806 to 1815, published a critical edition of the Sanskrit lexicon *Amarakosha*. H.H. Wilson, secretary of the Society during roughly the same period, translated the Puranas into English and published an edition of Kalhana's *Rajatarangini*. He also brought out the three-volume *Theatre of the Hindus*, which was translated into German and French. Sir John Shore, who succeeded Jones as president of the Society in 1794, published an abridged English version of the *Yoga Vasistha*. The Society was given permanent premises when in 1805, the government gifted it land at the corner of Park Street and Chowringhee, where it is housed even today. It built up an excellent library and also started a public museum in 1814.

This curiosity, even respect, for Indian culture was not confined to Calcutta. When in 1805, the Mission of William Carey in nearby Serampore asked for monetary assistance to translate the Sanskrit Ramayana, it was given 5,500 rupees. A branch of the Asiatic Society was opened in Bombay in 1803. A clutch of Orientalists were active in Madras too. Reading Persian classics was a favourite pastime for Charles Metcalfe, the British Resident in Delhi. William Fraser, who succeeded him, knew Urdu and Persian like a native and had an excellent library of Persian and Arabic books. Many among the British composed Persian and Urdu couplets; some even adopted a *takhallus* or pen name of their own—Joseph Bensley 'Fana', George Puech 'Shor' and Alexander Heatherley 'Azad'.

The difference of opinion between the Anglicists and the Orientalists was, therefore, real and prolonged. H.H. Wilson wrote to a Bengali friend in 1835 that 'it is a visionary absurdity to think of making English the language of India'.[12] He had his supporters in London as well. Charles William Wynn, the president of the Board of Control of the East India Company from 1822 to 1828, was quite appalled at the attempt to force Indians to adopt English. John Cam Hobhouse, who assumed the presidency later, wrote to Lord Auckland in the spring of 1836 that 'there is a strong party here who think that the rights of conquest do not extend to the destruction of language, and who believe it would be extremely impolitic to withhold all support from the propagation of Oriental learning'.[13] James Prinsep, who was the Secretary of the Asiatic Society in 1833, and who would in 1837 achieve the landmark breakthrough of deciphering the Brahmi script, enabling the Ashokan edicts to be read for the first time, protested the 'ultra radical subversion of all that now exists'.

Also perfect foils to Macaulay were Britishers like Sir Alexander Johnston. Born in India in 1775, Johnston learnt Tamil, Telugu and Hindustani, and as the president of the Council in Ceylon (1811), helped found a branch of the Asiatic Society there. Later, he became a member of the Judicial Committee of the Privy Council. In one of his reports from Ceylon, he made the point that the Indians 'had made the same progress in logic and metaphysics by 1500 B.C. as the Greeks, possessed centuries before the Greeks laws equal to, and in some areas, superior to theirs, possessed early knowledge of the numeral system which had proved to be essential for the achievements of Kepler, Newton, La Place and Napier, and devised astronomical tables of great scientific worth around 3000 B.C.'[14] Even after Macaulay's infamous 'Minute' became policy, there were those who disagreed. In 1853, H.H. Wilson tried to analyse why Macaulay went wrong. 'I have great respect for Mr Macaulay's talents,' he told the House of Lords Select Committee, 'but he was new in India, and knew nothing of the people; he spoke only from what he saw immediately around him, which has been the great source of the mistakes committed by the advocates of English exclusively. They have known nothing of the country: they have not known what the people want; they only know the people of the large towns, where English is of use and is effectively cultivated.'[15]

Macaulay's will prevailed in spite of such opposition because his attitude was in sync with the newly consolidated political ascendancy of the East India Company. The assertion of cultural supremacy is always related to political power. In the tentative phase of the Company's military forays in India, its employees were less bigoted and more flexible in their cultural interactions. By the time Macaulay arrived, the Company's paramountcy was near complete. Siraj-ud-Daula had been defeated at Plassey in 1757; Mir Qasim had capitulated at Buxar in 1764, and soon thereafter, the Mughal Emperor Shah Alam II had granted Diwani, or suzerainty, over Bengal, Bihar and Orissa in perpetuity to Clive. Tipu Sultan of Mysore had been routed in 1799, and the Marathas in 1803 and again in 1819. With the defeat of the French in 1761, there was no outside power to challenge British supremacy in India. It is to the credit of the Orientalists that they retained a considerable degree of cultural broadmindedness in spite of these British victories on the battlefield. But even they were never in doubt that they represented a civilisation meant to rule. The earnest and high-minded members of the Asiatic Society investigating Indian culture did not allow a non-European to join the Society until 1829, forty-five years after it was founded, even though the translations and compilations they turned out were greatly dependent upon an army of Indian experts in Sanskrit, Arabic and Persian. On arrival in Calcutta in 1814, around the same time that Colebrooke's critical edition of the *Amarakosha* was published, Lord Hastings noted in his journal: 'The Hindu appears a being nearly limited to mere animal functions, and even in them indifferent, [possessing] no higher intellect than a dog, an elephant or a monkey.'[16]

The dichotomy between the diligent appreciation of Indian antiquity and comments such as these can only be understood in the context of the swagger that political power gives even to cultural appreciation. The Company had material wealth and military might. Even its minor functionaries were surrounded by a battery of native servants—khidmutgars, durbans, syces, dhobis, bhistis (water carriers), hircarras (messengers), punkah-wallahs, palanquin-bearers, doreahs (dog keepers and walkers), malis, khansamas, ayahs and sweepers. Such a milieu was a natural incubator for notions of cultural, even moral, superiority and, increasingly, racial arrogance. Indians were always referred to as 'blacks' (Clive had noted with wry satisfaction that of the seventy or so casualties the Company had suffered at Plassey, most were 'blacks'), but now the derogatory word 'nigger' came into vogue. Lieutenant-Colonel H.B. Henderson, who served in India in the first half of the nineteenth century, and published his recollections in 1829, summed up the attitude of many Company officials: 'No native, however high his rank, ought to approach within a yard of an Englishman; and every time an English shakes hands with a Babu he shakes the basis on which our ascendancy stands.'[17]

Macaulay, the author of the 'Minute on Education in India', was a quintessential product of this process of British conquest and political and economic ascendancy. He drew a princely salary of £10,000 a year and spent less than £100 annually on the army of servants he employed; he kept house, as he admitted himself, more handsomely than any other member of the Council; as a part of his daily routine he read French and Greek to his sister Hannah after lunch; in the evenings he went out in his carriage for a drive along the riverfront, with servants running alongside. With unlimited arrogance and complete conviction he could thus say: 'Give a boy *Robinson Crusoe*. That's worth all the grammar of rhetoric and logic in the world.' And, in his 'Minute on Education', he could write: 'It is, I believe, no exaggeration to say that all the historical information which has been collected from all the books written in the Sanskrit language is less valuable than what may be found in the most paltry abridgements used at preparatory schools in England. In every branch of physical or moral philosophy the relative position is nearly the same.'[18]

Macaulay's brother-in-law, George Trevelyan, was, if anything, even more contemptuous of the culture of the natives and more convinced of the need to bring in English as quickly as possible as the sole medium of instruction. Macaulay, a bachelor himself, had come to Calcutta with his sister, Hannah, whom he loved dearly. Trevelyan, a young officer of the Company, met her socially soon after their arrival. In December 1834, they were married, and Trevelyan moved into Macaulay's home. Trevelyan was imbued with a missionary zeal to 'uplift' the natives. Macaulay noted that his 'mind is full of schemes of moral and political improvement and his zeal boils over in his talk. … His topics, even in courtship, are steam navigation and the education of the natives.' One of Trevelyan's pet causes was to replace the scripts of all the Indian languages by the Roman script, so as to end the 'curse of Babel', and help the formation of a national literature wholly based upon the civilised world of Europe. According to him, there was no synonym in the local languages for words like 'virtue' or 'public spirit' or 'patriotism' or 'honour'. In 1834, after the adoption as government policy of his brother-in-law's 'Minute', Trevelyan predicted that Lord Bentinck would be remembered for posterity because 'in his time the Oriental mania which broke out under Lord Wellesley's government; advanced under Lord Minto's; was in the height of its career under Lord Hasting's; and began to flag under Lord Amherst's, has completely exhausted itself.'[19]

The crucial aspect to introspect about is what impact this dismissal of their language and literature had on the Indians themselves. The vast majority, illiterate and impoverished under their new rulers as they were under many of the previous ones, were of course condemned to uncritical servility and not equipped to follow the arguments between the Anglicists and the Orientalists. But what about the educated Indian elite, who were knowledgeable about their literary and cultural heritage and should have been sensitive to the contempt with which it was being treated? The debate among the British was carried out in the open and for a considerable period of time; to every statement from the Orientalists, there was a spirited riposte from the opposite side. When William Jones compared Kalidasa to Shakespeare, Trevelyan countered by saying that 'the more popular forms of [Oriental literature] are marked by the greatest immorality and impurity'. The utilitarian James Mill argued that the 'lyricism and sentiment in Indian drama' was 'a mark of a self-indulgent society', and this in turn was the 'product of a despotic state'. Refined people would not, Mill argued, countenance the marriage that took place in the forest in Kalidasa's *Abhijnana Shakuntalam* between the heroine and her lover, where sinfully 'two lovers contract from the desire of amorous embraces'. Trevelyan was emphatic that the British did not need to spend any money to publish 'erotic Sanskrit dramas teaching lechery in its most seductive forms'.

Were the members of the Indian elite outraged by this? Did they protest the arbitrary imposition of a foreign language and the trashing of their own, or did they become colluders in the perpetuation of the Company's agenda? An instructive way to try and understand the response of the Indian elite is to study the life of perhaps the most famous of its then members, Raja Ram Mohan Roy. The purpose is not to pass judgement on the well-intentioned choices he made. Individuals are a product of their times and circumstances, and it is unfair to judge them in hindsight without taking that into account.

But even so, it is useful to explore the subtle and direct ways in which colonial rule co-opts the ruled and makes them accessories in its project. Under the imperial gaze of the ruler, the victims go through a complex process of emotions—resentment, denial, loss of self-worth, acquiescence, emulation and, ultimately, capitulation. They are often unable to distinguish between the erosion of self-respect and the pursuit of material incentives, between long-term loss and short-term gain, and between what they need to retain and what they must reject from their own inheritance. The discourse within the ruling group on what is the best course for them has a mesmerising and beguiling effect. They genuinely believe that their own interests are at the centre of this debate, and that the view that finally prevails is in their best interest. The subtext to this process of cultural co-option is, of course, power, but the victims does not see it so starkly. They believe that the choices they are making is of their own free will, and that the adoption of elements of the ruler's culture is their rightful destiny.

Ram Mohan Roy was born in 1772 in the village of Radhanagar in Hooghly district. His father claimed descent from Narottam Thakur, a prominent follower of the fifteenth-century Vaishnava saint, Chaitanya. His mother's forbears were chief priests of the Sakta sect, and she spent her last years in the Jagannath Temple at Puri. Roy was himself very religious, and indeed contemplated becoming a sanyasi at the age of fourteen. It is said that he would not even drink water without first reciting a chapter of the *Bhagwata Purana*. His early education was in Bengali, and by the age of fifteen he had mastered Sanskrit, Arabic and Persian. He did not learn English until he was twenty-four, and his first introduction to Western culture and literature was almost a decade later when he took up employment in the East India Company as an assistant to a minor functionary, John Digby. As a hardworking clerk in the Rangpur collectorate, Roy was treated well by Digby, who had apparently asked his British colleagues not to keep him standing in their presence, something which even the highest-placed natives were expected to do.

After ten years of service, Roy took voluntary retirement and settled down in Calcutta in a house he had built in the European style. The inclination of a few among the Bengali elite to adopt Western lifestyles had already been noted with smug satisfaction by the British. Bishop Reginald Hebber recorded that they had begun to decorate their houses with Corinthian pillars and acquire English-style furniture. In Calcutta, Roy organised the Atmiya Sabha, where members of the Bengali elite would meet to discuss ways to uplift Indians from the degradation they had fallen into. The desire of some urbanised and wealthy natives in Calcutta to study European literature and science had become quite vocal, and Roy helped David Hare, an English merchant, and Sir Hyde East, Chief Justice of Bengal, to set up Hindu College, whose avowed purpose was to *abjure* Hindu theology and metaphysics in favour of Western history, literature and natural sciences.

On 11 December 1823, Roy wrote a petition to Governor-General Lord Amherst against the teaching of Sanskrit and for the introduction of Western sciences. The document makes for remarkable reading:

> The Sanskrit language, so difficult that almost a lifetime is necessary for its perfect acquisition, is well known to have been for ages a

lamentable check on the diffusion of knowledge; and the learning concealed under this almost impervious veil is far from sufficient to reward the labour of acquiring it … no improvement can be expected from inducing young men to consume a dozen of years of the most valuable period of their lives in acquiring the Byakaran of Sanskrit Grammar. For instance, in learning to discuss such points as the following: khad, signifying to eat, khaduti, he or she or it eats, Query, whether does the word khaduti, taken as a whole, convey the meaning he, or she, or it eats or are separate parts of this meaning conveyed by distinct portions of the word? As if in the English language it were asked, how much meaning is there in the word eat, how much in the S, and is the whole meaning of the word conveyed by these portions of it distinctly, or by them taken jointly?

Neither can such improvements arise from such speculations as the following, which are the themes suggested by the Vedant: In what manner is the soul absorbed in the Deity? What relation does it bear to the divine essence? Nor will youths be fitted to be better members of society by the Vedantic doctrines which teach them to believe that all visible things have no real existence. … Again, no material benefit can be derived by the student of the Meemangsa from knowing what it is that makes the killer of the goat sinless on pronouncing certain passages of the Veda. … Again, the student of the Nyaya Shastra cannot be said to have improved his mind after he learned into how many ideal classes the objects in the Universe are divided, and what speculative relation the soul bears to the body, the body to the soul, the eye to the ear etc.[20]

Roy's motivations in writing this petition were laudable. He wanted the study of Western mathematics, chemistry and anatomy, clearly more advanced at this time than Indian science, to be available to Indian students. He argued for European teachers and for educational institutions to have the necessary books and scientific instruments for this new curriculum. But the important point is that in order to ask for this he had *to ridicule his own civilisation and heritage*. As a learned student of Sanskrit, he must have known that the language was not confined only to the futile tedium of splitting infinitives—Panini's majestic work on Sanskrit grammar, the *Ashtadhyayi*, with which the history of linguistics begins, was written in the fourth century BCE, at a time when the British were centuries away from speaking a coherent language. The six systems of Hindu philosophy constitute one of the most sophisticated metaphysical structures the world has known, and even as he dismissed the *Nyaya Shastra*, Roy must have been aware of the brilliance of this second-century CE text that deals, through its emphasis on debate and example, with the science of correct knowledge. Again, as a student of Vedanta, Roy could not have been ignorant of the fact that Adi Shankaracharya's speculation on the real and the unreal was in essence a deeply insightful inquiry into the nature of reality.

The irony is that only a few years before his petition to Amherst, Roy had authored scholarly works on the *Kena, Isha, Katha* and *Mandukya Upanishads*, and brought out a compendium of the Vedanta doctrines, the *Vedantasara*. What, then, made him damn his linguistic and philosophical heritage so spectacularly? If it was a tactical ploy to gain the support of British authorities or to rebut his critics within the orthodox Hindu establishment, it must nevertheless have been deeply humiliating to endorse the superficial yet relentless criticism of his culture by the rulers.

For the British, of course, Roy was an important ally: 'that enlightened native', as William Bentinck referred to him. It is interesting to note that in Macaulay's infamous 'Minute', one of the examples he gives to rubbish India's ancient civilisation is taken straight from Roy's petition. In his letter, Roy had reduced the legacy of the Mimamsa school of philosophy merely to passages that need to be recited to expiate the killing of a goat; a decade later Macaulay wrote that all that the 'Hindoos' learnt from studying their texts was how 'to purify themselves after touching an ass or what text of the Vedas they are to repeat to expiate the crime of killing a goat'.

Perhaps the most celebrated cause espoused by Roy was for the abolition of Sati. It is said that the sight of his brother's widow being burnt alive on her husband's funeral pyre created a sense of deep sorrow and revulsion in him. In 1818, he issued his first pamphlet denouncing the custom, and cited Hindu sacred literature as sanction for his viewpoint. Two years later, he issued another polemic, this time quoting Hindu law. This was followed by the publication of a booklet entitled *Brief Remarks Regarding Modern Encroachments on the Ancient Rights of Females According to the Hindu Law of Inheritance*. The Bengali paper he brought out, *Sambad Kaumudi*, was equally vocal in its condemnation. On this issue, Roy was an eloquent and very genuine social reformer, seeking to rid his society of inhuman practices for which the fanatically orthodox claimed religious sanction. Naturally, the British were supportive of such a campaign, not the least because it reinforced their claim that they were dealing with a barbaric and depraved people who needed to be saved from themselves. In his study of the ideologies of the Raj, Professor Thomas Metcalfe of the University of Cambridge emphasises that 'the dramatic representations of these evils was essential to the self-image of the Raj'. 'Few of their activities in India,' he writes, 'gave the British greater satisfaction than this vision of themselves as the reformers of Indian morality.'[21] Lord Bentinck, who steered the Act abolishing Sati in 1829, had a larger-than-life statue commissioned showing him dramatically rescuing an Indian woman from the funeral pyre. This piece of sculpture can still be seen in the compound of the Victoria Memorial Museum, but was at that time placed publicly in Calcutta.

Sati was indeed a heinous custom. But it is important to understand the contradictions and cynicism that influenced the British's intervention in the issue. When the British were still consolidating their rule in the subcontinent, they were happy to ignore issues like Sati that were to become so central to their civilising mission once they had established their military and political supremacy and wanted to buttress that with the notion of moral and intellectual superiority. In his 1829 report, 'On Ritual Murder in India', Bentinck wrote: 'When we had powerful neighbours and had greater reason to doubt our own security, expediency might recommend an indirect and more cautious proceeding, but now that we are supreme my opinion is decidedly in favour of an open, avowed, and general prohibition.' Actually, in 1813, the British had *legalised* Sati. While there was never any consensus even among upper-caste Hindus about scriptural sanction for the practice of Sati, the British authorities legitimised it by saying that it did.

Several Hindu scholars and reformers had been speaking against the practice of Sati and highlighting that it was not enjoined in any religious text that a widow burn herself on her husband's pyre. Among them were Mritunjay Vidyalankar, Gourisankara Bhattacharya, Kalinath Roy Chowdhury, besides others. They were all ignored and the 1813 law was passed. Later, too, reformers continued to work against the practice of Sati—chief among them, of course, was Ram Mohan Roy. Many of them understood the true nature of Sati, as a social aberration, and knew that the best way to fight it was from within, through reform. Ram Mohan Roy himself was not in favour of official intervention and had advised Bentinck *against* British intervention and legislation. It was valuable advice and he felt strongly about it. Yet, when Regulation XVII of 1829 abolishing Sati was promulgated, he gave it uncritical, unqualified and public support.

It is also important to remember that Sati was never as widespread or as rampant as the public campaign orchestrated against it would suggest. The British talked about numbers in the thousands, and that it was the practice among all Hindus across the subcontinent— Bentinck, in his 'On Ritual Murder in India', wrote: 'I have no doubt that the conscientious belief of every order of Hindus, with few exceptions, regards [Sati] as sacred', without of course providing any basis for his conviction. However, in records and writings of the time, there is enough evidence to the contrary, and several contemporary scholars have written about this—most notably, Anand A. Yang and Lata Mani. The incidence of Sati was largely limited to certain castes, even families, and was almost unknown outside parts of eastern and northern India. Between 1815 and 1828, 63 per cent of all recorded acts of Sati took place in Calcutta Division (interestingly, this was the then seat of colonial power).[22] In 1824, looking at the data compiled by the British themselves, of the 250,000 women who became widows in the Bengal Presidency, the number of those reported to have burned themselves was 600—that is 0.2 per cent of the overall number of widows.[23] The data for Varanasi, the most holy of cities for Hindus, is even more revealing. The incidence of Sati was very limited here, and 'the Banaras magistrate noted with surprise—in an obvious ethnocentric manner—that only 125 cases had occurred in the nine years between 1820 and 1828'.[24] Clearly, Sati was 'a localised, secular phenomenon, not a universal, religious one'.[25] But the British exaggerated it since it could be used to discredit the Hindu way of life and legitimise British rule. After the regulation abolishing Sati was promulgated, the prominent missionary William Carey wrote that 'for the first time during twenty centuries ... the Ganges flowed unblooded to the sea.'[26]

A similar case of deliberate colonial exaggeration and misrepresentation was that of the so-called thugs. The thugs were ordinary dacoits, but not even a tenth as exotic or pervasive as the British made them out to be. Although largely confined to a small region of north India, they were projected as a threat of such magnitude and reach that an observer would not have been wrong in believing that all of Indian society was representative of their violence and duplicity. Plays were made on them and sensationalist novels written on their secretive and murderous activities; indeed, the word 'thug' entered the English language. 'The campaign against Sati,' Professor Metcalfe concludes, 'reinforced notions of Indian women as helpless victims of religion, while lurid tales of the doings of the thugs powerfully reinforced the idea of Indians as treacherous and unreliable.'[27]

Roy was probably unaware that his idealism suited the larger purposes of British rule so well. Protests against their own culture by the natives provided the moral ground on which the British sought to build their imperial edifice. They appropriated and twisted the well-intentioned and often genuinely reformist campaigns of Indian intellectuals in order to give ideological justification to their empire. The denigration of the Sanskrit language, and the culture and philosophy associated with it, devalued an entire civilisational heritage and thus strengthened the rulers' project of imposing their own culture and language on the ruled. There was, of course, much that was wrong at that time with the practice of Hindu religion and the social customs it sanctioned. But selective focus on the most barbaric of these was vital collateral evidence to support the colonial contention that they were dealing with a sunken civilisation that only their rule could hope to salvage. Perhaps Roy can't be blamed for being co-opted into this imperial game, but it is crucial to understand the subtext of his interaction in such matters with the British, and their selective support for his reformist initiatives.

For his own society and religion, Roy was a scriptural non-conformist, a brave and enlightened man. In 1828, he set up the Brahmo Samaj, founded on the principles of one God and universal brotherhood beyond distinctions of caste or creed. Such an approach was a revolt against the social practices of his time. But in his dealings with the British, he compromised his independence and individuality, and let himself be co-opted into endorsing the vision they wanted the natives to have of themselves. 'Rammohan Roy had an unbounded faith in the sense of justice and goodness of the British government,' writes the historian R.C. Mazumdar, 'and accepted the British rule as an act of Divine Providence … and glorified the role played by them for civilizing the Indians.' On 15 December 1829, in a meeting at the Calcutta Town Hall, Roy publicly stated that 'the greater our intercourse with European gentleman, the greater will be our improvement in literary, social and political affairs'. He even went on to praise the British Indigo planters, the effects of whose rapacious rack-renting on the lives of farmers and farm workers in Bihar and Bengal were already apparent. 'There may be some partial injury done by the indigo planters,' Roy said, 'but on the whole they have performed more good to the generality of the natives of this country than any other class of Europeans whether or not out of service.' Around this time, he also wrote to the French botanist and geologist, Victor Jacquemont: 'Conquest is very rarely an evil when the conquering people are more civilized than the conquered, because the former brings to the latter the benefits of civilization. India requires many more years of English civilization so that she may not have many things to lose while she is reclaiming her political independence.'

Many of the contradictions that colonialism creates are mirrored vividly in the life of Roy. He was a scholar of Hindu thought and philosophy, yet publicly ridiculed its concepts. A master of the Sanskrit language, he openly condemned its learning and teaching—and yet, when attacked by the missionaries for his thoughts on the Gospel, he was forced to defend himself by citing examples from the Vedanta, whose legacy he had otherwise dismissed. His stated aim was to revive the fortunes of his countrymen; yet he made a declaration at the House of Commons on the need for Indians to be ruled in perpetuity by the British. An ardent believer in the civilising role of British rule, he was forced to protest against the uncivilised behaviour of British officials. While he paid open tribute to the justice and liberality of British laws, his appeal against the arbitrary censorship imposed by them, or their unjust treatment of the Mughal king in Delhi, never elicited a response.

In his personal life, Roy was caught in the not unfamiliar existential dilemma of the colonised. It is said that he had two houses in Calcutta, one in which everything was Western except him, and the other in which everything was Indian except him. A man committed to reforming Hindu society, he dedicated his petition against Sati to Lady Hastings. He made it his mission to oppose the blind orthodoxies of the Hindu religion, yet took along Hindu servants to cook his food, and two cows to provide him pure milk, during a voyage to England. Eager to fulfil his long-standing desire to visit England, a country he so openly admired, he was greatly inconvenienced on the ship when he could not find an open fire on which his meals could be made in accordance with Brahmanical notions of purity. While he was immensely gratified to have been received in audience by the English king, and, indeed, *argued for India to have a mixed community enriched by European stock*, he objected to being attended by English nurses during his last days in Bristol. On his deathbed, he expressed a wish not to be buried in a cemetery or with Christian rites, yet he was buried and not cremated. His memorial was designed by a Britisher, but its costs were defrayed by an Indian who did not, however, think it necessary to have anything inscribed on the monument in Bengali or Sanskrit, the two languages Roy knew better than any other.

Roy was both the creation and the victim of colonial policy. To be successful, such a policy must create the illusion of choice before the native, and give to its brute military power a softer tone of deliberation, fairness and liberality. It must be able to co-opt the natives into perpetuating its designs, often without them knowing it. And it must be able to both sense, and engage with, their aspirations and dissatisfactions in a manner that actually furthers the ruler's objectives but convinces the ruled that this is in their interest. It is most unlikely that a person as learned and intelligent as Roy would have become such an articulate acolyte of the British if the latter had aggressively and simplistically dismissed everything Indian and forced the native elite at the point of a gun to learn English.

The developments of Western science in the nineteenth century and their application in everyday life were something that many educated Indians admired and wanted to emulate. The learning of English was seen as a means to acquiring this new scientific learning. But the British administrators had their own, very different, reasons for imposing their language on the people of India. Their basic purpose was not to nurture Indian Einsteins of the future but to create a bank of English-knowing clerks for the immediate present. After all, had the objective been to expose the natives to scientific learning, this could have been done as easily—and more effectively— by translating Euclid into Sanskrit or the vernacular languages. The projection of English as the only linguistic vehicle to science and technology had a far more pragmatic subtext. A handful of Britishers may have conquered most of India by superior arms and chicanery, but they could not administer and control it without a subservient regiment of babus who could understand and speak their language. Lord Bentinck said so openly—he needed Indians in judicial and administrative posts in order to cut costs, because the numbers of his compatriots was limited and the salaries they demanded were higher. The Anglicists, who claimed that English alone could uplift the natives, were his ideological allies, but both they and he were quite happy if the language skills of their new students remained at perfunctory levels, functional but nowhere near literary fluency. It was enough if the natives learned sufficient English to get by, so that they could, to recall again Macaulay's famous phrase, play the role of intermediaries. The policy was to wean them away from their own languages while equipping them inadequately in the coloniser's; to 'improve' them through a familiarity with a 'civilised' tongue, but to ensure that familiarity did not equal ownership or empowerment.

The success of this policy lay in gradually restricting higher job opportunities to only those who knew English. Two years after Macaulay's 'Minute', Viceroy Auckland noted that Indians were responding well to this bait, and the realisation was sinking in that without English 'success in commerce and advancement in private and in public shall become more difficult'. At the pinnacle of the colonial administrative structure were the covenanted civil services. Macaulay thought that ultimately some Indians might qualify for it, although at present there were none 'whom it would be a kindness to the Native population to place'.

Macaulay also believed that the introduction of English would dilute the religious loyalties of the natives. In a letter to his father dated 12 October 1836, he wrote: 'No Hindoo, who has received an English education, ever remains sincerely attached to his religion. Some continue to profess it as a matter of policy; but many profess themselves as pure Deists; and some embrace Christianity. It is my firm belief that if our plans of education are followed up, there will not be a single idolator among the respectable classes in Bengal thirty years hence.'[28] This was perhaps the only aspect where Macaulay was off the mark. 'Hindoos' were far more complex and clever than he thought. They were not beyond giving the impression that they held their religion in lesser esteem in order to get a job or a promotion or admission to an English-teaching institution. But very few of them actually converted to Christianity. However, there is little doubt that they became less attached to their language and less confident about their own culture and lifestyle, and this was quite in conformity with expectations. In 1825, the *Oriental Herald* had, in a piece ponderously titled 'On the Inefficiency of the Means Now in Use for the Propagation of Christianity', argued that the need of the hour was to 'teach them (the natives) to despise the barbarous splendour of their ancient princes … and make them look to this country with that veneration which the youthful student feels for the classical soil of Greece'.[29]

Language, thus, became a strategic tool to achieve a variety of ends, none of which had anything to do with making the natives speak English of a literary standard. In an essay he wrote in 1838 titled 'On the Education of the People of India', George Trevelyan was both frank and remarkably prescient. With the teaching of English, he argued, the ruled would themselves have a stake in English protection and instruction. 'The natives will not rise against us because we shall stoop to raise them,' he wrote, and if British rule ever ended, the introduction of English would enable the rulers to 'exchange profitable subjects for still more profitable allies'.[30] Not surprisingly, those who had reached the greatest proficiency in English remained the most loyal to the British in the uprising of 1857. George Campbell, a young official in India, wrote in 1853: 'The classes most advanced in English education, and who talk like newspapers, are not yet those from whom we have anything to fear.'[31]

Campbell's assessment was not wishful thinking but based on careful observation. The young, eager recruits to English-medium schools were the most easily persuaded about the superiority of Western civilisation. Nobinchunder Das, a student of Hooghly College at Calcutta in the 1850s, wrote in an essay that 'those short days of Asiatic glory and superiority are gone, the stream of civilization has taken an opposite course; before it flowed from Asia to Europe, now, but with more than its pristine vigour and rapidity, it flows from Europe into Asia. ... Both in ancient and modern times Europe has been the seat of philosophy and civilization. England ... is particularly engaged in the cause of Indian improvement. She not only carries on commerce with India, but she is ardently employed in instructing the natives in the arts and sciences, in history and political economy, and, in fact, in everything that is cultivated to elevate their understanding, meliorate their condition, and increase their resources. ... The English are to us what the Romans were to the English.'[32]

Nobinchunder Das must have, no doubt, gone on to do well in his studies and probably succeeded against stiff competition to become a clerk in the British administration. Although his knowledge of English was good, to the British he must have still appeared as someone who 'talks like newspapers'. People speak like newspapers when they are not speaking their own language. They learn the big words, but can rarely acquire the fluency and effortlessness of the connecting spaces, and this is noticed by those to whom the language belongs. Speaking before a select committee of the House of Lords in 1853, George Trevelyan exulted that the Hindus spoke purer English 'than we speak ourselves for they take it from the purest models; they speak the language of the *Spectator*, such English as is never spoken in England.'[33] Trevelyan was paying tribute less to the kind of English the Indians spoke, and more to their ability to perform like programmed fleas to the linguistic music set by the rulers. His comment reflected a sense of genuine pride in the outcome of the linguistic policy of the British that had created caricatures who spoke the language not as it was spoken in England, but in its 'purest' form, as in newspapers like the *Spectator*. It was a tribute too to the seriousness with which their subjects set themselves to learn the alien language. Macaulay was surprised to note that the students of Hindu College had learnt 'by heart the names of all the dramatists of the time of Elizabeth and James the First, dramatists of whose works they in all probability will never see a copy'.[34] More than a century later, when Nirad Chaudhuri made his first trip to England in the 1950s, he was surprised that a group of Englishmen had to be told who Thomas Beckett was and what *The Black Prince* was, when he himself had 'learned about both in a jungle of East Bengal before I was twelve'.[35] The natives were nothing if not diligent, and the British were delighted that the most diligent among them had picked up more of bookish English than they were strictly required to in order to fulfil their role as clerical intermediaries. But for all their dedication and diligence, they remained linguistic curiosities to the rulers, adept students whose incongruity was least apparent to themselves.

The Kenyan Nobel Laureate, Professor Wangari Mathai once told me that it was only the colonial rulers who truly understood the importance of a language. That is why it was the first thing they took away. Not felicity, but competence, often at very basic levels, was the acquisition of the overwhelming majority of the new English-speaking Indians. A very small number could be held up for having learnt the language to some degree of eloquence. And the idea that English-language skills would filter down to the masses was not really feasible and, in any case, was never implemented seriously. What did emerge was an English-speaking elite, largely restricted to the administrative and professional classes. Of these, the most ubiquitous was the babu, still defined in the Webster's dictionary as 'A native clerk who writes English.' The Bengali writer Bankim Chandra Chatterji wrote caustically in 1873: 'The baboos will be indefatigable in talk, experts in a particular foreign language, and hostile to their mother tongue. ... Some highly intelligent baboos will be born who will be unable to converse in their mother tongue. ... Like Vishnu they will have ten incarnations, namely clerk, teacher, Brahmo, accountant, doctor, lawyer, magistrate, landlord, editor and unemployed. ... Baboos will consume water at home, alcohol at friends', abuses at the prostitutes' and humiliation at the employer's.'[36]

As more and more educated Indians persevered to pick up English, it took a perceptive Englishman, Lord Curzon, who came to India as Governor-General in 1899, to understand what had really happened.

The emphasis on rote, he observed, was the result of making English the condition for government employment. He noticed too the ensuing contempt for the vernacular languages, and deplored the decline of elementary education in the mother tongue. All this, he said, was due to the 'cold breath of Macaulay's rhetoric'. Curzon's remarks were not official British policy, of course. His concern was that of an acute and knowledgeable observer, and it was expressed as an obiter dictum, not as a resolve to reverse Macaulay's vision and the policies based on it. As an imperial power, Britain had no reason at all to question Macaulay's triumphant assertion to the British Parliament in July 1853 that his 'Minute' had indeed 'made a great revolution'.

Colonial rule made a serious dent in the linguistic genius of Hindu civilisation. For millennia, this civilisation had thrived not only through the vehicle of Sanskrit, but also in the vibrancy of the regional languages, as was spectacularly evident during the Bhakti movement. Now, they were made to feel that their own languages were completely inferior, less than relevant, not the best medium for creative expression, something to be spoken in the informal intimacy of personal intercourse but not worthy of high intellectual discourse, for which English was the befitting and modern medium, especially since knowledge of English was expressly linked to employment and upward social mobility. Such an immeasurable loss to the country was a major consequence of Macaulay's vision and deliberate colonial policy thereafter, and its ill-effects can be felt even today.

The second goal of the British rulers was to ridicule native culture and creativity, so as to prove the credentials of their own civilisation. The short-lived earlier attempt by some Britishers to objectively discover and evaluate the genius of ancient India was conclusively buried by Macaulay's derisive view on everything native. In the decades that followed, it became standard colonial policy to reinforce this disdainful—if ignorant—critique. Later, a definitive theory was built to support this belief. A favourite theory of the rulers was that Indian creativity had no claim to distinction or greatness except for those elements that had come to India from outside. In particular,

Greek influence, the consequence of Alexander's brief invasion of the Punjab in 326 BCE, and represented by the art of Gandhara, was touted to be far superior to anything produced in India itself. Alexander Cunningham, the first British Director of Archaeology, wrote extensively about the pivotal role of Greece in inspiring the best in Indian art; the historian Vincent Smith, whose books I studied in school, argued that Gandhara was vastly superior to the Mathura school; and Lord Curzon, in his speech at the Asiatic Society in February 1900, pronounced that the majority of Indian antiquities were 'exotics, imported into the country in the train of conquerors, who had learnt their architectural lessons in Persia, in Central Asia, in Arabia, in Afghanistan'.[37]

The interesting fact is that such sweeping generalisations were based on supposedly widespread field studies and research. For instance, W. Erskine published a scholarly treatise on the cave temples at Ellora, and acquired sufficient knowledge of Hindu iconography to correctly identify the three faces of Siva in the statue of Maheshamurthi. But he still felt that 'the execution and finishing of the figures in general ... are often very defective, in no instance being possessed of striking excellence. The figures have something of rudeness and want of finish, the proportions are sometimes lost, the attitudes forced, and everything indicates the infancy of art.'[38] Such 'scholarly' denunciations emboldened later critics to be bluntly dismissive. George Birdwood, widely regarded as one of the most influential art critics in late nineteenth century Britain, once compared an exquisite Gupta period image of the Buddha to a 'boiled svet pudding', and came to the conclusion that in seventy-eight years of the study of art, he had not come across anything in India that gave expression to 'the good, the beautiful and the true'.[39] The British judged Indian art and architecture from a ruler's conviction that their principles of aesthetics and of shape and form were the ideal; from this point of view, Indian architecture was, as James Fergusson stated in his *History of Indian and Eastern Architecture*, 'a mistake nothing can redeem'. The beautiful temples of the south had no appeal for him, for they lacked 'those lofty aims and noble results which constitute the merit and greatness of true architectural art'.[40] The Madurai temple he found particularly barbarous: 'the most vulgar building in all of India', while Sanchi 'showed neither delicacy nor precision'.[41]

Birdwood also wrote in 1910 that 'sculpture and painting are unknown as fine arts in India'. Such an astounding statement, rubbishing centuries of achievements as seen, for instance, in the exquisite Chola bronzes, had the backing of historians like Vincent Smith, who wrote condescendingly in 1889 that the Ajanta murals did not compare favourably 'with the world's masterpieces—no Indian art work does—but they are entitled to a respectable place among the second or third class'.[42]

Other art forms, like music and dance, came under hostile scrutiny too. Most British observers mistook all forms of classical dance to be a variation either of the 'nautch' or an extension of the Devadasi system, depraved and barely distinguishable from prostitution. Indian classical music represented such a stark contrast to Western musical traditions that it provoked hardly any appreciation or patronage, and the soulful elaboration of the raga was curtly dismissed by one Englishman as little better than a 'sleepy lullaby'. Apart from the colonial imperative to show that the people they ruled were undeveloped in their creative expressions, there was, as the historian Partha Mitter writes, a genuine gap in comprehension between two alien cultures: 'Nowhere can this clash of the two essentially different, even antithetical, cultural and aesthetic values be better studied than in European interpretations of Hindu sculpture, painting and architecture.'[43]

Colonial amnesia occurs when the ruled continue to fete and admire those who contemptuously dismiss their culture and civilisation. The adulation by most elite Indians for Edwin Lutyens (1869–1944), who designed the Viceroy's palace, now called the Rashtrapati Bhavan, and is credited along with his colleague, Herbet Baker, for designing New Delhi—'Lutyens' Delhi'—is a remarkable case in point. If there was one person who was the most outspoken and virulent critic of almost everything about Indian creativity and aesthetics, it was Lutyens. But he still receives near veneration by educated Indians as a visionary architect who, as Wikipedia's write-up (probably written by an Indian) says, 'is known for imaginatively adopting traditional architectural styles to the requirements of his times'.

Continuing long-established colonial derision, Lutyens' most vocal condemnation was about Indian architecture. 'Personally I do not believe there is any real Indian architecture or any great tradition,' he wrote. 'They are just spurts by various mushroom dynasties with as much intellect in them as any other art nouveau. ... And then it is ultimately the building style of children.'[44] He was convinced that anything at all redeemable in Indian architecture was due to the influence of the West, but even that was destroyed by the natives. 'The Hindus knew little and the Mughals little more of any ethic of construction and art in relation to them. The Mughals took Italian forms and mutilated them.'[45] The Mughal style of building was in his view little more than 'cumbrous ill-constructed buildings covered with a veneer of stone and marble and very tiresome to the Western intelligence'. Not surprisingly, his comments were scathingly dismissive of almost all the architectural landmarks in India, displaying a complete lack of sensitivity to the lifestyles of other socio-cultural traditions. He ridiculed the beautifully carved throne in the Diwan-i-Khas of the Red Fort in Delhi because it would only allow a man to 'squat cross-legged'. The exquisite panels in pietra dura of birds and animals he called 'tommy rot'. The Indian technique of joining marble slabs was plain 'nonsense'. About the Qutub he wondered, 'Why should we throw away the lovely subtlety of a Greek column for this uncouth and careless and unknowing and unseeing shape?'[46] The ancient city of Mandu in central India was to him 'childish and quite inconsequent and built to destroy itself', somewhat picturesque but 'with no intellect', good only for those 'who wear no clothes and want no furniture ... freakish monstrosities, ruthless and squalid with no real nicety'.[47] The Hindu temples and Buddhist shrines along the ghats in Banaras appeared like 'a cactus or children's toy tree on a steep mountainside, decorated at the top with flags on crazy bamboo poles.'[48] Holkar's palace in Bombay was 'very vulgar', and the palace at Udaipur 'barbaric'. The imposing Bikaner Fort was 'a large barbaric pile with some good lacquer work and other decorations inside. Some of it was too awful for words. Gods, Goddesses, Kings carved and jewelled and painted—no gollywog could better it.'[49] The Elephanta caves almost passed muster: 'Rather wonderful and some evidence of real beauty,' he conceded. 'But how can you achieve beauty with a Ganesha …?'[50]

Even the magnificent Taj Mahal did not amount to much for this man. 'People go head over heels with their admiration for the Taj,' he lectured to his wife, 'but compared to the great Greeks, Byzantines, Romans, even men of the calibre of Mansard, Wren etc., it is small but very costly beer, and alongside the Egyptians it is evanescent. … The third dimension seems beyond [the natives'] philosophy and they never get beyond carpet patterns and their carpets … inspire their architecture.'[51] The incandescent beauty of one of the wonders of the world on a full moon night left our finicky aesthete unmoved. The Taj by moonlight 'becomes so bald and indefinite', he wrote. 'It is wonderful but not architecture. … And so it is with all these Indian builders. Anything really admirable has been done by an Italian or a Chinaman. For the rest it is all pattern—just the same as any carpet hung up. The buildings are tents in stone and little more. Elaborated to howdahs, stone buildings which when put up are carved and carved and carved without any relation to the stone, its purpose or location. The Indians of today have no sense of construction decorated.'[52] The denunciation allows for no doubt. It is consistently and categorically hostile. His basic premise is that India has no architecture worth the name, only 'veneered joinery in stone, concrete and marble on a gigantic scale … but no real architecture and nothing is built to last, not even the Taj'.[53]

The Indian craftsmen he was compelled to work with drove him to despair. There were painters from Bengal at work at the Viceroy's Palace, but Lutyens felt that they could hardly draw. 'They know only the most terrible patterns and those nerve wracking sodden gods and goddesses and to be mysterious and godlike you must draw everything wrong—foolishly methodless. Thank Very God of Very God that he wrought not our world on such lines.'[54] When the furnishings were being done, he thought the French and English materials made 'the Indian stuff and materials look silly'. As he inspected his handiwork in the finishing stages, he observed how 'careless the Indians were … forever damaging things and the messes they make! Horrible! … And the Indian never finishes anything and breaks fifty per cent of what he temporarily fixes.'[55] He wanted to buy a Buddha for his wife but nothing came up to par. 'Lord, how ugly everything Indian and Anglo-Indian is,' he despaired. He wanted to somehow educate Indian craftsmen, but felt the task was quite futile. 'I feel sure it's no use blunting one's own sense of righteousness by stooping to the inefficiencies of an atrophied architecture.'[56]

In evidence here is a sweeping disdain, an implacable belief that his civilisation is inherently superior, and undisguised contempt for 'the natives'. Well into the twentieth century, this was a bit extreme even for diehard British imperialists. In a person outside of politics and trained in the arts, one would have expected to find some understanding, however small, of the culture of the country where he had come to work. But this was ruled out; Lutyens' mind was closed. 'I cannot allow the supremacy of the Eastern over the Western mind,' he declared. 'The Chinaman is an exception perhaps, but the Hindus and Muslims are mere children at the game.'[57] This attitude influenced Lutyens' work, of course, but also his interactions with Indians, even when they sometimes came from a background he approved. In a letter dated 27 February 1929, he recalls meeting 'a Pandit Nehru' at a party. This was Motilal Nehru, and since it appeared to Lutyens that he was not without 'some wit', he invited him to lunch. From the description of what transpired, the repast was mostly a monologue by the host on the decline of Indian arts, and how 'deplorably behind [the] times' they were. The construction of the Viceroy's Palace was essentially 'an education to the Indian mason and craftsman,' he told his guest, who—apparently—confessed that this angle to Lutyens' enterprise had not struck him. 'The only live thing in India [is] half-baked statesmanship and agitation,' declared the master builder over coffee and port. It was a rather satisfying lunch, especially since Lutyens felt that Motilal was interested in what he said, and was, therefore, an agreeable kind of person. 'He is a dear old man, drinks whisky, port etc., mutton, everything. A black coat and Jodhpurs on which I drew buttons so that he looked exactly like an English bishop. And that was all that he was fit for if he didn't help India in her material world.'[58] Not surprisingly, the greatest concentration of Indian motifs—elephant legs and sandstone bells— is found in the service entrance and the guardhouse of the Rashtrapati Bhavan. The few other tokenisms like the occasional use of chhajjas, chhatris and jaalis, and temple bell motifs are essentially drowned out by Lutyens' conviction that the only building suitable would be the classic European style, with the massive Corinthian columns dominating the façade of the building and the vaulted Durbar Hall patterned on Hadrian's Pantheon.

The reason why colonialism was such a deeply dislocating event was that its sustained critique was *internalised* by its victims. Since the denigration came from the rulers, it found effortless projection and no organised opposition; the entire paraphernalia of the state— including the educational institutions and curriculum and English as the officially sponsored and imposed medium of instruction—was available to disseminate this denigration and give it sanctity. Moreover, the denunciation came with the tag of scholarship, wherein obvious colonial bias was camouflaged with extensive field studies and tomes of data. The colonial historians and arbiters of art did not purport to give off-the-cuff opinions, they did not pronounce their verdict as one-line imperial dictates; their dismissal wore the garb of study and research and so-called 'comparative' analysis. The tragedy was that the local populace, more often than not, accepted this denigration; books on Indian art and architecture authored by British historians were standard texts in schools till many years after 1947. This entire body of one-sided criticism and dismissal seeped into the mentality of the educated Indians and, in particular, the elite.

The degree to which this unrelenting critique succeeded in influencing Indians can be gauged from the writings of a foreign observer, a remarkably observant Englishman. Ernest Beinfield Havell was the principal of the Government School of Art in Calcutta. He had worked with Abanindranath Tagore and written books on Indian sculpture and painting, on Banaras and on the principles of Indian art. In 1912, he penned a strongly worded polemic[59] on how British rule had subverted the artistic traditions of India, severing the Indian educated classes from their cultural roots and reducing them to little more than mindless mimics of Western fashions and mores. Havell noticed 'a curious want of discrimination in wealthy and aristocratic Indians, who in the intimate domestic life still kept up more or less Indian artistic traditions, but kept one part of their home in a quasi-European fashion'. 'It is this want of pride and want of faith in their own traditional culture on the part of the upper classes of India,' he said, 'which has been much more destructive to Indian art than the ignorance or indifference of Europeans.' Nothing, he argued, is more intellectually depressing than the sense of 'constitutional inferiority' that seems to have possessed Indians. 'The surrender of all their artistic traditions, which so many educated Indians have been content to make is an intellectual and moral loss for which all European science and literature cannot compensate them, nor will the fullest measure of political liberty ... restore to them what they lose by that surrender.' The great scourge eating into the creative faculties of educated Indians was the inclination to mimic European artistic traditions. This imitative faculty, Havell argued, was encouraged by the British educational system. 'Anglo-Indian education being imitative cannot be of any use to Indian art. The fact that Indian art has been totally ignored in the Anglo-Indian scheme of education has tended to hasten its decay only because it has on that account led English educated Indians to regard it with indifference.'

One can discern in Havell's comments a genuine sense of

outrage at the degree to which the legatees of a great civilisation had emasculated their cultural identity. His overriding motivation was to jolt them out of their colonised sensibilities. 'Let your homes,' he said, 'be built by Indian master builders schooled in the Shilpa-Shastras; let the furniture in your houses be of Indian design; let the teachings of the epics be taught to children and painted, as in the past, on the walls of schools and buildings; let the old chitrashalas be revived and patronized by the rich and the powerful.' He was exasperated by the proclivity of English-educated Indians to present to their European guests 'no higher domestic ideal than that of a London boarding house, and speak of their fellow countrymen who keep to the Indian tradition of domestic life as "jungly" folk.' Being at the helm of a leading educational institution, he interacted with those who were the principal beneficiaries of British education, and could see—with the objectivity that only a foreign observer could have—how far they were adrift from the animating spirit of their own cultural ethos. 'Indians will certainly gain immensely, not only morally and intellectually but also politically,' he stressed, 'by ceasing to imitate European fashions indiscriminately, for this very lack of discrimination which educated Indians have shown discredits them in the eyes of Europe. ... As long as their chief ambition is to become successful imitators of what Europe does, they will remain in a state of political inferiority—and rightly so, for indiscriminate imitation is an admission of inferiority which inevitably depreciates the power of initiative and prevents the development of all the creative faculties.'

In such situations, historical memory becomes episodic, the intervening periods blanketed in a haze of collective amnesia. For the colonised, the past does not have a benevolent, easily accessible continuum with the present. It becomes a template for either denial or rejection or overemphasis or amnesia, and this disequilibrium continues much after the rulers have left.

The manner in which the image of Krishna in his manifestation as the divine lover was sanitised provides an excellent illustration of this phenomenon. In Hinduism, Krishna is regarded as the purna avatar, the complete incarnation, because he incorporates within himself all the sixteen attributes of human refinement, including the sringara rasa—the erotic. His role as the divine lover is in sync with the four highest purusharthas or goals of life enjoined in the Hindu world view—dharma (right conduct), artha (the pursuit of material well-being), kama (the pursuit of desire) and moksha (salvation). If Krishna's romantic dalliance as a boy with Radha and the gopis of Vrindavan is a validation of kama, his conduct as the Pandavas' adviser in the Mahabharata is a validation of artha; and in the Gita-upadesha—during his sermon to Arjuna on selfless duty—he is the personification of dharma. The sringara rasa, therefore, is only one aspect of a many-splendoured personality that exemplifies the ideal life. The concept of Krishna as a lover was part of such an integrated, pragmatic and balanced world view, linking the sacred and the profane in a joyous celebration of life. It was certainly not evidence of some primitive hedonism or mindless carnality.

The British, however, viewed the entire lore of Krishna, the lover, with either ridicule or disgust. By the mid-nineteenth century, the British, weaned on the evangelical fervour of Charles Grant and William Wilberforce and the utilitarian credo of the Mills brothers, were emphatic in their assessment of India as the dark land of heathens wallowing in immorality and evil. Considerable attention was devoted to juxtaposing the Christian ethic and value system with the 'depraved' moral fibre of the natives. The Hindus, to them, were 'tied to hateful, horrible beliefs and customs—unmentionable thoughts'. Their world of darkness was filled with 'lust' and their culture had no 'moral codes—tolerating both polyandry and polygamy and countenancing the greatest sensuousness'. Their form of worship was 'to a very large extent disgusting and even immoral', and the Hindu himself suffered from 'unparalleled sexual degradation'. In the eyes of the Christian Literary Society of Madras, Krishna, quite simply, was an adulterer and fornicator. In 1862, Sir Mathew Sausse, a British judge of the Bombay High Court, pronounced a judgement in which he saw the rasaleela—the enactment of Krishna's dance with the gopis—as only a means of encouraging adultery: 'All songs connected with the worship of Krishna which were brought before us, were of an amorous character. … In these songs as well as stories both written and traditional, which later are treated as of a religious character, the subject of sexual intercourse is most prominent. Adultery is made familiar to the minds of all; it is nowhere discouraged or denounced, but on the contrary, in some stories, those persons who have committed that great moral and social offence are commended.'[60]

It was not Krishna alone who was the target of British ridicule—it was entire Hinduism as a religion. As far back as 1584, Ralph Fitch, Queen Elizabeth's envoy to Akbar, was appalled to see Hindu idols, describing them as 'blacke and evell favoured, their mouths monstrous, their eares gilded and full of jewels'. Christian missionaries were given a free hand by 1813. Their entry was prepared for by a volley of statements in Britain, and by the British in India, deriding Hinduism. A good example of this is what Robert Southey, later the Poet Laureate of England, had to say in 1810: 'The religion of the Hindoos … of all false religions is the most monstrous in its fables, and most fatal in its effects'.[61] Interestingly, Southey had never visited India, so what he was giving voice to was not based on personal observation but simply on an overweening sense of generalised contempt for Hinduism, and every aspect of Hindu civilisation. William Wilberforce fully backed the need for missionaries because, as he said in a speech in the House of Commons in 1813, 'our religion is sublime, pure and beneficent (while) theirs is mean, licentious and cruel'. For him, Hindu gods were 'absolute monsters of lust, injustice, wickedness and cruelty', Hinduism was 'the most enormous and tormenting superstition that ever harassed and degraded any portion of mankind', and Hindus 'the most enslaved portion of the human race'.

The British were never in any doubt that they were not only rulers but conquering proselytisers. To sustain this belief, they needed to heap derision on the faith to which most Indians belonged. In such an appraisal, there could be no scope for the short-lived admiration for Hindu religious texts and aspects of Hindu civilisation expressed initially by some British members of the Asiatic Society who had taken the trouble to study and translate important texts from Hindu religion and culture. The imperative was to make the natives ashamed of their religion, to make them believe that it was primitive, full of prejudice and superstition, and outdated vis-à-vis the needs of a 'scientific outlook' and 'European modernity', which alone were the path of the future. In so doing, they had to devalue, and even dismiss Hinduism as an obstruction to enlightened progress, and ridicule it, since it was the most important anchor preventing Hindus from more fully embracing the civilising Christian domination by England. British critique was reinforced by other eminent European academics. Immanuel Kant (1724–1804), one of the most influential figures of modern Western philosophy, wrote: 'Indians have a dominating taste for the grotesque. … Their religion consists of grotesqueries. Idols of monstrous form, the priceless tooth of the mighty monkey Hanuman, the unnatural atonements of the fakirs (heathen mendicant friars) and so forth are in their taste.'[62] Another great German philosopher, Friedrich Hegel (1770–1831), pronounced in his *Lectures on the History of Philosophy*: 'If we had formerly the satisfaction of believing in the antiquity of the Indian wisdom and holding it in respect, we now have ascertained through being acquainted with the great astronomical figures of the Indians, the inaccuracy of all figures quoted. Nothing can be more confused, nothing more imperfect than the chronology of the Indians.'[63] Hegel, therefore, felt that an inferior culture such as that of the Indians deserved to be colonised: 'The British, or rather the East India Company, are the masters of India because it is the fatal destiny of Asian empires to subject themselves to the Europeans.'[64]

The Hindu revivalist movements of the nineteenth century, of which the most important were the Brahmo Samaj (founded by Raja Ram Mohan Roy in 1830) and the Arya Samaj (founded by Dayanand Saraswati in 1875), were motivated by noble intentions—

to cleanse India's social and religious legacy of the many distortions that had crept into it over centuries. But in doing so, they sought also to gain respectability in the eyes of the British and 'raise' themselves to better absorb the new ideas of science and liberalism represented by the coloniser. Hence, the thrust of their reforming endeavours was to jettison from their collective religious heritage any and all elements that were likely to invite criticism from an Anglo-Christian perspective. Ram Mohan Roy was also very supportive of Christian missionaries entering the field of education. Reverend Alexander Duff of the Church of Scotland was one of the first to respond. When he had difficulty in finding premises for his school, Ram Mohan put a hall at his disposal. On the first day, a Bible was placed in the hands of the children, but Roy placated the protesting parents and students. Three hundred applicants had come for admission in a hall that could accommodate only a hundred and twenty. According to Duff, the students begged to be taken in. This is how he records their pleas: '"Me want read your good books, oh, take me"; "Me good boy"; "Me poor boy"; "Me know your commandments: 'Thou shalt have no other gods before me', oh, take me"; "Oh take me, and I pray for you".'[65] Indeed, the Brahmo ideology 'imbibed quite a bit of Christianity (particularly its Unitarian form) along with some Deism of the European Enlightenment. The third generation (Brahmo) Samaj leader Keshub Chandra Sen (1838–1884) professed a Christian-like veneration of Jesus of Nazareth and interiorized the Christian concept of man's profound sinfulness,'[66] so antithetical to Hindu philosophy.

The Arya Samaj was the most influential reform movement under British rule. Its impulses were motivated by the genuine desire to rid the practice of Hinduism of some of its accumulated evils, including superstition, prejudice, caste discrimination and gender disparity. But, the impact of the colonial critique of Hinduism can be easily discerned in several aspects of its doctrine. Dayanand Saraswati, who founded the Samaj, came from a traditional Hindu family. His father was an ardent devotee of Shiva, as was Dayanand to begin with. It is said that as a child he sat up the whole night in obeisance on Shivratri. However, his faith was ruptured because he saw a rat eating the prasad offered to Shiva—if the Lord could not protect himself against a rat, how could he be the saviour of the world? This was the question that arose in young Dayanand's mind.

Such anecdotal logic is used to explain Dayanand Saraswati's disillusionment with many of Hinduism tenets. But, while the Arya Samaj was a movement for change from within, much of this change was also prompted by the religion of the rulers, and their critique of Hinduism. Since Christianity had only one religious text, the Bible, the Arya Samaj too rejected all other texts of Hinduism except the Vedas, which were considered as shruti, or revealed texts. Since the British looked down upon idol worship, the Samaj rejected idolatry. (Incidentally, C.F. Andrews recounts a dialogue between Gandhi and Rabindranath Tagore, where Gandhi defends idols, arguing that people are 'incapable of raising themselves immediately to abstract ideas'.[67]) The rulers thought that Hinduism is little else except ritualism, and the Samaj expressed itself against worship in temples. The British were contemptuous of the proliferation of 'weird' Hindu gods and goddesses; expectedly, the Samaj endorsed a strict monotheism and rejected the notion of a personal god, considering even Rama and Krishna to be just historical figures and not deities. The British stood for the advent of science and modernity, so the Samaj emphasised the importance of science *as part of religious practice*. A good Hindu, Dayanand argued, 'should have practical training in [the] Sciences, learn the proper handling of instruments, master their mechanism, and know how to use them,' quite forgetting that Hindu civilisation had created milestones in scientific research long before Europe. Christianity was a proselytising religion so the Samaj too advocated proselytisation through the Shuddhi movement. Christianity looked down upon other faiths, so the Samaj also had derogatory things to say about all other religions—Sikhism, Buddhism, Jainism, Islam and Christianity—abjuring the Hindu tradition of respect for other faiths.

A movement that was primarily a *reaction* to the unrelenting and scathing critique by the rulers, was bound to have mutilating contradictions. Hence, while the Samaj valorises the Vedas as the sole infallible texts of the Hindus, it ignores many other foundational texts—so natural to an eclectic and discursive religion like Hinduism—such as the Bhagwad Gita, the *Brahma Sutras* and the six systems of Hindu philosophy. Besides, there is an arbitrariness in the selection from the Vedas themselves—Vedic philosophy is considered paramount, but texts like the Brahmanas, which are manuals of ritual and religious rites and are a part of the Vedas, are summarily overlooked. In rejecting the notion of a personal god, the Arya Samaj rejected the carefully crafted philosophical synthesis between the nirguna and the saguna, and confined to the dustbin the devotional fervour of the Bhakti movement. In the pursuit of a imitative monotheism, the Samaj curtly dismissed the epics—the Ramayana and the Mahabharata. Clearly, the Arya Samaj's world view was shaped not only by a genuine conviction that Hinduism needed reform, but also by the categories in which such a 'reformed' religion could win the approval of the ruler's gaze. Wendy Doniger calls it 'a kind of colonial and religious Stockholm syndrome', where, as a consequence of the transparent admiration for the culture of the colonisers, many highly placed Hindus 'swallowed the Protestant line themselves and not only gained a *new* appreciation of those aspects of Hinduism that the British approved of (the Gita, the Upanishads, monism) but became ashamed of those aspects that the British scorned (much of the path or rebirth, polytheism, the earthy and erotic aspects) and even developed new forms of Hinduism, such as the Arya Samaj and Brahmo Samaj, heavily influenced by British Protestantism'.[68]

Even those imbued with a fierce nationalistic spirit often found it difficult to escape the connection between patriotism, the colonial experience and the need to exorcise some aspect of the past. For instance, the fact that Hindu gods had goddesses as consorts, and that the power of shakti as symbolised in the Devi, which was an essential aspect of divinity, was now seen as a minus when juxtaposed with the Christian deification of a singular male god. The British consistently derided their Indian subjects for being too effeminate. The historian Robert Orme proclaimed, soon after the East India Company arrived in India, that the Hindu is 'the most effeminate inhabitant of the globe'. The dhoti worn by Bengali men was dismissed as a woman's dress; Indian men were described as completely lacking 'manly self-control' (their diet, of which rice was a major part, was considered one possible reason for this affliction). Baden-Powell, who founded the Scout Movement in 1908, and who is uncritically valorised by many military-minded Indian men to this day, was convinced that Indian boys needed a strong muscular infusion, for they were 'singularly without character by nature', and bereft of any notion of self-discipline or honour. A classic example showing how this critique was internalised even by individuals who were otherwise the proponents of a virile nationalism can be seen in the reaction of Bankim Chandra Chatterjee (1838–1896) to the lyrical genius of Jayadeva's Sanskrit classic *Gita Govinda*: 'From the beginning to the end,' Bankim lamented, 'it does not contain a single expression of manly feeling—of womanly feelings there is a great deal. ... I do not deny his high poetical merits in a certain sense of exquisite imagery ... but that does not make him less the poet of an effeminate and sensual race.'[69]

The point is that colonial rule, while politically humiliating, was far more harmful in the long run for the change in perceptions it wrought in Hindus themselves about their religion and culture. 'Scholars have noted a pattern in which colonized people take on the mask that the colonizer creates in the image of the colonized, mimicking the colonizer's perception of the colonized.'[70] This syndrome plays out in a myriad ways, where the 'native' becomes only the object of the ruler's gaze rather than an autonomous entity, and long-established traditions of belief and creativity are mutilated.

For instance, in the field of painting, soon after the consolidation of British rule in the second half of the eighteenth century, there was a great demand for lifelike images of the 'natives' and their 'exotic' culture for the viewing pleasure of friends and family back home.

Initially this demand was met by a select group of British artists who travelled to India to paint its people, monuments and scenery. William Hodges visited India over 1780–1783 and released his *Select Views of India* in 1787; he was followed by the uncle and nephew duo of Thomas and William Daniell, who produced the celebrated six-volume series of aquatints, *Oriental Scenery*. Other significant landscape and portrait artists included William Simpson, Edward Lear and Emily Eden, Tilly Kettle, John Zoffany, Robert Home and George Chinnery.

The works of these artists fuelled a growing curiosity in Britain, and to cope with this demand a need was felt to develop an atelier of Indian artists who could paint in the same genre and style as their masters. Indian artists were available for hire; they were in need of money because of the reduced patronage from members of the Indian royalty, who were, expectedly, more attracted to the British artists; and, they were willing and quick to adapt to the new stylistic requirements. Thus was created the Company School of Painting, wherein a great many Indian painters adjusted their own tradition and training to adopt the style and technique favoured by the British, for a British audience. At the behest of their British patrons and the occasional Indian royal, they produced, from about the mid-eighteenth century to the mid-nineteenth, a large body of work about themselves—their monuments, people, costumes, festivals, occupations, nautch girls, crafts, et al. —but in a style that was alien and for the needs of a foreign audience.

This was the first 'oscillation', a movement away from the artistic continuity that could have unfolded in normal circumstances. The Company School was not without merit, but it was an imposition, an artificial construct that was not the result of synthesis or of normal creative evolution, and, therefore, the *process* that it entailed needs to be analysed. When people are the subjects of their own culture, their creative expression has self-assuredness and spontaneity, so they create a unique and effective language of communication even when the grammar is imperfect because the idiom is authentic. But when people become objects of a foreign culture, a huge transformation takes place. Suddenly, a creative work is judged not for its intrinsic value, or for the heritage it is sourced from and is a part of, but for the degree to which it is comprehensible and conforms to the outsider's culture. The process is all the more mutilating if the outsider belongs to the dominant political or military power of the time, and there is prejudice and condescension in the gaze. When this happens, spontaneity reduces itself to self-conscious mediocrity; creativity seeks to qualify itself; authenticity gives way to imitation; self-assurance is replaced by denial. An entire culture attempts to reinterpret itself in terms that will somehow win the dominant outsider's approval. The objectified people then thrive only as exotica; their historic role becomes that of the observed; everything external about them—and nothing of intrinsic value—is collated, classified and investigated. They finally end up as caricatures, divorced from their own cultural milieu and perpetually alien—in spite of their best efforts at emulation—to the world of the outsider.

This interruption of natural artistic evolution, this 'oscillation', is verifiable—the imposition of British preference did not, after all, take place on a blank template. The painted pottery of the Indus Valley dates back to 3000 BCE, and reveals an already developed sense of line and colour. Alexander Gottlieb Baumgarten coined the word 'aesthetics' in 1735 but about two thousand years earlier, the *Natya Shastra*—as I have discussed—had analysed the structure of aesthetics and the rasa or emotions it produced. In the specific area of painting, several ancient Indian texts exist. The *Vishnudharmottara*, written in the second century, is a detailed treatise on the rules of painting, including the choice of materials, techniques and colours. The emphasis, even at this early stage, is on how the depiction needs to bring out the inner essence rather than merely a physical representation. Thus, specific colours are recommended to evoke the different moods or rasas—white for hasya (comic), dark blue for sringara (sensual), red for rudra (anger), black for bhayanak (fearsome), grey for karuna (compassion), yellowish white for vira (heroic) and yellow for adbhuta (marvel and awe). Bhittichitra, the art of making paintings on walls, was common throughout the ancient period, and the frescoes and murals of Ajanta—representing the apogee of this tradition—were made during the rule of the Guptas in the fifth and sixth centuries. Evidence that this tradition continued can be seen in the Ellora paintings of the eighth and tenth centuries, and in the medieval-era murals in the palaces of Kerala and Rajputana and the Jain temples of Gujarat.

A new element was added to this repertoire with the coming of the Mughals. In the sixteenth century, Emperor Akbar set up an imperial atelier, inviting the best artists from all over India to his court. In time, this royal patronage produced a fusion of Hindu and Persian art that consolidated itself under the rule of his successors, Jahangir and Shahjahan. The Mughal artistic oeuvre was extensive, and included paintings of flora and fauna, landscapes, portraits and illustrated manuscripts. Some of the best works were in the miniature style, which spread from the Mughal court to the Hindu kingdoms of Rajasthan and those in the Himalayan foothills. The themes of these artists were from their own milieu and history—a great many of the works dealt with the romance of Radha and Krishna, but collections on other subjects, such as the classical ragas—the Raagmala miniatures—or the changing seasons—the Barahmasas—were equally significant.

The imposition of British artistic requirements has to be seen in this context in order to understand the exact nature of the rupture in tradition and cultural evolution. Unable, and unwilling, to consider any world view other than their own, the British could not understand that the artists who painted the murals of Ajanta were less concerned with the exact physical representation of a form than with the inner spirit animating it. Their verdict, then, was that Indians could not draw well enough and needed to be trained. There was no question of providing patronage to existing artistic skills; the exclusive focus was on replacing them with the prevalent European art traditions. When, therefore, William Dalrymple says that 'Mughal technique, rendered with English watercolour on English paper, produced the Company

School of Art',[71] one is mystified. His assessment casually sanitises the colonial project, making it out to be an exchange between equals, thus adding to the prevailing trend towards revisionism that catalogued the glories of the Empire and presented colonial policies as either enlightened intervention or imperial benevolence. India had, over centuries, absorbed myriads of external influences, but this interaction with the British was different because it was based not on dialogue but on dictate, on rejection rather than interaction, thereby obliterating the possibility of a synthesis that would enrich both cultures. As Shakti Maira, the erudite art historian, says: 'Till British colonisation, Indian art … had its phases, movements and developments. There was a reshaping by patrons, as happened in the Mughal period, with their preference for a more religiously appropriate, non-figurative, more floral or more Persian art, yet this seems to have added to the range of art made in India. Rather than uproot or replace earlier or non-Islamic art, something was added. Temples and a wide range of art continued that showed no crisis of confidence that it was inferior, primitive, unskilled, un-progressive or banal. All this happened with the British, and the contemporary art scene has still not completely recovered from the lack of self-worth that came from what happened to India at that time.'[72]

If the Company School wrenched artists away from their themes and techniques to create an entire generation of visual clerks, the formal art schools set up in Bombay and Calcutta in the mid-nineteenth century set out to train Indian artists in the 'Royal Academy' style of painting. The J.J School of Art, named after the first Indian to be conferred a baronetcy, Sir Jamsetjee Jeejebhoy, who provided the school an initial grant of a hundred thousand rupees, was founded in March 1857. Lockwood Kipling was its first principal, and his son, the writer Rudyard Kipling, was born on the campus. The Government School of Art in Calcutta was founded in 1864, with H.H. Locke as its first principal. A generation of painters graduated from these schools, having learnt from British academicians about the superior principles of European art. The evangelical purpose of 'upgrading' Indian artists so that they could conform to and be inspired by European standards was never in doubt. The J.J. School, in its first annual report, spoke of the tendency of Indian artists 'to repeat traditional compositions which have come down to them from a distant age without refreshing or even glancing at real life. Hence they degenerate instead of improving. The grotesque images with the shapes of men and animals in all parts of the Hindu temple are irredeemably bad. Their sculptured foliage is purely abstract in character. It seems that the safest way of attempting to regenerate this defective and artificial manner of design without destroying what it has inherited from European schools of art is to set the student to copy faithfully the objects of nature, men and women. ... Thus a school of design would in time arise, native in the best sense, owing its sense of accuracy, truth, and natural beauty to European inspiration but moulding its material into purely Indian types.'

The Bengal School of the late nineteenth century was born as a reaction to this manifest colonial bias in art, and marked the second 'oscillation', this time in the opposite direction, towards precolonial artistic traditions. The movement began under the patronage of E.B. Havell, the principal of the Calcutta Art College from 1896 to 1905. Havell, as I have discussed earlier, was convinced about the need for Indians to go back to their own traditions. With Abanindranath Tagore, a cousin of Rabindranath Tagore, whom he had appointed as the vice principal, he set about clearing the college of its copies of mediocre European pictures and plaster casts of Greek models. The revivalist ideology of the Bengal School was greatly influenced by the philosophy and heritage of India's past, and drew inspiration from the Hindu epics, the Ajanta frescoes and Mughal and Rajput miniatures. It was a conscious effort to set the clock back, and support came from unexpected quarters. A group of Japanese painters who visited Calcutta at the turn of the twentieth century, of whom the most prominent was Kakuzo Okakura, added their opposition to the mindless imitation of the West, and gave demonstrations on how to paint on silk and paper in the style of Ajanta.

It is a commentary on the contradictions that colonialism creates that the high-minded intentions of the Bengal School did not have universal support among Indians themselves. The students of the Calcutta College went on strike and the local press was equally critical, condemning any invocation of India's past in preference to western modernity as retrogressive. This ideological confusion — where what is Western is considered relevant even if it is alien, and what is indigenous is perceived irrelevant — is among the most insidious consequences of colonialism. Of course, any attempt at revivalism has a tendency to be extreme, and some of the criticism of Abanindranath and his devoted followers was not entirely off the mark. Mukul Dey, the learned art critic, and principal of the Government College at Calcutta in the 1960s, rightly points out that the Bengal School artists 'were in the beginning somewhat afraid of modern life, lest they should be drawn merely into imitative representation. This led them to avoid landscapes or portraits, the representation of present day objects or events, so their work remained somewhat artificial, in the sense that it was not the outcome of their own actual experiences, but rather of a dreamland which they made real by giving it colour and form. ... Painting was found to be the best medium for expressing this dream life of theirs, and so the first group of Abanindranath's disciples completely neglected other mediums of art such as sculpture, architecture, or means of reproduction like lithography, woodcut, etching etc. Oil paintings were also disliked as being too decidedly European.'

The puritanical awkwardness of the Bengal School mellowed in time; artists like Nandalal Bose and Jamini Roy dexterously dipped into the folk idiom and created works that had considerable aesthetic appeal without the straitjacketed self-consciousness of the early years. But the deliberate glorification of a precolonial past was bound to create its own antibodies. The third 'oscillation' took place much later, after Independence, when leading painters in many parts of the country rebelled against both the revivalism of the Bengal School and the Royal Academy style taught in the government art colleges. This led to the Progressive Artists Group (PAG), founded in 1947 by F.N. Souza, K.H. Ara and S.H. Raza, and included M.F. Husain, H.A. Gade and S.K. Bakre.

The three 'oscillations' in Indian art since the arrival of the British were a direct consequence of colonial distortion. The Company School, which set off the chain reaction, constituted a wrenching away from the past; the Bengal School was an attempt to return to it; and the Progressive Artists Group and its offshoots constituted an angry denial of both the imposition of colonial techniques and an uncritically resurrected past. For over a hundred and fifty years, therefore, Indian art was only about *reaction*, not about normal evolutionary *progression*. The latter was a luxury only the colonising power could enjoy. Within that evolutionary progression there could be radical changes, such as, for instance, Dadaism, Cubism and the entire corpus of the European avant-garde, but these changes came from stimuli within, not as a reaction to what was imposed from outside. The contrast with the options available to the colonised is vivid—Indian artists had little option but to suppress their natural artistic heritage to conform to the requirement of the Company School; the well-meaning pioneers of the Bengal School could think of little else than to try and eliminate that colonial imposition by blindly reverting to the past; and the imperative before Souza and others like him was only to rebel against the two induced reactions. The Indian masters of the Company School, who painted market scenes and religious fairs and processions and made lifelike images of barbers and ironsmiths and weavers for the curiosity of foreigners, were caricaturing themselves against their will. The Bengal artists who were reluctant to experiment with anything that was not an element of their glorified past were, by the very acceptance of this limitation, caricaturing their potential. And the Progressive Artists in Bombay, seeking the anarchic freedom of the unconditioned, were, in the very process of denying their past, unknowingly caricaturing their rebellious vision of the future. All the artists of the PAG and similar post-Independence groups, and in particular, the firebrand Souza, were heavily and unnaturally influenced by European modernism, leading the art critic John Bergman to comment that Souza 'straddles many traditions but serves none'.

I have dealt at length with one area of creative expression—painting—only to illustrate how colonial rule impacts the memory and evolution of artistic traditions of ancient civilisations. It converts the confident legatees of a highly evolved aesthetic into helpless but willing accessories of the ruler's culture, and forces them to adapt to that compulsion in a manner that is—even in its most well-intentioned manifestation—a distortion.

If the wanton destruction by the Turkic invaders—and by the Muslim dynasties in India that followed it—traumatised the natural evolution of Hindu civilisation and deprived it of many of its most valuable cultural artefacts, British rule colonised the Hindu mind and robbed it of self-worth and esteem. It produced an army of willing accomplices for the perpetuation of the civilisational domination of the colonising power, and this process was all the more ironical because—in most cases—it was done with the cooperation of the victims, who had successfully been convinced that their past was primitive or irrelevant or a liability, and that salvation lay only in emulating the cultural, economic and political paradigm of the rulers. Hinduism survived the Islamic onslaught by reinventing itself, in which the democratisation and decentralisation by the Bhakti movement played a very significant role. Undoubtedly, there were areas of cultural synthesis that took place with Islam that enriched both cultures, but that did not obliterate the degree of challenge that Hinduism and Hindu culture faced for its very survival. British rule, on the other hand, did not lead to any significant Indianisation of the rulers; the assimilation by the British rulers into the Indian idiom was far more limited than in the case of Muslim rule. However, the penetration of the British project to colonise the mind of the natives was far deeper—in the vital areas of language, creativity, thought processes and the derogation of their own religion. I have provided snapshots of how this colonisation worked in the case of key individuals and in the larger processes that unfolded in parallel. Ultimately, British conquest was used by the rulers as a means to devalue, debase and demean Hinduism and Hindu civilisation in the eyes of Hindus themselves. As Kapila Vatsyayan insightfully puts it: 'We became the objects of our own viewing and not the subjects of our living. The Upanishadic view of the bhokta and the drishta—the experience and the watcher—were replaced by a decontextualisation of our categories of thought and speech from the life we lived. A definite fissure had taken place in the minds of many who first utilised the intellectual baggage of the "other" to understand the "self" … we began to look at ourselves as the vestiges of a dead past, the precious evidence of archaeology.'[73]

The psychological consequences of this—especially for a civilisation that was among the most refined and sophisticated in the world—have left a lasting imprint, and continue to cast a baneful shadow even today, decades after political independence in 1947.

6

THE CHALLENGE OF THE MODERN REPUBLIC

India gained independence on 15 August 1947. It resolved to become a republic on 26 January 1950, when the country's constitution was adopted. The freedom struggle, although not a monolith, was largely helmed by the iconic Mahatma Gandhi. The departure of the British was preceded by the horrific nightmare of the Partition. Pakistan, a Muslim-majority nation, was born. Millions of people were displaced, with large numbers of Muslims heading towards Pakistan, and Hindus from there coming to India. Unimaginable violence and brutality accompanied this tectonic movement of people.

Since the early days of the freedom movement, there was a fear among some Muslims that their position would be vulnerable after Independence in a Hindu-majority India. Syed Ahmad Khan, a leading voice among Muslim intellectuals, who founded the Aligarh Muslim University in 1886, was among the first to voice his apprehensions on this score. When a Muslim, Badruddin Tyabji, was elected the president of the Indian National Congress in 1887, he opposed it on the grounds that any attempt at Hindu–Muslim unity would be disadvantageous to the Muslims since they were an educationally and economically insecure minority, and would be swamped by the overwhelming Hindu majority.

The conservative Deoband seminary opened in 1866, with the avowed aim of spearheading Muslim revivalism. In 1906, a delegation of Muslim leaders—called the Shimla Deputation—met Lord Minto, the British viceroy, and demanded separate electorates for Muslims and a higher representation for Muslims than their population warranted. The British, who were rather adept at the divide-and-rule game, accepted most of what the Muslims wanted, and the Muslim League was born in the same year. In 1930, the famous poet Mohammad Iqbal clearly spoke of the idea of a separate nation for Muslims in the north-west, where they were in a majority. In 1940, the Muslim League, led by Mohammad Ali Jinnah, passed a resolution for the creation of Pakistan. The inevitable happened in 1947, and Bharat, that is India, was partitioned to create two separate states.

The purpose here is not to provide a detailed or chronological account of what led to Partition. Perhaps the Congress too made mistakes, such as when it rejected a possible accommodation with the Muslim League in 1937, or in 1946, when it spurned the creation of three sub-federations within a united India, as proposed by Jinnah, on the basis of Muslim-majority areas. Certainly, the British viceroy, Lord Mountbatten, seemed to have been convinced rather prematurely about the inevitability of the creation of Pakistan, and played a key role in persuading Congress leaders to accept it. However, even after Pakistan was created, and a great many Muslims migrated to it, a substantial number stayed behind to constitute India's largest minority.

For the first time after the Turkic invasion in the twelfth century CE and the British conquest in the eighteenth century CE, in 1947, Hindus became the dominant force in their country in terms of their numerical majority. But this new and heady freedom was also bounded by the terms of the republic as expressly laid down in the Constitution. The task ahead was to build a new India on the debris of the subjugation of the past, and as part of that goal, to also—at least that was the expectation of most Hindus—to reclaim for Hindu civilisation its due place in the discourse and practice of the new nation. What should this have entailed, what challenges and provocations lay in the way, to what extent has this aspiration succeeded, where has it failed and what more needs to be done, are things that we need to think and reflect about.

Colonised nations need to reclaim their history, especially after achieving independence. This is necessary because the colonial power seeks to obliterate and distort that history, and as I have discussed in the previous chapter, the British did so with spectacular success. Hindus—along with all Indians—were made to feel inferior not only with regard to their religion but also their civilisation, and the relentless critique created a co-opted elite that was—true to Macaulay's prophetic vision—an accomplice in amplifying this message. English spoken with the right fluency and accent, and modernity defined in Western terms, were the attributes of this class, and those who constituted it were the role models for other aspirants to upward mobility.

Although that may not have been the conscious intent of mass leaders like Mahatma Gandhi or Nehru, these anglicised elite were the ones who inherited the reins of power from the British. Its members had benefitted the most from the avenues of education under colonial rule; many of them had been educated in premier educational institutions in England; they were prominent in the upper echelons of the bureaucracy, the legal profession, academia, the armed forces and the corporate sector; and they usually came from a background of greater wealth, social status and belonged to an 'old-boys' network'. For this class, even if the British had left, their institutions, language, social mores, cultural habits and definitions of modernity remained, and they continued to carry a general disdain for India's civilisational past. These 'brown sahebs' were presumed to be the best equipped legatees to step into the shoes of the departing British.

In this assumption, they had a surprising if unintentional ally in Jawaharlal Nehru, India's first prime minister. It has become the fashion these days for some people to demonise Nehru. This is certainly not the intent here. Yet the truth is that—as he himself admitted in his *An Autobiography*—he was in temperament and exposure far closer to the British than to his own people. He had studied in Harrow and Cambridge, and spent almost all his formative years in England. Interestingly, Nehru was insightful enough to notice the insular nature of the anglicised class. The early membership of the Indian National Congress, founded in 1885 by an Englishman, A.O. Hume, was largely of people from this background. When they met to discuss public issues, such as the desirability of greater representation for Indians in administrative and legislative bodies, the conversation was in English in settings reminiscent of a British drawing room. Nehru attended the Bankipore session of the Congress in 1912 and recalled: 'It was very much an English-knowing upper-class affair where morning coats and well-pressed trousers were greatly in evidence. Essentially it was a social gathering with no political excitement or tension.'[1]

Nehru also noticed the Indians who found employment in the sarkar, particularly at the slightly elevated echelons, tried in some manner to model themselves on their English superiors. 'This official and Service atmosphere invaded and set the tone for almost all Indian middle-class life, especially the English-knowing intelligentsia. ... Professional men, lawyers, doctors and others succumbed to it. All these people lived in a world apart, cut off from the masses and even the lower middle class.'[2] As always, the emulation of the British was accompanied by a denigration of what was Indian. Nehru wrote that even in a relatively small city like Allahabad, his father, Motilal, 'was attracted to Western dress and other Western ways at a time when it was uncommon for Indians to take to them except in big cities like Calcutta and Bombay. ... He had a feeling that his countrymen had fallen low and almost deserved what they got. ... He looked to the West and felt greatly attracted by Western progress, and thought that this would come through an association with England.'[3]

Given his educational and family background, English had become Nehru's first language, and he was perceptive enough to note why this had happened. 'The British had created,' he wrote in his autobiography, 'a new caste or class in India, the English educated class, which lived in a world of its own, cut off from the mass of the population.' He was critical about the importance given to English by the privileged. 'Some people imagine that English is likely to become the lingua franca of India. That seems to me a fantastic conception, except in respect of a handful of upper-class intelligentsia. It has no relation to the problem of mass education and culture. It may be ... that English will become increasingly a language used for technical, scientific and business communications, and especially for international contacts … but if we are to have a balanced view of the world we must not confine ourselves to English spectacles.'[4]

As early as 1925, the Congress had adopted a resolution that its proceedings would be conducted, as far as possible, in Hindustani. But, given the linguistic predilections of the pan-Indian leadership of the freedom movement, little progress was made in the implementation of the resolution, and English remained the official language of the Congress.

The dependence on English of those who were at the forefront of the freedom movement only grew over the years. This was partly understandable, because their interlocutors were British, and the memorandums and petitions had to be in English. But it is significant that Lord Mountbatten, the last viceroy in India, thought that these people often came across as even more British than the British. Delivering the second Jawaharlal Nehru Memorial Lecture in 1968, Mountbatten reminisced: 'They were all professional lawyers steeped in the law and especially in British constitutional law. In this respect they were almost more British than the British. They were all masters of the English language, indeed of a clearer and purer prose than many of our British politicians. It was not only Churchill who carried on the traditions of Gibbon and Macaulay. The classical polish of Nehru's written and spoken word was truly memorable.'[5]

The advent of Mohandas Karamchand Gandhi gave to India's freedom movement a more radical agenda and a mass following. Nehru became his devoted lieutenant, and with his leftist leanings sought to steer the nationalist upsurge towards structural change in favour of the urban poor and the peasantry. The more pragmatic Gandhi was often a check on Nehru's revolutionary zeal, but both of them were in complete agreement on the role of English in the free India for which they were working. In a remarkably strong and reasoned statement, Gandhi spoke his mind as early as 1921:

It is my considered opinion that English education in the manner it has been given has emasculated the English-educated Indians, it has put a severe strain upon the Indian students' nervous energy, and has made of us imitators. The process of displacing the vernacular has been one of the saddest chapters in the British connection. Ram Mohan Rai would have been a greater reformer and Lokmanya Tilak would have been a greater scholar, if they had not to start with the handicap of having to think in English and transmit their thoughts chiefly in English. ... No country can become a nation by producing a race of translators. Of all the superstitions that affect India, none is so great as that a knowledge of the English language is necessary for imbibing ideas of liberty and developing accuracy of thought.[6]

Gandhi's views did not change over time. In 1944, just a few years before Independence, he spoke in a similar vein, but this time with a sense of foreboding about the consequences for the future: 'Our love of the English language in preference to our own mother tongue has caused a deep chasm between the educated and the politically minded classes and the masses. We flounder when we make the vain attempt to express abstruse thoughts in the mother tongue. ... The result has been disastrous. ... We are too near our own times to correctly measure the disservice caused to India by the neglect of its great languages.'[7]

Gandhi realised from the beginning itself that in order to defeat the intent of the colonisers and their dismissive legacy about Indian civilisation, it was essential to be oneself, rooted in the soil, and not appear as mimic men. In *Hind Swaraj*, he wrote: 'It is only those Indians ... who conscientiously believe that Indian civilization is the best, and that European is a nine days' wonder, who can speak without being frightened to the English.'[8]

It is for this reason that Gandhi chose to be Indian in dress, custom, diet and deportment, shunning the debasing emulation of the rulers, and following the cultural idiom of his soil. He could speak the Queen's English when required, but wrote his first book, *Hind Swaraj*, in Gujarati as a conscious decision. His effortless ability to belong to his own milieu, so different from the upper class of Indians of the times, who were at best poor copies of the British, enabled him to meet the British on terms of *cultural* equality, and often took them by surprise, leaving them bewildered and psychologically defeated. Charles Smith, who was Mountbatten's valet and butler in India, recalls what happened when Gandhi came one afternoon for tea at the Viceroy's Palace. The tables in the garden were laden with scones and sandwiches, but he smiled benignly at his hosts and chose 'to eat a bowl of curds he had brought with him. He even persuaded Lord Louis to sample a mouthful! His Lordship bravely swallowed it, but gracefully declined the offer for more.'[9] On another occasion, Gandhi responded to the urgent summons of Mountbatten in his own inimitable way. 'Judge of my astonished delight,' Mountbatten recorded, 'on my finding him enter my study with his finger to his lips to indicate that it was his day of silence. So I did all the talking. He scribbled a few friendly notes on the back of used envelopes.'[10] There was also the occasion—once again at the Viceroy's Palace—when during a lunch break, Gandhi spread out a chattai on the ground and sat down to eat. A horrified British official kept this note: 'I remember Gandhi squatting on the floor and after a while a girl coming in with some filthy yellow stuff which he started eating without as much as a by your leave.'[11]

Such idiosyncrasies, if that is how some would wish to see them, were not only about the superiority of goat's curd over scones, or the virtues of silence or the merits of sitting on the floor while eating. They were symbolic of a revolution of spirit, a proclamation of intent, that even under British subjugation he would meet with the rulers as *himself*. This was, of course, obvious in Gandhi's choice of khadi, the way he built his ashrams and, above all, his conscious immersion in his own civilisational ethos and—as I shall discuss later—acquisition of knowledge about it. And yet, his ambition for independent India to reclaim its own civilisational heritage, remained substantially unfulfilled. Notwithstanding Nehru's railing against the English language—and all that it stood for in cultural terms—at the stroke of the midnight hour on the night of 14 August 1947, when India finally broke the chains of British bondage, Nehru's first words to the millions across the country waiting with bated breath to hear one of the most towering leaders of the freedom movement, were in English. 'Long years ago we made a tryst with destiny,' he said. 'And now the time has come to redeem that pledge.' He spoke with eloquence and passion and a transparent sense of destiny. But, unfortunately, only a minuscule elite could understand what he was saying. Even the intermediaries created as a result of Macaulay's policy could not really be trusted to understand or spell 'tryst' correctly. It was truly an ironic situation—an Indian leader choosing to speak to his own people at the moment of freedom not in his own language but in that of the ruler, fully aware that most of his compatriots would not understand what he was saying, and yet, nobody—not those who listened without understanding, nor those who listened but understood only partially because their comprehension was limited to their clerical knowledge of English, nor the handful who, like Nehru, could speak the language with fluency and felicity—thought this to be unusual. Nehru spoke in a language whose idiom and emotional quotient could hardly touch the people. Had Nehru spoken in Hindi, large numbers in southern or eastern or some other parts of India may still not have understood all that he would have said. But at least the language would have been of the soil, of a country they could now truly call free and their own, rather than the language of the very conquerors whose departure they were celebrating.

As the first prime minister of independent India, Nehru played an admirable role in leading the young nation, and preventing it from dissembling or—as many thought would happen—from disintegrating. But in one way, Nehru's view of India's past was of dismissal and impatience, an impediment to India's push for progress and modernity. In this sense, he was a product of colonial prejudice, and had internalised—like so many others of the anglicised elite—the superficial but deliberate disdain of Indian culture, and specifically Hindu civilisation. His commitment to India's freedom was never in doubt, but in spite of himself, he could not but manifest key aspects of the colonial appraisal. 'It was natural and inevitable that Indian nationalism should resent alien rule,' he wrote in *An Autobiography*, 'and yet it was curious how large numbers of our intelligentsia … accepted, consciously or unconsciously, the British ideology of Empire. … The history and economics and other subjects that were taught in the schools and colleges were written entirely from the British imperial view-point, and laid stress on our numerous failings in the past. … We accepted to some extent this distorted version, and even when we resisted it instinctively we were influenced by it.'[12] Without doubt, Nehru must not have wanted to be influenced by the colonial critique of India's past, but because he was extraordinarily perceptive he could understand why this could happen even against one's will. Thus a yearning for a modernity heavily influenced by Western notions, and a rejection of the past strongly influenced by colonial assessments, became key elements of his world view, and appeared recurrently in his well-intentioned exhortations to the Indian people.

For Nehru, the future of India had to be fashioned unencumbered by the burden of the past. In his writings and speeches, this conviction often reduced itself to a black-and-white representation where, mimicking colonial vocabulary, India's past became some kind of dark cesspool threatening to hold the country back from progress towards the shining utopia of a rational, industrial and scientific state. 'India must break with much of her past and not allow it to dominate the present,' he wrote in his book titled, ironically enough, *The Discovery of India*. 'Our lives are encumbered with the dead wood of the past; all that is dead and has served its purpose must go.'[13] He railed against the 'dust and dirt of ages' that had mutilated India's image, and the 'excrescences and abortions that have twisted and petrified her spirit, set it in rigid frames and stunted her growth'.[14] Tradition for him was of little value, because it was overlaid by 'dead thought and ceremonial', and was irredeemably debilitated by the 'woeful accumulation of superstitions and degrading custom'.[15] 'We have to get out,' he exhorted, 'of traditional ways of thought and living which, for all the good they must have done in a past age ... have ceased to have significance today.'[16]

The interesting thing is that Nehru's emphatic rejection of the old and traditional did not suppress the tendency—common to the colonised—to romanticise the *remote* past, and re-invoke it in near mythical terms, as something that was once pure and unsullied but had 'fallen' over the ages. Nehru, in fact, admitted that he could not resist the temptation to conjure India as Bharat Mata or Mother India—a very old but beautiful lady, imbued with nobility and greatness, her beauty 'wrought out from within upon the flesh, the deposit, little cell by cell, of strange thoughts and fantastic reveries and exquisite passions'.[17] The syndrome was familiar and predictable—rejection, in conformity with the critique of the coloniser, and glorification in response to that critique. In the case of Nehru, however, the sentimentalism about the past was definitely subsidiary to his belief that India needed to free itself from its hold. The newly independent nation of which he was the leader must, he was convinced, put on a new garment, for the old was torn and tattered beyond repair.

The reclamation of the wisdoms and refinements of India's ancient past and Hindu civilisation became a victim of this mindset of the most important person who was at the helm during the formative years of independent India. He had his allies in the anglicised class, most notably in the bureaucracy. The Indian Civil Service set up by the British, where Indians could qualify provided they were role models for the kind of 'intelligent' natives who could serve the Empire, was scrapped but was replaced with little or no change in the criteria for qualification, by the Indian Administrative Service. The established members of the elite had a vested interest in perpetuating the old systems in which they were masters. Lip service was paid to India's glorious past, but little was done to integrate it with the national policy.

For decades after Independence, the educational curriculum in schools and universities continued on colonial lines. Gandhi had warned about the dangers of the colonial education system—designed to entrench the ruler's perspective—as far back as 1921: 'It should be remembered that there has been only one system of education before the country for the past fifty years, and only one medium of expression forced on the country. We have, therefore, no data before us as to what we would have been but for the education in the existing schools and colleges. This, however, we know, that India is poorer than fifty years ago. ... The system of education is its most defective part. It was conceived and born in error, for the English rulers honestly believed the indigenous system to be worse than useless. It has been nurtured in sin, for the tendency has been to dwarf the Indian body, mind, and soul.'[18]

Thus, our history books made little mention of great Hindu kings like Krishnadevaraya of the Vijayanagara dynasty, or of Raja Raja Chola I. No attempt was made to focus on the political insights of Kautilya's *Arthashastra,* or the *Shanti Parva* of the Mahabharata. Textbooks on Indian history continued to be written mostly by British scholars. Leaders like Shivaji and Maharana Pratap were relegated to the background. There was the constant fear that the teaching of history should not become 'communal' by giving disproportionate space to the role of Hindu leaders in opposing Muslim rule. Subjects such as an investigation into the antiquity of ancient India were considered undesirable, as they may lead to Hindu 'glorification'. The unprecedented renaissance of the bhakti period, lasting six centuries and producing some of the most exquisite devotional poetry, was eclipsed by political chronologies of the Mughal empire. Students learnt about the geography of England before they learnt the basics about their own country. English remained the medium of instruction, especially of elite schools, and schools where this was not the case, or where the means to do so were inadequate, were looked down upon, its products derisively categorised as 'Hindi-medium types'.

Philosophy and metaphysics—the great contributions of Hindu and Indic civilisation—were sidelined, and Western thought dominated the curriculums of philosophy departments. Except for a handful of academics, students were ignorant about the audacity of thought of philosophers like Jaimini, Kapila, Gautama, Kanada, Patanjali and Adi Shankaracharya, to name but a few. Little was done to recall the great cerebral eclecticism of the Hindu period, both in terms of thought and practice. The great achievements of Nalanda hardly figured in teaching courses. Science was taught without almost any reference to the great strides taken in this field by Indian mathematicians and astronomers. English literature courses were sought after, but there was no systemic way to impart knowledge on Panini's seminal work on grammar, the *Ashtadhyayi*, the scores of other works on etymology and linguistic construct and the classics in Sanskrit and other Indian languages. Some schools made a feeble attempt to teach Sanskrit, but the literary corpus of the language was but footnotes in the curriculum. Plays of Shakespeare were taught but Kalidasa ignored. The great epics, Ramayana and Mahabharata, were hardly analysed, and the exquisite lyricism and philosophy of Tulsidasa's *Ramcharitmanas* was largely confined to the piety of individual households. So many wisdoms of the past, such as the four ashrams of life, the nishkama karma of the Bhagwad Gita and the remarkably balanced four purusharthas or goals of life—which were secular areas of study—were considered unfit for academic scrutiny.

There was unforgiveable amnesia in the area of culture and creativity. Bharat's *Natya Shastra*, perhaps the world's first comprehensive compendium of the arts, was largely confined to anonymity. India's seminal contribution on aesthetics, the theory of rasa—again perhaps a pioneer in the world—was little known even to students of specialised schools of art. The curriculum of art colleges even today still remains largely based on Western notions of form and proportion, with no effort to integrate the foundational works on artistic creativity of ancient India. Theatre schools, like the National School of Drama, had curriculums which made but a passing reference to the prodigious work done in this field by Hindu scholars thousands of years ago.

Architecture was taught without even a cursory knowledge of

important treatises like the *Vastu Shastra*. No attempt was made to revert to an indigenous aesthetic idiom that incorporated our own notions of building. A spectacular example of forsaking our own and imitating the West was in the choice of Charles-Edouard Jeanneret (1887–1965), the Swiss–French architect more famously known as Le Corbusier, to design the new city of Chandigarh. The invitation to him provides a dramatic illustration of how, for the colonised, the future and the past are seen as irrevocably opposed, leaving only one choice—a past that must be rejected or a future without the past. Corbusier had very little to recommend him for designing an Indian city except that he was White, Western and perceived to be ultra-modern. The interesting thing, of course, is that his modernity was not acceptable to his own countrymen, and none of his futuristic plans were actually built in France or anywhere else in Europe. But destiny took a turn for the Frenchman. Far away in India, a country about which he knew very little, a person no less than the prime minister decided that he would be the best person to create a new city symbolic of the modernity India wanted to adopt. In his official notes and letters, Nehru referred to Corbusier as 'a genius of world reputation' and 'one of the biggest architects in the world'. He had no problems about Corbusier's ultra-radical ideas, or the fact that they had been rejected on aesthetic and sociological grounds in his own country, France, and elsewhere. His requirement was for the new city to be sanitised of the cultural identifications of the past, because this alone would provide concrete proof of India's desire and capability for modernity, especially to the Western world. The architectural historian Vikramaditya Prakash (whose father, Aditya Prakash, also an architect, was a part of Corbusier's team of Indian architects) has insightfully observed: 'While the emergence into modernity is accepted in the West as part of the continuing devolution of its own history, in postcolonial India, modernity inevitably signifies a break with its own history, and the superiority of the West.'[19] Those who thought that one could be modern without excluding the past were, for Nehru, simply 'bogged down in their narrow-mindedness'.

'Especially in India,' he felt, 'people are so steeped in old customs and habits that often they cannot understand new ideas.'[20] Speaking at the Institution of Engineers, he argued that Chandigarh was important because it was symbolic of 'not being tied down to what had been done by our forefathers and the like but thinking out in new terms … not in terms of rules and regulations laid down by our ancestors… unfettered by the traditions of the past, a symbol of the nation's faith in the future'.

Examples of these kinds of choices are near endless. India gained political freedom in 1947, but its cultural colonisation persisted. When people are ruptured from their heritage, they are essentially rootless, not always lacking proficiency in their specific area of work, but essentially deracinated, mimic people, inured to another's culture more than their own. Hindu civilisation was based on moulik soch or original thought, where each aspect of creativity was studied, examined, interrogated, discussed and experimented upon in the search for excellence. But when this great legacy was summarily devalued and looked upon as a liability to modernity, it left an entire people adrift from their cultural moorings, lacking authenticity and becoming a derivative people.

This cultural disconnect is often visible to a foreigner, even in small things—as one foreign journalist queried me—like the distribution of only English newspapers on an airplane. The disjunct becomes apparent in the shabby state of the infrastructure of culture in a country where culture was the yardstick of excellence for millennia. Today, even more than seventy years after Independence, there are few, if any, world-class auditoriums and conference centres in the country, and those that exist are mostly in poor condition. New Delhi, the capital of the Indian republic, has only one auditorium of more than two thousand capacity, the Siri Fort, and it is in deplorable condition; an air of musty neglect hangs over it, and no one seems to care that its stage and light equipment is horribly out of date. Our museums, the repositories of so much of our heritage, remain in visible neglect. There is no proper display, no worthwhile scholarship, no cataloguing commensurate with international standards and no sense of pride in our priceless artefacts that would make us give them the attention and funds they deserve.

The state of our monuments is not much better. The colonial devaluation of history has its most visible manifestation in the manner in which Indians treat their monuments, leaving them—apart from a few high-profile structures—dilapidated, overrun, illegally occupied, defaced and neglected. The National Gallery of Modern Art (NGMA), located in a monumental colonial building in the heart of New Delhi, has one of the richest collections of contemporary Indian art, but, in the land of Ajanta, gets a paltry 30,000 visitors annually. Its branch in Mumbai, the financial capital of the country, gets even less. Even if mechanical comparisons are not applicable, an idea of what is being lost can be gauged by the fact that the Museum of Modern Art in New York gets some 2.5 million visitors a year at $30 a ticket; the Louvre in Paris as many at €12.5 per head; and the Tate in London four million at £20 per person.

Because of the rupture with creative traditions, and partly because of foreign influences (to which postcolonial societies are disproportionately susceptible), we are witnessing today an onslaught on the basic tenets of much of our priceless classical heritage which is quite unprecedented. The centrepiece of Indian classical music is, of course, the raga, a melodic (not harmonic, as in Western classical music) scheme composed of a given structure of notes. The raga, through its slow elaboration, is meant, as I have discussed earlier, to evoke a mood, redolent of the different seasons or the different times of the day or of different emotions. It is a remarkably intricate structure that allows the artist a great deal of creative freedom, within a framework of inflexible rules, for slow and careful elaboration. However, many leading exponents of the genre today, whether vocalists or instrumentalists, seem to have no inclination to patiently develop the spirit of a raga in their performances. In a manner more appropriate in an adolescent pop band, they are often in a hurry to race through the initial slow phases of a composition to reach the fast-paced crescendo, thereby foundationally mutilating the genre.

The excuse given, that this is what appeals to the audience, is fundamentally untenable. Since time immemorial, great musicians have attempted to mould and educate their audience; and cultured societies cannot claim to be so if their role models are adept only at practising the policy of least resistance. If audiences do not know better and judge a classical artist only by his or her ability to emulate the beat of popular music, they need to be educated. Some pioneering work to this end has been done by SPIC MACAY (Society for the Promotion of Indian Classical Music and Culture Amongst Youth) set up by Dr Kiran Seth in 1977. Their campaign to take the legacy of classical music to schools and colleges and expose the young to some of its best exponents has made a difference, but is not enough. Classical musicians continue to mostly pander to the lowest common denominator, and the danger of a centuries' old tradition gradually emasculating itself is growing. Undeniably, classical soirees, earlier confined to the salons of the rich or the royal, have over time seen a welcome democratisation, with ordinary people having greater access to performances. But the widening of the audience, and the concomitant commercialisation, requires greater vigilance to ensure that the basics are not diluted.

Classical dance has many artists of great talent, who have spent entire lifetimes dedicated to their artistic skills. But it is a sad commentary that even the finest dancers, who represent a tradition refined over thousands of years, find it difficult to fill an auditorium. More often than not (with some venues in Chennai during the winter season being exceptions), the shows are not ticketed because people, including those who can well afford to, are not willing to pay. More of the young, especially girls, are learning classical dance today, but a leading dancer once told me that their knowledge of the language, literature, mythology, symbolism and philosophy underlying the dance compositions is unacceptably perfunctory, and they are content to cursorily learn only the technique of dance. The essential point is that, like classical music, classical dance is by definition a complex form of creative expression, encompassing not only pure dance but theatre, mime, music, poetry and, above all, rasa. It cannot be reduced to a technical simplicity without destroying its soul. For instance, a student of Kathak who is not steeped in the lore of Radha and Krishna and has no knowledge of Braj—the offshoot of Hindi in which much of the poetry of their celestial love is written—can only perform the dance mechanically. An intrinsic part of all classical dances is abhinaya, the portrayal of emotion. Only a dancer who has studied the poetry that is at the heart of a dance composition, and has a knowledge of the music and the raga in which it is being sung and is, over and above this, familiar with the philosophy and mythology underpinning the composition, can make the authentic emotional investment that abhinaya requires.

In civilisations where the creative tradition has not been so abruptly broken, or where an organised effort has been made to reinvest in that tradition, there is a sensible balance between popular and classical culture. In London, Hyde Park gets thousands of people when there is a pop group performing, but the theatres for Western classical music, too, have people queuing up for tickets. In a mature cultural civilisation, audience appreciation cannot be about monoculture; the popular must flourish *with*, and not at the cost of, the classical. This requires concerted effort to expose people to the richness of their culture, educate them about its intricacies and the prodigious thought that has gone into the creation of that art form. And this is precisely what has not been done in modern India. The less people know, the less they hear or watch, the more ignorant they are about that genre of art. The scope of appreciation is thus reduced not because tastes have irrevocably changed but because they have not been adequately cultivated. What prevents at least some more of the hundred-odd FM radio and satellite TV channels in India from hosting at least a weekly programme of Indian classical music, or lecture-demonstrations on classical dance? Few schools, including the government-run Kendriya Vidyalayas, have a subject on art or art appreciation in the senior classes. If the young are not exposed to art, where will the discriminating and knowledgeable audience, so necessary to sustain and develop culture in any country, come from? The late Ramnivas Mirdha, who was the president of the Sangeet Natak Akademi, once lamented to me that this ancient land may be losing the ability to create the rasiks who can appreciate culture and help promote and nourish it. He said that if the country's GDP falls by a percentage or two, it will recover, but if the country's culture is neglected, the damage would be irreparable.

Experiments with our established and highly evolved ancient art forms, where rules and principles were codified over centuries, need to be carried out only by those who are rooted in that tradition and know the limits of what can change and what cannot. When the famous Stanislavski and Nemirovich-Danchenko Moscow Academic Music Theatre in Russia sought to stage Kalidas's *Shakuntalam* in the 1970s, the veteran Kathak dancer Maya Rao, who was recruited as an adviser, found that the most difficult part was to make the Russian ballerinas walk on their feet and not on their toes. Certain forms of dance suit certain body types, and it is ridiculous to deny this. The world may be flat, but not everything lends itself to 'fusion'. Dancers from the classical tradition need not cut themselves off from what is happening in dance internationally, and certainly there cannot be a case for unthinking insularity. But it is precisely because they are the legatees of a centuries' old tradition that the transition must be made very carefully. To land enthusiastically but clumsily on the floor of somebody else's dance tradition, without considering what can be assimilated and what cannot, does injustice to both the authenticity of the old and the potential of the new.

The state of contemporary Indian theatre is even sadder. Lillete Dubey, the well-known theatre person and actress, once used a phrase, perhaps unconsciously, that is incredibly apt. Speaking about the shoe-string budgets and lack of professionalism that plague Hindi theatre, she said the productions look rather 'apologetic'. The word captures perfectly the shabby, half-hearted and diffident state of theatre in India. There are a few — just a few — well-known playwrights, and even among them, those who have a national following can be counted on the fingers of one hand. There is little funding, no committed audiences, except perhaps in Maharashtra and Bengal, and very little original work of high quality—this in the land of Kalidasa, whose plays were being staged two thousand years ago on sophisticated principles of drama developed a couple of hundred years earlier. India is nowhere near having its own Broadway, or an audience that would queue up to buy tickets for a good play.

The humanities departments of the universities are mostly cesspools of mediocrity, where original thinking is discouraged and learning by rote is encouraged. Teachers who can engage the minds of the young with fresh ideas and concepts are rare, and there are few students willing to go beyond the routine preparation for exams. Our Institutes of Technology (IITs) and some of our medical colleges compare favourably with those in the rest of the world, but great civilisations cannot be reduced to an unsustainable linear simplicity—good engineers and doctors and little else. This bias has ensured that the humanities sections of an overwhelming majority of our universities are obviously substandard. There is hardly any original output; doctoral works are usually collations of secondary material, laboriously footnoted to give the illusion of research. With the exception of some elite institutions, a pervasive sense of shabby weariness informs these departments. Gunnar Myrdal, who wrote a monumental work in the mid-1960s on the unfolding drama of development in Asian countries, had noticed this malaise even then. His comments cover South Asia as a whole, but have a special relevance to India:

> Every Western visitor to South Asian universities is struck by the uncritical attitude of the average student: he expects the professor and the textbooks (often only certain pages are prescribed reading) to impart to him the knowledge he needs, and accepts what is offered to him without much intellectual effort of his own. ... His submissiveness in this respect stands in curious contrast to his readiness to protest if he feels that requirements in examinations are unduly taxing. ... Teaching in South Asian schools at all levels

tend to discourage independent thinking and the growth of that inquisitive and experimental bent of mind that is so essential for development. It is directed toward enabling students to pass examinations and obtain degrees and, possibly, admittance to the next level of schools. A degree is the object pursued, rather than the knowledge and skills to which the degree should testify.[21]

Contrast this with Hieun Tsang's description of the Nalanda University in the seventh century, and the dramatic decline in excellence becomes vivid. Our ancient universities, immersed in the cerebral milieu of those times, stressed mimamsa or intellectual investigation and dialogue on issues. Today, education has become a simplistic byword only for a degree. This can be understood given the pressures to find employment, but what cannot be condoned is the near complete absence of creativity, or the absence of any sustained attempt to radically restructure our educational institutions so that students can move beyond learning by rote to knowledge through application of the mind—the hallmark of Hindu civilisation. As Ashis Nandy, the noted sociologist, says: 'Schooling is the chosen instrument of alienation. The brightest children are snatched away from familiar surroundings to be introduced in schools based on the Western model. When they leave, they speak the language of the colonizer and can no longer communicate with their own people.'[22] The New Education Policy of 2020 has finally taken a positive decision on schools adopting the mother tongue in a child's formative years in school, but on the whole this is too little too late, and hardly commensurate with the basic structural reform that this sector has been crying out for since 1947.

There are, indeed, some areas where Indian culture has made a mark. One of them is our film industry, which has grown in confidence and output, and acquired popularity abroad as well, especially in countries where there is a significant population of people of Indian origin. But very few of the thousand or so films that India makes every year are of good quality, and a great many are straight lifts of Hollywood productions. Innumerable websites give graphic details of this plagiaristic orgy, listing film after film, many of them hits, which have liberally 'borrowed' from some foreign film's story, music and screenplay, often without acknowledgement. The same syndrome afflicts film music. This is particularly painful because songs are the distinguishing feature of Indian films, and were of a very high quality—both for their lyrics and composition—in the early years.

Why does the Indian film industry need to copy so much? Of course, there are people of great artistic calibre within it who would wince at this blatant infringement of copyright. However, even they sometimes get co-opted into the great copying game. True, the industry has to keep commercial considerations in mind, but so does film-making anywhere in the world. Do our plagiarists believe that the audiences of India will never know? Do they genuinely believe that a cut-and-paste job is a good enough substitute for creativity? And are they happy at this devaluation, so long as the copied film turns out to be a moneymaker? Why have the standards of one of the oldest—and certainly the most prolific—film industry in the world fallen to this extent? Are Indian story writers incapable of developing an original plot of their own? Why do producers and directors and musicians knowingly devalue their creative credentials and acquiesce by taking this shoddy, unethical shortcut? These are questions that need to be asked, even as we take legitimate pride in the expansion of the film industry and its growing appeal worldwide. Pan Nalin, a perceptive commentator, who is also a filmmaker, has deep reservations about the very name 'Bollywood'. 'It's like calling Narayana Murthy Nill Mates.' The sad part is that the industry seems proud to be branded as 'Bollywood'. 'Indian cinema,' Nalin says, 'needs to do much more than that to be global. If India has mythology bigger than mangas, sagas bigger than *Star Wars*, legends larger than *Lord of the Rings*, then why do we look to the west for imitation?' As against the rampant imitation in Bollywood, he asks the valid counter-question: 'Does anyone know of any Indian story or film being remade in Hollywood?' The truth, he points out, is emphatically the opposite. 'Hundreds of Bollywood movies are a direct imitation of Hollywood movies. Movies with songs and dance are a part of our existence. But why do they fail to become universal? … If the Italians invented neo-realism in cinema, the Germans expressionism, the French new wave, then what did we invent? Bollywood?' Palin concludes, 'Indian cinema will be global only if takes root in Indian soil and then grows like a banyan tree sprouting roots in other countries. Ages ago our stories were universal. If not, a child in Indonesia would not be watching Ramayana today. Our stories were timeless. If not, Tibetans would not be reciting [the] Tantras.'[23]

Indian paintings appear to be finally getting their value on the international stage. From a paltry turnover of five crore rupees in 1997, the art market is today estimated at over one thousand crores and, except for the recession due to Covid, is set to continue to grow at 35 per cent annually. The first real breakthrough came in 2002, when Masanari Fukuoka, the biggest collector of Indian art in Japan, bought Tyeb Mehta'a work *Celebration* for $317,500 at a Christie's auction in New York. In 2005, at Christie's again, it was another work of Mehta's—*Mahishasura*—that demolished the million-dollar barrier, selling for an unheard amount of over $1.5 million. Since then, works by several Indian artists—Amrita Sher-Gil, F.N. Souza, V.S. Gaitonde, M.F. Husain, Rameshwar Broota, S.H. Raza, Atul Dodiya, Subodh Gupta, to name just a few—have fetched high prices in the international art market.

But while all this is for the good, and has been cause for much euphoria, it is sobering to bear in mind that of the Asian nations, it is China and not India that is ruling the global art market. According to the Art Price Index, Chinese artists accounted for more than one-third of the hundred most expensive artists worldwide, claiming prices that rivalled top Western artists, including Jeff Koons and Damien Hirst. Not surprisingly, the Georges Pompidou Centre of Paris opened its branch in Shanghai in 2019.

The comparison with China is apt because, like India, it too is a continent-sized nation and has a cultural lineage as old. If Chinese artists, in spite of the setback of the Cultural Revolution, are selling at far higher prices, is the euphoria in India about the new international recognition of Indian art justified? It is true that sales at such prices are unprecedented, and worthy of celebration, but should not our hyperbolic reaction be indexed to parallel developments in art elsewhere? The recent successes should also provoke an assessment of the state of our hardware—do we have enough galleries and are they of internationally acceptable professional standards? And what is the state of our art scholarship? Do we have enough curators who have the professional training to ensure high standards and discover creativity? According to one estimate, there are only about 500 serious collectors in the country where the very rich (who can easily afford to buy our best art and provide much-needed patronage) easily number, at the very least, more than twenty million. As has been noted earlier, the country's biggest and probably most prestigious gallery—the National Gallery of Modern Art—gets no more than 30,000 visitors per year, including foreign tourists. Is contemporary art an isolated oasis, sealed off from wider public knowledge and appreciation, provoking interest only for the hefty amount some artist gets at an auction abroad?

If we are honest, the answers to these questions should be cause for genuine concern for a civilisation where countless treatises were written on the theory and practice of art, centuries before anywhere else in the world. What is distressing is that much of what passes for contemporary art—abstract art in particular—is plain imitation of Western trends. One development, especially, that of installation art, frankly borders very often on gimmickry, and is an embarrassing attempt to copy Western trends of 'found art', popularised among others by the French artist Marcel Duchamp (1887–1968). Duchamp's installation of a common urinal, which he titled *Fountain,* was selected in 2004 by 500 renowned artists and historians in the West as 'the most influential art work of the 20th century'! The elevation of common urinals may be comprehensible as part of a certain artistic evolution, but there is no need for Indians to be part of the panegyric. Moreover, installation art, embedded in our own cultural context, has a living tradition in the decorations for Indian festivals, marriages and a host of other celebrations that are part of the ebb and flow of everyday life.

My suspicion, though—and several leading artists I have spoken to seem to agree—is that most artists experimenting with installations are merely copying Western idiom and themes, and are encouraged by Western galleries and curators, and their hangers-on in India, to do just that—a genuinely worrying trend for a country that earlier used to be the initiator of creative excellence, not a mindless borrower.

One important reason why such developments go largely unquestioned is that there is hardly any scholarly evaluation of our own artistic principles, or discussion of what our aesthetic yardsticks should be. The curriculum of our art colleges is hopelessly outdated; they rely disproportionately on Western studio techniques and continue to make the invidious distinction between art and craft that is so completely a Western construct. As per Indian aesthetics, a work of art is to be judged by its quality, and not categorised by its origins. A painter making a Madhubani painting on the walls of a village home in Bihar is as much an artist as a sophisticated city-bred artist. When such distinctions are made mindlessly, there is the real danger of the vibrant and ancient folk art of India being decontextualised, wrenched away from its natural environment and promoted only as some rustic curiosity. Should this happen, a great tradition will lose its organic sustenance, and curl up and die.

But the real tragedy is that there is no serious discussion on any subject relating to art and culture in the media. Most newspapers and magazines have no space for learned reviews; or perhaps they don't have such space because there are very few learned reviewers. Much of the new activity we see on the art scene is thus like a hothouse plant, not without energy, but poorer for the absence of a lively and serious space for critical appraisal. The contrast with the West is stark. Their reviewers may have voted a common urinal as the most influential work of art in the twentieth century, but the business of critiques is taken very seriously. Reviewers enjoy both power and respect and command bulky sections in almost any serious publication with a mass readership. In India, some leading English newspapers, with pan-Indian readership, have done away with space for art and book reviews. It is a barren landscape, where informed discussion and debate on developments in the field of art and culture is almost non-existent. Indians may be argumentative in other matters, but in art and aesthetics—two areas where Hindu civilisation had few rivals—there is a general intellectual inertness that can only be described as uncultured.

The purpose here is to identify a malaise, and not tarnish the few honourable exceptions to the norm. Unless we take stock of the fact that a civilisation that structured itself—from the time of the Vedas and the Upanishads—on dialogue, enquiry and interrogation is today bereft of such a spirit in the vital area of creativity, we may grow in terms of our economic parameters but will remain stunted in civilisational terms. Why is it that the capital of a country with an ancient and rich history of the creative arts does not have—with the exception of two insignificant lanes named after Tansen and Kaifi Azmi—any roads or squares or gardens named after our ancient poets, musicians, painters and philosophers? The city of London is dotted with blue plaques commemorating homes where its scholars, artists and intellectuals lived. In Delhi, until recently, even the haveli of its greatest Urdu poet, Mirza Ghalib, was occupied by a kabadiwallah. For a civilisation that put such a high premium on aesthetics, why is it that at the famous Hampi festival of classical music and dance, the organisers have often brought in Bollywood performers, arguing that the audience would hardly respond to anything else, and made thermocol reproductions in garish colours of the monuments as stage backdrops?

There is something terribly wrong in all of this, and while genuine creative achievements deserve praise, we need to honestly reassess the art scene in its totality. Too often, our threshold for recognising achievements is too low. Our responses are still conditioned by the colonial experience, and often ignorant of the antiquity, distinctiveness and sophistication of our artistic traditions, we are happy to celebrate even the mediocre. More importantly, Western approbation is still something we hanker for. Rabindranath Tagore did not get his due in India until he won the Nobel prize for literature in 1913; the talents of the great sitar maestro Ravi Shankar excited Indians much more after he received the endorsement of The Beatles; Satyajit Ray languished until he won accolades in the West. International recognitions are important, but creatively confident nations attuned to their own legacies hardly make them almost the sole criteria for internal appreciation. Besides, no attempt has been made to assess the politics behind international awards. Mahatma Gandhi—the greatest messiah of peace in the world since centuries—was nominated for the Nobel prize several times but did not get it. One unmistakable symptom of co-option is the exaggerated importance given to the slightest criticism or approval emanating from the West. The first produces howls of protest, the second unwarranted jubilation. Hindus, if aware of their civilisational legacy, should have a greater sense of equilibrium, but they can only do this if they first reappropriate, in authentic terms, their own cultural space.

While there is no dearth of tributes to India's great ancient heritage, the blunt truth is that modern India has failed to reclaim that legacy. It has failed to convincingly convey to its citizens that they are the product and custodians of one of the world's most ancient civilisations, and that therefore it is a sin for them to be imitative or derivative, or to neglect what is their own in the blind pursuit of what is not. Any objective appraisal of our cultural institutions will bear this out. The ministry of culture (MoC) is inadequately budgeted, and even the meagre amount allocated is not fully spent; it is overrun by bureaucrats who rarely know anything about culture and mostly consider it a punishment posting—a telling commentary for a country whose calling card since the dawn of time was culture. Institutions like the Indian Council of Cultural Relations—which, like the British Council, the United States Information Service (USIS) of the Americans, the Goethe Institute of the Germans, Mexico's Cervantes Institute and China's Confucius Centres—is meant to propagate Indian culture abroad, has little or no money beyond what is needed for fixed administrative costs; the Akademies—Sahitya,

Sangeet Natak, Lalit Kala—are, frankly, just cesspools of politicking, with little to show for the mandate they were founded for. As of 31 March 2020, 262 out of 878 posts in the Akademies were lying vacant.

The willingness to meaningfully support culture has been absent in all governments thus far. Parliament's Standing Committee on Culture pointed out that in 2010–11, the actual expenditure by the MoC as a percentage of the GDP was as low as 0.017 per cent. What is surprising is that this pathetically low spend *reduced* to 0.012 in 2019–20. When the Bharatiya Janata Party (BJP) government came to power with an absolute majority in 2014, it was expected that—even if the party's outlook was avowedly sectarian—much more would be spent on culture, since one of the party's consistent themes was the need to resurrect India's cultural past. However, the facts reveal quite a different story. The allocation for the MoC in 2021 was ₹461 crores less than the previous year—a 15 per cent reduction. This came after a 30 per cent mid-year downward revision of the cultural budget in 2020. Even if the impact of the Covid pandemic is taken into account, the overall figures show that, if inflation is taken into account, there has been no growth in allocations to MoC in the last five years.

Modern India has the strange paradox of the political class singing paeans of praise for artists, writers and poets, but unwilling to do very much for their actual nurturing, support and growth. For instance, in 2016–17, the MoC under the scheme Award of Young Artists, could only select 283 artists; in 2019, this figure had gone up by a paltry 117; under another scheme to provide scholarships and pensions to artists, called the Kala Sanskriti Vikas Yojana, the amount to be paid for pensions was only ₹4,000 per month, and even for this the MoC could not identify more than around 3,000 beneficiaries. There is no social security net, no guarantee of assured income for artists, and when a crisis like the Covid pandemic occurs, their suffering is palpable. Even in 2021, the MoC does not have a comprehensive cultural directory to identify artists. A scheme to do this was launched in 2015 but has not yet taken off, and of the ₹43 crores allotted for it, only

₹1 crore has been spent. When the government is so apathetic, it can hardly inspire support from outside. Corporate Social Responsibility (CSR) spend dropped from ₹306 crores in 2016–17 to ₹48 crores in 2019–20. Further, the National Culture Fund (NCF), set up to enable private participation in cultural preservation, has been dormant.[24]

Compare this what some other nations are doing. The economically developed countries have cultural infrastructures that we may not be able to compete with. But many developing countries have shown a renewed commitment to the promotion of their culture. China has built over 150 modern galleries in Beijing, along with an art district with neatly cobbled streets and rows of street-side cafes. It was built on the eve of the Beijing Olympics, and is now a major tourist attraction. Even Shanghai boasts at least a hundred art galleries, and smaller towns throughout China are being encouraged to develop gallery districts. Additionally, the Chinese—who destroyed a considerable part of their classical heritage during the 'cultural revolution'—have determinedly decided to make amends and invest in over a hundred museums to world standards. Singapore, Thailand and the Philippines have taken the decision to invest in a dozen state-of-the-art museums each; Hong Kong has devised a new cultural plan which makes it spend several billion dollars each year, an unprecedented investment per capita for an area so small. The oil rich UAE has earmarked over $30 billion for museums and art programmes.

It is true that India faces competing budgetary priorities, but the real lament is that our country has never really viewed culture as a priority. The project for the restoration of our ancient culture through a mature, balanced but concerted policy has suffered due to two inimical extremes, often acting as a reaction to each other. The first, as I have discussed, sought to indiscriminately dismiss our ancient heritage—in the words of Nehru—as 'the dead wood of the past', and aspired for 'modernity' in Western terms, largely divorced from the wisdoms of our own civilisation. This approach dominated policy and attitudes of the entrenched power elite for decades after Independence. The second, sought to over-glorify the Hindu past, but in terms that ended up caricaturing it. Dinanath Batra is the generic representative of the latter approach. A pracharak or preacher of the Rashtriya Swayamsevak Sangh (RSS), he was appointed general secretary of the Sangh's schools network, Vidya Bharati, in 1980. Since then he has carried out a crusade to give Hindu India its 'due', and is ever vigilant to prevent any slur, real or imaginary, being cast on it, through the two organisations he founded—the Shiksha Bachao Andolan Samiti and the Shiksha Sanskriti Uthan Samiti.

From one perspective, Batra's evangelism may be justified, especially since his ideological opponents try and downplay the Hindu period. However, there is much that is downright immature in the way he goes about it. Batra wrote six books as supplementary literature for the state education curriculum in Gujarat. In these books, he argues that cars—as we know them today—used to ply in Vedic India. According to him they were called 'anashva rath'. He also asserts that modern stem cell research was known then, for otherwise how could a sage convert a mass of flesh into the hundred bodies of the Kauravas? Batra further claims that live television telecasts were present at the time of the Mahabharata some 4,000 years ago. To quote him: 'There is no doubt that the invention of TV goes back to this. ... In the Mahabharata, Sanjaya sitting inside a palace in Hastinapur and using his divya shakti (divine powers) would give a live telecast of the battle of the Mahabharata ... to the blind Dhritarashtra.'

Batra's avowed goals are Bharat Gaurav (Indian pride), Jeevan Mulya (the essence of life) and Samajik Chetna (social conscience). But these goals are hardly served by making absurd claims of this kind. The entire project to sensibly reclaim Hindu India's many-splendoured past is reduced to a laughing stock by such exaggerations, which are presented as facts rather than overenthusiastic surmises. This kind of presentation of history encourages other ridiculous examples of 'pride'. Plastic surgery, it is claimed, was known in ancient India because the trunk of an elephant was grafted on a human body in the form of Lord Ganesha. And that advanced artificial insemination was practised thousands of years ago since Kunti 'miraculously' conceived her sons without intercourse. And that the vimanas mentioned in some of our ancient Pauranic texts actually refer to real planes flying around the ancient skies.

The net outcome of such claims is not Bharat Gaurav, but a caricature of history. Hindu India, no doubt, established great milestones in scientific research, and I have discussed some of them in detail in this book. These are globally recognised to be incontrovertible indicators of a civilisation that invented the zero and discovered the Pythagoras theorem centuries before Pythagoras did. Apart from mathematics and astronomy, we saw pioneering scholarship in many other branches of science as well. A projection of these achievements, often unfortunately ignored in educational curriculums today, is required. But to use mythology—important for its wisdom and symbolism but not meant to be taken literally in every aspect—to claim that the frontiers of science today are only replications of what India already knew and had millennia ago, is farcical. Hindu India was known for its ability for cerebration, the profundity of its thought, its creative efflorescence and its willingness to go into the depths of an issue through interrogation and questioning. It would be embarrassed by this mocking of its real achievements.

The tragedy is that Batra's books have been prescribed for schoolchildren. This distortion of history could have a very damaging effect on impressionable minds, and certainly puts at risk the scientific temper of reasoning and pursuit of logic that ancient India was noteworthy for.

To reclaim Hindu India one has to know what it stood for. On the advice of Batra, Madhya Pradesh Chief Minister Shivraj Singh Chouhan removed sex education from the school curriculum on the grounds that it 'offended Indian values'. Does Batra know how sensibly liberated Hindu India was on matters of sex? Does one have to remind him that kama, or the balanced pursuit of the sensual, is a part of the four highest purusharthas Hindus devised millennia before modern Hindu revivalism got overwhelmed by Islamic notions of purdah and Victorian morality?

Batra was also in the forefront of the campaign for the removal of A.K. Ramanujan's essay, 'Three Hundred Ramayanas, Three Examples and Five Thoughts', from the syllabus of Delhi University. It is difficult to understand in what way this sensitive essay offended Batra. Unlike the Abrahamic faiths, Hinduism does not have only one prescribed religious text. Valmiki's Ramayana has been joyously adapted by Hindus in many versions not only in India but also abroad, in accordance with local customs and sentiment, but without diluting the essential thrust of its narrative. Given Hinduism's eclectic nature, it would have revelled in this diversity, and even if there were disputes or differences, these would have traditionally been resolved not by a ban but through shastrartha or civilised discourse. In a detailed note to the government's National Council of Educational Research and Training (NCERT), which oversees the content of textbooks for schools, Batra even railed against certain lines by Rabindranath Tagore and the great poet and writer, Ramdhari Singh Dinkar. His hypersensitive 'Hindu' psyche was incensed also by this couplet of Ghalib—Ham ko maalum hai jannat ki haqiqat lekin, dil ko khush rakhne ko Ghalib ye khayal achacha hai: I know what heaven is really about, but this thought is good to keep the heart happy. Is it Batra's case that Hinduism cannot countenance any doubts about the reality of heaven? He needs to be reminded that the Upanishads and the six systems of Hindu philosophy were in search of what could be the ultimate truth, not divinity in religious terms. In this sense, their profound ideation can technically be called atheistic; what then is the sanctity of heaven for Batra? Besides, quite clearly, Ghalib, who was essentially a Sufi mystic in outlook, is making fun of his own tribe of mullahs. And in the Bhagwad Gita, Krishna's presentation of heaven is very different from the Abrahamic religions. It appears that Batra does not understand that.

The line between legitimate pride in the past, and racism or xenophobia is thin. Batra comes close to crossing over to the wrong side when he attributes a quotation to Dr S. Radhakrishnan, the great philosopher and former president of India. According to Batra,

Dr Radhakrishnan said the following at a dinner to a British audience: 'Friends, one day God felt like making rotis. When he was cooking the rotis, the first one was cooked less and the English were born. The second one stayed longer on the fire and the Negroes were born. Alert after his two mistakes, when God went on to cook his third roti, it came out just right and Indians were born.'[25] To believe that philosopher–statesman Dr Radhakrishnan, one of the most distinguished academics of comparative religion of the twentieth century, who held the chair of the Spalding Professor of Eastern Religion and Ethics at University of Oxford, would say that the English are a half-baked race, and the 'Negroes' (an offensive term) an overcooked one, while the Indians are the perfect rotis or race, beggars imagination. Yet, for all of this, Batra's books are not only prescribed reading in BJP-ruled Gujarat, but he is also a member of the education committee in Haryana, an appointment made in 2014 when the BJP came to power in that state.

Dinanath Batra is probably well-intentioned—and some of his suggestions for amendments in NCERT books were relevant in correcting the distortions of leftist Hindu-phobic historians—but, on the whole, narratives such as these of Hindu pride do real damage to the far more serious and unfinished agenda of independent India— to reclaim the heritage of its neglected foundational years. Amish Tripathi puts his finger on the real reasons for phenomena like Batra. 'Now why do fantasies associated with our scientific past, like the supposed space travel to Mars, exist in India today? It's because there is an absence of genuine knowledge. Speculative theories proliferate in an environment of ignorance. We teach practically nothing about our own past scientific achievements in our schools! Our medical education begins with Greek medicine; we don't teach Indian medicine. Our mathematical education focuses on the Western development of Maths. We don't learn anything about Indian mathematicians, who are among the greatest in history and have produced seminal work. We need to teach ourselves about our own achievements. We need to draw inspiration from them. And build an achievement culture today that will make us worthy of our great ancestors.'[26]

✦

The approach to Hinduism is also a key strand in the fabric of India as it evolved after 1947. The freedom movement led by Mahatma Gandhi believed in respecting all faiths, and carrying together all the people of India, irrespective of creed. The horrific Hindu–Muslim religious violence that was a consequence of the Partition created new concerns for newly independent India. While Pakistan was carved out of Muslim-majority areas, Muslims who remained back in India still constituted the largest minority. The challenge for India was to create a nation where there would be social harmony, equal respect for all faiths and the freedom for all to follow their religious calling without hindrance. The founding fathers of the Constitution expressly enshrined this sentiment as a fundamental right, guaranteeing the 'freedom of conscience and free profession, practice and propagation of religion' (Article 25).

The intent of the Constitution was that the Republic must respect all faiths and remain neutral in its actions between faiths. It was explicit that India was to be a secular Republic, not a theocracy, in spite of Hindus being an overwhelming majority. At the same time, it was not the intent of the Constitution to label the practice of religion as contrary to the principle of secularism.

However, Jawaharlal Nehru considered religion per se to be of little value. He considered it a 'relic' of the past, coterminous with superstition and obscurantism, and inimical to the 'scientific temper' which must be the attribute of 'modern' people. 'Organized religion ... encourages a temper which is the very opposite to that of science,' he wrote in *The Discovery of India*. 'It produces narrowness and intolerance, credulity and superstition, emotionalism and irrationalism. It tends to close and limit the mind of man, and to produce the temper of a dependent, unfree person.'[27] His espousal of the scientific approach, and new knowledge based on new evidence and not preconceived theory, 'the hard discipline of the mind' as he put it, made him hostile even to the loftiness of thought of Hindu philosophy, which he described as 'vague and soft and flabby, not a rigorous discipline of the mind, but a surrender of mental faculties'.[28] A professed agnostic, he wrote in his last will and testament: 'I wish to declare with all earnestness that I do not want any religious ceremonies performed for me after my death. I do not believe in any such ceremonies and to submit to them, even as a matter of form, would be hypocrisy and an attempt to delude ourselves.' Of course, it is another matter that his last rites were performed with full Hindu rituals.

By contrast, Gandhi was, as Nehru himself put it, 'a Hindu to the depth of his innermost being'. During his first jail term in South Africa (January 1908), he read Vivekananda's *Raja Yoga*, and commentaries on *Yoga Sutra* and Bhagwad Gita. During his second incarceration (October–December 1908), he read the Bhagwad Gita almost every day. During his third imprisonment (February–May 1909), he read the Upanishads, *Manusmriti*, Patanjali's *Yoga Shastra* and reread the Gita. One of the first books published by his International Press in Phoenix, Natal, was an abridged version of Tulsidas's *Ramcharitmanas*, which he considered, as he wrote in his autobiography (*The Story of My Experiments with Truth*), 'the greatest books in all devotional literature'. The Ram Rajya described by Tulsidas was an utopia which Gandhi saw as derived from religion but transcending it. He did not, therefore, see anything wrong in espousing Ram Rajya as the ultimate goal for independent India. For Gandhi, Hinduism was the repository of great wisdom, and its profound philosophical insights provided him great strength and resilience during the freedom struggle. In fact, it can be argued that as he got more involved in the secular cause of India's freedom, his interest in his religious heritage grew. His study was deep, and some of his comments clearly bring this out. In the *Isha Upanishad*, a key shloka reads: 'All this is full. All that is full. From fullness, fullness comes. When fullness is taken away from fullness,

fullness still remains.' Gandhi was deeply moved by this shloka, and is believed to have said that he would happily forego every scripture in Hinduism if he could just keep this one shloka. In short, unlike Nehru, Gandhi did not see religion as an obstruction to modernity or progress. On the contrary, he wrote in *Hind Swaraj*: 'Religion is dear to me, and my first complaint is that India is becoming irreligious (dharam brasht). Here I am not thinking of the Hindu, the Mahomedan, or the Zoroastrian religion, but of that religion which underlies all religions. We are turning away from God.'[29]

There was another vital point of difference between Nehru and Gandhi. Nehru's support for secularism came from his belief that modern nations must separate the church from the state. He saw recent Western history as a vindication of this belief, where the role of the church became secondary to the principles of a liberal democracy. He was also influenced by Communist Soviet Union; socialism, for him, far more relevantly addressed the needs of progressive nations, while religion took them back to the dark age of superstition and prejudice. Any attempt by religion to intrude into the priorities of the state was a sign of regression. Since religion could not be eliminated—although Nehru probably wished that it could be—it was essential for the state to be neutral between all religions, and be a secular state. On the other hand, Gandhi immersed himself in all religions to distil the message of secularism. He believed that although religion had been the cause of much strife in history, the essential message of all religions was love and brotherhood. In his daily prayer meetings, he would have the hymns of all religions sung or recited. Thus, he did not think that because he was a Hindu he should despise those who were not. His impulse to secularism came from a genuine respect for all religions, and from his belief that religion itself gave the message for the harmonious coexistence of all faiths.

The problem, however, was that Nehru's disdain for religion was out of sync with the realities of India. Whether Nehru liked religion or not, it played a very important role in the lives of the people—including Hindus. Gandhi's passionate belief in the importance of respecting all faiths, or in ensuring that no faith should feel it is being discriminated against, also created—even before 1947—a resentment in a section of Hindus. They felt that either as a result of his unsustainable idealism or his 'opportunist' political pragmatism, he was pandering to the Muslims and being less than fair to Hindus. It is probably true that in the face of Britain's divide-and-rule policy and its attempt to widen the trust deficit between Hindus and Muslims, Gandhi sought to assuage Muslim alienation and preserve Hindu–Muslim unity in jointly taking on the British Empire.

But, in this process some of Gandhi's decisions were, frankly, inexplicable, and others less than impartial. Gandhi's support for the Khilafat Movement (1919–1924), which was a pan-Islamicist political protest campaign launched by Muslims to restore the Caliph of the Ottoman Empire based in Turkey, falls in the first category. The irony is that the movement collapsed by 1922 when Turkey itself moved towards a secular state under Kemal Ataturk. That was precisely Bhimrao Ambedkar's point. He wrote that those for whom the cause had been taken up in India had 'themselves favoured a republic and it was quite unjustifiable to compel the Turks to keep Turkey as a monarchy when they wanted to convert it into a republic'.[30] But Gandhi was adamant. In his speech to the Congress session in Calcutta in September 1920, he said: 'The Mussalmans of India cannot remain as honourable men and followers of the faith of their Prophet, if they do not vindicate its honour at any cost.' Gandhi's aim may have been political—to indicate to the Muslims that the Congress supported their concerns—but in practice, the use of a religious card only reinforced the sense of a separate identity among Muslims. Besides, many Hindus saw this as the first of a series of steps meant only to appease Muslims. The support to the Khilafat Movement, which was fundamentalist, extraterritorial, largely indifferent to the cause of India's independence and provided the nursery for the cause of Muslim separatism leading ultimately to the creation of Pakistan, could not be justified on any grounds.

Gandhi's refusal to unequivocally condemn the horrific barbarity of the Moplah rebellion in Malabar, Kerala, in August

1921, was decidedly partial, and seen as such by even his supportive contemporaries. Egged on by the Khilafat movement, Muslims in Kerala declared Khilafat kingdoms in some areas. The Moplahs were tenants at will of Hindu landlords, and while they may have had some agrarian grievances, the fanatical violence with which they attacked their employers was unpardonable. 'Mass murders of Hindu families, brutal rapes of women in front of their family members, murders of pregnant women, desecration of temples, cow slaughter, forcible conversions, pillage, arson and loot reigned till the British troops took control.'[31] But under Gandhi's influence, the Congress sought to downplay the outrage. Gandhi spoke of the 'brave God-fearing Moplahs' who had the right to fight for their religion, and instead sermonised Hindus who, he said, would not find themselves blameless once they investigate the causes of Moplah fanaticism. An angry Ambedkar wrote: 'Any person would have said that this was too heavy a price for Hindu-Moslem unity. But Mr Gandhi was so obsessed by the necessity of establishing Hindu-Moslem unity that he was prepared to make light of the doings of the Moplahs and Khilafists who were congratulating them.'[32]

Resentment among some Hindus was building up due to events earlier on too. Through 1907 and 1908, the Muslim leadership was vocal in its demand that Muslims should be given representation in elected bodies beyond their numerical strength. Apart from the apprehension that they would otherwise be swamped by a Hindu majority, there was also the provocative argument that Muslims, as a consequence of their 700-years-rule in India, were deserving of greater political weightage. As a result of this pressure, the Morley–Minto Reforms of 1909 agreed to the disproportionate representation of Muslims in councils, and also sanctioned separate Muslim electorates. In 1916, the Congress, under the Lucknow Pact, agreed to the demand of the Muslim League for over-representation of Muslims in legislatures and councils. The Government of India Act of 1919 formalised this decision, and soon thereafter the Congress gave up its opposition to the demand for separate electorates as well.

Many leaders within the Congress felt that such decisions were wrong. Madan Mohan Malviya (1861–1946), who served four times as the president of the Congress, was prominent among these. He opposed the separate electorates for Muslims under the Lucknow Pact of 1916, and also opposed the support of the Congress to the Khilafat Movement. He even resigned from the Congress in protest against the Communal Award made by the British in 1932. Malviya represented a strong opinion within the Congress that there was no need to be dismissive about one's religion, as Nehru was. He was a proud Hindu, and made no bones about it. He was the founder of the Akhil Bharatiya Hindu Mahasabha—a pan-Indian organisation for the promotion and preservation of Hinduism. Posterity will always remember him for his tenacity and determination in setting up the Benares Hindu University (BHU) in 1916, and he remained its vice chancellor from 1919 to 1938. As a politician, he did not think there was any contradiction in working for the well-being of those of his faith. In 1910, he had started the Hindi paper, *Maryada*; in 1936, he launched the publication of a magazine, *Sanatan Dharma*, from BHU, dedicated to religious and dharmic interests. Hindu symbols of reverence like the Ganga and cow welfare appealed to him, and he acted upon his beliefs. He founded the Ganga Mahasabha to oppose the damming of the river, and compelled the British to sign an agreement in 1916 called the Aviral Ganga Raksha Samjhauta. For the welfare of cows, he created a non-governmental organisation named Shri Mathura Vrindavana Hasanand Grehar Bhoomi in Vrindavana. Similarly, he started the tradition of aarti at Har-ki-Pauri in Rishikesh, which continues even today. It was Malviya again who, at the 1918 Congress session, dipped into the *Mundaka Upanishad* to give the slogan 'Satyameva Jayate', Truth Shall Prevail, which remains modern India's national slogan.

Leaders like Malviya were poles apart from Nehru's agnosticism and general suspicion of the Hindu faith. Representing a legitimate spectrum of opinion in the Congress, Malviya believed that if Hinduism had received a serious setback, first under Islamic rule and then due to the British conquest, it was now time to give it its due, and doing so did not entail any conflict with the policy of secularism.

There were others, however, like Vinayak Damodar Savarkar, who took this sentiment to another extreme. In May 1923, Savarkar's short essay, 'Essentials of Hindutva', was published. It is important to deconstruct and contextualise this polemic for the scattered ideas it contains and not see it exclusively as a call for a separate Hindu Rashtra. We can have little objection to Savarkar when he claims that the term 'Hindu' was recognised from ancient times, that a civilisation was associated with that name, that this civilisation was culturally cohesive, that—in spite of the caste system—it represented a larger ideological unity, that it evoked a sense of belonging to a jati, a nation bound by common blood, and that it was always associated with a defined geographical territory, recognised by our ancient texts—Bharatvarsha. A reading of *Hind Swaraj* would show that Mahatma Gandhi said much the same thing. However, Savarkar went beyond this to argue that only those people could lay claim to belonging to India for whom it was both pitrbhumi or a fatherland and the land of one's ancestors, and their divyabhumi or holy land. In saying this, he accepted that Hindus who had converted in the past to Islam or to Christianity could be Indian because their ancestors were born in India; but they had to be excluded because India was not their holy land since their religion had extraterritorial loyalties, centred in Mecca or the Vatican.

It is important to read Savarkar in the context of his times, and his own visceral reactions to certain events that unfolded just before he wrote his essay. Savarkar was completely against the support of the Congress to the Khilafat movement—as were many others, including those in the Congress. Vikram Sampath, who has written the most well-researched biography of Savarkar, admits that the 'Khilafat and the transnational allegiance must have weighed heavily on Vinayak's mind'.[33] Savarkar was also indignant about the attempts by Gandhi and the Congress to appease Muslims, and in particular the downplaying of the horrific violence by the Moplahs. Statements by some Muslim leaders about the incompatibility of Muslims and Hindus living as part of one nation, and the need, therefore, for Muslims to explore a future, separate from the 'dominance' of the Hindus, must have also had their impact on him. There were, as Sampath brings out, deeply personal reasons too — in his incarceration in the Andamans of over a decade, his jailors were rather brutal Muslims, adept at humiliation and torture, and Savarkar was their prime victim.

Thus, in the specific context in which he wrote his essay, Savarkar's outpouring must be seen more as a clarion call for Hindus to unite on the basis of their civilisational bonds, and less as an iron-cast advocacy of an exclusionist Hindu Rashtra. The latter forms a much smaller component of his overall views, and can be better understood as an emotional exaggeration prompted by the situation prevailing then, both personal and historical and, in particular, his anger at the support for the Khilafat movement. There was a pervasive feeling among many sections of Hindus that their culture and civilisation had been denigrated by the Islamic and British conquests, and it was time to reclaim it with pride and aggression. In voicing this sentiment, Savarkar was undoubtedly more strident than many others. To be so was, in fact, a part of his personality. Even when he was studying law in England, he was persuaded to the cause of violent revolution against the British, and was arrested and deported to India for this reason. On his way back, when the ship docked at Marseilles, he made a courageous but failed attempt to escape, and was rearrested. It is not difficult to understand why, for a man of such strong views and convictions, who underwent near continuous solitary confinement in the horrific jail conditions of Kala Pani in the Andamans for eleven years, there could have been an excess in the expression of his views, especially since the essay was penned when he was still in jail in Ratnagiri. There can, of course, be no condonation of his racist argument. However, it is significant that Savarkar himself dilutes his extremism when he writes: 'We are trying our best, *as we ought to*, to develop the consciousness of and a sense of attachment to the *greater whole*, whereby Hindus, Mohammedans, Parsis, Christians and Jews would feel as Indians first and every other thing afterwards [emphasis mine].'[34]

That Savarkar was a patriot was never in doubt. His burning passion was to see an India free from British rule, and he paid a very high price for the courage of his convictions. Gandhi, Sardar Patel and Bal Gangadhar Tilak petitioned the British government for his release. It is true that towards the end of his term in the Andamans, Savarkar requested the colonial power to grant him amnesty. However, for a man who had suffered so much, there was nothing unpatriotic about this, considering that at that time the Congress itself was looking not at throwing out the British but only greater autonomy under British rule. In recognition of his revolutionary patriotism, Prime Minister Indira Gandhi released a postage stamp in his memory in 1970. When the BJP was in power in 2002, the airport at Andamans was renamed as the Veer Savarkar airport, and a portrait of Savarkar unveiled in Parliament in 2003. In assessing the many aspects of Savarkar's legacy, we can do no better than quoting the reflective assessment of his painstaking biographer, Vikram Sampath:

> As the intellectual fountainhead of the ideology of Hindutva, Savarkar is undoubtedly one of the most contentious political thinkers and leaders of the twentieth century. Accounts of his long and stormy life have oscillated from glorifying hagiographies to reproachful demonization. The truth, as always, lies somewhere in between. … I was slowly to discover that Savarkar was a bundle of contradictions and a historian's enigma. He simultaneously means many things to many people. An alleged atheist and a staunch rationalist who strongly opposed orthodox Hindu beliefs and the caste system and dismissed cow worship as a mere superstition, Savarkar was also the most vocal political voice for the Hindu community through the entire course of the Indian freedom struggle.[35]

While obviously an admirer of Savarkar, Sampath is objective enough to admit that in judging Savarkar's overall impact, 'his flaws and follies need to be assessed in conjunction with his vision and philosophy.'[36]

In this context, Sampath very aptly quotes American historian John Noble Wilford: 'All works of history are interim reports. What people did in the past is not preserved in amber ... immutable though the ages. Each generation looks back and drawing from its own experience, presumes to find patterns that illuminate both past and present.'[37]

One direct consequence of Savarkar's Hindutva doctrine was the birth in 1925 of the ultra-Hindu organisation, the Rashtriya Swayamsevak Sangh (RSS). Its founder, Keshav Baliram Hedgewar, was greatly influenced by Savarkar's thoughts, and had met him in Ratnagiri prison. The avowed purpose of the RSS was to unite and strengthen the Hindu community which, as a result of its internal disunity, had allowed a handful of Britishers to conquer the vast land of India. Hindus, Hedgewar felt, lacked parakaram (valour) and a sense of pride in their ancient civilisational legacy. He was disillusioned with the support to the Khilafat movement, impatient with the slow pace of the freedom struggle and critical of the policy of ahimsa or non-violence. He, therefore, set up training shakhas or units to give physical strength to the Hindu community by equipping them with paramilitary skills to better defend themselves.

By its critics, the RSS is seen today as wholly communal, bent only on pursuing its dangerously divisive policy of creating a Hindu Rashtra. However, it is important that we evaluate this organisation objectively, and not brush under the historical carpet some of its other facets. It is true that the RSS was suspected of having a role in the assassination of Mahatma Gandhi, but it is also a fact that the judiciary acquitted it. In the immediate aftermath of the assassination, the RSS was banned on the recommendation of Home Minister Sardar Patel, but the ban was later lifted. During the Partition and thereafter, RSS cadres contributed to the rehabilitation of Hindu refugees and the distribution of aid and services. In 1949, no less a person than Dr Zakir Hussain, who would go on to become the president of India, gave a testimonial to it while addressing a Muslim audience in Monghyr, Bihar: 'The allegations against the RSS of violence and hatred against

Muslims are wholly false. Muslims should learn the lesson of mutual love, cooperation and organisation from RSS.'

During the 1962 war with China, the RSS contributed actively to the war effort, especially in providing support to the civil administration. This impressed Prime Minister Nehru, who invited the RSS to field a contingent of hundred swayamsevaks in the 1963 Republic Day Parade in New Delhi. The RSS also distinguished itself in assisting the government during the 1965 war with Pakistan. Prime Minister Lal Bahadur Shastri invited the then RSS chief, M.S. Golwalkar, to an all-party meet, and even allowed the RSS to relieve the burden of the Delhi police by taking up some of its duties. In the 1971 war with Bangladesh, RSS volunteers were the first to donate blood, and helped the army to dig trenches. There was almost universal praise for these patriotic services. Field Marshall Cariappa, the first chief of the Indian Army, was among those who paid a glowing tribute: 'RSS is my heart's work. My dear young man don't be disturbed. Look ahead! Go ahead! The country is standing in need of your services.' When Indira Gandhi imposed the infamous Emergency in 1977, it was the RSS cadres who clandestinely worked on a large scale for the restoration of democracy. The Gandhian leader, Jayaprakash Narayan, who was earlier a staunch critic of the RSS, acknowledged this: 'RSS is a revolutionary organisation. No other organisation in the country comes anywhere near it. It alone has the capacity to transform society and casteism, and wipe the tears from the eyes of the poor.'

M.S. Golwalkar, who succeeded Hedgewar in 1940 and was the longest-serving sarsanghchalak or head or the organisation, serving till his death in 1973, rightly spoke about the need of a Hindu renaissance; his advocacy of Vasudhaiva Kutumbukam, the ancient Hindu ideal which looks upon the entire world as one family, was laudable too.

But, Golwalkar is also responsible for giving Savarkar's vision of a Hindu Rashtra a decidedly racist tone. In his book, *We or Our Nationhood Defined*, he wrote, in the context of Hitler's pogrom against the Jews: 'To keep up the purity of the Race and its culture,

Germany shocked the world by her purging the country of the Semitic Races—the Jews. Race pride at its highest has been manifested here. Germany has also shown how well-nigh impossible it is for Races and cultures, having differences going to the roots, to be assimilated into one united whole, a good lesson for us in Hindustan to learn and profit by'. In the same book, he also advocated a Hindu Rashtra where there was no scope for those of other religions. 'The non-Hindu people of Hindustan must either adopt Hindu culture and languages, must learn and respect and hold in reverence the Hindu religion, must entertain no idea but of those of the glorification of the Hindu race and culture ... in a word they must cease to be foreigners; or may stay in the country, wholly subordinate to the Hindu nation, claiming nothing, deserving no privileges, far less any preferential treatment— not even citizen's rights.'

This dangerously xenophobic thinking in a country where, even if Hindus were the overwhelming majority, there were people in sufficiently large numbers of other religions, was a matter of deep concern. However, the freedom movement, the sway of Gandhi, and his inclusive vision, and the popularity of the Congress under Nehru and Patel, kept this kind of thinking largely on the fringes of an otherwise plural and secular vision as enshrined in the Constitution. But the trajectory of events as they unfolded in independent India would create the reasons why such fringe exclusionism would surface in a far more threatening manner in the national discourse.

In the initial years after 1947, Gandhi's eclectic religious faith and Nehru's supra-religious modernity was largely internalised by the opinion-making Indian middle class. The members of this class were not unhappy with the sanctity given by Gandhi to the religious domain. They were, by the sheer moral force of his persona, also deeply influenced by his advocacy of communal harmony. Nehru's vision of a modern and progressive state had its appeal too. But over the years, the disdain for religion by influential sections of the ruling elite began to create its own anti-bodies. Unfortunately, the strongest espousal of secularism seemed to emanate from a Westernised upper segment in the metropolitan cities whose transparent cultural rootlessness greatly weakened the credibility and impact of the message. Gandhi was a convincing spokesperson of communal harmony because he was thoroughly familiar with his own religion, the essential tenets of other religions and the idiom and substance of his civilisational legacy. But the anglicised elite, although liberal, had very little understanding or knowledge of their religion and culture. Their secularism, therefore, was often perceived to be a stance to be invoked, almost as a reflex, every time there was a whiff of religion. For some of its members, faith was tantamount to medievalism, and all religious practice the equivalent of ritual and superstition. Such a condescending dismissal began to be resented over time by large sections of Hindus who were proud of their religion, as also of their culture and civilisation.

Anger also built up by the perception that secularism was used selectively, in a manner tailored to appease Muslims but take Hindus for granted. Matters first came to a head on the question of the rebuilding of Somnath Temple in Gujarat. This temple had been repeatedly razed to the ground by Muslim rulers. In 1204, the Turkic invader Mahmud Ghazni looted the temple and shattered the holy Shivalinga; in 1299, Alauddin Khilji's general, Ulugh Khan, sacked the rebuilt temple; it was built again by Hindu kings, but destroyed a third time in 1395 by Zafar Khan, the last governor of Gujarat under the Delhi Sultanate; Mahmud Begada, the Sultan of Gujarat, brought it down again in 1451; the temple was yet again restored by Hindus, but finally demolished by Aurangzeb in 1665.

It is important to understand that rebuilding this temple, which was among the first Hindu temples to be destroyed by the Turkic invaders, was emotionally important for Hindus. Somnath houses the first of the twelve Shiva jyotirlingas where Shiva, it is believed, appeared as a blazing column of light representing the Supreme, undivided reality. The temple's repeated and fanatical vandalism, although a part of the historical past, was internalised by Hindus, making its reconstruction an emotive goal for which there was near universal support in the community. Hindus did not think that in an independent republic, restoring a place of worship so barbarously destroyed on so many occasions by Muslim rulers, was against secularism or religious harmony. In fact, they thought that this was the least that could be done to rectify past historical wrongs, and give back with pride to Hindus one of their most important religious sites.

Sardar Patel, the then home minister, initiated the process of rebuilding the temple in 1947; he was supported by cabinet colleague, K.M. Munshi; Gandhi gave his blessings to the project, but advised that the costs should be paid not from the government exchequer but by raising funds directly from the people. This advice was followed, and when the temple was renovated, the organisers invited Dr Rajendra Prasad, the first president of India, to inaugurate it. But Nehru thought that for the president of India to be present on such an occasion would be a violation of secularism, and send the wrong message to Muslims. On 2 March 1951, Nehru wrote to Dr Rajendra Prasad: 'I confess that I do not like the idea of your associating yourself with a spectacular opening of the Somnath Temple. This is not merely visiting a temple which can certainly be done by you or anyone else, but rather participating in a significant function which, unfortunately, has a number of implications.' On 10 March, Prasad clarified to Nehru that the Somnath Temple had been built entirely with private subscriptions, and he was not doing anything extraordinary if he associated himself with the function as he visited other places of worship when he felt inclined to do so. Undeterred, Nehru wrote again to Prasad on 22 April 1951, this time also referring to international disapproval: 'In criticism of policy in regard to it, we are asked how a secular government such as ours can associate itself with such a ceremony which is, in addition, revivalist in character.'

Dr Prasad did go ahead and inaugurate the restored temple in May 1951. But the opposition of Nehru to this was known publicly, and many Hindus felt that this was an unwarranted case of secularism being used primarily to assuage Muslim sentiments without adequately appreciating Hindu feelings, especially since the president was particular in stating that his participation in no way meant a dilution of his respect for all other religions. Perhaps Nehru, so soon after the Hindu–Muslim tensions of Partition, wanted to be extra careful not to do anything that may once again disturb religious harmony. He also felt that spending so much money on restoring a temple was a misplaced priority at a time when the economy was fragile. The basic difference was that Nehru believed that the state should not be involved in any way with religion, while Prasad, mirroring the Gandhian viewpoint, believed that respecting all religions was more important, and did not think that a belief in secularism negated the importance of personal faith. The bottom line, however, is that Nehru's views did not go down well with a large number of Hindus, including those in his own party. In fact, K.M. Munshi, who too had been accused by Nehru of encouraging Hindu revivalism, bluntly said so in a letter to Nehru: 'I can assure you that the "Collective Sub-conscious" of India today is happier with the scheme of reconstruction of Somnath ... than with many other things that we have done and are doing.'

A similar situation arose with Nehru's support for the amendment of Hindu personal law, through a series of four Acts relating to marriage, succession, adoption and guardianship, passed by Parliament in 1954–1956. It is not the intention here to discuss in any detail the merits or otherwise of the bills. In many aspects they were progressive, especially in conferring rights on women. However, we are dealing with the perception that they created in Hindus. Many of them were strongly opposed to the amendments, and felt that they were being singled out for changes in the time-tested tradition of their personal laws, when other communities, especially the Muslims, were being excluded. Article 44 of the Constitution enshrines a Uniform Civil Code as a part of the Directive Principles, desirable goals to be pursued by the government. If this goal was pursued without singling out only the Hindu community, it might have assuaged the resentment in the majority community, including within the Congress party itself. While Nehru had his way, it left the Hindus feeling that although they were the largest in number, their sentiments could be ridden rough-shod, while that of other communities were treated as sacrosanct.

This simmering discontent was accentuated by the feeling that Muslims were being appeased for purely vote-bank politics. Appeasement was probably not a part of a planned design, but in a first-past-the-post electoral system, political parties realised that the bulk support of one community could make the difference between winning and losing, especially in closely contested elections. The Hindus were never a monolith. They were divided along caste lines, and mostly voted accordingly. However, the Muslims realised soon enough that their support to any one party or group of parties could increase their bargaining strength in democratic politics. For instance, in Uttar Pradesh, the most populous state of the country, which sends the maximum number of representatives to Parliament, every sixth voter is a Muslim. In the united UP (before Uttarakhand was carved out from it), results in a fourth of the 400 constituencies depended on how the Muslims voted. Indeed, between 1977 and 1996, over a hundred constituencies elected Muslims to the state assembly. Nationwide, Muslims had a significant density in as many as 125 parliamentary constituencies, which constitute almost one-fourth of the House. Quickly enough, most political parties factored in such an important electoral consideration.

This led to many decisions which were clearly dictated only by the expediency of not alienating Muslim opinion. The most dramatic of these was the Shah Bano case in 1986, when Prime Minister Rajiv Gandhi, in order not to displease Muslims, passed an Ordinance to overrule an eminently sensible decision by the Supreme Court upholding the provision of payment of maintenance to a divorced Muslim woman. Shah Bano was a sixty-two-year-old woman with five children. Her husband, Mohammad Ahmad Khan, an affluent lawyer in Indore, had married again and left Shah Bano and her children without any monetary support. When she filed for maintenance under the Criminal Procedure Code, he summarily divorced her through the primitive triple talaq route, and claimed that since she was no longer his wife, he had no obligation to pay her anything. Shah Bano fought for her rights legally, and in 1985, the Supreme Court ruled in her favour.

The judgment triggered a predictable furore in orthodox Muslim opinion. The conservative All India Muslim Personal Law Board organised a series of protests, arguing that the judgment was an erosion of Muslim personal law. It appears that initially Rajiv Gandhi was inclined to go with the Supreme Court's judgment, but was later persuaded by 'seasoned' Congress leaders, and influential journalist–politicians like M.J. Akbar,[38] that this would do great harm to the party's electoral prospects, where Muslim support was critical. Accordingly, in 1986, the Parliament passed the Muslim Women (Protection of Rights on Divorce Act) which nullified the Supreme Court ruling, and restricted the payment of maintenance to a divorced Muslim woman only for the period of iddat, or until ninety days after the divorce. Arif Mohammad Khan, a cabinet colleague of Rajiv Gandhi, resigned from both the party and his post in protest against this completely unwarranted capitulation. Across the country, ordinary citizens, and especially Hindus, rightly felt that this was a blatant example of appeasement for vote-bank politics. Hindus were outraged that while their personal law could be amended by Nehru, his party under his own grandson was not willing to show the same resolve where Muslims were concerned. Besides, secular women groups were appalled at the betrayal of gender rights. There was widespread feeling that Muslim personal law was harshly discriminatory to women, and that summary divorce through the pronouncement of triple talaq, was contrary to every value held by a modern republic espousing the cause of equality of women.

Hindu anger was also fuelled by the ethnic cleansing of Kashmiri Hindus—mostly Pandits—from Jammu and Kashmir as a result of anti-Hindu pogroms in the years following 1989. These were ruthlessly carried out by Muslim insurgent movements spearheaded by the Jammu and Kashmir Liberation Front and the Muslim United Front. By some estimates, some 600,000 Hindus were forced to flee their ancestral homes in the Valley, and anywhere between 400 to 1,000 were killed, accompanied by the large-scale destruction of Hindu properties. An entire people were displaced from their place of birth and ancestry. What was conspicuous was the absence of any real outrage on the part of influential voices in the liberal spectrum, who otherwise were in the forefront for the protection of human rights, especially of the Muslims.

The movement by the BJP in 1992 for the reconstruction of a Ram temple in Ayodhya, at the place where Lord Ram was believed to have been born, further catalysed this growing Hindu dissatisfaction. The site was disputed since a mosque had been built there in the fifteenth century by the first Mughal king, Babur. As had happened in the case of so many other temples, a great many Hindus believed that the mosque had been constructed after destroying an existing temple at that site. The rath yatra to Ayodhya, begun by BJP leader L.K. Advani from Somnath in 1990, was meant to correct this historical wrong. It was a master card to galvanise and consolidate Hindu opinion in support of an emotive religious cause.

Apart from resentment over the policies of appeasement, the Hindu community, and in particular its influential middle class, was by this time psychologically predisposed to religious revivalism for a variety of other reasons linked to irreversible changes in the structures of traditional society.

Firstly, increased economic opportunities and mobility had led to a breakdown of the extended family, and this induced a hankering for some transcendent institution which could, through the medium of common belief, resurrect a sense of community.

Secondly, for many across urban India, the degree and scope of change in the course of one generation was both tremendous and often traumatic. It was not unusual for persons to do their schooling in a village and college in a nearby town and then find a job in an unfamiliar and faraway metropolis. Telescoped in a decade were the changes of a century—a new environment, new technologies, new values, new skills, new expectations and new lifestyles. Religion, by invoking the certitudes and simplicities of an idealised past, provided the most accessible crutch to stand up to the unpredictably of this rapid and demanding transformation.

Thirdly, the frenzy of a million individual endeavours in the thrust and grasp of India's urban sprawl created a pervasive feeling of being alone in a naturally hostile world, a world that was Darwinian in the survival of the fittest. The feeling of being abandoned in a sea of constant strife and competition rendered the individual susceptible to any institution which posited countervalues of assurance and certainty.

Fourthly, the landscape of urban India was singularly deficient in institutions of community interaction. The upwardly mobile often found themselves living in unfamiliar neighbourhoods without knowing who their neighbour was; joy and grief had become largely nuclear phenomena. Once again, religion was the refuge against this impersonal social structure.

Fifthly, in a situation where cynicism and corruption seemed to have compromised almost every secular institution, the appeal of religion, as the repository of absolute values, could not but grow. Thus, it would be fairly accurate to say that when the BJP made its call for Hindus—Garv se kaho hum Hindu hain: Say with pride that you are a Hindu, it found a responsive resonance in most of them, tired of hiding their religious feelings because of the Nehruvian definition of secularism as an aversion to the practice of religion.

This does not mean that when L.K. Advani began his rath yatra, much of Hindu India was in the throes of religious revivalism. But what it did mean was that under the awning of progress and modernisation projected by secular India, there existed, contrary to the illusions of an overly Westernised elite, a strong undercurrent wanting the rectification of wrongs done to Hinduism. Even then, when the rath yatra led to the demolition of the Babri Masjid in December 1992, the dominant feeling was one of shock and disapproval. When the Masjid fell, an entire generation of Hindus, weaned on the commitment to secularism, woke up to the debris of their own assumptions. Shock was followed generally by a sense of guilt; but guilt was not necessarily followed by a sense of remorse. Instead, there was, in many cases, an attempt to overcome guilt by a two-step manoeuvre—condemnation of the act of demolition, and an even more militant assertion of the reasons justifying the rise of Hindu assertiveness.

Although the Ram Janambhoomi agitation did not immediately lead to the rise of a triumphant Hindu radicalism, there is little doubt that it gave it a significant fillip. The electoral gains that the BJP made in the immediate aftermath of the Masjid demolition were neither lasting nor of a magnitude to bring it to power. This had to wait till 1998, when the charismatic Atal Bihari Vajpayee led the BJP to power for the first time in India's history. Vajpayee was a product of the RSS, but was far from being a hardcore Hindutva-wadi. He had no qualms in claiming to be a proud Hindu or working for Hindu revivalism, but was pragmatic enough to understand that in a country like India, where there were millions of people of other faiths scattered all over the country, a policy of rigid exclusionism would be disastrous. His liberalism was thus as much a matter of his innate personality as it was an enlightened accommodation with the realities of India.

By contrast, it is ominous how many other iconic leaders in the BJP—and earlier in the Bharatiya Jan Sangh—interpreted their fealty to Hinduism and Hindus largely in terms of hatred of Muslims. Deendayal Upadhyaya (1916–1968) was among the tallest leaders of the Jan Sangh, and his philosophy of 'integral humanism' was adopted as the ideology of the Sangh's successor organisation, the BJP. As a part of his vision of integral humanism, Deendayal posited the notion of 'chiti', or the soul of a nation, which was his most original contribution. Deendayal's view was that each nation has a soul of its own. In this respect, chiti probably corresponds to the German concept of zeitgeist, which argues that each era has a unique spirit that sets it apart from others. This uniqueness reflects the dominant ideals and beliefs of a society. Deendayal had clarified that his articulation of chiti was meant to bring out the most positive or constructive content of each nation. He had also stressed that chiti is faith-neutral, and that, as per his definition of integral humanism, people have the full right to follow their respective faiths. It was his belief that Hinduism is inherently tolerant and assimilative in character. As he clarified in 1962, 'So long as Hinduism is alive there is no danger to Islam. A Hindu does not discriminate between Ram and Allah. He recites Vishnu Sahasranam in the daily schedule, he will be too happy to add one or two names to the thousand terms attributed to God Vishnu. The concept of Hindu nation is neither negative, nor reactionary, nor territorial, it is a cultural and civilizational concept connoting positive direction.'

But while Upadhyaya made the case of inclusion—at least in principle—it is significant that he still reiterated the need for a 'Hindu nation', and his actual views were intolerant, with little sensitivity to faiths other than Hinduism. In a speech in 1952, he said: 'There exists only one culture here. There are no separate cultures here for Muslims and Christians. Culture is not related to mode of worship or sect; it is related to the country. Kabir, Jayasi and Raskhan should serve as models for Muslims. Today their centre of loyalty is outside Bharat. The Muslims must completely change their sentiment and view.'[39] It was the same language which Savarkar and Golwalkar use, although the philosophy of integral humanism sought to put a gloss over it. In 1965, the year that he articulated the concept of integral humanism, Upadhyaya said: 'Some argue that Muslims are our brothers and should not be called foreigners. Arguing the same way, why is Aurangzeb, who lived and utilized the wealth here, regarded a foreign ruler? Are not Moghul kings to be treated as foreigners? ... Akbar may have been great but he was not ours. We speak of having become free after a thousand years of slavery. This simply means that during Akbar's reign we were in bondage.'[40] The essential message was that Muslims were—and are—foreigners in India, and their only redemption lay in becoming Hindu in terms of their culture, outlook and values. In articulating such an exclusionist view, Deendayal was going beyond even Savarkar's concept of a Hindu Rashtra. Savarkar accepted that those Muslims whose ancestors had lived in India for generations were entitled to be Indians. He excluded them on the grounds that their religious loyalties were extraterritorial. Savarkar's extremist views could be contextualised—as I have discussed—as being an emotional

339

overreaction to the specific events around the 1920s when he wrote his polemic on Hindutva, and when independence from British rule was still a remote possibility. But Upadhyaya's ideology, which has been officially adopted by the BJP, was articulated decades *after* Independence, when the multicultural and multireligious character of India was accepted as a reality and guaranteed by the Constitution.

Atal Bihari Vajpayee lost the elections in 2004, and the BJP remained out of power at the centre for the next decade when the Congress-led United Progressive Alliance (UPA) was in office. In 2014, Narendra Modi led the BJP to an unprecedented, absolute majority in the Lok Sabha for the first time in India's history. Given the BJP's consistent support for Hindu-related causes, this assumption of political power could, one would have thought, lend support to the rediscovery of the great wisdoms and historical experience of Hindu civilisation. It could have led to the long-awaited Hindu renaissance, with institutional encouragement being given, within the framework of the Constitution, for Hindus to learn more about their past refinements, their culture and their remarkable cerebral output, as also the consideration and implementation of much needed reforms within Hindu society that would make it modern, progressive, egalitarian and gender-sensitive, while remaining culturally rooted.

For a man accused of allegedly enabling the mass murder of Muslims in the horrific Gujarat riots of 2002, Modi began promisingly with an inclusive slogan—Sabka Saath, Sabka Vikas. This raised hopes that the BJP under his helmsmanship would temper its majoritarian agenda, and carry all Indians irrespective of their caste and creed in the interests of expeditious economic development. I have discussed the causes for Hindu resentment in the decades after Independence—and even before—and the general rise in Hindu assertiveness. No doubt, apart from the disenchantment with the lacklustre second term of the UPA government, it was precisely these sentiments that contributed to the spectacular win of the BJP. However, the hope that the responsibilities imposed by political power would make the BJP restrict its sectarian evangelism, eschew its ultra-Hindu aggression, jettison its ostrich-like pursuit of the outdated, unconstitutional and impractical goal of creating a Hindu Rashtra and work for a genuine Hindu renaissance compatible with the goals of a modern republic, have been largely belied.

Whatever the slogans and speeches of the top BJP and RSS leadership to the contrary, the fact of the matter is that they have been complicit and collusive in seriously eroding India's commitment to pluralism, religious harmony, respect for all faiths, civilised dialogue and rule of law. The BJP's strategy has been to consolidate Hindu votes by promoting the divide between Hindus and Muslims on the basis of religion. Both in the 2014 and 2019 parliamentary elections, the BJP won with an absolute majority of seats but there was not a single Muslim among its winning candidates, certainly a first for any triumphant political party in the history of Indian democracy. Around 98 per cent of cow-related lynchings since 2010 occurred after 2014; 86 per cent of the victims were Muslims; and, the majority of these incidents took place in BJP-ruled states. Cow vigilantes made no secret of their adherence to violent 'Hindutva' groups, and proudly posted videos compelling their helpless victims to recite 'Jai Shri Ram'. Several BJP politicians justified such attacks, prosecution was unforgivably tardy, and often the victims were booked before any action was taken against the perpetrators. Many of these attacks were based on mere suspicion—later proven unfounded. Mohammad Ikhlaq in UP lost his life in 2015 in precisely this way. There was also unbelievable cruelty, totally alien to Hindu tradition even in dealing with 'adversaries'. In 2016, in Jharkhand, vigilantes beat up a Muslim cattle trader and a twelve-year-old boy travelling to an animal fair. Their badly bruised bodies were found hanging from a tree with their hands tied behind them. Pehlu Khan, a farmer in Haryana, was killed in April 2017 for transporting a cow he had legally bought in an animal husbandry sale. Video footage shows him pleading for his life as his attackers continue to thrash him while chanting the names of Hindu gods. The 'triumphal' video was shot by his attackers, as proof of their great 'defence' of Hinduism. Pehlu Khan named his killers before his died, but in spite of this and the video footage, they were acquitted even as the Haryana police showed great alacrity in pursuing a case filed against Khan.

There is enough evidence to support the perception that the BJP and its affiliated organisations were merely tokenistic in disapproving such incidents. The PM, who'd coined the slogan 'Sabka Saath, Sabka Vikas', often took days to express mild disapproval of such gory killings. Ministers in the government who referred to Muslims as 'haramzade'—bastards—were but gently ticked off. No action was taken against those—seen on video—openly telling people not to buy vegetables from Muslim vendors during Covid times. There was a prominent minister who publicly garlanded those accused of lynching. Many more such incidents can be narrated. The essential point is that the national consensus—backed by the express mandate of the Constitution—for India to be a nation where there is respect for all faiths is under threat, and is being replaced by a brittle tension in which Muslims have become the target of lumpen right-wing elements who seem to have the tacit backing of the state. There were even members of parliament (MPs) who publicly praised Nathuram Godse, the man who assassinated Mahatma Gandhi, while others made no secret of the fact that they would be happy to build a temple in the assassin's name.

This pervasive atmosphere of intolerance empowered a new rhetoric, where anybody who differed with the BJP was labelled a 'Pakistani' or a 'Pakistani agent', or dubbed anti-national, or a traitor or lacking patriotism. This in turn provided sanction to those who believed that they have the right to take the law into their own hands to deal with such 'traitors'. New 'protectors' of Hinduism came up, whose knowledge about the religion was in inverse proportion to their aggression. In a spectacular denial of the great Hindu tradition of dialogue and discussion to resolve differences, they believed that they had the right to shoot dead anyone—including Hindus—who in their ignorant opinion were 'harming' Hinduism. Thus, rationalists like Professor M.M. Kalburgi, former Vice Chancellor of Kannada

University, Hampi, in Karnataka, who argued against idol worship, was shot dead in August 2015; Narendra Dabholkar, social activist, rationalist and crusader against religious superstition, who founded the Maharashtra Andhashraddha Nirmoolan Samiti, was murdered in August 2013; Govind Pansare, author of a bestselling biography of Shivaji, was killed in February 2015; and journalist Gauri Lankesh, who spoke and wrote fearlessly against the extremist Hindu right, and worked for Dalit and tribal rights, was assassinated in September 2017.

Another very dangerous consequence of this misguided Hindu 'revivalism' was the imposition of a 'moral code' for Hindu women. Fanatical groups like the Sri Ram Sene felt they could barge into bars or restaurants and humiliate and attack women in the name of enforcing orthodox and patriarchal notions of how 'chaste' Hindu women should behave. Young couples in parks were harangued and humiliated for betraying 'Hindu values'. It was a bizarre case of the imposition of Victorian morality on a civilisation which—as we have seen in detail—recognised kama as a part of an enlightened and balanced life, and as among the four highest goals of life. The 'Love Jihad' Act, pushed through by Chief Minister Yogi Adityanath in UP, and emulated in other BJP-ruled states, not only demonises all Muslim men, but also nullifies the free choice of adult Hindu women to marry whomsoever they wish. Forced conversions of Hindus is wrong, and there are provisions in the existing law to counter it. But assuming that all interfaith marriages are a result of coercion or fraudulent conversion, is a totally unwarranted conclusion, leading to the justifiable inference that the real aim of the supporters of the bill is only to fan Hindu–Muslim hostility. Besides, the attempt to infantilise Hindu women, and make them behave in accordance with asinine orthodoxies akin to Talibani fiats, is downright repulsive.

The prescriptive element that the new, so-called evangelists of Hinduism are bringing in is anathema for most Hindus. Hinduism has always been a way of life. Hindus don't like to be told what to do and what not to do, what to eat and what to drink, what to wear and how to behave, what to watch and what to read, who to meet and who not to, how to practise their religion and how to be good Hindus. Hindus living in the twenty-first century, especially those of the middle class, have gone far beyond the insular diktats of this new breed of 'mentors', seeking to drag the republic back to a horribly distorted 'utopia' of their narrow, conformist, patriarchal and conservative imagination.

The real danger is that we are witnessing the emergence of a lumpen leadership that believes that it has a monopoly to interpret Hinduism and Hindu civilisation. Since time immemorial, Hindus have faced many travails and setbacks but have survived them by drawing upon the great strengths of their culture: tradition and faith. Even in the greatest adversity, Hinduism have never allowed its core cerebration and idealism to be compromised. Under Muslim rule, Hindus carried out one of the most remarkable processes of creative democratisation and decentralisation through the Bhakti movement. The British conquest led to a deep introspection on what reforms Hinduism needed, and prompted stalwarts who were knowledgeable about their legacy to consider ways of reinventing their faith. But, under BJP rule starting 2014, the attack has come from within. The complicity of the top BJP leadership in the uncontrolled radicalisation of Hindutva politics has led to the empowerment of the lowest common denominator within Hinduism. It has given the leadership of the great Hindu civilisation to the rabble, and unleashed forces that in their misplaced evangelism are trampling with impunity upon the delicate and refined tapestry and enormous wisdoms of the very faith and civilisation such forces claim to defend.

This is a consequence which must very deeply concern all right-thinking Hindus. The first task in this process is to understand what this newly empowered lumpen leadership stands for, what are its distinguishing features and what is the texture of its thought processes. Firstly, it is characterised by a singular lack of knowledge about the nuances, complexities and intellectual grandeur of Hinduism. Secondly—and for precisely this reason—it is averse to dialogue, discussion and debate. Its debilitatingly simplistic certitudes are doctrinaire, even fanatical, and it views with deep suspicion anyone who has a point of view to the contrary. Thirdly, it has no compunction in resorting to violence to impose its views. This predilection towards violence is accentuated when its representatives are in a mob. Fourthly, it is highly conservative and orthodox in its interpretation of Hinduism, supportive of inequitable existing hierarchies, and completely unexposed to the liberality of thought that is the quintessential feature of Hinduism. Fifthly, it is deeply patriarchal, believing that women should accept their subordinate position and conform to stereotypical notions of so-called 'Hindu' values, which essentially means that men should decide what they should wear, who they should meet, what they should drink or eat and what kind of relationships they can have. Sixthly, the dominant emotion is hatred of the 'other', others being defined as primarily Muslim, but also including all those who are not part of its smug circle of like-minded largely upper-caste brethren. This hatred is collectively fuelled by a simulated sense of besiegement, a perennial feeling of insecurity, where the conjured projection is that traditional citadels of social entitlement are under attack and need to be defended or resurrected. Seventhly, it is animated by the need to revive India's great Hindu past, but its knowledge of what this really is, is highly superficial, consisting—as I have discussed—a make-believe world of airplanes and cars in the past, thereby devaluing the real achievements and refinements of ancient India. Eighthly, it has scant regard for the rule of law. It believes that such niceties are the crutches of the weak, and have little or no application to those who are fighting for bigger causes like 'protecting' Hinduism, especially since they have the perceived backing of the powers that be. Ninthly, it has little problem in conflating religion with patriotism. Through the prism of this narrow polarity, only a Hindu can be patriotic, while the patriotism of all others is suspect. And tenthly, it is particularly porous to false information so long as it buttresses its preconceived world view. As part of this process, it has no compunction in wilfully purveying false news to win more supporters to its cause.

The fact that Hinduism and Hindu civilisation is now sought to be led by such a lumpen class, should make even the BJP worry. From the beginning, the BJP–RSS leadership took a position of strategic ambivalence to the rise of this class, through a policy of both encouragement and denial. Such an approach enabled it to reap political dividends, while allowing it to ostensibly distance itself from some of its more outrageous and lawless actions. But however fine-tuned this strategy may have been intended, in reality the occasional mild-mannered condemnation was of little use in reigning such elements, while the conspicuous silence or covert encouragement only served to strengthen it further. Hinduism and Hindu civilisation are thus faced with a real crisis, where instead of the genuine Hindu renaissance that should have unfolded, we are witnessing the hate-filled trivialisation of that great legacy.

The goal of a Hindu Rashtra, which has been an article of faith of the BJP–RSS, needs to be objectively studied. Ordinary Hindus must ask whether, even if such a goal is hypothetically desirable, is it practical? Although Hindus constitute the overwhelming majority in India, people of other faiths have also resided here for centuries and are equal citizens of the republic. The Muslims are the largest minority, accounting for 14 per cent of the population, or some 180 million people. In a letter to chief ministers in 1947, Jawaharlal Nehru stated the issue bluntly: 'We have a Muslim minority who are so large in numbers that they cannot go anywhere else. They have got to live in India. That is the basic fact about which there can be no argument.' Nehru's personal commitment to a secular India was unwavering, as was that of Mahatma Gandhi, and this was undoubtedly of considerable importance in the early years after 1947 in resisting the lurch towards communal politics. But the bedrock of the secular vision was the simple truth—far more comprehensible to the average Hindu than the complexities of ideology or principle— that there is no way to survive or flourish except by learning to live with each other.

Moreover, Muslims in India are not confined to one geographical area, and are dispersed throughout the country. In Jammu and Kashmir they are in a majority (65 per cent); in UP they number some 40 million or close to 20 per cent of the population, and in Bihar 18 million or 17 per cent of the population. In the states of Assam (34.22 per cent), West Bengal (27.01 per cent) and Kerala (25.56 per cent), their presence is significantly large. They are also a sizeable proportion of the population in Jharkhand (14.53 per cent), Karnataka (12.92 per cent), Maharashtra (11.54 per cent), Rajasthan (9.07 per cent) and Gujarat (9.06 per cent). Even Christians, who constitute around 2 per cent of the population, are more than the combined population of Hungary and Greece.

The creation of a Hindu Rashtra would entail either expelling these very large minorities, which is unfeasible, or subjugating them as second-class citizens, which is a recipe for disaster. Quite apart from the violent mutilation of the Constitution, it would lead to perennial social instability, unmitigated religious strife, endemic community conflict and a state of public volatility that would put an end to the peace and harmony so necessary for progress and prosperity. Is this in the interests of Hindus? I would think not. Even though the BJP–RSS leadership often publicly aver to the contrary, the foot soldiers they have empowered continue to live in a time warp trying to make Savarkar's dream come true. Redressing the legitimate grievances of Hindus is one thing; making them the cannon fodder for a political goal that is patently unworkable, outdated and against the self-interest of the vast majority of Hindus themselves, is another.

The Citizenship Amendment Act (CAA), passed by Parliament in December 2019, hyphenated—as repeatedly stressed by Home Minister Amit Shah, including on the floor of the House—with the National Register of Citizens (NRC), is the latest example of the BJP's continued push towards religious strife ostensibly in the interests of Hindus. The CAA has a laudable intent—to give citizenship to Hindus, Sikhs, Buddhists, Jains, Parsis and Christians, who entered India before the end of December 2014 as a result of religious persecution in Afghanistan, Bangladesh and Pakistan. The Muslims are not included in this list, making religion for the first time a criterion for citizenship under the law. The NRC, which Home Minister Amit Shah emphasised would be implemented across India in conjunction with the CAA, aims to make a list of genuine citizens weeding out illegal immigrants. Those who would not be able to meet stringent birth and identity proof requirements to prove this—and there could be millions in India who may not be able to because of poverty and illiteracy—would be given an amnesty if they alleged that they were refugees from religious persecution elsewhere. But such an amnesty would not be available to Muslims. The purpose here is not to discuss the merit or demerit of a NRC; many countries have it, and an argument can even be made that it is a valid administrative tool for identifying legal citizens. But in India, and specifically in the context in which the NRC was being sought to be implemented, the intent became starkly clear—to render stateless or disenfranchise large sections of the Muslim population, and put them in detention centres, several of which were already being built in anticipation. Predictably, there was considerable outrage across India—not only among Muslims but also Hindus—on the intent and consequence of such a hare-brained scheme. In the face of the nationwide protests, the government downplayed its narrative on the NRC. Both PM Modi and Amit Shah backtracked on their earlier adamancy to implement it immediately, stating that the cabinet had not even discussed it.

The crux of the matter is that the attempt by the Hindu ultra-right to whip up Hindus to become some kind of jihadis fighting a religious war, and encourage them to become intolerant and violent to people of other faiths, is alien to Hindus, repugnant to their civilisational values and a distortion of Hinduism and its eclecticism. It is a matter of historical record that Hindus have not been hostile to other faiths. The reason quite simply is that they were not afraid of them. The Jews lived peaceably in India before they did anywhere else. Muslim traders from the Arab countries practised their faith undisturbed in Kerala more than a thousand years ago. The Parsis came in the seventh century and the Christians in the fourth. The tolerance and sense of accommodation Hinduism has always shown does not compromise its right to be assertive against injustice, nor does it make Hindus inert or passive, but only adds to that remarkable, self-assured strength that has made Hinduism a truly sanatan dharma. The attempt thus to make Hinduism a clone of the brittle Semitic faiths is fraught with danger, for it threatens the very foundations which makes Hinduism stand apart. The acceptance of harmony and pluralism—as ends in themselves—is not a dilution of Hinduism, but a sign of its tensile resilience and, indeed, a recognition of what Hindu philosophy has always been about. As Mahatma Gandhi wrote: 'If I know Hinduism at all, it is essentially inclusive and ever-growing, ever responsive. It gives the freest scope to imagination, speculation and reason'.[41]

Trying to 'reinvent' Hinduism and make it akin to Wahabism, is an act of sacrilege. As I have discussed in the earlier chapter on Hindu philosophy, Hinduism's world view is governed by the seminal Rig Vedic injunction—Ekam sat vipra bahudah vadanthi: The truth is one, wise people call it by different names. This inherent openness to diversity is based on the fact that rigid dogmatism devalues the intellect, while eclecticism of spirit expands the boundaries of cerebral exploration. Hindus were not less rooted in their own faith; but Hinduism accepted that so long as the goal was the ultimate truth, there could be several paths to reach it. Non-Hindus were free to follow their own paths just as, within its own fold, Hinduism allowed for many different points of view, like that of the Charvakas, who even rejected the fundamentals of the mainstream faith. This breadth of vision is Hinduism's calling card to the world, and has been the key to it even when it was at the receiving end of proselytising faiths like Islam and Christianity.

One of the greatest voices of Hinduism in the modern era, Swami Vivekananda, emphasised precisely this in his famous speech on 11 September 1893 at the Parliament of World Religions in Chicago: 'I am proud to belong to a religion which has taught the world both tolerance and universal acceptance. We believe not only in universal toleration, but we accept all religions as true. ... I will quote to you, brethren, a few lines from a hymn which I remember to have repeated from earliest childhood, which is every day repeated by millions of human beings: As the different streams having their sources in different places all mingle their water in the sea, so, O Lord, the different paths which men take through different tendencies, various though they appear, crooked or straight, all lead to Thee.'

Swami Vivekananda's belief in religious pluralism, *as a defining characteristic of Hinduism*, was also inspired from the practice and beliefs of his mentor, the iconic saint, Swami Ramakrishna, about whom he wrote: 'He wanted to understand what other religions were like. ... He found a Mohammedan saint and placed himself under him; he underwent the disciplines prescribed by him, and to his astonishment found that when faithfully carried out, these devotional methods led him to the same goal he had already attained. He gathered similar experience from following the true religion of Jesus the Christ. ... Thus, from actual experience he came to know that the goal of every religion is the same.'

Not surprisingly, Swami Vivekananda was impatient with the narrow orthodoxies of some Hindus. When one of them questioned his decision to stay with a Muslim friend in Mount Abu, his retort was sharp: 'Sir, what do you mean? I am a Sannyasin. I am above all your social conventions. I can dine even with a Bhangi. I am not afraid of God, because He sanctions it. I am not afraid of the scriptures, because they allow it. But I am afraid of you people and your society. *You know nothing of God and the scriptures*. I see Brahman everywhere manifested through even the meanest creature. For me there is nothing high or low. Shiva! Shiva! [emphasis mine].'[42]

When the Swami spoke about his critics not knowing anything about God and the scriptures, he was correct. The problem with Hindu hardliners today is that they don't know enough of the very religion that they consider their duty to defend. If hatred of the 'other' was Hinduism's dominant emotion, why would the Upanishads say— Anno bhadra kritavo yantu vishvataha: Let good thoughts flow to us from all directions? If religious exclusion was the defining belief of Hinduism, why would our ancient seers stress—Udar charitanam vasudhaiva kutumbukam: For the big-hearted, the entire world is a family? The *Narada Bhakti Sutra*, containing aphorisms of the great sage Narada, could not be clearer: 'It is not proper to enter into a controversy about God, or spiritual truths, or about comparative merits of different devotees. For there is room for diversity in views; no one view based upon mere reasons is conclusive in itself.' King Ashoka, in his Rock Edict XII, makes the same plea: 'Beloved of the Gods, King Piyadasi, desires that there should be growth in the essentials of all religions. Growth in essentials can be done in different ways, but all of them have as their root, restraint in speech, that is, not praising one's own religion, or condemning the religion of others. ... By so doing, one's own religion benefits, and so do other religions, while doing otherwise harms one's own religion and the religion of others.' In Tulsidas's *Ramcharitmanas*, Shri Rama, whom these zealots randomly invoke when indulging in lawlessness and violence, uttered the ultimate verity of Hinduism when he told Lakshman—Par hita saris dharam nahin bhai, par peeda sam nahin athmai: There is no greater dharma than the welfare of others, and no greater sin than injury to others.

Resentment against some of the injustices done to Hinduism in the past may have its reasons. But, hatred and violence cannot become the defining features of a religion which rejects them both. Moreover, these sentiments are completely counterproductive in a modern republic whose stated goal is respect towards all faiths, and which aspires for progress and prosperity, whose sine qua non is social peace and harmony. That is why, one of modern India's great entrepreneurs, Narayana Murthy, categorically says: 'The founding fathers of independent India wanted a nation where every religion would flourish and every voice would be heard. Thus, India, very rightly adopted secularism as its credo.' That is also why the Shankaracharya of Sringeri, Jagadguru Bharathi Teertha Mahaswami, on a visit to the Buddhist shrine at Sarnath in 1994, declared: 'The principles of non-violence, compassion, truth, self-restraint and purity were meant for every individual; one might go to a temple, vihara or church, but the faith and belief were the same.'[43]

What Hindus need today is a true renaissance, in keeping with its essential nature, intellectual grandeur and remarkable refinements. The term Hindutva stands discredited because of the illiterate bigotry that is sanctioned in its name. *Hindutva must be replaced by Hindu-satya, the truth about Hinduism.* The first step of Hindu-satya is to pursue reform within Hinduism. If there was one thing that united both Savarkar and Mahatma Gandhi, it was the need to cleanse Hinduism of some of the oppressive distortions that have come to infest it. But this part of Savarkar's message is largely ignored by his fervent but ill-informed acolytes today. The truth is that where transformation of Hinduism into a modern and progressive religion was concerned, Savarkar was nothing short of revolutionary. Although born into an orthodox Chitpawan Brahmin community, he was resolutely against the caste system and its exploitative discrimination, and the practice of untouchability. 'The claim to glory on the mere basis of one's birth, and not worth,' he wrote, 'is an utterly erroneous and futile one—a national foolishness so to say.' His dismissal of scriptural injunctions to uphold what needed to change was equally strong. 'Fossilizing oneself to scriptural injunctions ... is another idiocy. These scriptures, often self-contradictory, were created by human beings and were relevant in a particular context and in a particular society. With all due respect to them, they need to be discarded as and when society evolves, and new rules and laws that are relevant to contemporary times need to be codified. ... Thus, I reverentially bow my head to the vast, Himalayan corpus of Sanskrit literature of the Shrutis, Smritis, Puranas, Itihasas as they have shaped our Hindu mind over centuries. I will not allow them to become fetters in my feet and retard my progress towards modernity, but instead draw inspiration from them to move ahead on modern, scientific terms.'[44]

Savarkar identified seven fetters that Hindus needed to unshackle themselves from. These, in his own words, are:

1. *Vedoktabandi*: The exclusivity of access to Vedic literature and rituals to only the Brahmin community must be immediately dissolved. Vedic literature is civilisational knowledge for the entire human race and India's unique gift to humankind.
2. *Vyavasayabandi*: An individual's choice of profession must be left entirely to him or her, based on their aptitude and capability.
3. *Sparshabandi*: The practice of untouchability is a sin, a blot on humanity, and nothing can justify it.
4. *Samudrabandi*: The day we forbade crossing the seas to go to foreign lands and deemed it a loss of caste heralded our collapse on various fronts.
5. *Shuddhibandi*: The folly of disallowing reconversions to Hinduism is a self-destructive one. ... I have nothing against those who convert to another faith by sheer conviction.
6. *Rotibandi*: Unshackling ourselves from this one thoughtless fetter—the belief that one loses one's caste through inter-caste dining—can liberate us as a society.
7. *Betibandi*: The intemperate practice of abolishing inter-caste marriage has caused our Hindu society a lot of harm. ... Instead of demonizing such marriages, they must be honoured.

It is quite clear that in Savarkar's vision for the resurrection of Hindus and Hinduism, a very significant element was the reform needed within Hinduism. In pursuing this, he was more than prepared to invite the wrath of orthodox Hindus. For instance, he was against cow worship:

Elevating an animal that eats garbage and indiscriminately passes excreta anywhere and everywhere to the status of a goddess is in my view insulting to both humanity as well as divinity. On the one hand we consider scholarly human beings like Ambedkar or saints like Chokha Mela as impure due to their caste; but on the other hand the urine of an animal suddenly becomes soul purifying for us! Is this not a great fallacy and contradiction? Our ancestors might have elevated the cow to a divine status to induce a sense of responsibility towards its protection. But we took that too literally. We should bear in mind that the cow is an object of utility for the human being and not vice versa. Doing so degrades the status of human beings. The object of worship should be greater than its worshipper.

The same iconoclastic spirit informs Savarkar's views on food and eating meat:

Religion is in the heart, the soul, the spirit; not the stomach! There is no food that is prohibited. Anything that is healthy, nutritious and tasty must be generously and merrily indulged in, no matter who has cooked it or where it was available. The whole world has robbed us and feasted on our grains—have they all turned Hindu? How then does a Hindu dining with a Muslim make him lose his caste?

Gandhi did believe in cow protection, but shared the same impatience towards fanatics who would resort to mindless violence on this cause. 'Am I, then, to fight with or kill a Mahomedan in order to save a cow?' he asks in *Hind Swaraj*. 'In doing so, I would become an enemy as well of the cow as of the Mahomedan. … Who protects the cow from destruction when they cruelly ill-treat her? Who ever reasons with the Hindus when they mercilessly belabour the progeny of the cow with their sticks?'[45]

Gandhi was against the inequities of the caste system, although he was possibly not as emphatic as Savarkar for its total abolition. In *Young India*, in 1933, he wrote: 'I have frequently said that I do not believe in caste in the modern sense. Assumption of superiority by any person over any other is a sin against God and man. Thus caste, in so far as it connotes distinction in status, is an evil.' Gandhi's essential goal was to bring about a greater sense of egalitarianism in Hinduism. 'In the eyes of religion, all men are equal. Learning, intellect or riches, do not entitle one to claim superiority over those who are lacking in these.'[46] On the need to abolish untouchability, he was nothing short of a crusader, founding the Harijan Sewak Sangh, and carrying out a relentless campaign for the abolition of this pernicious practice. A religion, he wrote as early as 1915, which justifies untouchability 'stinks in my nostrils. This certainly cannot be the Hindu religion.' Swami Vivekananda also drew sharp attention to the inequities within Hinduism: 'No religion on earth preaches the dignity of humanity in such a lofty strain as Hinduism, and no religion on earth treads upon the necks of the poor and the low in such a fashion as Hinduism.... We have the doctrine of Vedanta, but we have not the power to reduce it in practice. In our books there is the doctrine of universal equality, but in work we make great distinction. It was in India that unselfish and disinterested work of the most exalted type was preached, but in practice we are awfully cruel, awfully heartless....'[47]

Indeed, it would be a fair inference that Hindu revivalism under British rule, although incomplete, and during the freedom movement, had a dominant message for social reform within Hinduism. In voicing such a sentiment, the inspiration came from much earlier. The powerful Bhakti movement carried a strong message for equality and brotherhood, and the need to rid Hinduism of Brahminical oppression, caste discrimination, superstition and ritualism. Post the Bhakti movement, and prior to the freedom movement, powerful social reformers like Mahatma Jyotiba Govind Phule (1827–1890), who himself was a Dalit, formed the Satyashodak Samaj for the upliftment of the oppressed classes. He also started the first school for women in Pune in 1848. The most powerful voice among the Dalits was, of course, that of Dr B.R. Ambedkar (1891–1956)—jurist, economist, politician and social reformer. In 1936, he wrote his passionate tract, *Annihilation of Caste*, and later converted to Buddhism in protest against the oppression of the caste system. As independent India's first minister for law and justice, he is considered the chief architect of the Indian Constitution. The Constitution of the Indian Republic abolished untouchability and proclaimed the equality of all men and women under law. Article 14 and 15 of the Constitution—part of the chapter on fundamental rights—state categorically: 'The State shall not deny to any person equality before the law or the equal protection of laws within the territory of India. The State shall not discriminate against any citizen on grounds only of religion, race, caste, sex, place of birth or any of them.'

Yet, the truth is that Hindu society even today is unacceptably casteist and discriminatory. It is not that nothing has changed. Certainly, the asphyxiating stranglehold of the caste system has somewhat diluted and Dalits are more politically empowered, but there is still rampant social oppression. According to the National Crime Records Bureau (NCRB), 45,935 crimes against Dalits were reported in 2019. This was a 7.8 per cent increase over 2018. According to this report, a crime against a Dalit is committed every fifteen minutes and six Dalit women are raped every day. Shockingly, the conviction rate for the perpetrators is very low: 25.2 per cent in 2009, and 22.8 per cent in 2018. Such statistics only reveal the tip of the iceberg of reported cases; unreported cases must be many more.

The cases of atrocities that were reported and did surface in the media portray a shocking state of affairs. I give some instances, not for sensationalism, but to bring home the point that caste discrimination is still pervasive and nationwide. In July 2016, seven members of a Dalit family, who were skinning a dead cow—a 'menial' task consigned to Dalits—were attacked by upper-caste cow vigilantes near Una, Gujarat. They were tied to the cars of the attackers and publicly flogged with sticks and iron rods. Four of them were subsequently forcibly brought to Una town and stripped and assaulted again in public. The assailants recorded a video and circulated it on social media. The incident caused a huge public uproar. A charge sheet against the alleged perpetrators was filed in July 2018, but so far no one has been convicted.

In December 2017, a bright young PhD student of University of Hyderabad, Rohit Vemula, who was a member of the Ambedkar Students Association, committed suicide. In his suicide note, he said that he did so because he could not bear any more the discrimination in the university against Dalits and lower castes. In April 2019, a young Dalit man was thrashed to death in Tehri, Uttarakhand, for eating in front of upper castes at a wedding ceremony. In June 2019, a Dalit minor was stripped and beaten to death in Pali, Rajasthan, by upper-caste men for trying to enter a temple. In July 2020, a Dalit man was stripped and beaten up in Karnataka's Vijaypura district for touching an upper-caste person's motorbike. In December 2020, a twenty-five-year-old Dalit man was beaten to death in Chhatarpur, Madhya Pradesh, for touching food meant for the upper castes. In the same month, a Dalit groom was forced to get down from a horse at Shivpur in Rajasthan. These are snapshots to show how deep the malaise still is. In the past, states like UP, Bihar and MP saw caste wars, with hundreds killed in the insane battle between upper and lower castes. Fortunately, such mass killings are seen less now, but social oppression still exists, and it affects not only the Dalits but also those from the backward classes.

This curse of oppressive disunity within Hinduism, which sanctions discrimination against some 160 million Dalits (and backward classes) on access to clean water, places of worship and schools has to be put to an end. A Hindu society where one Hindu intimidates or kills another on the basis of caste should have been consigned to the dustbin of history long ago. Affirmative action, through the policy of reservations, has helped in empowering the weakest sections of society; the dynamics of democratic politics has also given a voice to the lower castes because their votes matter, and they are willing to unite and fight for their right to be heard. But the real imperative is for a foundational change in the mindset of Hindus that makes them realise that caste discrimination is not only illegal but also a highly undesirable and outdated legacy of the past which has no place in a modern democratic society, and which ends up only dividing and weakening Hindus. After all, one of the central tenets of Hindu philosophy is that the same consciousness is in one and all, and therefore, there can be no basis for discrimination on the basis of human-made hierarchies.

A second taint on Hinduism is the persistence of oppressive male patriarchy and gender discrimination. As I have discussed, in the most influential school of Hindu philosophy, Advaita, the Almighty—Brahman—is itself beyond gender categories, and is visualised as pure consciousness. Hinduism, at the level of religious practice, must also be one of the few faiths which gives such a prime place to Devi, the goddess, and considers her equal to—if not greater—than her male counterpart. I have also referred to evidence regarding the respect and honour accorded to women in ancient times. But today, it seems that, while we venerate the female, Shakti, we do not accord the necessary respect to women who are the very symbol of that energy. Undoubtedly, many women have broken out of the patriarchal mould of our society and excelled in a wide variety of fields, bringing pride and glory to India. Access of education to girls has substantially increased, and progressive laws have been enacted to ensure gender rights, leading to some change in mindsets. But, equally, there are large numbers of women—especially in rural areas—who remain victims of male domination, who enforce strict rules of marriage, dress, conduct and sexual choices. Bhishma, in the *Anushasan Parva* of the Mahabharata says: 'The daughter, O King, has been ordained in the scriptures to be equal to the son.' Yet, it is a matter of shame that, in spite of the legal provisions against it, India has one of the highest rates of female foeticide and infanticide in the world, and Hindus are complicit in this dastardly crime. One reason why sons are preferred is because of the pernicious practice of payment of dowry in the marriage of a daughter. Mahatma Gandhi had said: 'Any young man, who makes dowry a condition to marriage, discredits his education and his country, and dishonours womanhood.' Dowry is banned under the Dowry Prohibition Act of 1961, and other provisions of the Indian Penal Code. However, regrettably, it is still a widely prevalent practice.

Patriarchy is inextricably linked in many ways to caste hierarchies. 'Honour' killings, in the name of punishing women (and men) for violating the rules of caste, are not uncommon in today's India. The Hathras case in UP in September 2020, where a nineteen-year-old Dalit girl was brutally raped and killed allegedly by higher-caste perpetrators, is a vivid example of the intersection between the assault on women and caste hierarchies. Child marriage is another blot. According to the 2011 census, 12 million children were married before the age of 10, of which 84 per cent were Hindus, and 80 per cent of illiterate children who married before the age of 10 were girls. Although child marriage is legally prohibited, 102 million girls—30 per cent of the female population—married before the age of 18, according to the same census. What this means is that Hindu society is willingly colluding in denying women within its fold from reaching their full potential, and thus depriving itself of a huge reservoir of talent. According to the NCRB, crimes against women showed an increase of 7.3 per cent in 2019 compared to 2018. A majority of these cases related to domestic violence by the husband or his relatives. Such statistics are not segregated according to religion, but there is no doubt that Hindu men too are guilty of the use of force against women, especially under the influence of alcohol, and in mistreating their wives.

Hindu society needs to introspect on this undesirable state of affairs. The time has come for major reforms within Hinduism that allows the actual conduct of Hindus in their everyday lives to match the civilisational legacy they are and should be proud of. This cannot be achieved only through laws, especially in an unequal society where the more vulnerable are unable to seek their protection in the same measure as the more powerful are able to flout them. As I have emphasised, the reforms that Hinduism needs can only come about when Hindus themselves are convinced of their need. Hindus must bridge the gap between the achievements of the past and the imperatives of the present. The history of Hindus may be littered with pioneering landmarks in the areas of philosophy, spirituality, arts and science, but that same history is marred and loses credibility in the face of indubitable empirical evidence of rampant inequity and discrimination today.

Even worse are attempts to justify this inequality and exploitation in the name of sanctioned tradition. No tradition, however hoary, can militate against the basic dignity of human beings and the egalitarianism which is the hallmark of modern and progressive societies. If those who want to work for Hindu revivalism would devote their real energies to working for much-needed change in Hindu society, they would contribute far more to the proud reassertion of their faith. For this noble cause, they would find enough material within Hinduism. The goal must be not to blindly resurrect the ancient past but to re-create Hindu society in the present by drawing upon the abundant wisdoms in Hinduism in the past. As Sri Aurobindo, the towering intellectual who made no secret of being a proud Hindu, writes: 'We should recognize without any sophisticated denial those things in our creeds of life and social institutions which are in themselves mistaken and some of them indefensible, things weakening to our national life, degrading to our civilization, dishonouring to our culture.'[48]

A second imperative is for Hindus to become more knowledgeable about their own civilisation. The blunt truth is that Hindus, in general, are as proud of their past as they are ignorant about what exactly it is. Very few among them have taken the trouble to read the basic texts of their faith. Nor do they know, except very superficially, about the achievements of their legacy in the secular realm. Partly, this is so because Hinduism is not a prescriptive faith and allows its followers to practise it in almost any manner they choose. Most Hindus see—rightly—their religion as a way of life, of which they can be proud participants even if they don't know the profundities of its philosophical tradition, and the deep symbolisms behind even ordinary rituals. Partly, it is also because the educational curriculum is deeply flawed and does not include information about ideas and concepts and achievements, which it should; and partly it is because parents and family members who could impart such knowledge are as ignorant as their wards. When this happens, a reflex glorification of the past sits comfortably with the absence of the vibrant intellectual energy that should be its real consequence. It is Sri Aurobindo again who puts his finger on it: 'There is a rapid cessation of the old free intellectual activity, a slumber of the scientific and the critical mind as well as the creative institution; what remains becomes more and more a repetition of ill-informed fragments of past knowledge. There is a petrification of the mind and life in the relics of the forms which a great intellectual past had created.'[49]

When I wrote my book on Adi Shankaracharya, many readers who read the book with interest did not know until then when the great thinker was born, or what he wrote about. This lack of curiosity, and the resulting ignorance about our past, has become the bane of Hindu society, leading to a double jeopardy. Firstly, Hindus are volitionally wrenched away from so much that is of such great value in their own history and culture. A treasure house is before them, but they have little desire to enter and reclaim it, and are the poorer for it. The great danger is that people who are so ill-informed about their own culture ultimately become derivative, photocopies of someone else's, 'modern' in an imitative sense and culturally rootless. Nothing can harm Hindu civilisation more than the lack of interest of its own legatees in the range and loftiness of what is their inheritance.

As I have discussed at length, the cultural and intellectual reclamation that should have followed Independence in 1947 did not happen. If this had been done—in an enlightened manner without xenophobia or bigotry—we would by now have a generation that knows much more about the real achievements of Hindu civilisation. Instead, we are now witnessing a movement of Hindu revivalism which is blatantly geared towards short-term political dividends, and replete with intolerance and hatred that is anathema to the very spirit and substance of Hinduism.

This brings us to the second jeopardy. Superficially informed Hindus are in no position to confront the illiterate bigotry of the self-anointed new 'protectors' of Hinduism. Knowledge is a great enabler. Anyone who has studied Hinduism, or acquired even a basic familiarity about its lofty eclecticism and deep cerebration, would laugh out of the room those who seek to conflate this great faith only with violence and exclusion. But Hindus, disarmed by lack of knowledge, become cannon fodder more easily in the hands of ignorant evangelists.

The real Hindu renaissance will take place when Hindus in vast numbers make the effort to rediscover their religion and civilisation. That knowledge will enable them to resurrect Hindu society in terms of true renewal, a renewal of spirit and substance, and allow them to build, along with all the other great faiths that have a home in this ancient land, a modern India that is democratic but also rooted in the great wisdoms of its past. As Adi Shankaracharya said—Satyam Jnanam, Anantam Brahman: Knowledge is Truth; Brahman is Eternal. For a civilisation that goes back to the dawn of time, and is based on moulik soch, the power of original thought, there can be no greater tribute than to rediscover it.

The imperative of the future is for this process to begin. This was the vision of people like Sri Aurobindo who sought meaningful Hindu revivalism: 'And now survival itself becomes impossible without expansion. If we are to live at all, we must resume India's great interrupted endeavour; we must take up boldly and execute thoroughly in the individual and in the society, in the spiritual and the mundane life, in philosophy and religion, in art and literature, in thought, in political and economic and social formulation the full and unlimited vision of her highest spirit and knowledge.'[50] Sanatan dharma will survive and flourish when its followers make the effort to know, in the real sense, the reasons for its invincibility. And, with that knowledge, let India awake to its future greatness—modern, progressive, prosperous, humane, tolerant, inclusive and rooted in the great wisdoms of its past.

Let us chant the Hindu mantra for peace and prosperity:

Om saha navavatu saha nau bhunaktu,
Sah viryam karava vahai.
Tejasvin nau adhitam astu ma vidvishavahai,
Om Shanti, Shanti, Shanti.

Together may we be protected, together may we celebrate,
Together may we grow from strength to strength.
May our knowledge be illuminated, and take us away from hate,
Om, let there be peace all around and within me.

Notes

1. HINDU CIVILISATION: MYTH OR REALITY?

1. Gurcharan Das, *The Difficulty of Being Good* (Penguin, 2009), p. xxxv.
2. Amartya Sen, *The Argumentative Indian* (Penguin, 2005), pp. ix–x.
3. Ibid., pp. xi–x.
4. Romila Thapar, *The Penguin History of Early India* (Penguin, 2003), p. 20.
5. Ibid., p. 21.
6. Jawaharlal Nehru, *My Life and My Prisons*.
7. Ibid.
8. A.B. Shah and C.R.M. Rao, *Tradition and Modernity in India* (Manaktalas, 1965), p. 15.
9. Richard Lannoy, *The Speaking Tree* (OUP, 1971), p. 415.
10. Upinder Singh, *A History of Ancient and Medieval India: From the Stone Age to the 12th Century* (Dorling Kindersley, 2008), p. 3.
11. Wendy Doniger, *The Hindus: An Alternative History* (Penguin, 2009), p. 30.
12. Ibid.
13. Ibid.
14. Sunil Khilnani, *The Idea of India* (Hamish Hamilton, 1997), p. 154.
15. Ibid.
16. Romila Thapar, *The Penguin History of Early India*, op. cit., p. 20.
17. Sanjay Subrahmanyam, *Is Indian Civilization a Myth* (Permanent Black, 2013), p. 1.
18. Ibid.
19. Ibid., p. 4.
20. Ibid., p. 7.
21. Ibid.

22. Sunil Khilnani, *The Idea of India*, op. cit., p. 169.
23. Upinder Singh, *A History of Ancient and Medieval India*, op. cit., p. 3.
24. Sunil Khilnani, *The Idea of India*, op. cit., p. 156.
25. Ibid., p. 157.
26. Kautilya, *Arthashastra*, edited, rearranged, translated and introduced by L.N. Rangarajan (Penguin, 1992), p. 628.
27. Koenraad Elst, *Decolonizing the Hindu Mind* (Rupa, 2001), p. 457.
28. Amish, *Immortal India: Young Country, Timeless Civilisation* (Westland, 2017), p. 184.
29. Mahatma Gandhi, *Hind Swaraj*, edited by Anthony Parel (Cambridge University Press, 1997), pp. 48–49.
30. Aurobindo, *India's Rebirth*, p. 173.
31. Amartya Sen, 'The Vision that Worked', *Times Literary Supplement*, 8 August 1997.
32. Ibid., p. 67.
33. Arun Shourie, *A Secular Agenda* (Rupa, 2005), p. 9.
34. Ibid., p. 14.
35. Koenraad Elst, *Decolonizing the Hindu Mind*, op. cit., p. 462.
36. Sudhir Kakar and Katharina Kakar, *The Indians* (Penguin, 2007), p. 4.
37. Fernand Braudel, *A History of Civilizations* (Penguin, 1987), p. xxxviii.
38. Romila Thapar, *The Penguin History of Early India*, op. cit., pp. 18–19.
39. Koenraad Elst, *Decolonizing the Hindu Mind*, op. cit., p. 30.
40. Romila Thapar, *The Penguin History of Early India*, op. cit., p. 19.
41. Amartya Sen, *The Argumentative Indian*, op. cit., p. 56.
42. Ibid., p. 57.
43. Ibid., p. 354.
44. Ibid.
45. R.C. Majumdar, *Ancient India* (Motilal Banarsidass, 1952), p. 455.
46. Amartya Sen, *The Argumentative Indian*, op. cit., p. 84.
47. Ibid., p. 54.
48. Ibid., pp. 352–353.
49. Romila Thapar, *The Penguin History of Early India*, op. cit., p. 3.
50. Upinder Singh, *A History of Ancient and Medieval India*, op. cit., pp. 455–456.
51. Ibid., p. 518.
52. Ibid., p. 463.
53. Ibid., p. 521.
54. Wendy Doniger, *The Hindus*, op. cit., p. 349.
55. Ibid., p. 45.

56. Copyright Benoy K. Behl, from his audio commentary for the documentary film *Ancient India* (2004), with gratitude for permission to reproduce it.

57. Richard Lannoy, *The Speaking Tree*, op. cit., p. xviii.

58. Ibid., p. 336.

59. Wendy Doniger, *On Hinduism* (Aleph, 2013), p. 3.

60. Ibid.

61. Ibid., p. 4.

62. Ibid.

63. Ibid., p. xi.

64. Amartya Sen, *The Argumentative Indian*, op. cit., p. 310.

65. Ibid., p. 23.

66. Romila Thapar, *The Penguin History of Early India*, op. cit., p. xxiv.

67. Vinay Dharwadkar, ed., *The Collected Essays of A.K. Ramanujan* (OUP, 1999), p. 7.

68. Ibid., p. 38.

69. Rajiv Malhotra, *Being Different* (HarperCollins, 2011), p. 8.

70. Ibid., p. 182.

71. Ibid., p. 215.

72. Ibid.

73. Amartya Sen, *The Argumentative Indian*, op. cit., p. 310.

74. Sanjeev Sanyal, *India in the Age of Ideas* (Westland, 2018), p. 6.

75. Rabindranath Tagore, *Swadeshi Samaj* (1904).

76. Upinder Singh, *A History of Ancient and Medieval India*, op. cit., p. 179.

77. Romila Thapar, 'The Rigveda: Encapsulating Social Change' in K.N. Panikkar, Terence J. Byres and Utsa Patnaik (eds), *The Making of History, Essays Presented to Irfan Habib* (Tulika, 2002), p. 12.

78. Michel Danino, *The Lost River: On the Trail of the Sarasvati* (Penguin, 2010), p. 35.

79. Ibid., p. 254.

80. Ibid.

81. Ibid., p. 265.

82. Ibid., p. 266.

83. Tony Joseph, *Early Indians* (Juggernaut, 2018), p. 230.

84. Upinder Singh, *A History of Ancient and Medieval India*, op. cit., p. 134.

85. Michel Danino, *The Lost River*, op. cit., p. 213.

86. Stella Kramrisch, *The Art of India through the Ages* (Phoenix Books, 1954), p. 10.

87. John Marshall (ed.), *Mohenjodaro and the Indus Civilization*, vol. 1 (Arthur Probsthain, 1931), p. vi.

88. John Stratton Hawley and Donna Marie Wulff, *Devi: The Goddesses of India* (Aleph, 2017), p. 2.
89. Michel Danino, *The Lost River*, op. cit., p. 233.
90. Upinder Singh, A *History of Ancient and Medieval India*, op. cit., p. 186.
91. Ibid., p. 187.
92. Romila Thapar, *The Penguin History of Early India*, op. cit., pp. 14–15.
93. Sanjeev Sanyal, *Land of Seven Rivers* (Penguin, 2012), p. 55–56.
94. R.C. Majumdar, *Ancient India* (Motilal Banarasidass, 10th reprint, 2018), p. 27.
95. Michel Danino, *The Lost River*, op. cit., p. 269.
96. Ibid., p. 270.
97. Suraj Bhan, 'The Aryanization of the Indus Civilization', in *The Making of History: Essays Presented to Irfan Habib*, op. cit., p. 52.
98. Amartya Sen, *The Argumentative Indian*, op. cit., pp. 66–67.
99. Tony Joseph, *Early Indians*, op. cit., pp. 162–163.
100. Karl Marx, in an article written for an American newspaper in 1853. See Rajiv Malhotra, *Being Different*, op. cit., pp. 318–319.
101. Romila Thapar, *The Penguin History of Early India*, op. cit., pp. 8–9.
102. Upinder Singh, A *History of Ancient and Medieval India*, op. cit., p. 8.
103. Amartya Sen, *The Argumentative Indian*, op. cit., p. 158.

2. THE AUDACITY OF THOUGHT

1. Mahatma Gandhi, *Hind Swaraj*, op. cit., p. 66.
2. Rabindranath Tagore, *The Message of Indian History* (1902).
3. Sri Aurobindo, *The Renaissance in India and Other Essays on Indian Culture* (Sri Aurobindo Ashram Pondicherry, 1997), pp. 10–13.
4. Lin Yu Tang, *Wisdom of India* (Jaico, 1956), p. 4.
5. Octavio Paz, *In Light of India* (Harcourt Bruce and Company, New York, 1997), p. 185
6. Wendy Doniger (trans.), *The Rig Veda* (Penguin, 1981), pp. 25–26.
7. There are many exemplary translations of the Upanishads but for flow of language and composition, I have chosen the one by Eknath Easwaran, *The Upanishads*, first published by the Blue Mountain Center of Meditation in 1987.
8. K.M. Sen, *Hinduism* (Penguin, 1961), p. 80.
9. Y. Keshava Menon, *The Mind of Adi Shankaracharya* (Jaico, 1976), p. 5.
10. There are some who believe that Mandana Mishra was a resident of modern-day Bihar. However, my research, as detailed in my book

Adi Shankaracharya: Hinduism's Greatest Thinker (Tranquebar, 2018), favours the view that he belonged to Mahishmati in Madhya Pradesh.

11. There is a little debate among some scholars whether Bharati was Mandana Mishra's wife, but the bulk of academic opinion as well as popular belief accepts that she was, so this controversy, if there is one at all, need not detain us.

12. S. Radhakrishnan, *Indian Philosophy*, vol. 1 (George Allen & Unwin, 1977), p. 281.

13. Rajiv Malhotra, *The Battle for Sanskrit* (HarperCollins, 2016), p. 121.

14. Amartya Sen, *The Argumentative Indian*, op. cit., pp. xi–xii.

15. Gurcharan Das, *The Difficulty of Being Good*, op. cit., p. 286.

16. George Cardona, 'Traditions and Argumentation: Tensions among Some Early Thinkers and Their Backgrounds', Paper presented at the *Infinity Foundation Colloquium*, 2003.

17. Pavan K. Varma, *Adi Shankaracharya: Hinduism's Greatest Thinker*, op. cit., p. 142.

18. M. Hiriyanna, *Outlines of Indian Philosophy*, George (Allen and Unwin, 1973), p. 386.

19. Ibid., p. 387.

20. Wendy Doniger, *On Hinduism*, op. cit., p. 153.

21. Ibid., p. 152.

22. Ibid.

23. Ibid., p. 196.

24. Ibid., p. 197.

25. Ibid., p. 196.

26. Kapila Vatsyayan, *Arrested Movement: Sculpture and Painting* (Wisdom Tree, 2007), p. 77.

27. U.R. Ananthamurthy, 'What does Translation Mean in India?' in *Culture and the Making of Identity in Contemporary India*, edited by Kamala Ganesh and Usha Thakkar (Sage, 2005), p. 133.

28. Ananda K. Coomaraswamy, *The Dance of Shiva* (The Noonday Press, 1969), p. 78.

29. Fritjof Capra, *The Tao of Physics* (Flamingo, 1976), p. 271.

30. John Stratton Hawley and Donna Marie Wulff (eds), *Devi: The Goddesses of India* (Aleph, 2017), p. 26.

31. Sri Sharada Peetham, *The Greatness of Sringeri*, Sri Sri Jagadguru Mahasamsthanam Dakshinamnaya, February, 2012, p. 15.

32. John Statton Hawley and Donna Marie Wulff (eds), *Devi*, op. cit., p. 12.

33. This rendering, and the following extracts from the Gita have been

taken from the lyrical translation of Juan Mascaro, first published in 1962, and republished by Penguin India in 1994.

3. THE REALM OF IDEAS

1. Stella Kramrisch, *The Art of India*, op. cit., p. 14.
2. Kapila Vatsyayan, *The Square and the Circle of the Indian Arts* (Roli Books, 1997), p. 3.
3. Shakti Maira, *Towards Ananda: Rethinking Indian Art and Aesthetics* (Penguin, 2006), p. 4.
4. Harsha V. Dehejia, *The Beautifully Indian Hindu Mind* (D.K. Printworld, India, 2020), p. 48.
5. Stella Kramrisch, *The Art of India*, op. cit., pp. 26–27.
6. Kapila Vatsyayan, *The Square and the Circle of Indian Arts*, op. cit.
7. Ibid., p. 39.
8. Stella Kramrisch, *The Art of India*, op. cit., p. 9.
9. Kapila Vatsyayan, *The Square and the Circle of Indian Arts*, op. cit., p. 39.
10. Kapila Vatsyayan, 'From Interior Landscapes into Cyber Space: Fluidity and Dynamics of Tradition', in *Culture and the Making of Identity in Contemporary India*, edited by Kamala Ganesh and Usha Thakkar (Sage, 2005), p. 40.
11. Harsha V. Dehejia, *The Beautifully Indian Hindu Mind*, op. cit., p. 260.
12. Alka Pande, *Masterpieces of Indian Art* (Roli Books, 2004), p. 150.
13. A.K. Ramanujan (tr.), *Speaking of Siva* (Penguin Classics, 1985), pp. 19–20.
14. Stella Kramrisch, *The Art of India*, op. cit., p. 10.
15. Kapila Vatsyayan, *The Square and the Circle of Indian Arts*, op. cit., p. 27.
16. Ibid., pp. 26–28.
17. P.S. Rawson, 'Early Art and Architecture', in *A Cultural History of India*, edited by A.L. Basham (OUP, 1975), p. 204.
18. Quoted by Kapila Vatsyayan in *The Square and the Circle of Indian Arts*, op cit., p. 81.
19. Kapila Vatsyayan, *Arrested Movement*, op. cit., p. 13.
20. Rajiv Malhotra, *Being Different*, op. cit., p. 180.
21. Debu Chaudhuri, *Classical Music (Incredible India)* (Wisdom Tree, 2007), p. 5.
22. Shakti Maira, *Towards Ananda*, op. cit., pp. 35–36.
23. A.K. Warder, 'Classical Literature', in *A Cultural History of India*, edited by A.L. Basham, op. cit., p. 171.
24. Wendy Doniger, *The Hindus*, op. cit., p. 5.
25. Rajiv Malhotra, *Being Different*, op. cit., p. 37.

26. Rajiv Malhotra, *The Battle for Sanskrit*, op. cit., p. 30.

27. Upinder Singh, *A History of Ancient and Early Medieval India*, op. cit., pp. 526–527.

28. Pavan K. Varma, *Yudhishtar and Draupadi: A Tale of Love, Passion and the Riddles of Existence* (Penguin, 1996), pp. 62–83.

29. Romila Thapar, *The Penguin History of Early India*, op. cit., p. 33.

30. Upinder Singh, *A History of Ancient and Medieval India*, op. cit., p. 8.

31. Fernand Braudel, *A History of Civilizations* (Penguin, 1987), p. 225.

32. Ibid.

33. R.C. Majumdar, *Ancient India*, op. cit., p. 87.

34. Wendy Doniger, *The Hindus*, op. cit., p. 207.

35. Richard Lannoy, *The Speaking Tree*, op. cit., p. 295.

36. C. Panduranga Bhatta and Pragyan Rath, *The Art of Leading in a Borderless World* (Bloomsbury, 2020), p. 49.

37. Mahabharata, *Vana Parva*, 207.77.

38. Ibid., 131.11.

39. Mahabharata: *dharmasya tattvam nihitam guhayam*. See also Gurcharan Das, *The Difficulty of Being Good*, op. cit. p. xliii.

40. Vinay Dharwadkar, *The Collected Essays*, op. cit., p. 48.

41. Mahabharata, *kalah pachati bhutani sarvani*. XVII. 1.3.

42. Kamala Subramaniam (ed. and trans.), *The Mahabharata* (Bharatiya Vidya Bhavan, 1982), pp. 135–136.

43. Ibid.

44. A.L. Basham, *The Wonder That Was India: A Survey of the Culture of the Indian Sub-continent before the Coming of the Muslims* (Fontana Books, in association with Rupa & Co., 1971), p. 307.

45. Kautilya, *The Arthashastra*, op. cit., p. 145.

46. Chaturvedi Badrinath, *Dharma: Hinduism and Religions in India*, edited by Tulsi Badrinath (Penguin-Viking, 2019), pp. 11–12.

47. A.L. Basham, *The Wonder That Was India*, op. cit., pp. 217–218.

48. P.S. Rawson, 'Early Art and Architecture', in *A Cultural History of India*, edited by A.L. Basham, op. cit., p. 210.

49. Quoted in John Dowson, *A Classical Dictionary of Hindu Mythology and Religion, Geography, History, and Literature* (Trübner & Company, 1983).

50. Quoted in Lee Siegel, *Sacred and Profane Dimensions of Love in the Indian Tradition, as Exemplified in the* Gitagovinda *of Jayadeva* (OUP, 1978), p. 14.

51. Ibid., p. 16.

52. Quoted in John Dowson, op. cit., p. 146.

53. Quoted in Pavan K. Varma, *Krishna: The Playful Divine* (Viking, 1993), p. 53.

54. Quoted in Pavan K. Varma, *Krishna: The Playful Divine*, op. cit., p. 54.

55. Ibid., p. 55.

56. Kapila Vatsyayan, *Kamasutra*, translated by Sir Richard Burton and F.F. Arbuthnot (London, 1883, Reprint 1988), p. 23.

57. Harsh Madhusudan and Rajeev Mantri, *A New Idea of India* (Westland, 2020), p. 2.

58. Hieun Tsang, quoted in R.C. Majumdar, *Ancient India* (Motilal Banarsidass Publishers, 1952, Reprint 2018), p. 453.

59. Koenraad Elst, *Decolonizing the Hindu Mind*, op. cit., pp. 29–30.

60. Carl Sagan, interviewed in *New India Digest*, March 1997.

61. H.J.J. Winter, 'Science', in A.L. Basham (ed.), *A Cultural History of India*, op. cit., p. 154.

62. Ibid., pp. 147–148.

63. D. Mackenzie Brown, The White Umbrella (University of California Press, 1953), p. 37.

64. Quoted in Richard Lannoy, *The Speaking Tree*, op. cit., p. 319.

65. Ibid., pp. 319–320.

66. C. Panduranga Bhatta and Pragyan Rath, *The Art of Leading in a Borderless World*, op. cit., p. 50.

67. A.L. Basham, *The Wonder That Was India*, op. cit., pp. 88–89.

68. Upinder Singh, *A History of Ancient and Medieval India*, op. cit., p. 203, quoting Wendy Doniger O'Flaherty, *The Rig Veda: An Anthology* (Penguin, Middlesex, 1986).

69. Richard Lannoy, *The Speaking Tree*, op. cit., p. 143.

70. Tony Joseph, Early Indians, op. cit., p. 213.

71. Amartya Sen, *The Argumentative Indian*, op. cit., pp. 10–11.

72. Amish, *Immortal India*, op. cit., p. 81.

73. Wendy Doniger, *The Hindus*, op. cit., p. 86.

74. Romila Thapar, *The Penguin History of Early India*, op. cit., p. 10.

75. See Chaturvedi Badrinath, *Dharma*, op. cit., pp. 14–15.

76. Quoted also in R.C. Majumdar, *Ancient India*, op. cit., p. 146.

77. Quoted in Wendy Doniger, *On Hinduism*, op. cit., p. 260. See also Wendy Doniger with Brian K. Smith (trans.), *The Laws of Manu* (Penguin, 1991).

78. The Laws of Manu (4.147-9, 9.3). Quoted in Wendy Doniger, *On Hinduism*, op. cit., p. 260. See also Wendy Doniger with Brian K. Smith (trans.), *The Laws of Manu*, op cit.

79. Ibid., p. 260; (5.154–64).

4. THE ISLAMIC CONQUEST

1. Jawaharlal Nehru, *Glimpses of World History* (Jawaharlal Nehru Memorial Fund, 1982 reprint), p. 155.
2. A.K. Warder, 'Classical Literature', in *A Cultural History of India*, edited by A.L. Basham, op. cit., p. 193.
3. Will Durant, *The Story of Civilization*, vol. 1 (1972), p. 459.
4. Heinrich Zimmer, *Art of Indian Asia*, vol. 1 (Princeton University Press, 1983), p. 201.
5. Amartya Sen, *The Argumentative Indian*, op. cit., p. 58.
6. Ibid., p. 314.
7. Ibid., p. 58.
8. Sita Ram Goel, *Hindu Temples: What Happened to Them* (Voice of India, 2019).
9. Ibid., vol. 1, p. 32.
10. Sita Ram Goel, *Hindu Temples*, op. cit., pp. 19–20.
11. Wendy Doniger, *The Hindus*, op. cit., p. 536.
12. Amartya Sen, *The Argumentative Indian*, op. cit., p. 18.
13. Ibid., p. 60.
14. Quoted by William Dalrymple in *The Guardian* (UK), 20 March 2004.
15. Tarun Tejpal, 'Christianity Didn't Damage India Like Islam', *Outlook*, 15 November 1999.
16. Ibid.
17. Ibid.
18. Willian Dalrymple, 'Trapped in the Ruins', *The Guardian*, 20 March 2004, with excerpts from his book *White Mughals* (Harper Perennial, 2002).
19. *The Guardian* (UK), 20 March 2004.
20. Quoted by Aakar Patel, in *Islam and Prejudice: Why Girish Karnad Is Wrong about Islam*, Blog on Firstpost.com, 11 November 2012.
21. Ibid.
22. David Gilmartin and Bruce Lawrence, *Beyond Turk and Hindu* (University Press of Florida, 2000), quoted in *The Guardian* (UK), 20 March 2004.
23. Ibid.
24. Amish, *Immortal India*, op. cit., p. 138.
25. A.J. Appasamy (ed.), *Temple Bells: Readings From Hindu Religious Literature* (Association Press, 1930).

26. J.T.F. Jordens, 'Medieval Hindu Devotionalism', in *A Cultural History of India*, edited by A.L. Basham, op. cit., p. 269.
27. A.J. Appasamy, *Temple Bells*, op. cit., p. 63.
28. Deben Bhattacharya (trans.), *Love Songs of Chandidas, the Rebel Poet-Priest of Bengal* (George Allen & Unwin, 1967), p. 57.
29. Bihari, *The Satasai*, translated by K.P. Bahadur (Penguin Books/ UNESCO, 1992), p. 46.
30. J.S. Hawley, *Surdas, Poet, Singer, Saint* (1982), p. 65.
31. J.T.F. Jordens, 'Medieval Hindu Devotionalism', op. cit., p. 274.
32. Rabindranath Tagore (trans.), *One Hundred Poems of Kabir* (Macmillan, London, 1962).
33. Ibid, Poem number XLII.
34. Ibid, Poem No II.
35. A.K. Ramanujan (trans.), 'Basavanna' in *Speaking of Shiva* (Penguin, 1973), p. 19.
36. Ibid., p. 28.
37. A.K. Ramanujan (trans.), 'Allama Prabhu', in *Speaking of Shiva*, op. cit., p. 147.
38. L.D. Barnett (trans.), 'Nannaya', in *The Heart of India: Sketches in the History of Hindu Religion and Morals* (Wisdom of the East series, 1913), pp. 111–112.
39. Friedhelm Hardy, *Viraha-Bhakti: The Early History of Krishna Devotion in South India* (OUP India, 1973), p. 420.
40. Rana Fulop-Miller, *Saints that Moved the World* (Thomas Y. Crowell, 1945), p. 175.
41. Ibid., pp. 424–425.
42. A.J. Alston (trans.), *The Devotional Poems of Mirabai* (Motilal Banarasidass, 1980).
43. Ibid.
44, Ibid.
45. Norman Cutler (trans.), 'Karaikkalammaiyar', in *Songs of Experience: The Poetics of Tamil Devotion* (Indiana University Press, 1987), p. 121.
46. A.K. Ramanujan (trans.), 'Mahadeviyakka', in *Speaking of Shiva*, op. cit., pp. 112–113.
47. Ibid., p. 116.
48. Ibid., pp. 48–49.
49. A.J. Alston (trans.), 'Introduction' in *The Devotional Poems of Mirabai*, op. cit., p. 25.
50. Milton Singer (ed.), *Krishna: Myths, Rites, and Attitudes* (East-West Centre Press, 1966), p. 133.

51. Chaturvedi Badrinath, *Dharma*, op. cit., p. 88.
52. Vinay Dharwadkar, ed., *The Collected Essays*, op. cit., p. 271.

5. BRITISH RULE AND ITS AFTERMATH

1. Macaulay's 'Minute on Education', 2 February 1835.
2. Ibid.
3. Ibid.
4. Ibid.
5. Ibid.
6. Ibid.
7. Ibid.
8. Ibid.
9. Ibid.
10. Cited in Pavan K. Varma, *Becoming India*, op. cit., p. 32.
11. William Jones, *Collected Works*, Vol III, p. 34.
12. John Clive, *Thomas Babington Macaulay: The Shaping of the Historian* (Martin Secker & Warburg, 1973), p. 359.
13. Ibid., p. 390.
14. Ibid., p. 398.
15. Parliamentary Papers, XXXII (1852–1853), pp. 263–264.
16. Lawrence James, *Raj: The Making and Unmaking of British India* (Little, Brown, 1997), p. 158.
17. Ibid., p. 157.
18. Macaulay's 'Minute on Education', 2 February 1835.
19. John Clive, *Thomas Babington Macaulay*, op. cit., p. 344.
20. This quotation, and other details relating to Ram Mohan Roy's life, are sourced inter alia from V. Mahadevan and S.K. Krishnamurthi's book, *Raja Ram Mohan Roy and Lord William Bentinck* (Longmans, 1929), and R.C Mazumdar's learned essay on Roy (Asiatic Society, 1972).
21. Thomas R. Metcalfe, *The Indian Empire and the Beginnings of Modern Society: Ideologies of the Raj*, The New Cambridge History of India, vol. III, pt. 4 (Cambridge University Press, 1994), p. 96.
22. Lata Mani, *Contentious Traditions: The Debate on Sati in Colonial India* (University of California Press, 1998), p. 22.
23. Anand A. Yang, 'Whose Sati: Widow Burning in Early-Nineteenth-Century India', *Women and Social Reform in Modern India: A Reader*, edited by Tanika Sarkar and Sumit Sarkar (Indiana University Press, 2008), p. 28.

24. Ibid.

25. Lata Mani, *Contentious Traditions*, op. cit.

26. George Smith, *The Life of William Carey, Shoemaker & Missionary* (The Echo Library, 2006), p. 162.

27. Thomas R. Metcalfe, *The Indian Empire and the Beginnings of Modern Society*, op. cit., p. 96.

28. John Clive, *Thomas Babington Macaulay*, op. cit., p. 410.

29. Quoted in Gauri Viswanathan, *Masks of Conquest: Literary Study of British Rule in India* (Columbia University Press, 1989), p. 6.

30. John Clive, *Thomas Babington Macaulay*, op. cit., p. 409.

31. Thomas R. Metcalfe, *The Indian Empire and the Beginnings of Modern Society: Ideologies of the Raj*, op. cit., p. 49.

32. Gauri Viswanathan, op. cit., p. 139.

33. John Clive, *Thomas Babington Macaulay*, op. cit., p. 408.

34. Ibid., p. 403.

35. Nirad C. Chaudhuri, *A Passage to England*, p. 188.

36. Ashis Nandy, *At the Edge of Psychology: Essays in Politics and Culture* (OUP India, 1980), p. 60.

37. Sir Thomas Raleigh (ed.), *Lord Curzon in India* (1906), p. 182.

38. W. Erskine, *Account of the Cave Temples of Elephanta*, TLSB, I, 1819, p. 198.

39. Thomas R. Metcalfe, *The Indian Empire and the Beginnings of Modern Society*, op. cit., p. 92.

40. Ibid., p. 87.

41. Partha Mitter, *Much Maligned Monsters: History of European Reactions to Indian Art* (Clarendon Press, 1977), p. 267.

42. Ibid., p. 158.

43. Ibid., p. vii.

44. Ibid., p. 251.

45. Ibid., p. 271.

46. Ibid., p. 279.

47. Ibid., pp. 268–269.

48. Ibid., p. 292.

49. Ibid., p. 295.

50. Ibid., p. 323.

51. Ibid., p. 332.

52. Ibid., p. 280.

53. Ibid., p. 250.

54. Ibid., p. 416.

55. Ibid., p. 414.
56. Ibid., p. 280.
57. Ibid., p. 271.
58. Ibid., p. 419.
59. E.B. Havell, *The Basis for Artistic and Industrial Revival in India* (The Theosophist Press, 1912).
60. Karsandas Mulji, 'Appendix' in *History of the Sect of Maharajas, or Vallabhacharyas in Western India* (Trubner & Co., 1865).
61. Wendy Doniger, *The Hindus*, op. cit., p. 591.
62. Rajiv Malhotra, *Being Different*, op. cit., p. 204.
63. Ibid., p. 317.
64. Ibid., p. 317.
65. Gauri Viswanathan, op cit. p. 51.
66. Koenraad Elst, *Decolonizing the Hindu Mind*, op. cit., p. 103.
67. Amartya Sen, *The Argumentative Indian*, op. cit., p. 92.
68. Wendy Doniger, *The Hindus*, op. cit., p. 597.
69. Quoted by Barbara Miller, 'The Divine Duality of Radha and Krishna', in J.S. Hawley and D.M. Wulff (eds), *The Divine Consort* (Berkeley Religious Studies Series, 1982), p. 25.
70. Ibid., p. 591.
71. *Outlook*, 17 September 2007.
72. Shakti Maira, *Towards Ananda*, op. cit., p. 22.
73. Kapila Vatsyayan, 'From Interior Landscapes into Cyber Space: Fluidity and Dynamics of Tradition', in *Culture and the Making of Identity in Contemporary India*, op. cit., p. 44.

6. THE CHALLENGE OF THE MODERN REPUBLIC

1. Jawaharlal Nehru, *An Autobiography* (1980), p. 23.
2. Ibid., p. 29.
3. Ibid., pp. 3, 5, 24.
4. Jawaharlal Nehru, *The Discovery of India* (1956) pp. 413–414.
5. Lord Mountbatten, 'Reflections on the Transfer of Power and Jawaharlal Nehru', *2nd Jawaharlal Nehru Memorial Lecture* (Cambridge University Press), p. 12.
6. *Young India*, 27 April 1921, p. 130.
7. Mohandas Karamchand Gandhi, *Constructive Programme: Its Meaning and Place* (Navjivan Press, 1944), p. 16.
8. Mahatma Gandhi, *Hind Swaraj*, op. cit., p. 116.

9. Charles Smith, *Fifty Years with Mountbatten* (Sidgwick & Jackson, 1980), p. 79.
10. Lord Louis Mountbatten, *Reflections on the Transfer of Power and Jawaharlal Nehru*, op. cit., p. 32.
11. Rober Grant Irving, *Indian Summer: Lutyens, Baker and Imperial Delhi* (Yale University Press, 1981), p. 186.
12. Jawaharlal Nehru, *An Autobiography* (Jawaharlal Nehru Memorial Fund/OUP, 1997), p. 426.
13. Jawaharlal Nehru, *The Discovery of India* (Jawaharlal Nehru Memorial Fund/OUP, 1997), p. 509.
14. Ibid., p. 510.
15. Jawaharlal Nehru, *An Autobiography*, op. cit., p. 429.
16. Jawaharlal Nehru, *The Discovery of India*, op. cit., p. 510.
17. Jawaharlal Nehru, *An Autobiography*, op. cit., p. 429.
18. *The Collected Works of Mahatma Gandhi* (Navjivan, 1944), pp. 42–43.
19. Vikramaditya Prakash, *Chandigarh's Le Corbusier: The Struggle for Modernity in Postcolonial India* (Mapin, 2002), p. 27.
20. *Selected Works of Jawaharlal Nehru* (Second Series), NMML, Vol 28, p. 2.
21. Gunnar Myrdal, *Asian Drama: An Inquiry into the Poverty of Nations*, vol. 3 (Penguin, UK, 1968), pp., 1645–1646.
22. Ashis Nandy, 'Propagating an Indian Model', *Sunday Mail*, 14 January 1990.
23. Pan Nalin, in *The Times of India*, 16 July 2006.
24. Padmapriya Janakiraman and Maansi Verma, 'Culture Needs More Government Support', *Hindustan Times*, 14 February 2021.
25. Dinanath Batra, *Prerna Deep*, p. 8.
26. Amish, *Immortal India*, op. cit., p. 51.
27. Jawaharlal Nehru, *The Discovery of India*, op cit., p. 513.
28. Quoted by Barkha Dutt, *Hindustan Times*, February 2008.
29. Mahatma Gandhi, *Hind Swaraj*, op. cit., p. 43.
30. B.R. Ambedkar, *Pakistan or the Partition of India* (Samyak Prakashan, 2013), pp. 165–166.
31. Vikram Sampath, *Savarkar: Echoes from a Forgotten Past 1883–1924* (Penguin-Viking, 2019), p. 401.
32. B.R. Ambedkar, *Pakistan or the Partition of India*, op. cit. pp. 177–178.
33. Vikram Sampath, *Savarkar: Echoes from a Forgotten Past*, op. cit., p. 417.
34. Aakar Patel, *Our Hindu Rashtra: What It Is. How We Got Here* (Westland, 2020), p. 88.

35. Vikarm Sampath, *Savarkar: Echoes From a Forgotten Past*, op. cit., p. xvi.
36. Ibid., p. xvii.
37. Ibid., p. xviii.
38. Wajahat Habibullah, *My Years With Rajiv: Triumph and Tragedy* (Westland, 2020), p. 100.
39. Aakar Patel, *Our Hindu Rashtra*, op. cit., p. 109.
40. Ibid., p. 115.
41. Gandhi, *The Collected Works* (Navjivan Publishing House, Ahmedabad, 1958–94), vol 25, p. 178.
42. In a speech at St. George's Cathedral, on 17 September 1947. Quoted by Chaturvedi Badrinath, *Dharma: Hinduism and Religions in India*, op. cit, p. 97.
43. C. Panduranga Bhatta and Pragyan Rath, 'Religious Pluralism is the Need of the Hour', in *The Art of Leading in a Borderless World*, op. cit., pp. 199–201.
44. These quotes, and the ones that follow, from Savarkar have been cited in Vikram Sampath's book, *Savarkar: Echoes from a Forgotten Past*, op. cit., pp. 421–432, where he has summarized the writings of Savarkar on this subject.
45. Mahatma Gandhi, *Hind Swaraj*, op. cit., p. 40.
46. *The Hindu*, 19 April 1945.
47. Swami Vivekananda, Letter dated 6 April 1897 to Sarala Ghoshl, *SV Letters*, p. 324.
48. Sri Aurobindo, *The Renaissance in India and Other Essays on Indian Culture* (Sri Aurobindo Ashram, 1997), p. 89.
49. Ibid., p. 14.
50. Ibid., p. 91.

Index

Udbhata, 120, 137
uncertainty, doctrine of, 83
Uniform Civil Code, 333
United Progressive Alliance (UPA), 340
universal equality, doctrine of, 355
untouchability
    abolition of, 355
    practice of, 352, 354
    untouchables, 208
Upadhyaya, Deendayal, 338–339
    concept of a Hindu Rashtra, 339
upamana (analogy), 69
Upanishads, 26, 34, 63–64, 73–74, 108–
    109, 204, 311
    Advaita philosophy of, 81
    Aham Brahmasmi mahavakya, 103
    Brahman–Atman of, 110
    Brihadaranyaka Upanishad, 164,
      183
    Chandogya Upanishad, 65–66
    conceptualisation of Brahman, 67
    cosmic design of, 82
    Great Sentences of, 64
    injunctions of, 78
    Isha Upanishad, 66, 320
    Katha Upanishad, 64
    on lingam as a sign of That, 97
    Mundaka Upanishad, 64–65, 324
    philosophy of, 67
    Shanti Mantra of, 173
    Taittiriya Upanishad, 66
    teachings of, 73
    Vastu Sutra Upanishad, 117
    view of the bhokta and the drishta,
      284
Urdu language, 194, 203, 241, 311
Uttara Mimansha Sutra, 68, 73

Vaisheshika Mimamsa, 69
Vaisheshika school of the sage Kanada, 69
Vaishnava school of bhakti, 213, 216
Vaishno Devi, 102
Vajpayee, Atal Bihari, 338, 340
Vakapadiya (Bhartrihari), 138
vaka shakti, 80
Vakataka kings, 29
vakrata (curvature), 136
Vakyapadiya (Bhartrihari), 80

Vallabhacharya (Vallabha), 213
Vamana, 136
Varahamihira, 172
vardushikas (money lenders), 163
varnikabhanga, 124
Varttika, 138
Vastu Shastra, 45, 124, 174, 299
Vasudhaiva Kutumbukam, 78, 329, 351
Vatsyayan, Kapila, 123, 284
Vayu Purana, 132
Vedanta, 63, 82–83, 87–88, 355
Vedantasara, 249
Vedanta Sutra, 73
Vedantic monism, 218
Vedas, types of, 62
Vedic age, 63
Vedic culture, glorification of, 49–50
Vedic Dharma and culture, 50
Vedic India, 315
Vedic rites and rituals, practice and
    interpretation of, 72
Vedic ritualism, performance of, 77
vedoktabandi, 353
Vemula, Rohit, 356
Venn diagram, of intersecting circles of
    concept, beliefs and practices, 32
vernacular languages, 207–208, 236
    British contempt for, 260
vibhatsa bhava, 119
vibhava (determinants), 119
Viceroy's Palace, *see* Rashtrapati Bhavan
Victoria Memorial Museum, 250
Vidya Bharati, 315
Vidyapati, 210
Vijayanagar kingdom, 199–200, 297
Vaishnava bhakti, 222
Vijnanavada, 82
Vikramaditya VI, 169
vimarsha, process of, 104
vira bhava, 119
Virashaiva devotional movement, 219
vishist advaita, doctrine of, 88, 222
Vishnudharmottara, 122–124, 132, 277
Vishnu, Lord, 92, 124, 165, 207, 339
    adishesha, 118
    avatars of, 29, 86, 99, 213
Vishnu Purana, 89, 99, 168
Vishnu Sahasranama, 93